D1295376

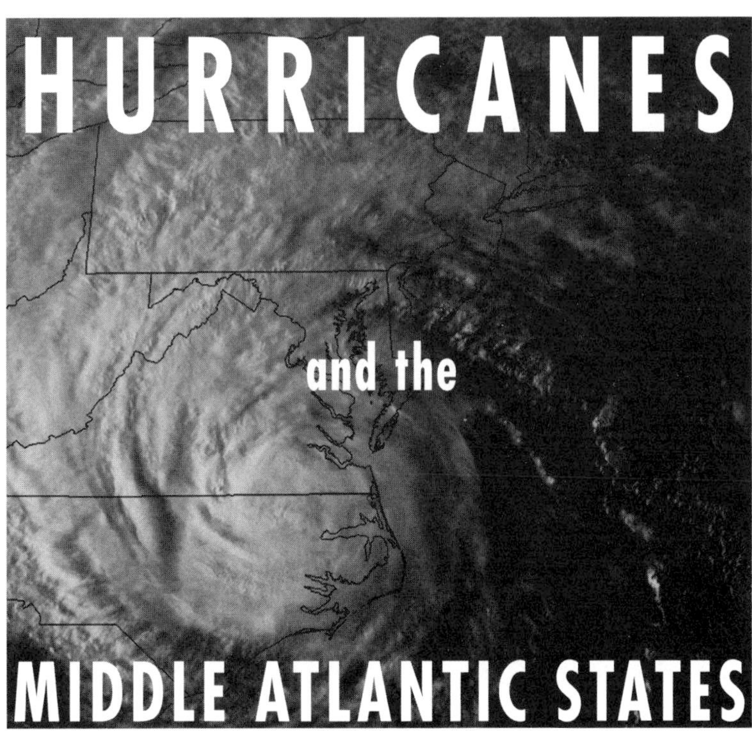
HURRICANES
and the
MIDDLE ATLANTIC STATES

HURRICANES

and the

MIDDLE ATLANTIC STATES

Rick Schwartz

EDITORS: **Al Karr, Kevin Myatt**

GRAPHIC DESIGNERS: **Tracylee Hertzog, Meredith McDanal-Piemme**

BLUE DIAMOND BOOKS
Springfield, Virginia

HURRICANES and the MIDDLE ATLANTIC STATES

Published by: BLUE DIAMOND BOOKS
6516 China Grove Ct.
Alexandria, Virginia 22310
www.bluediamondbooks.com

Printed by Cushing-Malloy, Ann Arbor, Michigan

Publisher's Cataloging-in-Publication
Schwartz, Rick, 1955-
Hurricanes and the Middle Atlantic States / Rick Schwartz ; editors, Al Karr, Kevin Myatt; graphic designers, Tracylee Hertzog, Meredith McDanal-Piemme. -- 1st ed.
p. cm.
Includes bibliographical references and index.
LCCN 2006906485
ISBN-13: 978-0-9786280-0-0
ISBN-10: 0-9786280-0-4

1. Hurricanes--Middle Atlantic States. 2. Middle Atlantic States--Climate. I. Title.

QC944.S39 2007 551.55'20974
QBI07-600155

Manufactured in the United States of America

First Edition
First Printing August 2007

07 08 09 10 5 4 3 2 1

Front cover photograph: Satellite photograph of Hurricane Isabel/NOAA
Rear cover photographs: Isabel 2003 by Kevin Ambrose, Hurricane Donna/NOAA

To order a copy of *Hurricanes and the Middle Atlantic States*:
Send a check, bank check or money order for $32.95 (postpaid) to Blue Diamond Books, 6516 China Grove Ct., Alexandria, VA 22310. Virginia residents add $1.50 sales tax.

For additional information or to purchase by credit card visit
www.midatlantichurricanes.com or www.bluediamondbooks.com

ACKNOWLEDGMENTS

Hurricanes and the Middle Atlantic States grew out of my interest in weather and history. Assembling a book was not easy. The effort required six years.

Peter Gajary, Stan Rossen and John Windolph deserve special mention. We've tracked hurricanes, chased a few and spent endless hours discussing them for more than 30 years. Their inspiration and input is reflected throughout the book. At the start of the project, they told me to write a book I'd be thrilled to read. I did.

Thank you to the following weather enthusiasts: Keith Allen, Thomas Blackburn, Kevin Shaw, Brian Smith and Kevin Ambrose.

Thanks to Herbert Saffir for supplying background information on the Saffir-Simpson hurricane intensity scale.

Editors Kevin Myatt and Albert Karr helped sculpt *Hurricanes and the Middle Atlantic States*. Mr. Myatt is a copy editor and weather columnist for *The Roanoke Times*. Mr. Karr has been a freelance writer since 1997. Before that, he had a 40-year career with *The Wall Street Journal* as a writer and editor.

I would like to acknowledge the support of my colleagues at Vance International, particularly Sam Carmen, who reviewed the manuscript and offered suggestions.

Much appreciation to friends and family.

Historical societies provided much information and many photographs. Special thanks to Art Buswell of the Colonial Beach, Va., Historical Society, Jim Campbell of the Greater Cape May, N.J., Historical Society, Beth Colosimo of the New Jersey Archives, Wendy Garner of the Federalsburg, Md., Historical Society, Kate Myer of the Historical Society of Kent County, Md., Allen "Boo" Pergament of the Atlantic City, N.J., Historical Society, and Harriet Stout of the Chesapeake Beach, Md., Railway Museum.

Resurrecting hurricane history required resources from many libraries and organizations. While it is impossible to list all staff members who assisted, the following individuals merit recognition: Clark Gilman and Christopher Tucker of the New Jersey Department of Environmental Protection, Peggy McPhillips, the Norfolk, Va., city historian (Norfolk Public Library), Robert Schopp, U.S. Geological Survey—a New Jersey district surface-water specialist, and Gary Schuchardt, the director of regional emergency management services for the Hampton Roads, Va., Planning District Commission.

Tracylee Hertzog, Meredith McDanal-Piemme and Dawn Buchert of Springfield (Va.) Printing and Graphics helped design this book. Their work is showcased on the cover and following pages.

I salute the contributors, interviewees and others who aided in creating this reference. As a result, *Hurricanes and the Middle Atlantic States* offers a unique window to the past, a foundation for future research and a good read.

— Rick Schwartz

hatever serves to prove the kinship of all humanity, however widely separated by time or space, is of historical value and, if in generations to come, these plain records of the obscure doings of everyday people shall give the life of our day another touch of reality for them, they have not been written in vain.

Rebecca T. Miller
Annals of Sandy Spring, Md.
June 1909

CONTENTS

CONTENTS
(HURRICANE LISTING)

Dual dates are included for hurricanes prior to 1752. The calendar system used in the British Empire changed that year. Great Britain adopted the Gregorian calendar on September 14, 1752, replacing the Julian calendar. At that time, an additional number of days based on the century were added to the historical record. Ten days were appended to the period from March 1, 1500 to February 18, 1700. (For example, the hurricane of August 27, 1667—old style—occurred on September 6, new style.) An 11-day addition applied from February 19, 1700 to September 3, 1752. The Gregorian calendar remains in use.

CONTENTS
(HURRICANE LISTING)

NOR'EASTERS:

PREFACE

"In short, had the storm continued but a few hours more, the present view must satisfy every sensible person that this part of America would have ceased to exist."

Excerpt—letter from Virginia (1769)

"Hurricanes don't happen here."

Comment by a resident of Virginia (2006)

The Middle Atlantic region of the United States (Delaware, Maryland, New Jersey, Pennsylvania, Virginia and Washington, D.C.) may go for years without a major hurricane. But make no mistake, hurricanes happen there. They batter the coast; some also strike inland. Consider the following:

- Since 1954, more than 60 named tropical storms or hurricanes tracked through or within 100 miles of the Middle Atlantic states. From 1886 to 2003, 75 hurricanes or their remnants passed over or close to Maryland. That's a frequency similar to Delaware, New Jersey and Pennsylvania. Virginia had even more.
- Many hurricanes bring one or more of the following: damaging winds, torrential rain, tidal flooding and destructive tornadoes. Property losses caused by an even modest storm continue to rise.
- Devastating wind events are not limited to the coast. About twice each century a hurricane carries an extended swath of hurricane-force winds far inland. Other tropical cyclones bring gales that cause widespread power outages, downed trees and countless problems.

The Mid-Atlantic holds a unique place in the hurricane belt, a section of the United States that includes coastal states from Texas to Maine. It has its own brand of variability, which continually challenges forecasters. It has its own brand of risks.

Hurricanes and the Middle Atlantic States is a reference that describes the variability and risks. Specifically:

1) It profiles historic storms. Past hurricanes provide clues for the future—a kind of crystal ball. Information within is a starting point for further discovery. Looking back enables us to plan and prepare more effectively.

2) It provides a basis for comparison. Are tropical cyclones becoming more frequent and powerful? Is there historical precedent for a particular type of event?

3) It offers a chronological guide to significant storms and serves as a tool for research and decision-making. What areas were impacted? How did residents respond? What remains to be done?

This book fills a void and while providing considerable detail goes beyond statistics to share encounters of those caught in a storm's embrace. Here is a collection of tales gleaned from articles, books, journals and interviews. Stories of how individuals and communities have reacted before, during and after a visit by the mightiest storm on earth. There are heroes, ordinary people who have done extraordinary things.

Recent centuries have brought amazing natural events to the region.

***

This book began, in a sense, on September 15, 1967. The Weather Bureau issued a hurricane watch for much of New Jersey as Hurricane Doria threatened to make landfall.

New Jersey? Hurricanes happened in faraway places like Florida. Not in my hometown of Edison.

The weather that afternoon was late summer gorgeous. It hardly seemed possible that the next morning would bring unforgettable wind and rain.

In fact, the following day dawned sunny with Doria nowhere in sight. It weakened, slipped south before landfall, became a middling tropical storm and left behind apologetic forecasters. Nevertheless, I was intrigued by even the possibility that a hurricane *could* visit my locality. I've been fascinated with the big storms ever since.

A hunt for information followed—anything I could find. Despite abundant material on hurricanes in general, details about those affecting New Jersey proved elusive. There seemingly existed a gap between Cape Hatteras, N.C., and New York City. One popular weather text bluntly stated, "The Middle Atlantic states, with the possible exception of the Virginia Capes, are normally considered outside the hurricane belt."

Shortly thereafter, I moved to the Washington, D.C., area and continued my search. Over time, I discovered snippets of the region's hurricane history. There were the photos of devastation caused by Hurricane Hazel in 1954 exhibited at a waterfront restaurant along the lower Potomac River in Maryland. Or a marker outside a church in central Maryland, which mentioned, "almost destroyed by a hurricane in 1896."

Of course, there were storms that came my way. They had names like Floyd and Isabel—hurricanes that did what Doria didn't.

Residents of the Middle Atlantic states: This is *your* hurricane history. Events on the following pages offer profound lessons and a guide for the future. Hurricane history continually shouts, "Build on a flood or tidal plain, abuse the land, be lax about building construction and safety codes, or about ensuring sound infrastructure—there will be consequences!"

There is much to learn, choices to consider, lessons to apply. With a growing population and ever-increasing commercial development, with a rising sea and the potential consequences of global warming, challenges have never been greater. Collective memory fades after several decades and nearly vanishes in a few more. Lessons learned and a resolve to fare better next time are frequently lost. Must we repeat this cycle?

"Hurricanes don't happen here." Sadly, few residents have knowledge of the Mid-Atlantic's hurricane past. Yet, the region will be tested again and again. Storms such as Floyd, Isabel and their kind may go by a different name tomorrow; but rest assured, there will be a tomorrow.

— Rick Schwartz

INTRODUCTION

ind, rain, storm surge and tornado. These are the destructive threats wielded by a tropical cyclone. An overview of each:

WIND

During each century there arrive storms like no other—inland hurricanes. They are the Mid-Atlantic equivalent of the great California earthquake, the "Big One." The region is due for another.

Inland hurricanes carry destructive winds hundreds of miles from the sea. A mixture of tropical and non-tropical elements, the systems weaken slowly, spreading unforgettable devastation.

Hurricane Hazel in 1954 was the last tropical cyclone to bring extended hurricane-force winds to interior sections of the Mid-Atlantic. Similar events also occurred in 1667, 1724, 1769, 1775, 1821, 1878 and 1896. When the next inland hurricane arrives, expect the following:

- Several hours of 30-40 mph gusts before a spike. Sustained winds may climb to 70-80 mph, with gusts of 80-100 mph. Dangerous levels typically persist for an hour or two.

In the aftermath anticipate:

- Countless trees uprooted. Hurricanes are among nature's tools for pruning Eastern forests.
- Widespread utility outages including electrical and telephone service, and possibly the loss of safe drinking water.
- Many shattered windows, toppled chimneys and damaged roofs. Fragile, shoddy, or otherwise sub-standard construction is at greatest risk.
- A shortage of home repair supplies, bottled water and other necessities. Hiring reputable contractors for fix-up work may prove a herculean task.
- Traffic headaches in urban areas. Motorists will experience lengthy delays as a result of fallen power lines and trees, darkened traffic lights and legions of sightseers.
- Heavy loss of crops, numerous barns damaged or blown down, and serious harm to fences and outbuildings.
- Areas west of the center will have lighter winds but considerably more rain than sections to the east. Flash flooding, downed trees and power outages promise to make the hurricane memorable to those on the so-called "weak" side of the storm.

Hurricane Andrew, which devastated Florida and Louisiana in 1992, ranks among the costliest single-storm weather disasters in U.S. history, with at least $27 billion in property losses. A blow similar to Hazel could top this. While its winds wouldn't equal Andrew's statistically, the hurricane *would seem* like an Andrew on the James, Potomac or Susquehanna to a population unaccustomed to such fury.

Other tropical cyclones will bring less wind. However, the Middle Atlantic states face a more acute risk than southern states like Florida. Winds of similar strength cause greater damage.

The region's broadleafed, shallow-rooted trees are easy prey for strong winds. Even a 50 mph gust can topple a leafy oak. Florida's ubiquitous palms, on the other hand, have evolved to live with hurricanes.

The Mid-Atlantic faces greater susceptibility to wind losses because of less stringent building design and construction practices. Also a risk factor: Inhabitants of the separate regions have differing perspectives on the hurricane menace.

There has been a proliferation of development since Hazel. The Mid-Atlantic region has a population largely ignorant of the area's hurricane history. The next Hazel is due.

RAIN

Hurricane-induced flooding from excessive rainfall is responsible for more deaths in the Middle Atlantic states than wind, storm surge and tornadoes combined.

Tropical moisture lifts and cools as it plows into the Appalachian Mountains or a cold front. This process frequently produces heavier rainfall, dumping it on the headwaters of the region's great rivers.

Remnant systems that stall or crawl can drop double-digit totals over a large area. Even a storm that moves steadily can turn into a prodigious rainmaker as it interacts with the ocean, land and surrounding weather systems.

Many Mid-Atlantic towns and cities are wedded to floodplains. Periodic floods haunt their history. Similar events lie ahead.

Urban areas have a special risk during intense downpours. Burgeoning development makes flash flooding a serious threat. Concrete, asphalt and other impervious surfaces reduce the absorption of rainwater, increasing runoff. Mid-Atlantic cities often feature paved-over hillsides. The monsoonal deluge of a tropical system can quickly turn calamitous.

Hurricane-related rainfall is of particular concern in mountainous sections. Steep slopes allow rapid runoff. An extreme deluge can liquefy the soil generating deadly mudflows.

The Appalachians are an ancient mountain range and over the eons, overburden—soil, boulders, trees, and houses—have accumulated on bedrock. A study by the U.S. Geological Survey concluded that severe rainstorms are recurring phenomena, playing an important role in the erosion and formation of the landscape. Slides are triggered by cloudbursts dumping over 10 inches of rain—and sometimes more than 20 inches—within several hours on already saturated ground. Between 1844 and 1985 at least 51 major mudflow events impacted the mountains, according to the Geological Survey.

Flooding has an adverse and long-lasting environmental impact. Raging water carries an enormous load of pollutants, as well as nutrients that support harmful algae. Floods from tropical systems such as Hurricane Agnes in 1972 have devastated marine life, leaving a decades-long legacy.

***

Localities tend to prepare for the worst flood in memory and are stunned when a hurricane-related inundation exceeds past experience. Increased residential and commercial development, an altered shoreline or a dam breach, can make floodplain charts obsolete.

Adding to woes: Many property owners are stunned when they learn standard homeowner's insurance doesn't cover flood losses. Among the sadder plaints of storm victims, heard far too often, "We never dreamed water would reach us. We have no flood coverage…"

Hard-hit areas typically go through three phases after a disaster. First comes trauma, disbelief, depression. Then hope, "We'll build a better town!" Finally, there's recovery—

perhaps. After the initial adrenaline rush, the media spotlight, and an influx of aid and volunteers—when the crowd goes home—the challenge of renewal truly begins.

A weather calamity rarely results in the demise of a community, but it may exacerbate unsolved socio-economic problems and contribute to a long-term decline. Such a crisis tests residents' mettle. Recovery is not guaranteed. It must be earned.

STORM SURGE

Hurricanes periodically assault the Mid-Atlantic coast, generating a surge that attacks shoreline and overwhelms barrier islands. Storm surge events come in several varieties.

Hurricanes (and nor'easters) may linger, producing gales lasting more than a day. The sea rises gradually, peaking after several tidal cycles. The ocean relentlessly gobbles shoreline.

Stalled storms often cover a vast area. Their duration is difficult to predict. Past events have caught coastal communities napping, arriving without the fanfare and obvious menace of a major hurricane. Therein lies vulnerability.

Most barrier island evacuation plans call for a phased pullout based on the anticipated strength—wind speed—of an approaching hurricane. But it's likely that among the most destructive Mid-Atlantic coastal storms of the 21st century will be minimal hurricanes or strong nor'easters that anchor offshore and exercise erosive power through persistence.

Storm surges in the Mid-Atlantic have, on rare occasion, peaked with a series of enormously destructive breakers. These arrived during the eye's closest approach. In 1944, for instance, a hurricane slammed New Jersey with a tsunami-like wall of water described, variously, as one to three "tidal waves." Hurricanes during September 1821 and October 1878 produced a similar effect, targeting the Delmarva Peninsula and Delaware Bay.

A hurricane with a large sweep of gales, tracking between the Chesapeake Bay and Blue Ridge Mountains, produces tidal flooding throughout the bay region. Isabel, in 2003, and Fran, in 1996, are recent examples.

A rising ocean portends increased bouts of flooding in tidal sections, especially along the Chesapeake Bay. A recent report from the University of Maryland Center for Environmental Science concluded, "With a rate of relative sea level rise almost double the global average, the Chesapeake Bay will feel the effects of global sea level rise more acutely than other regions. Global warming is expected to be accompanied by an increase in the frequency and intensity of tropical storms such as hurricanes and this combined with relative sea level rise suggests that the aftermath of Isabel may foreshadow the effects of these storms in the future."

TORNADO

"Tornadoes don't happen here. They happen elsewhere," said a disbelieving victim of a twister produced by Hurricane Ivan as she surveyed damage to her Maryland home.

The region's landscape—ocean, coastal plain, piedmont and mountains—and non-tropical weather systems create a brew of violent possibilities when they combine with hurricane remnants. Tornadoes are among the offspring.

Meteorologists once considered hurricane-spawned tornadoes rare. Actually, hurricanes often create a risk for twisters as they interact with surrounding weather systems.

Tornadoes and hurricanes attack the ground in differing ways. Tornadoes pull and twist. Hurricanes push. A tornado usually causes more structural damage than a hurricane when similar wind speeds blow for a comparable period. But a tornado only lasts for a minute or so in any location. A hurricane's straight-line winds can tear away for hours.

Pinpointing exactly where a hurricane-generated tornado will touch down is beyond our present knowledge. Eugene McCaul, a meteorologist and tornado researcher, puts the challenge and risk this way:

"Tropical cyclone tornadoes are often spawned by unusually small storm cells that may not appear particularly dangerous on weather radar, especially if the cells are located more than 60 miles from the radar. In addition, these small storms often tend to produce little or no lightning or thunder, and may not look very visually threatening to the average person. Furthermore, the tornadoes are often obscured by rain, and the storm cells spawning them may move rapidly, leaving little time to take evasive action once the threat has been perceived."

TROPICAL CYCLONES AND THE MIDDLE ATLANTIC REGION

Mid-Atlantic hurricane history suggests the following:

- The region experiences cyclical bouts of significant hurricane activity. Periods of increased storm activity occurred from 1876 to 1904, 1933 to 1961 and 1969 to 1979. It appears another busy cycle began in 1995.

- Hurricanes making landfall on the East Coast are an obvious threat to the Mid-Atlantic. Those striking the Gulf Coast also pose a menace. Such storms have reached the Middle Atlantic states producing enormous flooding, destructive windstorms and deadly tornadoes.

- Major hurricanes seem to retain a hidden energy that may erupt two or three days after landfall, resulting in a variety of severe weather.

- There is scant evidence that tropical cyclones visiting the Mid-Atlantic region are getting stronger or arriving with greater frequency. However, such systems process, transfer and disperse excess atmospheric heat. Therefore, a warmer climate may lead to more frequent and powerful hurricanes.

  (Perhaps, the 2005 hurricane season reflected this. The 27 tropical cyclones eclipsed the previous high of 21, which occurred in 1933. There were also an unprecedented 15 hurricanes, including the most intense ever measured in the Atlantic basin.)

  — But a caveat. Our understanding of the long-term consequences of global climate change is limited. It seems logical that greater warmth will generate increased hurricane activity. Nevertheless, such a conclusion may prove premature. In fact, some of the most severe Atlantic hurricanes of the past 400 years occurred during the "Little Ice Age." This regime of cooler global temperatures spanned the 14th century until the mid-19th century.

If a warmer climate leads to more dangerous hurricanes, the result may not manifest as an extreme Category 5-type storm, at least not in the Mid-Atlantic region. Instead, something less than unique may do something unique, such as a major hurricane making landfall in a section that has never known a similar encounter.

Even if future hurricanes are no worse than those of the past expect many significant events.

HURRICANES: AN OVERVIEW

he playwright William Shakespeare knew the violent storms as *tempests*. In subsequent centuries, hurricanes went by a variety of terms, anything from *equinoctial gales* to *West Indies tornadoes*.

Call them what you will. Tornadoes may blow harder, and nor'easters might encompass a greater domain, but for combined size and fury nothing beats a hurricane.

The meteorological definition, according to the National Hurricane Center:

"Hurricanes are giant whirlwinds in which air moves in a large, tightening spiral around a center of extreme low pressure, reaching maximum velocity in a circular band extending outward 20 or 30 miles from the rim of the eye. This circulation is counterclockwise in the Northern Hemisphere, and clockwise in the Southern Hemisphere. Near the eye, hurricane winds may gust to more than 200 miles per hour, and the entire storm dominates the ocean surface and lower atmosphere over tens of thousands of square miles."

The eyewall, a turbulent area containing the most violent winds, surrounds the eye, or hub, of a hurricane. It is a spectacular band of wind and rain encompassing a column of dry air. At the juncture, calamity meets calm.

Inside the eye, little or no wind and an absence of rain belie conditions a short distance away. The sun appears in a clear sky or peeks through thin overcast. A "stadium effect," tiered clouds soaring far into the atmosphere, may flank a well-developed eye.

The average diameter is about 20 miles. However, the size of the eye varies from less than 10 miles to more than 50. (The diameter does not necessarily correlate to the strength of surrounding winds.) Size, shape and dynamics are in constant flux.

After the eye passes, the wind usually returns to its former strength or a bit stronger, blowing from the opposite direction. The transition takes only a few minutes. Air pressure rises rapidly. The greatest concentration of strong winds is usually in the right front quadrant of circulation (northeast in a storm moving in a northerly direction). However, the location of the highest wind varies in relation to the eye. An immutable rule: Each hurricane is unique.

The eye contains the lowest barometric pressure—a leveling off after a steep dive in the eyewall.

"The biggest change in pressure occurs across the eyewall," said Richard Pasch, a meteorologist at the National Hurricane Center. "Within the eye, there are some pressure differences, with the lowest pressure usually found near the geometric center.

"The bottom line is that where the largest changes in surface pressure are occurring, the surface wind speeds are the strongest. This is because the hurricane's wind circulation is in balance with the pressure field. So, within the eye, where winds are relatively light, pressure changes are much smaller than they are in the eyewall where winds are much stronger."

A moat, a corridor of modest, gusty winds and little or no rain separates the eyewall from outer rainbands. Outer rainbands provide squally weather that generally lasts less than an hour.

***

Despite impressive power, hurricanes rely on fragile and changeable ingredients. Among them:

- A closed wind circulation, which can gather heat, energy and moisture through contact with mild ocean waters. Sea surface temperatures of about 80 degrees or higher foster growth and development. Water should be at least this warm to a depth of approximately 150 feet.

- A wind pattern near the ocean surface that spirals air inward. Bands of thunderstorms form. They coalesce and rotate around a core of lowest pressure.

- A warm central core (warmer than the surrounding area) surrounded by feeder bands. These carry energizing heat and moisture to the center of circulation.

Several conditions weaken hurricanes. Upper-level wind shear five to eight miles above the surface may blow the tops off thunderstorms or otherwise disrupt a tropical cyclone's structure. Sea surface temperatures cooler than 80 degrees rob storms of life-giving warmth. A jaunt over land cuts necessary surface warmth and moisture. Friction inhibits circulation. Adjacent weather systems, particularly in middle and northern latitudes, may interfere with structure and circulation.

Tropical cyclones develop (and dissipate) in stages including:

Disturbance: a tropical weather system of organized/organizing persistent thunderstorms. It is generally 100 to 300 nautical miles in diameter. Tropical cyclones, whether a disturbance or something greater, are not linked to a weather front. To be classified as a disturbance, a system must maintain its identity for at least 24 hours.

Depression: a tropical cyclone in which the maximum sustained surface wind speed is 38 mph or less.[1]

Storm: a tropical cyclone in which the maximum sustained surface wind speed ranges from 39 mph to 73 mph. As a tropical storm nears hurricane force, an eye forms.

Hurricane: a tropical cyclone in which the maximum sustained surface wind speed is 74 mph or more. Spiral limbs encompass a diameter of 100 to more than 500 miles. Cloud tops often reach 50,000 feet.

Extratropical Storm: a low pressure system with more non-tropical than tropical features. For instance, the system may retain feeder bands although the eye is no longer discernible. An extratropical storm is primarily fueled by temperature differences between two or more air masses. In contrast, a tropical cyclone is maintained by the extraction of heat energy from the ocean.

Hurricanes serve vital purposes.

They are thermal engines that move tropical air northward, transporting excessive concentrations of heat from the tropics and sub-tropics. The earth's climate constantly strives for equilibrium—not too hot, not too cold. Hurricanes provide a critical relief valve from excessive heat. They assist in maintaining the narrow limits of hot and cold that make the planet livable.

Most hurricanes are benign. Indeed, an appreciable number never affect land. Those that do often supply needed rainfall, making critical contributions to late-summer moisture, ensuring adequate groundwater. Some initiate an end to a drought.

This book focuses on a minority, the highly destructive hurricanes. Many other storms have been more helpful than harmful.

---

[1] The U.S. Weather Service uses a one-minute averaging time for reporting 'sustained' winds. The maximum sustained wind mentioned in an advisory of the National Hurricane Center is the highest one-minute surface wind occurring within the circulation of a tropical cyclone. Observations are based on a reading at the standard meteorological height of 33 feet. (Gusts are seconds-long wind peaks. Typically, a hurricane's peak gust is 20-25 percent higher than a one-minute sustained wind.)

SEASONALITY, FREQUENCY AND DURATION

The Atlantic hurricane season officially begins on June 1 and ends November 30. An average of 10 tropical cyclones form each year; about six become hurricanes. Only one tropical cyclone occurred in 1890 and 1914, and a record 27 developed during 2005.[2]

Most appear during August and September. The earliest hurricane in the Atlantic basin developed on March 7, 1908, and the latest appeared on December 31, 1954. That storm continued into January 1955, dissipating in the southeastern Caribbean Sea on the 5th. During the closing days of December 2005, and in early January 2006, Tropical Storm Zeta roamed the Atlantic northeast of Puerto Rico.

Tropical cyclones impact at least part of the Middle Atlantic region nearly every year. The annual average occurrence is slightly greater than one. However, seven arrived in 1893 and six visited during 2004. Notable hurricanes have affected the Middle Atlantic states as early as June 3 (1825) and as late as December 2 (1925).

Activity that begins early in the season often foretells future visits. When a tropical cyclone impacts the Mid-Atlantic before August 31, one or more follow about 60 percent of the time.

Nearly every Atlantic hurricane forms between the latitudes of 10 and 35 degrees north. Early and late-season storms usually develop in the Gulf of Mexico and western Caribbean. Incubation grounds expand north and east during July and August. Some of the most powerful tropical cyclones originate in the eastern Atlantic near the Cape Verde Islands off the western coast of Africa. August and September are the primary months for "Cape Verde hurricanes."

Tropical cyclones travel at an average of 15 mph. However, speed ranges from nearly stationary to about 70 mph. The fastest hurricanes often appear after Labor Day.

The average lifespan of a tropical cyclone is 10 days, but some dissipate within two or three days. A rare few have survived for more than four weeks.

STORM SURGE

A storm surge produces the costliest hurricane-related damage along the coast. The phenomenon is characterized by an abnormal rise in the sea created by a hurricane. Its height is the difference between the observed level of the sea surface and the level that would have occurred in the absence of the storm.

The ocean rises in the eye of a hurricane as a result of prolonged, intense swirling winds and low barometric pressure. This dome or bulge, generally less than two feet over the open ocean, increases substantially as it presses into shallow water near the coast. Strong winds and the eye carry the surge ashore. Water usually increases steadily, gathering momentum as the center nears. The worst generally occurs as the eye comes ashore or makes its closest approach to land. The highest surge heights in the United States have ranged up to 25 feet.

The following factors contribute to the height of the storm surge:

1) The response of the sea level to lowered surface pressure at the hurricane's center.
2) The strength and distance of maximum winds from the center.
3) The near-shore water depth in the landfall area.
4) The stage of astronomical tides at landfall.

---

[2] Our improving ability to recognize potential hurricanes at their earliest stages (via satellites, air reconnaissance, etc.) makes historical comparability problematic and has contributed to a rise in the annual average.

THE SAFFIR-SIMPSON HURRICANE INTENSITY SCALE

A challenge since the days of Christopher Columbus: How does one describe a hurricane's strength in a way that's generally understood?

The most widely used standard today is the Saffir-Simpson hurricane intensity scale. Named for its designers, Herbert Saffir, a structural engineer, and Robert Simpson, a former director of the National Hurricane Center, the scale offers five ascending categories based on winds and anticipated damage and storm surge. Categories 3, 4 and 5 are classified as "major hurricanes."

"I took into account the various degrees of structural damage I had noted in inspecting and investigating past hurricane damage," explained Saffir. "It was originally designed by me as part of a report that I was commissioned to do by the United Nations on low cost housing throughout the world that was subject to hurricanes. Simpson added the tidal surge categories."

The increments enable forecasters to gauge destructive potential as a tropical cyclone develops, peaks and diminishes. The scale also facilitates historical comparison.

According to Saffir, "The public can reap the greatest benefit from the scale by being knowledgeable as to the different degrees of potential structural damage and tidal surge, and by understanding that the force, and resultant damage exerted by wind, increases as the square of the wind increases. In other words, if the wind velocity doubles, the force exerted increases four times (with resultant structural damage)."

Landfalling Category 5 hurricanes, the strongest tropical cyclones, are rare. Only three came ashore in the United States during the 20th century, with two striking Florida (the Labor Day Hurricane of 1935 and Andrew in 1992) and one slamming Mississippi (Camille in 1969).

Many hurricanes attaining major status at sea weaken as they approach land. For example, Hurricane Isabel in 2003 became a Category 5 well out in the Atlantic Ocean but struck North Carolina as a Category 2.

"Much of the damage from Hurricane Isabel came as a result of uprooted trees," Saffir said. "Tree damage caused tremendous effect on the infrastructure, power lines, communications, individual residences, etc. If the full Category 5 hurricane had made landfall in North Carolina, it would have caused utter devastation along its track in North Carolina, Virginia and Maryland. Almost nothing in that area is designed to withstand a Category 5 hurricane."

The Saffir-Simpson Scale includes:

CATEGORY 1

Winds: 74-95 mph. **Barometric pressure:** greater than 28.94 inches. **Storm surge:** generally 4-5 ft. above normal.

Damage primarily to shrubbery, trees, foliage, and unanchored mobile homes. No real damage to other structures. Some damage to poorly constructed signs. Also, minor coastal road flooding and pier damage, with some small craft in exposed anchorages torn from moorings.

CATEGORY 2

Winds: 96-110 mph. **Barometric pressure:** 28.50-28.91 inches. **Storm surge:** generally 6-8 ft. above normal.

Some damage to roofing materials and some window and door damage. Considerable damage to shrubbery and trees, with some trees blown down. Considerable damage to mobile homes, poorly constructed signs, and piers. Marinas flooded. Coastal and low-lying escape routes flood 2-4 hours before arrival of the hurricane center (eye).

CATEGORY 3

Winds: 111-130 mph. **Barometric pressure:** 27.91-28.47 inches. **Storm surge:** generally 9-12 ft. above normal.

Some structural damage to small residences and utility buildings, with a minor amount of curtainwall failures. Foliage blown off trees and large trees blown down. Mobile homes and poorly constructed signs are destroyed. Flooding on the coast destroys smaller structures, with larger structures damaged by battering from floating debris. Terrain continuously lower than 5 ft. above mean sea level may be flooded inland eight miles or more.

CATEGORY 4

Winds: 131-155 mph. **Barometric pressure:** 27.17-27.88 inches. **Storm surge:** generally 13-18 ft. above normal.

More extensive curtainwall failures, with some complete roof failures on small residences. Shrubs, trees and all signs are blown down. Complete destruction of mobile homes. Extensive damage to doors and windows. Low-lying escape routes may be cut by rising water 3-5 hours before arrival of the hurricane center. Major damage to lower floors of structures near the shore. Terrain lower than 10 ft. above sea level may be flooded requiring massive evacuation of residential areas as far inland as six miles.

(The strongest hurricane-related wind measured in the Mid-Atlantic region occurred during the Great Atlantic Hurricane of 1944. Cape Henry, Va., registered a sustained wind of 134 mph and an estimated peak gust of 150 mph.)

CATEGORY 5

Winds: greater than 155 mph. **Barometric pressure:** less than 27.17 inches. **Storm surge:** generally greater than 18 ft. above normal.

Complete roof failure on many residences and industrial buildings. Some complete building failures, with small utility buildings blown over or away. All shrubs, trees, and signs blown down. Complete destruction of mobile homes. Severe and extensive window and door damage. Low-lying escape routes are cut by rising water 3-5 hours before arrival of the hurricane center. Major damage to lower floors of all structures located less than 15 ft. above sea level and within 500 yards of the shoreline. Massive evacuation required for residential areas on low ground within 5-10 miles of the shoreline.

(The strongest Category 5 hurricanes have produced sustained winds of 180-200 mph. In 2005, Hurricane Wilma established the Atlantic basin record for the lowest surface air pressure, 26.05 inches, while churning through the western Caribbean. Sustained winds at sea level likely reached 185 mph. The world record for minimum barometric pressure belongs to Typhoon Tip, 25.69 inches, in the western Pacific Ocean during 1979. Tip had sustained winds of nearly 200 mph. Gales encompassed 650 miles.)

TORNADOES

Many hurricanes produce tornadoes. Most twisters form in the right front quadrant (usually northeast). They typically travel in the direction of their parent rainband. Hurricane spawned tornadoes usually develop from embedded 'mini-supercells'—unstable convective clouds reaching heights of 30-35,000 feet, compared to 40,000 feet or more for their non-tropical tornadic counterparts.

Remnant systems often produce tornadoes as they churn through the Middle Atlantic states. A few tropical cyclones generate outbreaks. Hurricane David (1979) spawned 34 tornadoes along the East Coast, with many touching down in Virginia, Maryland and Pennsylvania. Hurricanes Frances, Ivan and Jeanne in 2004 spun-off dozens of tornadoes in the Mid-Atlantic region.

Hurricane-spawned tornadoes are usually short-lived, carving paths narrower than 200 yards wide. They generally travel fewer than 10 miles. But there have been notable exceptions. A tornado during August 1888, for example, journeyed almost continuously from near Washington, D.C., to beyond Wilmington, Del., a distance of more than 80 miles.

Roger Edwards, a forecaster with the Storm Prediction Center in Norman, Okla., is researching hurricane-spawned twisters.

"Right now we have two major challenging questions in forecasting tropical cyclone tornadoes," Edwards said. "Why do some tropical cyclones produce almost no supercells and tornadoes when they seem to have all the ingredients? The answer to this question would help us to make tornado watch areas for landfalling tropical events become smaller, more accurate and more useful."

Another critical question, according to Edwards: "What's the difference between supercells that produce tornadoes and those that don't? If we can better answer this question we can issue far fewer false-alarm tornado watches and warnings in tropical situations. This is so hard to measure because the differences seem to cover too small an area to observe and verify well, even with NEXRAD radar and all the other ways we try to measure hurricanes as they move inland."

The number of tornadoes seems to be increasing. However, much of the apparent rise is due to improved observation technology, better reporting and other non-atmospheric factors.

"The increased number of reported storms is due mostly to changes in society rather than atmospheric influences," says Joseph Schaefer, director of the National Weather Service Storm Prediction Center. "In addition to the advent of more precise Doppler radar, many other forces are at play: population increases in rural areas, an overall increase in weather awareness, improved communications, the spread of 'storm spotter' networks, and tracking of verification information."

THE FUJITA TORNADO INTENSITY SCALE

The Fujita Scale measures the intensity of tornadoes. It has been a standard for the National Weather Service since 1973. Introduced by Theodore Fujita (1920-1998), a professor at the University of Chicago, the Fujita Scale evaluates tornado strength based on wind speed and the degree of structural damage. Unlike the Saffir-Simpson Scale, the Fujita Scale is not used to gauge an event in progress. F0 is the weakest and F5 is the strongest although meteorologists have speculated on the possibility of an even stronger, F6, tornado.[3]

The Fujita Scale includes:

F0 (40-72 MPH)

Some damage to chimneys; breaks branches off trees; pushes over shallow-rooted trees; damages signboards.

F1 (73-112 MPH)

The lower limit is near the beginning of hurricane wind speed; peels surface off roofs; mobile homes pushed off foundations or overturned; moving autos pushed off the roads; attached garages may be destroyed.

F2 (113-157 MPH)

Considerable damage. Roofs torn off frame houses; mobile homes demolished; boxcars pushed over; large trees snapped or uprooted; light object missiles generated.

F3 (158-206 MPH)

The roof and some walls torn off well-constructed houses; trains overturned; most trees in forest uprooted.

F4 (207-260 MPH)

Well-constructed houses leveled; structures with weak foundations blown off for some distance; cars thrown and large missiles generated. (While there have been numerous hurricane-spawned F3 tornadoes during the past 50 years, only two F4's have been verified. There have been no confirmed F5's.)

F5 (261-318 MPH)

Strong frame houses lifted off foundations and carried considerable distances to disintegrate; automobile sized missiles fly through the air in excess of 100 meters; trees debarked; steel reinforced concrete structures badly damaged. F5 tornadoes produce the strongest winds on the planet.

[3] The National Weather Service plans changes to the Fujita Scale, effective in early 2007. The "Enhanced Fujita Scale" takes into account a greater range of tornadic effects and also attempts to better correlate tornadic winds with related destruction. The various "Fujita" or "F" levels will include updated descriptions and additional damage-based indicators. (Estimated wind measurements assume a three-second gust.) The Enhanced Fujita Scale includes: EF0 65-85 mph, EF1 86-110 mph, EF2 111-135 mph, EF3 136-165 mph, EF4 166-200, EF5 (greater than 200 mph—no maximum limit).

A HURRICANE BY ANY OTHER NAME...

Andrew, Floyd and Katrina. Names that bring to mind unforgettable images of wind and flood.

Hurricanes are the only type of weather system with a formal naming convention. A name is applied when a tropical depression develops winds of at least tropical storm strength, 39 mph or greater. The World Meteorological Organization, an agency of the United Nations, maintains separate alphabetical lists for eight hurricane-prone areas of the world.

The word "hurricane" originated from the language of the indigenous peoples of the Caribbean region. The Mayan's named their storm god "Hunraken," and the Taino people called their deity "Huracan." By the early 20th century, the following terms were synonymous with hurricane: *Cuban*, *Florida* or *West Indies* hurricane, and *cyclone*, *tropical cyclone*, *tornado*, *tropical twister*, *northeast storm*, *September gale, summer blizzard.*

Prior to our modern identification system, any destructive storm that ravaged Spanish-speaking lands in the Caribbean was given the name of the patron saint of the particular day it struck. Devastating hurricanes in the United States were often identified by the city or region most affected and/or the year. This custom lasted until the middle 20th century. Names were of little use except for historical reference.

During the late 19th century and first half of the 20th century, forecasters tracked storms by location, using coordinates of latitude and longitude. After World War II, the need to quickly and clearly inform the public of an approaching hurricane necessitated the use of short and distinctive identifiers.

Anecdotal evidence ascribes the concept of naming hurricanes to various origins, from an Australian meteorologist who gave them the names of politicians he disliked to the author George R. Stewart who took the name-game one step further in his novel, *Storm*. Published in 1941, the book's protagonist, a "junior meteorologist," gave female names to low pressure systems that he plotted on his weather maps.

The Weather Bureau began identifying hurricanes by military phonetic alphabet (Able, Baker, etc.) in 1950. Female names were introduced in 1953, with the same group used in 1954. However, annual repetition proved confusing. For instance, Hazel of 1953, a middling tropical storm, bore little resemblance to the destructive Hurricane Hazel of 1954.

The solution beginning in 1955 was four—later six—separate rosters rotated annually. Starting during 1979, lists included alternating male and female names of English, French and Spanish extraction. Assignations reflect the diversity of lands affected by Atlantic hurricanes.

Any country devastated by a particular hurricane can request that the World Meteorological Organization retire the storm's name (see Appendix B).

Tropical cyclones that cross into the Pacific basin from the Atlantic or vice-versa take on a new name based on the next available moniker on the list for that basin. Thus, Atlantic hurricane Cesar became Pacific hurricane Douglas after crossing Central America in 1996.

The annual North Atlantic roster includes 21 names. (The Greek alphabet was used in 2005 when the number of tropical cyclones exceeded 21.)[4]

Identifiers beginning with q, u, x, y and z are no longer included because of the scarcity of names starting with those letters. During the 1950s, however, they appeared in the yearly line-up. Thus, in 1956, Quenby, Ursel, Xina, Yola and Zenda made the list. It was Quinta, Undine, Xmay, Yasmin and Zita in 1957. Enough said.

ATLANTIC TROPICAL CYCLONES

2007: Andrea, Barry, Chantal, Dean, Erin, Felix, Gabrielle, Humberto, Ingrid, Jerry, Karen, Lorenzo, Melissa, Noel, Olga, Pablo, Rebekah, Sebastien, Tanya, Van, Wendy

2008: Arthur, Bertha, Cristobal, Dolly, Edouard, Fay, Gustav, Hanna, Ike, Josephine, Kyle, Laura, Marco, Nana, Omar, Paloma, Rene, Sally, Teddy, Vicky, Wilfred

[4] The Greek alphabet as used in 2005 included Alpha, Beta, Gamma, Delta, Epsilon and Zeta.

HURRICANES: FORECASTING HISTORY

"We are as yet in the infancy of meteorology as a science, great as have been the advances made in recent times. The day will no doubt come when we shall know the probable weather of the coming 24 hours with almost the same certainty with which we now foretell an eclipse."

—Henry Hallowell, Sandy Spring, Md., 1873

Meteorology has progressed considerably since Hallowell's day. The science has grown with discoveries, the invention of observational and forecasting tools, as well as ongoing research and wonder. Curiosity and skepticism have nourished progress.

The words of Joseph Henry, first secretary of the Smithsonian Institution, remain timely: "Indeed, meteorology has ever been an apple of contention, as if the violent commotions of the atmosphere induced a sympathetic effect in the minds of those who have attempted to study them."

There's no room for complacency. We have learned much about hurricanes. Much is unknown.

***

Soon after Christopher Columbus discovered America, he discovered hurricanes. The navigator encountered the fringe of a tropical cyclone on his second voyage to the New World in 1494. He spent the rest of his career learning how to predict and avoid the storms. Such knowledge likely saved his life in 1502.

Columbus took shelter in a protective cove on the island of Hispaniola when he observed the telltale signs of an approaching hurricane. A treasure fleet of 30 vessels ignored his warning and was annihilated. Only a single ship limped to Spain. It carried proceeds from the sale of the explorer's New World properties.

Since antiquity, destructive storms were considered divine retribution, a belief firmly rooted in colonial America. For example, after a pair of violent hurricanes in 1683, Increase Mather, one of New England's spiritual leaders, wrote:

"There is an awful intimation of Divine displeasure remarkable in this matter, inasmuch as August 8, a day of public humiliation, with fasting and prayer, was attended in (Connecticut), partly on the account of God's hand against them in the former flood, the next week after which the hand of God was stretched out over them again in the same way, in a more terrible manner than the first. It is also remarkable that so many places should suffer by inundations as this year it hath been; for at the very time the flood happened at Connecticut, there was a hurricane in Virginia, attended with a great exundation of the rivers there, so that their tobacco and their Indian corn is very much damnified."

An understanding of climate and hurricanes developed during the next two centuries, emerging as thinkers discarded age-old notions and scientists made sundry discoveries. A law of storms developed akin to assembling a jigsaw puzzle.

British scientist and mathematician Sir Isaac Newton postulated laws of motion during the late 1600s, laws of nature that applied to meteorology. During the 1700s, intellectuals proposed a variety of climatological explanations, challenging complacency dating back to Aristotle and ancient Greece. Benjamin Franklin's astute observations, for instance, encouraged speculation about lightning, the movement of storms and other weather phenomena.

Diarists began recording regular weather observations. The Reverend John Campanius of Swedes Fort, near Wilmington, Del., became the first colonist to collect data systematically when he kept daily records during 1644-45. Several of the United States' founding fathers, among them George Washington and Thomas Jefferson, included weather descriptions in their journals.

Shipmasters of the age learned to spot the signs of an approaching hurricane and knew that August, September and October brought the greatest risk. But they had no way to determine the strength, track and duration of a tropical menace. That shortcoming regularly cost the lives of crews and passengers.

Hurricanes bedeviled 18th century maritime commerce. In September 1775, for example, a hurricane off Newfoundland caught fishermen by surprise, resulting in the deaths of as many as 4,000. During 1780, "The Great Hurricane" tore through the northeastern Caribbean Sea scuttling opposing French and British fleets and sinking merchant ships. The nautical death toll exceeded 3,000 (and an estimated 20,000 people died on the region's islands).

National Association for the Advancement of Science

William Redfield

By the early 1800s, efforts to investigate tropical cyclones languished. A notable hurricane and prominent dispute between two unlikely adversaries accelerated the American quest for a law of storms.

William Redfield, a merchant from Middletown, Conn., witnessed the effects of the Great Norfolk and Long Island Hurricane of 1821 when he traveled through the state in the weeks that followed. Redfield noticed that the direction of tree fall created a counterclockwise pattern. A decade later, his observation and explanation appeared in the *American Journal of Science*. The article fired the opening salvo of what became a rancorous debate.

Redfield (1789-1857) spent the rest of his life trying to understand hurricanes (and other storms) and sharing his opinions with the public. Respected by colleagues, he served as the first president of the American Association for the Advancement of Science, now the largest scientific organization in the United States.

Whereas Redfield grew into the role of scientist and advocate, shunning flamboyance, James Pollard Espy (1785-1860) embraced the spotlight. As a young man, he switched teaching careers swapping classical languages for meteorology. His admirers dubbed him the "Storm King," a crown he wore with bemused pride. Espy lectured widely and was never shy with the pen.

He took aim at Redfield, challenging his ideas on hurricane dynamics and structure. Redfield believed that all fluid matter, such as atmospheric moisture, tended to run in whirls or circuits and that violent rotation generated and maintained storms. In other words, wind spun around a central point, set and kept in motion by the rotation of the earth. Conversely, Espy theorized that rising warm air, varying pressure, and the cooling and condensing of moist air fueled destructive weather phenomena. He believed that hurricane winds converged inward to a central location and soared skyward, just as hot air rises up a chimney.

Although other scientists offered competing (and erroneous) explanations of storm development, the Redfield-Espy controversy held center stage during the 1830s and 1840s. Both deduced pieces of the storm puzzle but neither realized that they only grasped part of the picture. Hurricanes rotate counterclockwise (Redfield). Air spirals into the center of tropical cyclones, which are fueled by warm air lifting and cooling (Espy).

Espy's influence proved long lasting. In 1824, he joined the faculty of the Franklin Institute in Philadelphia. He began gathering storm reports from volunteer observers around the United States and championed a national weather service. In 1842, Espy was appointed the government's first salaried meteorologist. His *Philosophy of Storms* became a standard reference of that era. Collaboration with the Smithsonian's Joseph Henry brought enduring results.

The men wanted to understand weather systems, particularly storms, and use the knowledge to create daily maps and forecasts. That required a national

National Portrait Gallery, Thomas Sully

James Espy

Joseph Henry

observer network. The idea also necessitated the timely dissemination of predictions, made possible with the invention of the telegraph in 1844. Espy worked with Henry to develop an observation and research project. In 1848, the Smithsonian Institution allocated $1,000 for the effort—its first scientific undertaking.

There was no shortage of volunteers. The program, however, faced unforeseen obstacles, including a challenge discussed in the Smithsonian's annual report of 1850:

"Since the date of the last report, the system particularly intended to investigate the nature of American storms, immediately under the care of this Institution, has been continued and improved both in the number of the stations, and, to some degree, in the character of the instruments.

"Appropriation was made to furnish a larger number of observation stations with barometers and thermometers, by distributing these instruments in some cases entirely at the expense of the Institution, and in others by offering them to the observers at half their original cost; but the demand was so great, and the loss by breakage in transmitting the instruments so frequent, that the appropriations were soon exhausted, and until we can afford to devote a large sum to the object, and employ a special agent to transport the articles to their destination, it will be inadvisable to attempt anything more in this way. Though the instruments employed by these observers in some cases cannot be relied on for giving absolute results, yet they serve a good purpose in determining changes of pressure and temperature, and the returns give all the varying phases of the sky."

The project thrived. Volunteers sent monthly reports by mail. A few provided daily observations by telegraph replete with assorted measurements and descriptions of atmospheric phenomena. The network operated from 1849 to 1874 and then merged with a new government weather office.[1]

By the late 1850s the Smithsonian exhibited a daily weather map, posting telegraphed weather observations. Espy, Henry and others began issuing forecasts, focusing on a few cities. The predictions covered 24 hours and were quite basic—rain or shine, high and low temperatures. Not much detail but consider the significance: The quality of a weather forecast is readily apparent. An inaccurate prediction brings public ridicule, if not hostility. For the first time, prognosticators had the confidence and level of understanding to be right more often than wrong and to offer something greater than mere speculation.

Continuous and increasingly widespread weather observations led to a more comprehensive picture of the nation's climate. In 1857, Lorin Blodget, using Smithsonian data, wrote *Climatology of the United States and of the Temperate Latitudes of the North American Continent*, an important meteorological reference book of the era.

The federal government joined the quest to record and track the nation's weather. President Ulysses S. Grant authorized creation of a government weather unit attached to the Army Signal Service. In November 1870, the section began collecting data and issuing daily maps and predictions for the eastern United States. (There was too little data from the West to forecast that region's weather.)

The military weather office became a civilian agency under the Department of Agriculture in 1891, designated the United States Weather Bureau.[2]

Mr. Hallowell, a diarist and weather observer, shared the excitement of his fellow enthusiasts when, during 1873, he penned:

---

[1] The National Weather Service still relies on a nationwide network of volunteers to provide basic data. "Cooperative observers" now number more than 12,000. They provide daily maximum and minimum temperatures, precipitation totals and other weather data.

[2] In 1940, the Weather Bureau was transferred from the Department of Agriculture to the Department of Commerce. The agency became the National Weather Service in 1971. (This book uses the name of the organization in effect at the time of a particular hurricane.)

"A great advance has been made in meteorological knowledge, and the public is beginning to reap some advantage from the long-continued labors of scientific men, commencing with Franklin, and ably seconded in latter days by Prof. Espy. By attentively watching the phenomena connected with rain, currents of air, changes in the height of the barometer, and other things, and by laboriously collating the results, a law of storms has been developed which by the aid of the telegraph in announcing changes as they occur over the country enables the central observer to give us the daily 'probabilities' that have proved so wonderfully accurate even this early in the experiment. By the cautionary signals on the Lakes and on the coast many lives and much property have been saved."

***

The 19th century saw significant advances in weather forecasting and a greater understanding of hurricanes. The following luminaries made notable contributions:

Francis Beaufort (1774-1857) Sir Francis Beaufort designed a wind estimation scale for nautical use that became an international standard. The Beaufort Scale is based on the wind's effect on the sea surface and sails. In 1838, the British Navy adopted the measure and its use became widespread. A visual tool, the Beaufort Scale required no special equipment. Gradations ranged from Force 0 to Force 12, a hurricane, a wind "which no canvas could withstand." The measure was eventually adapted for land use. (see Appendix A, the Beaufort Wind Force Scale)

Gustave-Gaspard Coriolis (1792-1843) In 1835, the French physicist published a paper that described what is today known as the Coriolis effect. Its essence: There exists a deflective force on all free-moving objects (including hurricanes) as a result of the earth's rotation. Deflection is to the right in the Northern Hemisphere and to the left in the Southern Hemisphere. Hurricanes require the spin imparted by the Coriolis effect.

William Reid (1791-1858) During the early 18th century, Reid wrote a reference popularly known as *The Law of Storms*. The book described and illustrated the quadrants of a hurricane, including the dangerous right front sector. Reid also established the Northern Hemisphere's first hurricane warning system.

Henry Piddington (1797-1858) Piddington built on William Reid's work. He coined the term "cyclone" (derived from the Greek word 'kyklos,'—coil of a snake) to describe all rotary storms. His influential reference, *The Sailor's Horn Book*, provided a basic understanding of the wind flow around a tropical cyclone. It assisted seafarers in avoiding the most violent sector of a hurricane. Piddington's book also suggested a maneuvering strategy to enable ships to make better time by advantageously negotiating the fringes of a hurricane.

Benito Viñes (1837-1893) The foremost authority on Atlantic hurricanes during the late 19th century. Viñes, a Jesuit priest, organized ongoing storm research as director of the meteorological observatory at the Royal College of Belén, in Havana, Cuba. He set up a model observational network and warning system on the island. His book, *Practical Hints in Regard to West Indian Hurricanes*, became the period's most incisive analysis of tropical cyclones. Father Viñes died in 1893, respected by meteorologists throughout the world.

Cleveland Abbe (1838-1916) The "father of the United States Weather Bureau." Abbe served as director of the Mitchell Astronomical Observatory in Cincinnati, Ohio, after the Civil War. He began issuing daily weather forecasts during 1869, one of the first meteorologists to do so. Abbe became the meteorologist-in-charge of the Army Signal Service's weather unit at its inception and was later appointed director of the Weather Bureau. He served until his death. Nicknamed "Old Probs," a reference to the term "probabilities," as forecasts were called in the early years of his tenure.

***

During the 20th century, new technology improved the quality of observations, forecasts and warnings. Important inventions included:

Radio: Guglielmo Marconi's "wireless telegraphy," radio, was less than a decade old when, in 1902, forecasts were transmitted to ships at sea. On December 3, 1905, the Weather Bureau received its first broadcast weather observation from an ocean going vessel. It received an initial report of a hurricane during 1909. Within a few years, radio enabled expanded and timely data collection from sea. It also provided forecasters a more effective way to issue weather warnings.

By the late 1930s, the radiosonde, an adaptation of radio technology, became an integral tool for upper-air weather soundings. A package of instruments attached to a balloon provided information on temperature, humidity and barometric pressure. Such observations improved the accuracy of storm forecasting. (Dropsondes, a variation of radiosondes, are dropped into hurricanes by reconnaissance aircraft, providing a wealth of data as they parachute to earth.)

Radar: Originally developed to track aircraft and introduced in 1942, radar proved adept at picking up cloud patterns. Astonished radar operators watched the spectral appearance of spiral feeder bands as a hurricane passed off the Mid-Atlantic coast during 1944. Beginning in 1955, the Weather Bureau began installing radar at forecast offices. Cape Hatteras, N.C., became an early site, a key location for tracking hurricanes. Radar continues as a valuable technology to observe, analyze and evaluate storms. Refinement has led to more precise and detailed information on approaching weather systems and timely watches and warnings.

Aircraft: The airplane has proven invaluable for probing the atmosphere. During World War II, for example, pilots inadvertently discovered jet streams—rivers of fast-moving air, steering currents for storms. A flight made on a dare led to a breakthrough in hurricane observation and tracking.

On July 27, 1943, Lt. Colonel Joseph Duckworth and his navigator, Lt. Ralph O'Hair, flew into a hurricane off the Texas coast. The trip went well. Confident that the storm wouldn't demolish his airplane, Duckworth made a second flight that day. Regular military sorties began in 1944.

Hurricane Hunters, the 53rd Weather Reconnaissance Squadron of the U.S. Air Force Reserve, based at Keesler Air Force Base in Biloxi, Miss., is tasked with flying into hurricanes. Flights gather position and intensity data, relaying vital information to the National Hurricane Center.

The National Oceanic and Atmospheric Administration (NOAA) also operates several airplanes. The fleet is based at MacDill Air Force Base in Tampa, Fla. According to NOAA:

"The United States Air Force planes are the workhorses of the hurricane hunting effort. They are often deployed to a forward base, such as Antigua, and carry out most of the reconnaissance of developing waves and depressions. Their mission in these situations is to look for signs of a closed circulation and any strengthening or organizing that the storm might be showing. This information is relayed by satellite to the National Hurricane Center for the hurricane specialists to evaluate.

"The NOAA planes are more highly instrumented and are generally reserved for hurricanes threatening

NOAA

Hurricane hunting.

landfall, especially on U.S. territory. They are also used to conduct scientific research on storms.

"The planes carry between six to fifteen people, both the flight crew and the meteorologists. Flight crews consist of a pilot, co-pilot, flight engineer, navigator, and electrical technicians. The weather crew might consist of a flight meteorologist, lead project scientist, cloud physicist, radar specialist and dropsonde operators.

"The primary purpose of reconnaissance is to track the center of circulation—these are the coordinates that the National Hurricane Center issues—and to measure the maximum winds. But the crews also evaluate the storm's size, structure and development. This information is also relayed to the National Hurricane Center via radio and satellite link. Most of this data, which is critical in determining the hurricane's threat, cannot be obtained from satellite observation."

Satellites: Beginning in 1960 with the launch of TIROS I (Television and Infrared Observations Satellite), the United States has maintained a weather eye in space. The satellite soon located a typhoon in the Pacific, relaying valuable photographs during the busy 1960 hurricane season. In 1961, TIROS III became the first satellite to locate a newly tropical cyclone. Satellites began pinpointing suspicious cloud clusters, making aircraft patrols more efficient.

The National Weather Service currently uses "Geostationary Operational Environmental Satellites," which remain above a given point on the equator, traveling at the same speed as the Earth's rotation. These sentinels provide a continuous view of the tropical Atlantic.

The Weather Service also deploys "Polar-orbiting Operational Environmental Satellites" to provide global coverage needed to support longer forecasts and weather models. The combination of geostationary and polar-orbiting satellites gives forecasters a window on evolving and interacting weather systems.

***

No invention has had a greater impact on hurricane forecasting than the computer. Meteorologists recognized its potential to gather myriad data and convert input into useful products.

The vast number-crunching capability of the computer gave life to an idea proposed in 1922. A British mathematician, Lewis Richardson, believed that mathematical methods might be applied to weather prediction. His book, *Weather Prediction by Numerical Process* intrigued meteorologists, but implementation seemed impossible. The proposed method used equations requiring a vast quantity of weather data. Richardson estimated that the number of calculations needed for an accurate daily product would require tens of thousands of workers with calculators laboring around the clock throughout the year. However, the visionary, who died in 1953, lived to see the technology that made his dream possible.

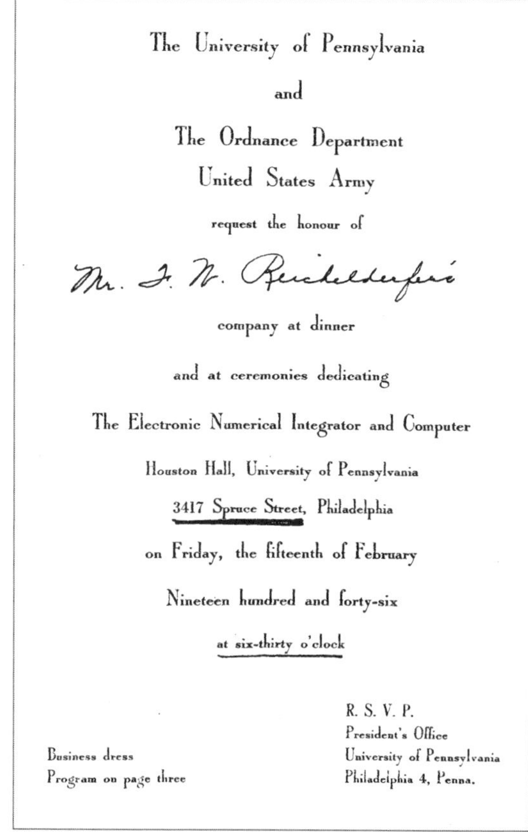

The University of Pennsylvania

and

The Ordnance Department

United States Army

request the honour of

Mr. F. W. Reichelderfer's

company at dinner

and at ceremonies dedicating

The Electronic Numerical Integrator and Computer

Houston Hall, University of Pennsylvania

3417 Spruce Street, Philadelphia

on Friday, the fifteenth of February

Nineteen hundred and forty-six

at six-thirty o'clock

R. S. V. P.
President's Office
University of Pennsylvania
Philadelphia 4, Penna.

Business dress
Program on page three

During February 1946, the director of the Weather Bureau, Francis Reichelderfer, attended the unveiling of the first computer, an ungainly 30-ton behemoth. The meteorologist scarcely contained his excitement as he grasped its potential. Reichelderfer wrote to the Secretary of Commerce:

"I attended the dedication ceremonies for the ENIAC (electronics numerical integrator and computer) at the Moore School of Electrical Engineering, University of Pennsylvania, Friday evening, and witnessed the demonstration of the computer. The ceremony was attended by approximately one hundred mathematicians and physicists representing various educational and research institutions throughout the country. The computer is impressive—it is capable of performing more than one million additions and subtractions of ten-figure numbers in five minutes, thus compressing computations that would require several weeks if done by hand, into a few minutes.

"We have had our eyes on the possibilities in this development for several months and have had conferences with the designers of the electronics computer for the purpose of determining how it can be applied to meteorology. Neither the electronics engineers nor the meteorologists are able to answer that question at the moment."

Reichelderfer went on to say, "The importance of this development, if it turns out to be possible, can scarcely be overestimated and we are going ahead with our investigation of the possibilities as rapidly as possible. We have been working with representatives of the RCA Laboratories for several months as well as with the ENIAC group at the University of Pennsylvania."

By the 1950s the Weather Bureau, academia and the military began researching and developing computer models based on numerical forecasting. That effort continues.

The computer modeling of hurricanes combines weather soundings with physical equations to generate predictions of storm behavior. Data comes from automated stations, observers, ships, weather balloons and other sources. Meteorologists analyze several different models. Some models focus on storm tracks while others anticipate intensity. Predictions differ because of varying atmospheric assumptions and the scope and parameters of data sampled. There is no universal standard.

The models' capabilities are hindered by limited knowledge of how the atmosphere works. Also, they are only run a few times each day and cannot take into account the many short-term changes in weather conditions. In addition, there remain large gaps in data coverage, and sometimes the observations themselves have errors. As a result, computers work with a limited view of the overall picture.

Models have proven most successful at offering guidance on hurricane tracks, especially within a 48-hour timeframe. They have been less reliable when forecasting intensity.

***

The Miami, Fla., office of the Weather Bureau was designated the National Hurricane Center in 1955. It was given primary responsibility for forecasting hurricanes in the Atlantic and eastern Pacific oceans. That year Congress authorized funding to create a research unit at the Weather Bureau, the National Hurricane Research Project.

Now known as the Hurricane Research Division, it is one of the National Weather Service's leading offices for tropical cyclone investigation. It works with the National Hurricane Center, other government agencies, universities and the private sector to increase understanding of tropical cyclones and improve predictions.

DIRECTORS OF THE NATIONAL HURRICANE CENTER

Grady Norton (Unofficial 1935-54)
Gordon Dunn (1955-67)
Robert Simpson (1968-73)
Neil Frank (1973-87)
Robert Sheets (1988-94)
Jerry Jarrel (Acting Director 1994-95)
Robert Burpee (1995-97)
Jerry Jarrel (Acting Director 1997-98/ Director 1998-2000)
Max Mayfield (2000-2007)
William Proenza (2007-)

***

The Tropical Prediction Center (TPC) in Miami, Fla., is home to the National Hurricane Center. The TPC generates and coordinates tropical cyclone forecasts for 24 countries in the Americas and Caribbean. It monitors the waters of the North Atlantic Ocean, Caribbean Sea, Gulf of Mexico and eastern North Pacific Ocean. Components include:

- The National Hurricane Center, which maintains a continuous watch on tropical cyclones. It prepares and issues forecasts, watches and warnings. The office conducts research to evaluate and improve forecasting techniques. It offers an outreach and education program that trains emergency managers and representatives from the many countries affected by hurricanes.

- The Tropical Analysis and Forecast Branch, which provides marine and aviation weather analysis, forecasts and warnings. It also produces satellite-based weather interpretation and rainfall estimates for the international community, including tropical cyclone position and intensity estimates.

- The Technical Support Branch, which monitors and maintains computer and communications systems. The office includes an applied research and techniques development unit, which develops tools and techniques for hurricane and tropical weather analysis and prediction.

The goal of the Tropical Prediction Center is "to save lives, mitigate property loss, and improve economic efficiency by issuing the best watches, warnings, forecasts and analyses of hazardous tropical weather, and by increasing our understanding of these hazards." It strives "to be America's calm, clear and trusted voice in the eye of the storm, and, with its partners, enable communities to be safe from tropical weather threats."

Put another way, to borrow the words of Henry Hallowell, "the day will no doubt come when we shall know the probable weather of the coming 24 hours (and more!) with almost the same certainty with which we now foretell an eclipse."

Photograph by Julio Ripoll

The Tropical Prediction Center, home to the National Hurricane Center. The building's fortress-like 10-inch-thick walls and squat architecture were made to withstand a Category 5 hurricane.

RADIO OPERATORS SAVE LIVES AND AID FORECASTERS

September 1979. A rough time for the newly independent Caribbean nation of St. Lucia. Hurricane David roared through, leaving many casualties. A British naval hospital ship was in the region but needed a formal request to assist. With the island's communications in shambles, permission seemed impossible. To the rescue: amateur (ham) radio and the National Hurricane Center.

Julio Ripoll, then a student at the University of Miami and ham radio enthusiast, had set up an experimental station at the hurricane office. He handled transmissions between the British ship and St. Lucia.

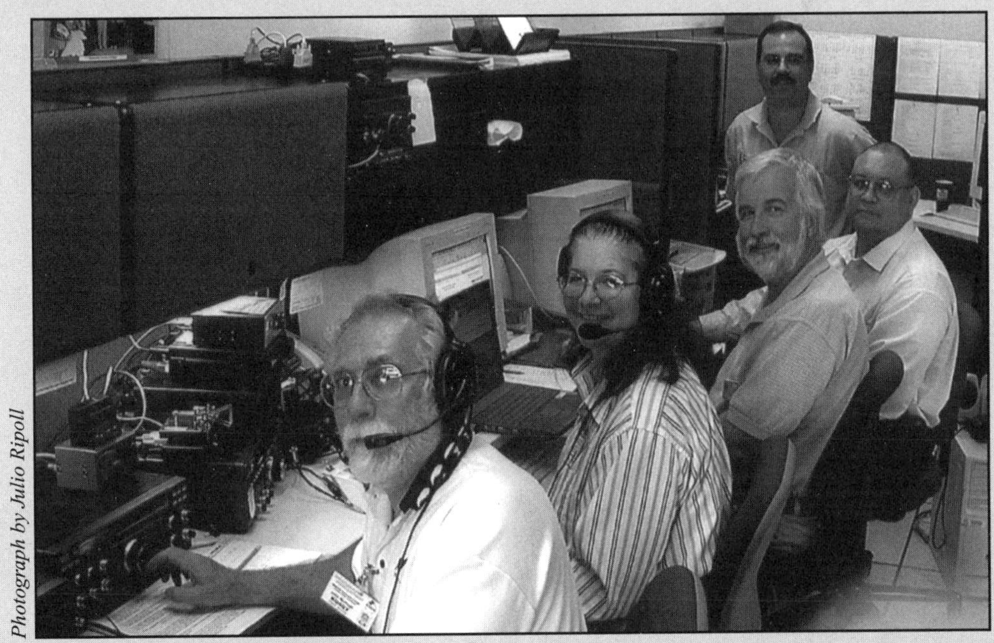

Photograph by Julio Ripoll

Amateur (ham) radio operators at the National Hurricane Center provide a vital link to storm-ravaged areas. On duty, from left: John McHugh, Joanne Carbana, David Knight, Caesar Carbana, Julio Ripoll

"The radio operator in St. Lucia said, 'Wait just a few minutes. I'll get the prime minister,' " said Ripoll, who was skeptical. "Believe it or not, 10 to 15 minutes went by and, to my surprise, the prime minister came on the air and gave the ship permission to land."

That success launched an ongoing effort. Ripoll is among dozens of volunteers who spend each hurricane season handling radio communications for the National Hurricane Center. Their station, WX4NHC, assists forecasters by sending and gathering information as storms approach and strike land. Operators receive broadcasts in English, Spanish and French.

"We get information not available elsewhere," Ripoll said. "Radio operators in affected areas give us what they see and hear. That adds a human touch."

Volunteers have diverse professional backgrounds. One is a meteorologist. Ripoll (WD4R) is employed as an architect. John McHugh (K4AG), the organization's coordinator, is a retired engineer. He sees his role this way:

"I'm like a mailman. I gather data and deliver it to the forecasters. I don't try to interpret it. I don't try to embellish it. I give it to them as received.

"Max (Mayfield, former director of the National Hurricane Center) has said, it's nice to know what's going on at 5,000 or 10,000 feet, but we *need* to know what's happening on the ground."

The use of amateur radio during weather emergencies isn't unique to the National Hurricane Center. Every National Weather Service field office has a Skywarn program that includes radio operators who observe and report severe weather. They and other trained spotters—volunteers who submit reports by telephone or computer—provide accounts of ground conditions.

The National Hurricane Center radio station provides a link to isolated regions. For example, during Hurricane Mitch—a monster that meandered through Central America in 1998—it received an alarming report from an observer at a lake on Mexico's Yucatan Peninsula.

"That operator told us that the water had retracted several hundred meters from the shore," said Ripoll. "People were venturing out on the lake bed. We knew that there'd be a rush of water back into the area once the eye passed. It could kill many people.

"We got on the air and broadcast a warning: 'We need everyone to get out of the lake bed!' It was relayed to the operator and the warning got out. We will never know whether we saved one life or many, but I believe that we helped save lives. That is just one of many instances where our work has saved lives."

The 2005 hurricane season proved to be the organization's busiest. Radio operators will never forget Hurricane Katrina, which made a personal visit.

"The eye went right over the Hurricane Center," Ripoll said. "I was on duty as the eye came over. That made for some excitement.

"When the eye came over, it got very calm. That's when one of the forecasters came into the radio room, very excited, and said, 'You've got to see this!' We ran to a vestibule and looked out a thick glass door. We were probably in the eye for 45 minutes. Then, the wind picked up within minutes. We saw the eyewall come across a field. We watched large palm fronds shoot like arrows when the wind returned."

The station remained on the air as Katrina struck and devastated sections of Louisiana and Mississippi.

"The National Weather Service office in Slidell (La.) lost all (normal) communication with the National Weather Service regional office and the National Hurricane Center," said Ripoll. "They had a ham radio operator in their office, and we were able to maintain a communications link for six critical hours. They gave us their peak wind readings and told us what was going on. At one point, the wind gusted to 138 mph. All the trees went down. They couldn't get out of the building because the trees were blocking everything. We talked to the operator throughout the whole thing.

"We also received reports from New Orleans, where people were standing on their roofs asking for rescue. We passed the information to Max Mayfield and to the FEMA office at the National Hurricane Center.

"After Katrina, most communications (in the hardest-hit areas) were out. There were no telephones, no cell phones, no computers. A lot of communication was done on ham radio. In many areas, that was the only link still operational."

As they've done so many times, amateur radio operators played a critical role during and after a storm.

"The old technology is rock-solid," Ripoll said. "That's why they've kept us around for 25 years. They've got state-of-the-art satellites, computers and all that. But sometimes they need (information) from a guy with a 100-watt ham radio running off a battery, with a wire hanging out his window."

"We're not in it for medals or glory," said McHugh. "We're the boys in the back room, rarely noticed. We do our thing and try to help."

HURRICANES
1600s

1609

July

"Now would I give a thousand furlongs of sea for an acre of barren ground—long heath, brown furze, anything. The wills above be done, but I would fain die a dry death."

— From *The Tempest* by William Shakespeare

amestown, Va., the initial permanent English settlement in America, was two years old when a fleet with 500 colonists embarked from Great Britain during June 1609. Weeks later, a hurricane roiled the western Atlantic, scattering the vessels. Most escaped the maelstrom but the flagship, *Sea Venture*, lurched toward a sinister place known as the "Isle of Divels."

It lodged on a reef. Those onboard safely reached shore. They arrived at a refuge discovered nearly a century earlier by the Spanish explorer, Juan Bermudez.

Expecting hell, the group found paradise. The only demons were those of the mind. According to their leader, Admiral George Somers, "All the fairies of the rockes were but flocks of birds, and all the devils of the woods were herds of swine."[1]

Food and water were abundant and the climate delightful. The castaways stayed through the winter and built two smaller vessels, the *Deliverance* and *Patience*. Some yearned to linger but Virginia's newly appointed governor, Sir Thomas Gates, insisted that everyone continue to America.

The party arrived in Jamestown during May 1610. They were greeted as if resurrected. In fact, it was the inhabitants of Jamestown who flirted with death during the previous winter. Life hung by a thread in the New World, a strand easily severed. Hunger decimated the colony during a period that became known as the "starving time." Only 60 gaunt settlers greeted spring from a population that once numbered several hundred.

The diversion of the *Sea Venture* saved its passengers—and likely preserved Jamestown.

The influx of newcomers provided leadership and bolstered the outpost. The group included John Rolfe, whose marriage to the Indian princess Pocahontas brought a critical period of peace and assistance between the colonists and area tribes. Rolfe's most enduring contribution, however, was raising a marketable strain of tobacco. The golden weed ensured Jamestown's survival and prosperity.

***

Shakespeare was an investor in the Virginia Company, sponsor of Jamestown. He knew the tale of the *Sea Venture*. Its mishap served as grist for the opening act—and inspiration for the closing scene—of his play, *The Tempest*.

The production debuted in 1611. It opened with a storm-tossed vessel miraculously spared disaster when blown upon a mysterious island. *The Tempest* concluded with a happy ending—not unlike that of the *Sea Venture*.

Library of Congress, R.A. Artlett

William Shakespeare found inspiration for *The Tempest* after a hurricane shipwrecked English settlers bound for Jamestown, Va.

[1] The British initially named the land "Somers Island." Later, Somers Island was changed to Bermuda in recognition of Juan Bermudez. Pigs found by the *Sea Venture* survivors were descendants of those left by Bermudez.

1667

September

THE YEAR OF THE HURRICANE

Virginia struggled financially until it found an economic savior in tobacco. Initially shipped to England in 1613, the weed became currency, a measure of wealth. Leaves could buy land, pay taxes or even purchase a spouse. From 100 to 150 pounds of it bought the trans-Atlantic passage of a bride.

At first, the English market absorbed all the colonists could send. But by mid-century London was awash. Prices plummeted. Planters debated ways to restore profitability. Finally, during 1666, the governors and respective legislatures of North Carolina, Virginia and Maryland agreed to an unprecedented one-year cessation of production effective in 1667.

Despite economic woes implementation proved elusive as Lord Baltimore, the proprietor of Maryland, held veto power over the province, which he exercised. However, no mortal could prevent a production cut, at least not in "the year of the hurricane."

A storm sliced through the Mid-Atlantic region on August 27 (Sept. 6). Fitful winds arose from the northeast. Dark clouds hurried through a troubled sky. The rains came, a little at first. Several sources tell of the calamity that followed.

"On the 27th of August followed the most dreadful Hurry Cane that ever the colony groaned under," wrote Thomas Ludwell, Virginia's colonial secretary. "It lasted 24 hours, began at North East and went around northerly till it came to west, and so till it came to South East, where it ceased. It was accompanied with a most violent rain but no thunder. The night of it was the most dismal time I ever knew or heard of, for the wind and rain raised so confused a noise, mixed with the continual cracks of falling houses.

"... The waves were impetuously beaten against the shores and by the violence forced, as it were, into all creeks, rivers and bays to so prodigious a height that it hazarded the drowning of many people who lived not in sight of the rivers, yet were forced to climb to the top of their houses to keep themselves above water.

"The waves carried all the foundations of the fort at Point Comfort into the river and most of our timber which was very chargeably brought thither to perfect it. Had it been finished and garrisoned, (it would have seemed like) they had been stormed by such an enemy as no power but Gods can restrain.[1]

"... The nearest computation is at least 10,000 houses blown down, all the Indian grain laid flat on the ground, all the Tobacco in the fields torn to pieces, and most of that which was in the houses perished with them. The fences about the cornfields were either blown down or beaten to the ground by trees that fell upon them. Before the owners could repair them the hogs & cattle got (into the fields) and in most places devoured much of what the storm had left."

By 1667, the crude dwellings of earlier years had given way to more substantial abodes. Nevertheless, the hurricane made shambles of entire neighborhoods. Virginia's governor, William Berkeley, acknowledged the disaster in a letter to Lord Arlington, secretary of state and colonial minister for Great Britain.

"... A mighty wind on 27 Aug. destroyed four-fifths of (our) tobacco and corn and blew down in two hours fifteen thousand houses in Virginia and Maryland."

The following article appeared in London during late 1667:

"Having this opportunity, I cannot but acquaint you with the Relation of a very strange Tempest which hath been in (Virginia), which began Aug. 27, and continued with such Violence that it overturned many Houses, burying in the Ruines much Goods and many people, beating to the ground (crops) in the Fields and blowing many Cattle that were near the Sea or Rivers into them. Whereby, unknown numbers have perished, to the great affliction of all people, few having escaped who have not suffered in their persons or Estates. Much corn was blown away and great quantities of Tobacco have been lost to the great damage of many and utter undoing of others. Neither did

[1] After a Dutch raid in the spring colonists fortified a wooden stockade, Fort Algernourne (which is now the site of historic Fort Monroe). When the Chesapeake Bay subsided, little more than a few stakes remained.

it end here, but the Trees were torn up by the roots, and in many places whole Woods blown down, so that (residents) cannot go from Plantation to Plantation.

"… The Tempest, for the time, was so furious that it hath made a general Desolation, overturning many Plantations, so that there was nothing that could stand its fury. We are now with all the industry imaginable repairing our shattered houses and gathering together what the Tempest hath left us. Although it was not alike Violent in all places, yet there is scarse any place in the whole Country where there is not left sufficient marks of its ruines. By the ships you will hear a particular of all our losses. …"

Few accounts of 17th century hurricanes survive. The event in 1667 is an exception, underscoring an extraordinary occurrence.

Unfortunately, there is no record of where the hurricane made landfall, its track and forward speed. A high-end Category 2 or a Category 3 coming ashore in southeastern Virginia could cause such havoc. A Category 4 making landfall in the vicinity of the North Carolina Outer Banks and tracking briskly to the north-northwest would also devastate the Chesapeake region.

Colonists had endured starvation, epidemics and warfare. Now they discovered a new threat. Nobody thought a hurricane possible so far inland.

The storm created a kinship, a reference point. Survivors spoke of events, "Before the year of the hurricane" and "After the year of the hurricane." Decades later, a younger generation might question the fantastic tales of wind and rain. Elders would glance at each other, smile sadly and nod knowingly.

1693

October

ACCOMACK STORM

"There happened a most violent storme in Virginia, which stopped the course of the ancient channels, and made some where there never were any: So that betwixt the bounds of Virginia and Newcastle in Pennsylvania, on the seaboard side, are many navigable rivers for sloops and small vessels."

Letter by a "Mr. Scarburgh"
(Transactions of the Royal Society—1694)

Hurricanes and nor'easters cause more shoreline erosion than any other weather systems. Scarburgh's words describing a storm during October 1693 could apply to more recent events such as the hurricane of August 1933, which carved the famous Ocean City, Md., inlet, or the Ash Wednesday nor'easter of March 1962. Each dallied off the Mid-Atlantic coast, altering beaches and creating channels "where there never were any." Relentless gales stoked increasing tides until an invasive sea washed over barrier islands. Severe coastal storms lasting days can transport a quantity of sand normally carried over a period of months or more.

Scarburgh's event is also known as the "Accomack Storm," a reference to the author's residence on the Virginia Eastern Shore. It cut inlets as far north as Fire Island, near New York City. Weather historians have described the blow as extremely powerful although little beyond Scarburgh's description exists. His account makes no mention of wind-related property losses. The tempest appears to have been a minimal hurricane or strong nor'easter that stalled offshore and produced destructive, erosive tides.

HURRICANES
1700s

1724

August

THE GREAT GUST

A pair of hurricanes brought notable wind and rain to the Mid-Atlantic during 1724. The first storm, the "Great Gust," arrived on August 12 (23). David Ludlum, the author of *Early American Hurricanes*, wrote:

"Though the severe tropical storm, which struck the Chesapeake Bay area of Virginia and Maryland in August 1724, produced a long-lasting impression, very few meteorological details have been preserved. The Virginia Gazette twenty years later in describing a December storm of 1744 remarked, 'The like has not been known in the Memory of Man, not even in the great Gust in the year 1724.' "

According to John Custis, who lived along the lower James River, "We have had such a violent flood of rain and prodigious gust of wind the like I do not believe ever happened since the universal deluge."

"Gust" meant hurricane. Widespread structural damage.

Did the Great Gust approach the stature of the hurricane of 1667? Did residents fear for their lives and the integrity of their homes? Only sketchy information survives. What is known is that the event remained a benchmark for decades.

Days later, another tropical system brought flooding to eastern sections of the Middle Atlantic. From the *American Weekly Mercury*:

"Philadelphia, August 20.

"On the 17th, 18th and 19th of this (month), we had a violent Storm of Wind and Rain, which has caused such a Fresh in our Creeks and Rivers that it has broke several of our best Mill Dams in this and our Neighboring Provinces, (particularly Col. Trents Mill at Penepack), and the Fresh is so strong that our Vessels in the Road have not Winded: Such a Fresh has not been known these Twenty Years."

***

The hurricane of 1724 is among several significant tropical cyclones to visit the Mid-Atlantic region during the late 1600s and early 1700s. Sparse records make identification and description difficult. Accounts suggest that major coastal storms occurred in August 1635, September 1675 and November 1706. Destructive hurricanes visited interior sections during August 1683 and October 1703.[1]

---

[1] Most information on early American hurricanes is found in period correspondence as American newspapers were scarce until the middle 1700s. The *Boston News-Letter*, which began on April 24, 1704, was the first newspaper in the colonies to be continuously published. By the time of the Great Gust of 1724, there were fewer than 10 regular publications.

1743

November

THE ECLIPSE HURRICANE/FRANKLIN'S STORM

Benjamin Franklin anticipated the lunar eclipse for months. On the day of the event, October 22 (Nov. 2), he was dismayed to observe an approaching storm. Franklin never saw the cloud-obscured eclipse but, instead, discerned an important meteorological principle.

Logic of the time held that a storm tracked in the direction of the prevailing wind. Philadelphia experienced a northeast gale, which meant that the system should have affected Boston first. However, Franklin learned that the residents of Boston had a wonderful view of the eclipse. The strong wind and heavy rain arrived shortly thereafter.

Franklin correctly theorized that wind direction doesn't necessarily govern storm movement. He mentioned his hypothesis in a letter to a friend, Jared Eliot, and also wrote, "The Storm did a great deal of Damage all along the Coast, for we had Accounts of it in the News Papers from Boston, Newport, New York, Maryland and Virginia. …"

Interior sections of the Mid-Atlantic and New England were spared the turmoil dealt the coast. Strong gales and a furious sea assaulted Rhode Island and Massachusetts. The tide at Boston reached its highest level in nearly 20 years.

The event left a historic footnote. John Winthrop, a professor at Harvard College in Cambridge, Mass., took the first known barometric reading of an American hurricane, recording a minimum central pressure of 29.35 inches.

***

In 2006, the 300th anniversary of Franklin's birth, it's worth recalling his contributions to meteorology. He wrote papers and letters on a wide range of atmospheric phenomena. He offered farsighted theories on storm movement and lightning. Investigation of the latter included his famous kite-flying experiment in 1752. It resulted in a practical invention, the lightning rod. (The Maryland State House still uses a Franklin lightning rod.)

The multi-talented Philadelphian wasn't afraid to shake up outdated notions.

Although a basic understanding of storm movement and circulation took another century, Franklin's comments on the Eclipse Hurricane were important. A prominent thinker raised questions about a long-accepted truism—one that was, quite simply, wrong.

National Portrait Gallery, Edward Fisher

Benjamin Franklin missed a storm-obscured lunar eclipse but discerned an important meteorological principle.

1749

October

Hurricanes impacting the Middle Atlantic coast don't come much stronger than that of October 7-8 (18-19), 1749. It left a lasting impression on the land and people of southeastern Virginia. The (Norfolk) *Virginia Gazette* chronicled the storm's passage:

"The wind began to blow hard, and at about one or two in the morning (Oct. 8) was very violent at N.E. with rain, and kept increasing. The hardest of the storm was from ten (a.m.) till two (p.m.) on Sunday. The tide rose 15 feet perpendicular higher than usual and forced ships ashore where the water was never before known to flow, many ships and other vessels being now so far from water, and some of them loaded too, that they will cost more than their worth to get them afloat, if it be practicable at any rate. Several ships on the docks were floated off; all the wharves and many warehouses are entirely carried away."

Also from the *Gazette*:

"Several gentlemen now at Norfolk, who were at Jamaica a few years ago when a terrible hurricane happened there, which destroyed many men of war, say this was much more violent than that. The tide kept continually fluxing, and at the rate of five knots an hour overflowed all the streets and has carried some small craft near a mile from the common high-water mark, and left some in cornfields.

"We hear from the upper part of the country that the great freshet of late has done great damage to the crops there.

"From the lower part of the country, that by a great gust of wind and rain, which happened on Sunday last, many people received considerable damage thereby; some houses being carried away by the high tides, and one whole family drowned.

"From Hampton, that the water rose four feet in the streets and that considerable damage is done to the shipping, several ships being drove on shore and some out to sea; the wind being so violent that it tore up large trees by the roots and snapped others in the middle. The like storm has not been known in the memory of our oldest men."

Big storms alter the coastline; the hurricane of 1749 left its imprint. A sandy rise remained behind, inside the Chesapeake Bay. It gradually grew and is now Willoughby Spit, a finger of land in Norfolk, home to 4,000 residents.

The hurricane veered northeast after battering Virginia. Gales whipped coastal sections of New Jersey and southern New England, uprooting trees and wrecking boats but causing less havoc than in the Old Dominion.

***

What kind of storm would generate a 15-foot rise on the lower Chesapeake Bay, a height equal to that of 1749?

"It would take a Category 4 hurricane moving in a north-northwest or west-northwest direction to produce the greatest tides," says Bill Sammler, warning coordination meteorologist at the National Weather Service forecast office in Wakefield, Va.

"This would be the worst possible case, as a Category 4 this far north is extremely rare," Sammler explained. "However, tidal departures of 15-17 feet above normal could be expected with such a storm. This is comparable to the tidal departures in the 1749 hurricane."

A tide 15 feet above normal? A harrowing thought. The highest tide during the 20th century rose about 10 feet above normal. More than 1.5 million people live in the vicinity of Hampton Roads. Emergency management officials warn that such a flood could displace more than a half-million people.

What if the storm came as a surprise? What if a seemingly minimal hurricane tapped a summer-warm ocean and exploded to a Category 3 or 4 at landfall? It might snare those who refused or were unable to evacuate. It might catch motorists as they crawled through horrific traffic jams.

The hurricane would likely track near the great urban centers of the Northeast bringing enormously destructive wind, rain and surge—possibly becoming one of the costliest natural disasters in U.S. history.

Is Hampton Roads a Mid-Atlantic New Orleans waiting for a Katrina?

Hurricane history suggests that a similar disaster could occur. Hampton Roads has faced several close encounters within the past century.

In 1933, a Category 2 hurricane made landfall 50 miles south of Virginia Beach. During 1936, another Category 2 churned to within 30 miles of Cape Henry. A last-minute jog to the northeast kept the eye—and the storm's fiercest winds—over the Atlantic. Storm surges generated by the hurricanes of 1933 and 1936 rank among the area's highest of the 20th century.

During September 2003, as Hurricane Isabel roared toward the East Coast, some computer track models suggested that the Category 5 storm might reach Virginia as a Category 3. It eventually slammed North Carolina, coming ashore 150 miles south of Norfolk as a Category 2.

A Katrina in Hampton Roads?

Landfall of an intense hurricane would bring winds in excess of 100 mph and an unforgettable storm surge, amplified as the sea funneled into the confined Chesapeake Bay. Specifics are left to the imagination but this much is certain: A major hurricane striking southeastern Virginia would be catastrophic.

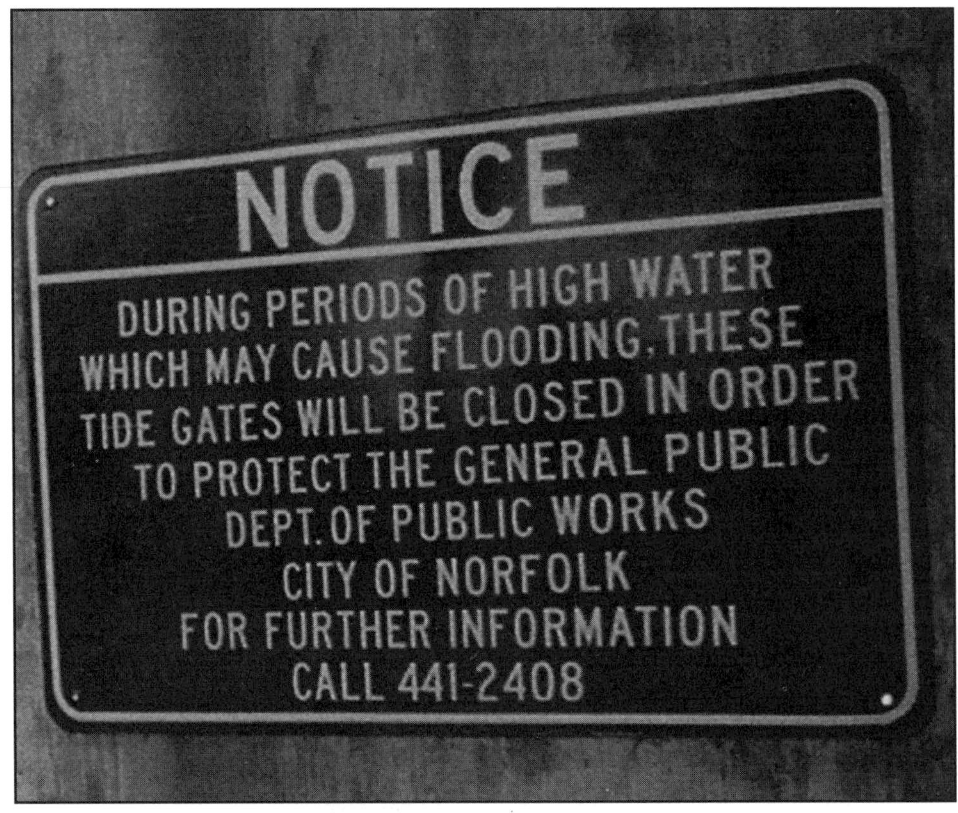

A flood wall 11 feet above sea level protects downtown Norfolk. Will it be enough?

NEW YORK CITY MAY SEE THE BIG ONE

What are the chances of a major—Category 3 or stronger—hurricane striking the other great coastal metropolis of the Mid-Atlantic, New York City?

No major hurricane has barreled from the ocean directly into New York City during the past 400 years. However, in 1821, 1893, 1960 and 1976 lesser hurricanes plowed through the vicinity. Damage was modest. Their tracks, however, suggest that something stronger could come ashore.

The Great New England Hurricane of 1938 made landfall 60 miles away. An additional four hours of westerly movement before the storm turned north might have brought its eye into the metropolitan area.

A Category 3 hurricane would deliver gusts greater than 140 mph, especially to upper levels of the city's many skyscrapers. Canyon-like streets would turn into deadly wind tunnels.

The right angle formed by the juncture of New York and New Jersey, and narrowing bays, could funnel a phenomenal storm surge. If the hurricane peaked near high tide, damage throughout the area would be staggering.

The populous Hudson River and Connecticut River valleys could experience disastrous flooding from heavy rainfall near the eye. Hurricane-force winds would carry far inland, possibly to Canada.

Three strength determination factors come into play as a storm approaches. Is the atmosphere conducive? Will proximity to land weaken the whirl before landfall? Are ocean temperatures supportive?

Category 3 hurricanes periodically track within 100 miles of New York City. They've always made landfall to the east, remained at sea or diminished before reaching the Big Apple. Cooler water temperatures and land's drag on circulation usually temper them. But a compact, fast-moving hurricane might power ashore with little loss of strength. And a warmer climate may produce favorable ocean temperatures off the New Jersey-New York coast offering a welcome mat for a meteorological monster.

NOAA

Waves striking a seawall during the Great New England Hurricane.

1769

September

THE GREAT CHESAPEAKE BAY HURRICANE

The shrieking winds, the shuddering of the house, were terrible enough. Now, as Vernon Hebb returned from surveying the shattered fields of his St. Mary's County, Md., farm, he wrote to his sister:

"Only a few days ago we had the most violent gale of wind that was ever known in the Memory of Man, for it has carried away allmost everything before it, and Ruined the Crops Intirely, and allmost everybody's Tobo (tobacco) Houses are Blown down. For my part (I have) lost a good deal, three Tobo Houses allmost full of Tobo, and allmost all the trees on my Land. I have not heard from your Plantation yet, tho' no Person has Escaped without some Loss."

The hurricane that terrorized eastern North Carolina and the Chesapeake Bay region on September 7-8 ranks among the strongest to invade the Middle Atlantic interior during the 18th century. It made landfall south of New Bern, N.C., wrecking the colonial capital. Tides rose 12 feet above normal, destroying ships, warehouses and dwellings. One resident opined, "To describe the Horrors of this Hurricane is beyond the Art of my Pen, therefore must leave it to you to form an Imagination of so terrible a Night."

Other accounts testify to the hurricane's ferocity, which likely tracked through the lower and middle Chesapeake Bay before turning northeast. From the *Virginia Gazette*:

"Williamsburg, September 14.

"Last Friday Morning, about one o'Clock, came on at North East a most dreadful Hurricane, attended with Rain, which came down in Torrents. It blew most violently from this quarter til between 10 and 11 o'Clock, then shifted to the North West, when the Storm increased, and continued, without any abatement, until about Dinner Time.

"The Damage done in the Country must be inconceivable, for the Corn is laid level with the Ground, and much of it destroyed; the Fodder is entirely gone. What Tobacco was in the Fields is quite spoiled, and that in Houses by their falling, and the Deluges of Rain which poured into them, greatly damaged, which might likewise be said of the Wheat.

"There was not a dry House in Town that Day, many old Houses were blown down and (many) trees. The Woods are entirely covered with fallen Trees, many of the largest Bulk, which has blocked up the Roads, so that there is no traveling with Carriages. The farther up the Country the fiercer the Storm was, and most of the Mills are destroyed, upwards of 50 we hear between this place and New Castle.

"From Hampton we hear that all the small Craft there are driven ashore. All the Shipping and small Vessels at Norfolk are aground, many of them dismasted; some of the Wharffs are gone, and others much damaged."

Farmers were extremely vulnerable. A hurricane on the eve of harvest meant financial disaster in an era when agriculture ruled the economy. It ravaged crops. Roads to market became quagmires rendered impassable by fallen trees. Winds leveled warehouses, barns and sheds, and destroyed commodities awaiting shipment. Boats and docks turned wreckage.

The following letter originated in Williamsburg, Va., on September 16, 1769. It was sent to John Norton, a London merchant:

"It is probable before this gets to Hand, you will have heard of the Misfortune which our Crops have met with. We had the 8th Instant the most violent Gust of Wind & Rain that the oldest Man I have seen ever remembers; I yesterday was told that it did not reach more than forty miles above (Richmond); those whose Plantations exceed that Distance, if they have escaped, were particularly fortunate, as all the Tobo. standing out where the Storm raged is totally destroy'd & tis generally thought that much is damaged in the Houses. Our corn is much injured, & the Fodder almost totally destroy'd. It was very lucky that Robertson & Outram were gone, as most of the Ships remaining in the Country were drove on Shore."

Stratford Hall Plantation, future birthplace of Confederate General Robert E. Lee, is the likely source of the following letter. The property, along the Virginia shore of the lower Potomac River, was located about 20 miles from the Hebb farm. Stratford Hall lost a mill, wharves and warehouses. From *The London Magazine/Gentleman's Monthly Intelligencer*:

"Sept. 11, 1769.

"On Thursday the 7th of this month, after many dreadful clouds, frightful in their imagined contents had been swagging about, as the fields loaded with their crops of corn and tobacco were very promising, and every thing most delightful to the poor, a wind at north east arose, and as soon as it had spread over the face of the heavens for one general rain, it died away till near bedtime, and then began to blow beyond the power of expression: it did not rain till two o'clock in the morning; but when the dissolving rains came on, every one had cause to wish for broad day to see but a chance to save themselves: for the strongest and newest built houses, by the violence of both wind and rain, were hardly a security for their dreadful effects.

"The water pouring down in such mighty torrents, some few thought of boring holes in their floors to give it vent; in this situation it continued till two in the afternoon, when the unhappy eye saw itself surrounded with the most deplorable destruction.

"Houses crashed down; fruit-trees of all kinds blown up; the woods laid mostly level. Our corn, not near hard for gathering, beaten flat to the earth; and, to be sure, in evident danger of rotting: the tobacco in the fields blown into shreds, that which was housed before the storm, quite crushed down and pounded, and the mills entirely destroyed, as far as the ear has at present reached.

"Numbers of vessels in every harbor bulged upon the shores; and some drove into the very ports by the extreme height of the tide except where the proprietors thought of boring holes through their bottoms and sinking them; for neither anchors or cables could stand the dreadful hurricane. A particular description of every loss would be tedious in such a general devastation; level fields, in many places, dissolved into deep gullies.

"In short, had the storm continued but a few hours more the present view must satisfy every sensible person that this part of America would have ceased to exist."

Annapolis trembled under nature's assault. The *Maryland Gazette*:

"The Rain beat through many houses in this City, the Walls of which were (up to) 14 Inches thick. In short, scarce anything has withstood the Violence

Robert E. Lee Memorial Association, Richard Cheek

"Had the storm continued but a few hours more, the present view must satisfy every sensible person that this part of America would have ceased to exist," wrote an observer after the Chesapeake Bay hurricane of 1769. The Stratford Hall plantation, home to the venerable Lee family, sustained widespread damage.

of the Tempest. Damage done by the Destruction of Buildings, Corn, Hay, Fodder, and Tobacco, can only be guessed at, but certainly amounts to many Thousands Sterling, and will be severely felt the ensuing Winter."

Fierce winds apparently remained concentrated near the storm's center, in the vicinity of Chesapeake Bay. George Washington, at Mount Vernon, didn't mention the event in his diary. Henry Muhlenberg, in Frederick, Md., about 75 miles west of the hurricane's track, recounted:

"September 8, Friday.

"Yesterday's heavy rain continued so that I was able, for once, to spend the entire day at home, alone, and devote my time to meditation and writing."

Philadelphia lay in the hurricane's path, as did central New Jersey. The *Pennsylvania Chronicle*:

"Numbers of Mill Dams are broke, and two Mills carried away. Several Vessels drove ashore in our River, and many in the Bay, we are fearful, have met the same Fate. We hear of terrible devastation in all Parts of the Country, various orchards being tore up, and great Quantities of Indian Corn and Buck Wheat destroyed, and that two Men were drowned."

Jacob Hiltzheimer of Philadelphia observed:

"September 9. Walked to Centre Woods, where I found above one hundred trees blown down."

Days after the hurricane Elizabeth Drinker traveled from Philadelphia to New York City via Trenton, Princeton and New Brunswick. She wrote, "The late N. East storm has done much damage; many Trees blown down; Bridges carried away by ye force of ye waters; and the Roads greatly hurt by it."

The hurricane continued northeast passing a short distance off the New England coast. Gales lashed New York City, Newport, R.I., and Boston, Mass. John Winthrop wrote of "a great storm of wind and rain" at Harvard College. Several vessels were driven ashore in Massachusetts Bay. Reverend Thomas Smith of Portland, Maine, described the event as "a dreadful N.E. storm."

***

The hurricane's impact lingered throughout the Chesapeake Bay region. Hebb, no doubt, expressed the sentiment of many planters when he lamented, "for indeed this is with much pain that I write, for Tobo all out and no Houses to put (it) in, and that all our Year's Work to be Lost in so little time is very shocking, and the loss is very grate all over Where I have heard."

1775

September

THE INDEPENDENCE HURRICANE

Early September 1775. Newspapers printed storm warnings of rebellion. In Massachusetts—at Concord, Lexington and Bunker Hill—rebels yanked the British lion's tail. Now colonists awaited a response expected any hour.

In the midst of crisis, a powerful hurricane swept the East Coast. It triggered one of the Revolutionary War's earliest confrontations in Virginia.

The whirl brushed the Georgia and South Carolina coasts on September 2 before making landfall in North Carolina. It sped through Virginia, Maryland and Pennsylvania. From the *Virginia Gazette*:

"WILLIAMSBURG, September 8.

"Every day last week it rained more or less and sometimes continued the chief part of the night; but on Saturday it never ceased pouring down, and towards noon the wind began to rise, which increased afterwards to a mere hurricane, it blowing most furiously from the N.E. till near 10 o'clock at night. Infinite damage has been done to the crops of corn and tobacco, much wheat spoiled in barns, a great number of trees blown down and almost every mill-dam in the country given way."

Virginian Landon Carter (1710-1778) wrote of the hurricane's fearsome passage. Carter's plantation, Sabine Hall, was located on the lower Rappahannock River. On Saturday, September 2, 1775, he penned:

"I thought the two spare pages in the last month—as it has rained ever since Sunday last—would have been enough to set down the rainy days; but it is not, for it rained all last night and all this day very much, and now it blows and rains, the Wind at Northeast and bids fair for a Gust. I have known 4 such Spells in my observation, all in August, that is, old stile, and all began moderately for several days and then at last began to tear away. But I, though (illegible writing), hope otherwise."

"About half after 3 (p.m.) the much suspected Gust began; it has now struck 6, and I wish I could say there were signs of it abating. The Wind is from North to Northeast and sometimes to Northwest with prodigious flows that drive vast sheets of rain before it, and make everything shake almost to their foundations.

"We have but one hope, and that is in a merciful God. It is true we can't plead for Protection from any goodness of ours; but his Mercy has always hitherto exceeded his Judgements. And may it do so now. It is only hoped we are not incorrigible offenders; our frailties often overbear us; but is not his wisdom satisfied that our hearts are good towards him, and though man is blessed with reason, yet how often is imperfection divested of all reason."

"Half past 9, a dreadful time. Gusts harder and all the weather side of my house in a float. I am obliged to get up. If the window sand bags or some such thing had been thought of before night, this leaking might in a great measure (have) been prevented."

"The violent Gust began to abate about two in the night. It cost me my Mill dam, in all, a vast damage. But I wish this may be all, for it carried every terror with it that could be conceived. And without a most Merciful God to Preserve us, it made me doubtful Whether anything would have stood it. I can't therefore but be thankful and greatly rejoice. Wind now every way, sometimes down. Poor man indeed! But the Lord is Gracious and merciful."

Morning found fodder, corn and tobacco flattened. Barns, sheds and fences littered the countryside. Carter counted his blessings despite considerable agricultural ruin. His family remained safe and Sabine Hall sustained only slight structural damage.

Not so for the recently completed Maryland State House in Annapolis. Wind claimed its roof. Copper sheeting rolled up "like scrolls of parchment," according to contemporary accounts, leaving the inside exposed to the elements. During the winter, rain and snow destroyed its elegant interior.

Annapolis endured two hurricanes in six years. Architects overseeing reconstruction planned for another. The rebuilt edifice included a sturdy wooden

Governor's Office, State of Maryland

A hurricane in 1775 claimed the roof of the Maryland State House. Today's wind resistant dome replaced it.

dome. It remains the most striking feature of the oldest state capitol building in continuous legislative use.

The foul weather reached southeastern Pennsylvania. Phineas Pemberton of Philadelphia wrote:

"Sept. 3—Stormy and showery. A violent gale of wind from NE to SE the preceding night with much heavy rain, lightning and thunder—a remarkably high tide in (the) Delaware this morning. Flying clouds & wind with sunshine at times P.M."

From *Dunlap's Maryland Gazette*:

"Philadelphia, Sept. 6.

"All last week we had squally weather and rain, but on Saturday evening it began to blow hard at N.E. and S.E. and by midnight increased to a hurricane, attended with heavy floods of rain, which raised the tide in our river higher than has been know there several years, and has occasioned much damage in the stores on the wharves, among sugar, salt and other perishable articles; wood, staves, plank, &c. was washed off the wharves, and many boats and small craft were sunk or beat to pieces."

Gales and torrential rain swept New England, but losses were less than in the Mid-Atlantic region.

The hurricane passed. Tension of war returned.

***

John Murray, Earl of Dunmore, the royal governor of Virginia, fled the capital, Williamsburg, in June. He remained in the area. Angry, frustrated and bitter, seeing the colony slipping away on his watch, Dunmore lashed out. He proposed sanctuary and freedom for slaves who joined his army, a threat that enflamed the conflict.[1]

Then came the hurricane—its winds a spark to gunpowder.

Two Royal Navy craft were among the vessels driven ashore in the lower Chesapeake Bay. The *Mercury*, a 20-gun warship, nearly sank as its crew battled the elements. It went aground in Norfolk harbor. The *Liberty*, a patrol boat, stranded near Hampton.

Locals soon burned the *Liberty* and captured most of its crew, including two escaped slaves. Then they eyed the *Mercury*.

Captain John McCartney commanded the ship. Easygoing and determined not to exacerbate rebel sentiment, he nevertheless angered everyone. Dunmore, incensed at McCartney's liberal approach, recommended that he be relieved of command and tried by a court-martial. Firebrands wrongly interpreted the captain's friendship as weakness, vulnerability. They proposed to seize and burn the *Mercury*. But McCartney remained loyal to his command. He sent the following message to the mayor of Norfolk:

"I am sent hither to be the guardian of a British colony; to protect His Majesty's governor, and all the loyal subjects in the province of Virginia. This is my duty, and should with it be known that my duty and inclination go hand in hand."

Ominously, he concluded, "More effectually to perform my part, I shall, the first opportunity, place His Majesty's ship under my command abreast of the town; and I shall assure you that not withstanding, I shall feel the utmost pain and reluctance in being compelled to use violent measures to preserve the persons and properties of His Majesty's subjects, yet, I most assuredly shall, if it becomes necessary, use the most coercive measures in my power to suppress all unlawful combinations and persecutions within the province of Virginia."

The price for the *Mercury*: Norfolk. McCartney positioned his guns accordingly.

For two weeks the factions edged toward fiery confrontation. Norfolk's mayor pleaded for restraint. Meanwhile, as the crew attempted to refit and float the *Mercury*, the *Kingfisher* arrived with McCartney's replacement and orders to take him into custody. Finally, on September 23, the *Mercury* sailed for Boston, defusing the situation.

Because of McCartney's resolute stand, charges were dropped.

As a result of the seizure and burning of the *Liberty*, the Royal Navy blockaded Hampton.

Lord Dunmore departed during 1776, effectively ending British rule in Virginia.

[1] In November 1775, Lord Dunmore offered emancipation to slaves willing to help suppress the rebellion. About 300 accepted. The "Ethiopian Regiment," as it was called, emblazoned on their shirts the motto, "Liberty to Slaves," even as "patriots" fought for their freedom. The unit departed Virginia with the rest of Dunmore's army in 1776. Most members settled in Canada or the Bahamas.

1785

September

WRECK OF THE *FAITHFUL STEWARD*

On the night of September 1, Irish immigrants on the *Faithful Steward* slept with dreams of waking up in America. After an arduous two-month sail across the Atlantic, they expected to greet Philadelphia on the morrow.

The sea roughened. South of Delaware Bay, near the Indian River Inlet, the *Faithful Steward* struck a shoal a few hundred yards from shore. Dawn saw a desperate situation with angry surf pounding the boat, promising watery death to those on board. Throughout the day, passengers and crew attempted to swim or ride debris to safety. Few succeeded. By evening, 68 survivors hugged the sand, remnants of 300.

They met a mixed reception. Some locals offered assistance. Most came to loot. Inhabitants of the Delaware shore and other isolated sections of the East Coast lived a hardscrabble life. Shipwrecks were fair game.

James McEntire lost family members and friends. Interviewed nearly a half-century later, McEntire bitterly recalled, "Many country people, on receiving intelligence of the shipwreck, hastened to the seashore fully prepared with wagons and negroes, not to aid in the cause of humanity, not to rescue their fellow human beings from the ruthless waves, not to console the bereaved or administer to their wants. No, but solely to plunder till they could plunder no more."

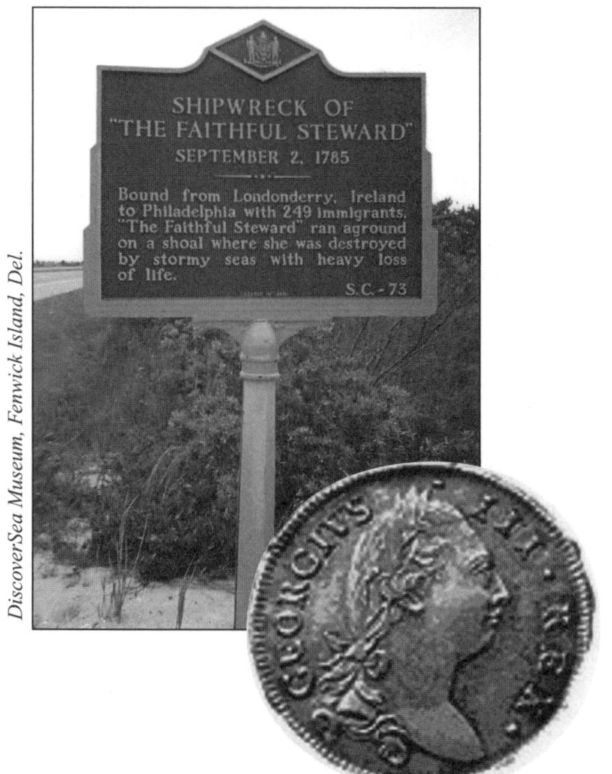

DiscoverSea Museum, Fenwick Island, Del.

Relic of the *Faithful Steward*

The disaster has been blamed on navigational error, but that does not explain the raging sea. Nor do contemporary accounts mention a storm or high winds in the area. What happened?

Hurricanes occurring within weeks of each other, journeying through the same geographic vicinity, often take parallel tracks. The western Atlantic was a prime conduit for tropical cyclones in September 1785. Less than three weeks after the loss of the *Faithful Steward* another hurricane brushed the Delmarva Peninsula.

Large storms generate waves propagating hundreds of miles, creating treacherous currents. A hurricane moved northwest of the Leeward Islands on August 31. By September 2, it may have tracked to within a few hundred miles of the *Faithful Steward*, producing powerful swells, nudging the vessel toward doom.

The *Faithful Steward* would have faded from history had it not carried a treasure. Barrels containing thousands of British half pennies and pennies lay below deck. The coppers were en route to the United States. They were a welcome addition to a coin-starved country lacking a mint. (Congress approved a monetary system during 1792. The U.S. mint began operation during 1793. In 1785, the nation depended on European and European colonial coinage.)

During the 1930s, members of the Civilian Conservation Corps and Coast Guard found hundreds of the coins in the vicinity of the Indian River Life-Saving Station. Others joined the hunt, which continues.

Relics date from 1774 to 1782. Rarely, silver or gold coins are discovered—most likely the life savings of those on the *Faithful Steward*. The best chance for finding treasure is after a hurricane or nor'easter.

The vessel is memorialized on a highway marker north of the Indian River Inlet. The adjacent strand is known as "Coin Beach."

September

THE GREAT COASTAL HURRICANE OF 1785

During the afternoon of September 24, an immigrant ship approached the Chesapeake Bay as a hurricane set in. Treacherous shoals, the bane of mariners since the settlement of Jamestown, lay beneath a menacing sea. The shipmaster, Captain Smith, dared not risk passage inside the Virginia capes—grounding meant disaster. He turned back into the Atlantic and met the elemental furies head-on.

"From blowing as described, a hurricane from the N.E., (the wind) fell calm," Smith said. "(We) loosened and sheeted home the mizzen top-sail, with an intent to keep the ship's head to the sea; the ocean at this instant appeared in a most surprising agitation, shipped a dreadful sea upon our starboard quarter, which hove the ship upon her broadside, and shifted all cargo to starboard, washed a man out of the main-top (it being 30 feet above our deck) and five from the deck, one of whom was our carpenter, carried away our quarter gallery rails, boats, binnacle, and, in short, everything that could possibly be moved. After being about ten minutes calm, the hurricane burst forth with enraged fury from the S.W. Our situation now became truly deplorable, without boats, with but half our hands, wrecked of all our masts, deprived of our compasses, the ship laboring and often overwhelmed with the most tremendous seas, expecting every instance to be dashed on the shoals of Hatteras."

The ship survived, besting a hurricane that thrashed the Virginia and North Carolina coasts. The *New Jersey Gazette* carried this account from Norfolk:

"A higher tide and severer storm were never known at this place than happened yesterday; the damages sustained thereby are immense; almost all the ships in the harbour were drove from their moorings, and many warehouses were entirely carried away; great quantities of salt, sugar, corn, lumber, and other merchandise are totally lost. The lower stories of many dwelling houses were quite filled with water."

And from neighboring Portsmouth:

"On Thursday, Friday and Saturday we had the most tremendous gale of wind ever known in this country, from N.E. to N.W. The whole town was (flooded) and numbers of vessels driven into the cornfields and woods; storehouses drifted from their foundations, and every kind of property floated with the tide."

Captain Smith returned to Norfolk and issued the following plea, which appeared in prominent newspapers:

"(My experience), I hope, will strike the attention of my countrymen towards erecting a lighthouse at Cape Henry to preserve the lives and property of thousands."

This hurricane and others convinced officials to construct the long-sought beacon. Cape Henry opened in 1792—the first commissioned public works building of the U.S. government. The lighthouse is now a museum.

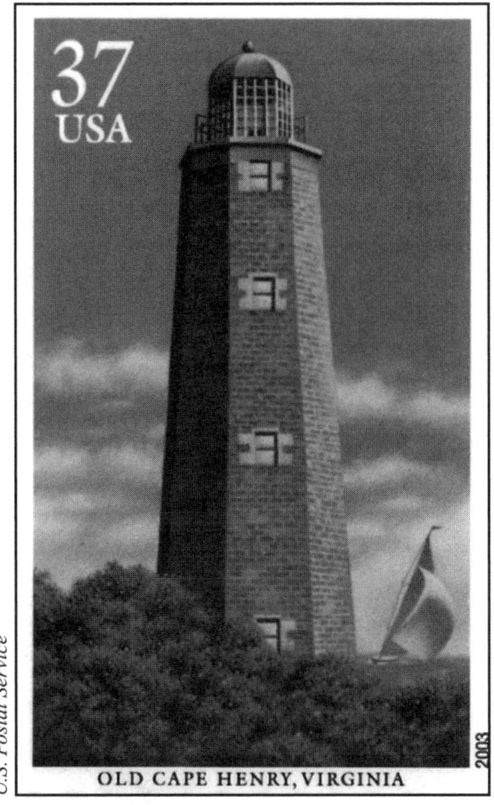

The Postal Service commemorated the old Cape Henry Lighthouse during 2003.

1788

July

GEORGE WASHINGTON'S HURRICANE

A hurricane that visited Mount Vernon on July 23-24 is sometimes referred to as "George Washington's Hurricane" because of the Virginian's descriptive narrative:

"Thursday 24th. Thermometer at 70 in the Morning—71 at Noon and 74 at Night—A very high No. Et. Wind all Night, which, this morning, being accompanied with Rain, became a hurricane—driving the Miniature Ship Federalist from her Moorings, and sinking her—blowing down some trees in the groves & about the houses—loosening the roots, & forcing many others to yield and dismantling most, in a greater or lesser degree of their Bows, & doing other and great mischief to the grain, grass (etc.) and not a little to my Mill race.

"In a word it was violent and severe—more so than has happened for many years. About Noon the Wind suddenly shifted from No. Et. to So. Wt. and blew the remaining part of the day as violently from that quarter. The tide about this time rose near or quite four feet higher than it was ever known to do driving Boats &ca. into fields where no tide had ever been heard of before—And (it is feared) has done infinite damage on the Wharves at Alexandria—Norfolk—Baltimore &ca."

The hurricane sideswiped Bermuda on July 19 before continuing west-northwest to North Carolina's Outer Banks and into Virginia. Days of easterly winds raised a huge tide along the Mid-Atlantic coast. The Chesapeake Bay region also bore the storm's worst. The *Independent Gazette* recounted a destructive passage through Norfolk, Va.:

"Wednesday last (23rd) the most violent storm ever known commenced at 1700 and continued for 9 hours—wind at start from N.E.—at 0300 it suddenly shifted to S. and blew a perfect hurricane, tearing up large trees by the roots, removing houses, throwing down chimneys, fences, etc., and laying the greatest part of the corn level. The tide was not so high as in 1785. Only two ships in Hampton Roads survived the gale."

From Portsmouth, the *Virginia Gazette*:

"On the 22nd we had a most violent gale of wind at N.E. which continued till 3 o'clock yesterday morning (July 24). The houses in town shook as if they would have fallen down. Most of the craft and other vessels were driven from their moorings; some of them into the very streets of Portsmouth."

A correspondent from Alexandria, Va., near Mount Vernon, wrote:

"On the evening of the 23rd instant, we had one of the most violent storms of wind and rain ever experienced here, which continued with unabating fury till the next day. The wind was at E.N.E. when the storm began, but changed suddenly to the southward bringing in the highest tide that was ever known in this river, and the damage done to tobacco, sugar, salt, &c. in the warehouses in this town is computed at $5,000. – Several inhabitants on the wharves were obliged to retire to their chambers, and some were taken out of their houses in boats."

An account from Baltimore, Md.:

"About twelve o'clock, on Wednesday night, commenced one of the most violent storms that has ever been experienced here since the memory of man. For upwards of twelve hours, the wind and rain were incessant, and such were the effects of their relentless rage that it threatened destruction to the wharves, stores and buildings."

The *New Jersey Gazette* reported:

"We hear from Baltimore, that on Wednesday (July 23) at night, came on the severest storm ever experienced there in this season of the year. The wind at E.N.E. blew with unabated fury (accompanied with heavy rain) for upwards of 12 hours, which occasioned a most dreadful inundation of the sea, that deluged all the wharves, stores, and low grounds near the Basin and at Fell's Point, producing a scene of devastation and horror not to be described. The industrious merchant beheld with unavailing regret the fruits of his toil and enterprise, in one moment, destroyed by the rage of combined elements."

The hurricane's fringe reached the foothills of the Blue Ridge. At Orange, Va., Colonel James Madison, father of the future president, observed, "great winds and rain all night." Storm remnants steadily weakened while passing through Pennsylvania and New York.

***

For all its bluster, was *George Washington's Hurricane* really a hurricane at Mount Vernon? Probably not, at least not by our current definition, which requires sustained winds of 74 mph or greater. A stronger hurricane followed a similar trajectory during August 1933. Steady winds in the vicinity of Mount Vernon peaked at about 50 mph.

But in Washington's day the definition of a hurricane was subjective. No formal wind scale defined an objective, statistically based, standard. Reliable anemometers were nearly a century away. The term depended on visual effects. A "hurricane" might describe any destructive wind event, tropical or not. In that sense, *George Washington's Hurricane* was a hurricane.

Library of Congress

The Washington family sheltered from the hurricane of 1788 at Mount Vernon.

1795

August

Thomas Jefferson kept a journal that included regular weather observations. He kept an almost unbroken record between 1776 and 1816. As a plantation owner, the variability of climate affected his life and livelihood.

Two hurricanes reached Virginia within 10 days during August 1795, ruining Jefferson's crops. On August 11, he said of the first, which struck August 2-3, "We have had a terrible storm which has thrown our corn generally prostrate. We shall be greatly at a loss in sowing wheat among it."

Jefferson wasn't alone.

"It appears that the late heavy rains have been general throughout the country," the *Maryland Gazette* reported. "The inundations caused thereby in the rivers, creeks, &c have been great in the extreme."

Flooding plagued much of Virginia, central Maryland and eastern Pennsylvania. Elizabeth Drinker of Philadelphia jotted in her diary:

"August 4. This evening's paper says: 'The rains for a few days past have been greater and the floods higher than ever before known in Pennsylvania. The mails and the public stages, which set out for different parts of the United States, were all obliged to return to the city, finding the roads impassable. The mails due this morning had not arrived when this Gazette was put to press.' "

Another hurricane invaded North Carolina and Virginia on August 13, bringing additional downpours and flooding. In the Old Dominion, many streams and rivers rose to levels not attained for decades.

The Appomattox River crested more than 12 feet above flood stage at Petersburg, the highest in at least 70 years. A correspondent for *Dunlap and Claypoole's American Daily Advertiser* related appalling conditions:

"A view from the heights is truly astonishing and curious to see sixty or a hundred houses up to their second stories and roofs in water, some partly carried away, and others falling. – We were put across in a rowboat from Blanford to Petersburg, and sailed among the houses, perhaps 15 or so feet above the street."

Jefferson bemoaned additional losses at his plantation, Monticello. "During the summer months of this year there were probably twice as many wet days as in common years, for nothing like it has ever been seen within the memory of man."

On August 18, he wrote to his son-in-law, Thomas Mann Randolph:

"I mentioned in my last the ravages committed by the rains. Since then we have had still worse. I imagine we never lost more soil than this summer. It is moderately estimated at a year's rent. Our crops of corn will be much shortened by the prostate and downed conditions of the plants, particularly of the tossil which can perform it's office of impregnation but partially and imperfectly."

On August 20, Jefferson concluded:

"We thought the storms and floods here very great till we heard from other quarters. It seems now they have been less with us than anywhere else. To the Northward as far as Pennsylvania. we learn there has been an almost universal destruction of mills and forges."

HURRICANES
1800s

1806

August

THE GREAT COASTAL HURRICANE OF 1806

ew disasters capture public attention like the sinking of a passenger ship. The loss of the *Rose-in-Bloom* during August 1806 made news for days—a compelling blend of pathos and heroism.

The vessel left Charleston, S.C., on August 16 bound for New York with 49 people onboard. A hurricane pursued. By Friday, August 22, a terrific thunderstorm foreshadowed trouble. The *Maryland Gazette* reported:

"At noon on that day, a storm arose of great violence attended with thunder and lightning so fierce and vivid as had rarely been witnessed, never exceeded, even by the oldest inhabitants of South Carolina who were on board. More need not be said of it than it appalled the hearts of the stout mariners, and made such an impression on their imaginations as to induce them to think there was a strong sulfurous stench about the vessel."

The transport reached the central New Jersey coast late Saturday. Squalls increased. A sandbar paralleling the state, located about 300-800 yards offshore, serves as graveyard for many vessels including the *Rose-in-Bloom*. The ship foundered near Barnegat Inlet shortly after midnight. Its crew fought to keep the wreck afloat. The *Maryland Gazette*:

"The only chance they appeared to have was to cut away the masts: but this was found to be impossible, neither ax nor hatchet to be had. Some persons, however, who had run up the side of the ship by the shrouds, contrived, with much labour and difficulty, having nothing but small pocket knives with which to do it, to cut away the lanyards, on the giving way of which, all the masts broke off short by the board. The ship now began to right gradually, but very slowly. The lading below as well as on deck being cotton, she was, so far fortunately, buoyant, and continued to float with her stern above water; so low however, as to be swept by the waves as they passed along."

The 21 people who perished were carried off by the sea or trapped in their cabins. Survivors clung to a precarious perch of canvas and wood. Land seemed too distant to risk swimming against deadly currents. There'd be no assistance from the sparsely settled shore.

Winds shifted and abated, the riotous sea subsided. Survivors endured an anguished night, scanning the horizon for a passing ship. Shortly before dawn, the group took cheer from a light to the east. But the beacon, their anticipated salvation, was simply the luminescent morning star. All yearned for radiant day. However, the hours after sunrise offered growing heat and thirst.

The ordeal continued until mid-morning. Suddenly, sails blossomed to the southeast. Two crew members mounted the remains of a mast and paddled toward the distant ship. They intercepted the British brig *Swift* on its way to St. John, Newfoundland. The *Swift* carried survivors to New York.

***

The *Rose-in-Bloom* fell victim to the Great Coastal Hurricane of 1806. The storm made landfall south of Wilmington, N.C., on August 21 before continuing a slow northeasterly drift—tracking 250 miles in 36 hours. The *Wilmington Gazette* stated that winds blew with "utmost violence" and tides rose to levels "without precedent."

The hurricane peaked at Norfolk on August 23. Vessels foundered. Wharves and warehouses flooded. Piers washed away.

Prolonged gales caused extensive beach erosion, altering the shoreline. Willoughby Spit (pop. 4,000), near the mouth of the Chesapeake Bay, became firmly established.

Squalls continued along the coast from the Delmarva Peninsula to Cape Cod. Rain cascaded like a waterfall on Martha's Vineyard, Mass. An observer in Edgartown reported an astonishing catch of 30 inches!

***

Days after the hurricane a letter signed by the *Rose-in-Bloom* survivors appeared in various newspapers, including the *Maryland Gazette*:

"New York, August 28, 1806.

Courtesy of NOAA, Department of Commerce

To Captain Richard Phelan, of the Brig Swift.

Sir,

For having under the blessings of God, rescued us from the wreck of the ship Rose-in-Bloom, we offer you our sincere thanks. When we were nearly exhausted by hunger, thirst, fatigue and cold, and clinging to the small part of the wreck, which was then not entirely under water, and without any prospect of possibly escaping from the watery grave into which we were fast descending, the appearance of your vessel resuscitated our drooping spirits, and made us consider you as destined by Heaven for our relief. Your altering course, sending off boats, and making great and prompt exertions to save us excite emotions of gratitude, which we will not attempt to describe. We request you do us the favour of accepting, as a small compensation for your great and benevolent services, one hundred (gold) guineas, and be assured that we shall rejoice in any occasion which may hereafter occur of (the money) being useful to yourself, your mate, Mr. M'Fee, or any of the crew of your vessel. We sincerely wish you safe passage to St. Johns—that in your passage through life you may not meet with any other gales than those of prosperity, and that you do justice to the sentiments of infinite gratitude with which we are your obliged servants."

Captain Phelan replied:

"I accept with strong emotions the testimony you have presented me of the remembrance you preserve of my services in taking you off the wreck. Not to have done what I did would have been a cause of the most severest and most lasting self-reproach; while the recollection of having been instrumental, under Providence, in saving so many valuable lives, will I assure you, be one of the greatest sources of happiness to me during the remainder of my existence. Accept my reciprocal good wishes."

1821

September

NORFOLK AND LONG ISLAND HURRICANE

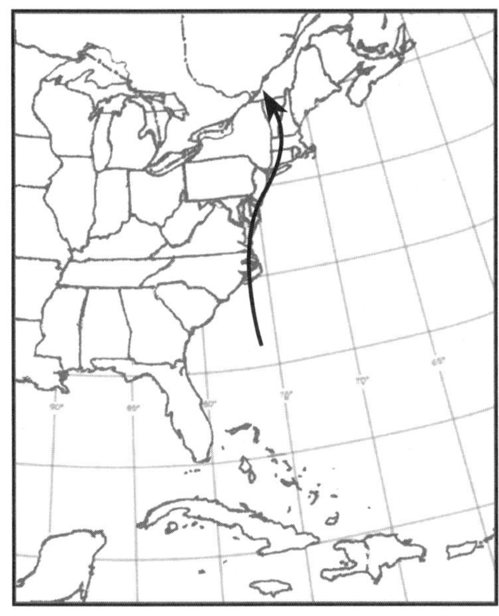

The summer of 1821 brought the worst of times to Norfolk, Va. Yellow fever stalked streets, alleyways and homes. Families fled the city to avoid the scourge. Those who stayed feared they would become victims of what one newspaper described as "the destroyer engaged in cutting short the thread of human life."

Then came a savage hurricane.

John Myers, a prominent merchant, wrote to his brother, Samuel, "Disease & death, which surround us, has no terrors like the fury of the tempest, for a short time."

Meteorologists refer to the storm of September 3, 1821, as the "Norfolk and Long Island Hurricane." In the lore of southeastern Virginia and the Delmarva Peninsula, however, it's the "Great September Gust."

After churning across eastern North Carolina on September 3, the storm tracked near the coastline from Virginia to New York.

Based on descriptions of damage and a comparison to Mid-Atlantic hurricanes of known intensity, the storm was likely of Category 2 strength in southeastern Virginia, along the Delmarva Peninsula and in southeastern New Jersey. It remained a strong Category 1 as it tracked along what is today the Garden State Parkway.

Nobody in the big winds' path would forget the mighty broadsides. Myers decried:

"We had an awful tempest. The damage done is great. The extent is not ascertained. Suffers many. Some severe. The papers give you a hasty & imperfect sketch. It is a scene that could not be described without detailing a thousand minutia. You must see it to believe. We have not a tree, shrub or fence standing."

The weather observer at Fort Norfolk logged:

"Violent hurricane commencing at 11 o'clock am from NE and continuing till 1 pm. Shifting winds (to the) NW. Damage to Norfolk houses, bridges, etc., incalculable."

The *Norfolk Herald* provided the following details:

"Among the rest of our misfortunes, we are grieved to state, that our town was on yesterday visited by a storm, or rather tornado, far surpassing in violence and calamitous consequences, any that it has ever experienced within the remembrance of the oldest inhabitants. The best description we are prepared to give of it at this moment can convey but an imperfect conception of its terrors.

"The morning was dark and gloomy, and about six o'clock the black and lowering clouds began to discharge their watery contents, not in gentle showers, but literally in torrents. At ten o'clock the rain abated for a few minutes, as if to collect itself for a more copious discharge; for it presently set in again with increased violence, and the wind commenced blowing a heavy gale from N.E., which continued to increase to a most alarming height.

"From half past 11 till half past 12, so great was the fury of the elements, that they seemed to threaten a general demolation of everything within their reach. During that period the scene they presented was truly awful. The deafening roar of the storm, with the mingled crashing of windows and falling of chimneys—the rapid rise of the tide threatening to inundate the town—the continuous cataracts of rain sweeping impetuously along, darkening the expanse of vision, and apparently confounding the 'heavens, earth and sea' in general chaos; together with now and then a glimpse caught through the gloom of ships forced from their moorings and driving with rapidity, as the mind might conjecture in such circumstances, to inevitable destruction."

The article continued, "About 12 o'clock the wind shifted round to N.W. but without abating its fury until half an hour after, when it ceased raining; the storm began to subside, and the water to recede. At four o'clock it changed to S.W. and the weather became calm and serene."

High water powered through the Chesapeake Bay. Thomas Crockett heard the stories of older residents and included (an erroneously dated) account in his book, *Facts and Fun: The Historical Outlines of Tangier Island,* published in 1890.

"On the 12th day of September, 1821, the wind blew a storm from the east and southeast; also all night, and until 1 o'clock on the 13th when suddenly the wind changed to northwest and blew a perfect hurricane, and the tide being very high, the hurricane brought the salt water from the Chesapeake Bay until it covered the Island. Even the highest land had three feet of water over it. This was ever known as the 'great September gust.' The land was not covered with salt water more than three hours, for the wind did not last longer than that."

John Elliott, who lived on a farm at Bradfords Neck near the village of Quinby on Virginia's Eastern Shore, was a youngster when the storm struck. Years later he reminisced:

"The wind continued to increase and still to increase. Two large willows stood in the yard, one near the barn, the other further off—they blew down. By that time I put my book by to notice the destruction: trees in every direction were falling, houses tumbling, roofs flying high in the air, the tides swelling. Such was the fearful condition that no one dared to venture out the door, expecting every moment that (the house) was about to fall.

"It continued to blow until the afternoon at which time a perfect calm ensued. All hands rushed out to see the destruction, which was terrible to behold: stables all down, corn houses unroofed, fences laid to the ground, fodder in ribbons.

"We had only time to look on the destruction when the wind came from the west, the opposite point from the morning's wind. It crested to a violent storm in a few minutes, harder than the former. It upended trees, many of them, and carried them the other way. The water in Machipongo (River that had been) filled by the east wind was taken in spray and carried across (Bradfords) Neck. This body of water piled up on the bleak shore and swept over the lower portions of the neck lands."

A relentless Atlantic swallowed barrier islands. The sea rose as much as 10 feet during the storm's advance, accompanied by a deadly surprise. A "tidal wave," as survivors called it, struck soon after passage of the eye, when the wind shifted and blew with renewed violence. An elderly resident of Chincoteague Island told of the horror in the April 1877 edition of *Scribner's Monthly:*

"A dull roar came nearer and nearer, and suddenly a solid mass of wind and rain and salt spray leaped upon the devoted island with a scream. Great pines bent for a moment, and then, groaning and shrieking, were torn from their centuried growth like wisps of straw and hurled one against another; houses were cut from their foundations and thrown headlong; and then a deeper roar swelled the noise of the tempest, and a monstrous wall of inky waters rushed with the speed of lightning toward the island. It struck Assateague, and in a moment half the land was a waste of seething foam and tossing pine trunks; the next instant it struck Chincoteague, and in an unbroken mass swept across the low south marsh flats, carrying away men and ponies like insects; rushing up the island, tearing its way through the stricken pine woods."

Five islanders drowned. Others narrowly escaped. One man was discovered hanging from a tree dangling by his waistband. Residents survived by fleeing to the rafters or rooftops of their homes.

The hurricane's eye passed over Cape Henlopen, Del., providing about 30 minutes of calm. Cape May, N.J., reported a lull lasting 15 minutes. As at Chincoteague, a sudden rush of water, an abrupt rise of the sea, swept the lower Delaware Bay. Charles Ludlum of South Dennis wrote of the storm's rampage through Cape May County:

"The morning of September 3d, 1821, commenced with a light wind from the west. There was nothing in the looks of the atmosphere that indicated bad weather. At about 9 o'clock the wind hauled round to the southeast, steadily increasing. At 11 o'clock it might be called a gale, at 12 it was blowing a hurricane with intermittent gusts that drove in doors and windows, blowing down outbuildings, trees, fences and overflowing the marshes between the beach and mainland. At this time it was difficult to stand without some support; no clouds were to be seen, but in their place was a universal haze like a thick fog.

"The salt spray of the sea was driven inland some miles so as to kill vegetation. At about (2:30 p.m.) it fell perfectly calm for about fifteen minutes, then the wind burst out from the northwest, the directly opposite quarter, and blew with increasing violence for about three hours, then gradually subsided, and by six o'clock had nearly ceased, and cleared off at sundown."

"… On our bay shore the tide was higher than on the seaside of the Cape by several feet; persons who witnessed the overflow said it came like a perpendicular wall some five feet high driven by the wind when it changed to the northwest. It came in an overwhelming surge. From the formation of the land in the cove in our bay, in the vicinity of Goshen and Dias Creek and Cedar Hammocks, the water was concentrated as a common center and the tide was higher there than anywhere along the shore; drift was lodged in the tree tops at the Cedar Hammocks nine feet high; in all probability the heave of the sea had something to do with this."

Gales shook southeastern Pennsylvania and most of New Jersey. High winds uprooted trees. Rainfall in Philadelphia, west of the hurricane's track, totaled 3.92 inches.

At Jersey City, "the wind was from the N.E. accompanied with hail and rain, which fell in torrents. Docks, wharves, piers, &c. &c. were all swept away."

The Norfolk and Long Island Hurricane is one of the few tropical cyclones to pass directly over New York City as an actual hurricane. Rainfall was light, only .87 inches. The barometer bottomed at an unimpressive 29.38 inches.

Structural damage was minor to moderate, with the brunt along the city's waterfront. The *New York Post* described the storm's effects:

"From Saturday morning till 4 o'clock yesterday afternoon (Monday), we were visited with repeated and copious showers of rain, accompanied by some loud peals of thunder and lightning, and an extreme dense atmosphere; the wind during the time veered and shifted to almost every point of the compass, when about half past four o'clock yesterday afternoon it came out from almost east, with all the violence and fury of a hurricane, and continued to about half past 8 last evening, throwing down chimneys, unroofing buildings, and prostrating trees in various directions. When the gale was at its height, it presented a most awful spectacle. The falling of slate from the roofs of buildings, and broken glass from windows, made it unsafe for anyone to venture into the streets."

A calm lasted about 15 minutes before winds shifted to the southwest. Hurricane-strength gusts ranged from New York City to Bridgeport, Conn., a distance of 50 miles. The storm continued through Connecticut, Massachusetts and Vermont, leaving downed trees and disheveled farmland.

Foul weather caused trouble for many but offered relief to some. Richmond, Baltimore and Washington welcomed a soaking rain. The *Washington National Intelligencer* (obviously unaware of events along the coast) rejoiced:

"After a long and oppressive drought we are now deluged with unceasing rains; but they are refreshing and useful. As it is an ill wind which blows nobody good, we may consider the converse of the proposition also true, and say that it is a good one which brings nobody any ill."

***

William Redfield, a businessman, visited different sections of Connecticut after the blow. He plotted the direction of downed trees and cornstalks, discovering a counter-clockwise pattern.

"This storm exhibited in the form of a great whirlwind," concluded Redfield in an article published by the respected *American Journal of Science*. His observation became an important link in the chain of discoveries leading to an understanding of hurricane structure and dynamics.

1822

September

Hurricane Hugo in 1989 astounded residents of Charlotte, N.C. Winds gusted to 90 mph nearly 200 miles from Charleston, S.C., where Hugo swept inland. Hurricanes didn't happen in Charlotte, or so went conventional wisdom.

North Carolinians living in central sections of the state likely felt similar dismay after the blow of September 1822. A fierce hurricane came ashore near Georgetown, S.C., on the 27th as, possibly, a Category 4 (the same strength as Hugo). It carved a path of destruction across central North Carolina and Virginia. Two hours of furious gusts unroofed houses and littered the countryside with downed trees.

From the *Richmond Enquirer*:

"We are informed by an intelligent gentleman from Raleigh, that in the direction of Fayetteville (N.C.) nearly one-half of the trees are suppose to have been bent or prostrated."

An *Enquirer* correspondent from Raleigh, N.C., wrote, "On Tuesday, the 24th, after a drought of several weeks, it commenced raining in this place, and continued, with very little intermission, until the Saturday morning following, when it terminated in a violent gale of wind, prostrating trees, fences, &c. We are informed that some of the roads leading to the city were literally covered with fallen trees, so as to render them almost impassable for carriages of any description."

The storm traversed southwestern Virginia. *The* (Lynchburg) *Virginian*:

"After a drought of several weeks, it commenced raining on Wednesday last, and continued to Saturday noon. The morning of that day set in with a very severe storm of wind and rain. Several chimneys were blown down, and a great number of trees torn up by the roots."

The south and north forks of the Staunton River rose "to the greatest height ever known," according to *The Virginian*. "Rain commenced on the evening of the 27th from easterly clouds, with high winds, and continued until the 28th, about 9 o'clock A.M. when Heaven was pleased to grant us a serene sky and shining sun. The consequences are serious and awful—mills, milldams and dwelling houses have shared the common loss."

Thomas Jefferson's granddaughter told of the effects at Monticello:

"We have had constant rains, and on (September 28) a violent storm which strewed the whole mountain top with broken boughs of trees, and tore one of our willows completely asunder."

***

The hurricane of 1822 gave rise to stories of the ghostly Gray Man of Pawleys Island. The strand, on the upper coast of South Carolina, is at the mercy of the big storm. Speculation on the Gray Man's origin differs, but accounts agree that the spirit portends a destructive hurricane.

Tales state that he appeared before the powerful blows of 1822, 1893, 1954 and 1989. The ghost vanished after urging residents to leave. Nearly two decades have passed since Hugo, the last major hurricane to pummel the area. The Gray Man may soon stir again.

Gray Man of Pawleys Island

1825

June

"June—too soon. July—stand by. August—look out you must. September—remember. October—all over." — A mariners' proverb

June *wasn't* too soon in 1825. On June 3-4, a hurricane tracked along the East Coast delivering a maritime disaster. Ships were snared by surprise. Numerous wrecks followed.

A hurricane crossed Cuba on June 1 and reached southeastern Virginia by June 3. The *Norfolk and Portsmouth Herald*:

"It is uncommon to hear of violent storms and hurricanes on any part of our extensive coast in the month of June; but we have to notice a visitation of stormy weather, which commenced about 9 o'clock on Friday night, rarely, if ever equaled in the memory of the oldest inhabitant. The storm of the 3d of September 1821 was perhaps rather more violent, but it lasted only three or four hours, while this continued with undiminished violence, from the hour we have stated until 12 o'clock on Saturday night, or about 27 hours."

The *Herald* reported that the tide "rose at least eighteen inches higher than it was ever known within the last 40 years."

The hurricane stayed off shore. At Philadelphia and New York City, it seemed the equivalent of a respectable nor'easter, bringing lengthy gales and heavy rain. The storm uprooted numerous trees in eastern sections of the Mid-Atlantic and caused scattered wind-related mischief. Nevertheless, casualties on land were few in contrast to those at sea.

Mariners negotiated a maelstrom, a nautical nightmare. Craft pitched and rolled as wind shrieked and whistled through cordage. Stinging rain and salt spray blinded sailors. A merciless ocean devoured hapless crews. Ponder the fate of the *William & Mary*. From the *Herald*:

"Fredericksburg, June 15. The (schooner) *American Coaster*, Capt. Gifford, June 6th, in lat. 37, 38, long. 75 15, on her way from New York to this place, fell in with part of a wreck, and picked up a boat 14 feet long, with Simon Parker's name on the inside, and *William & Mary* on the outside of the stern—one pump, one jib boom, and her mainmast broken off by the deck; main boom and gaft and mainsail altogether—no rigging on the mast—all hands supposed to be lost. From the marks on the boat, Capt. Gifford supposes *Wm. & Mary* was the vessel's name, and Simon Parker the Captain. He saw nothing more."

1846

October

GREAT HAVANA HURRICANE

A hurricane in October 1846 underscored the long-distance menace of tropical cyclones making landfall along the Gulf Coast. It devastated western Cuba and Key West, Fla., before barreling up the East Coast.

The blow that struck Cuba on October 11 ranks among the island's most destructive hurricanes of the century. It rampaged through the countryside and shattered the capital, Havana.

"The destruction in this, and the other cities heard from in the Island, of houses, crops, vessels, and of everything else," reported the U.S. consul Robert Campbell, "has been most calamitous, and unparalleled in the history of the Island. Many lives have been lost in this port and city. No house in the city has entirely escaped."

After leaving Cuba, the jaws of a possible Category 5 hurricane closed on Key West. When the fury

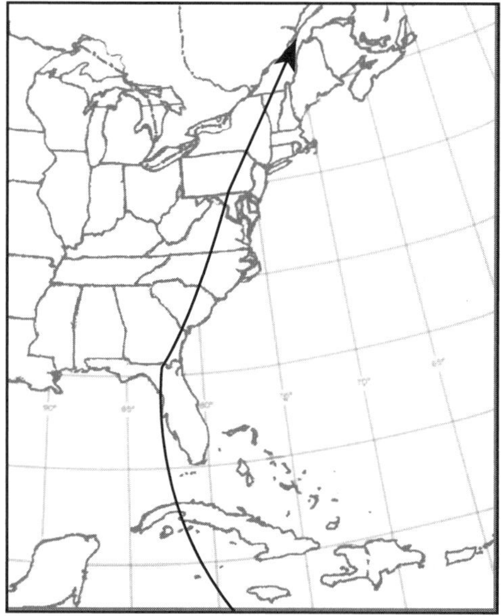

subsided, only six of the island's 600 dwellings remained livable. Lantern posts marked where the Key West Lighthouse stood.

The whirl advanced through northeastern Florida, plunging inland at Cedar Key. It became the second tropical system in five weeks to visit North Carolina, and tracked through the Middle Atlantic states on October 13.[1]

Southeast gales on October 13-14 caused memorable flooding along the Delaware Bay and it's tributaries. At Philadelphia, the Delaware River reached a height not attained since the Independence Hurricane of 1775. Flooding also occurred along the Chesapeake bay and its tidal tributaries. The *Alexandria Gazette*:

"The tide in the Potomac, at this place, on Tuesday, caused by the heavy blow, was one of the highest, if not the highest, ever witnessed by our citizens. The wind blew directly up the bay, which was the cause of this extraordinary rise."

Flooding along the non-tidal Potomac River, the result of heavy rain throughout the watershed, severely damaged the Chesapeake and Ohio Canal, one of the region's commercial arteries. Washington and Alexandria, victims of the destructive storm surge on October 13, suffered another inundation two days later as excess from the upper Potomac raced downstream.

Gales whipped the eastern half of Virginia, Maryland and Pennsylvania. Delaware and New Jersey also endured a notable storm.

Two years earlier, Samuel Morse tapped out the first telegraph message, "What hath God wrought?" A sentiment applicable to the hurricane of 1846. It became the first of many to tangle with the nation's telegraph network. Winds treated poles and wires like playthings, leaving them in shambles. Service along the main line, Washington-Baltimore-New York, remained out for days.

Flooding disrupted the nascent railroad system. Regular U.S. train service began in 1830. By 1846, the Mid-Atlantic boasted a large share of the nation's rail routes. Builders situated tracks along paths of least resistance, frequently river valleys. Why build over hills or mountains when lowlands offered a convenient alternative?

Subsequent floods were disastrous. The *Sentinel*, Woodstock, Va., detailed woes from the hurricane of 1846:

"The damage sustained by the Winchester and Potomac, Baltimore and Ohio, and other railroads in Maryland and Virginia is immense. Not only have many miles of these roads been covered with mud, timber, &c., but a large number of the principal bridges & watering places have been carried away by the floods, and those which have been left standing have been more or less injured."

***

Hurricanes making landfall along the Gulf Coast and tracking up the Eastern Seaboard—such as the storm of 1846—sometimes bring calamitous wind, rain and coastal flooding to the Middle Atlantic states. A Gulf Coast hurricane brought the worst windstorm to Richmond, Va., and Washington, D.C. (1896). A Gulf Coast hurricane spawned the Mid-Atlantic's most prolific tornado outbreak (2004). A long jaunt over land doesn't necessarily diminish the menace.

[1] A hurricane on September 7-8 demonstrated the sculpting ability of great storms. It carved Hatteras and Oregon inlets on the North Carolina Outer Banks.

1861

November

THE EXPEDITION HURRICANE

What a spectacle! During October 1861, with the Civil War in progress, the largest gathering of battleships ever assembled by the United States anchored in the lower Chesapeake Bay. The Northern press dubbed it "The Great Expedition," a flotilla of 77 vessels and 12,000 troops. Their mission: enforce the Anaconda Plan, a blockade to strangle Southern ports, cripple commerce and isolate the Confederacy. Their destination: a military secret.

The armada left on October 29. Hurricanes came late in 1861. One caught the fleet by surprise, threatening the mission and those at sea. Winds buffeted the ships as they sailed off North Carolina's Outer Banks. Two sank. The steamer *Belvidere* limped back to the Chesapeake Bay. An unidentified correspondent provided the following account:

"On Friday (November 1) we took (a) gale, which lasted until Saturday night, and a terrible gale it was. Never do I again wish to witness such a sight. It was, indeed, (awe-inspiring). We rode it out finely all day Friday, shipping a good deal of sea, and at noon speaking the flagship. At 4 o'clock we passed the steam-frigate *Wabash*; the gale increasing, darkness came at last, bringing us still heavier weather; the ocean rose mountains high, the rain fell in torrents, the lightning flashed, and the grand old ocean looked like one vast field of fire, each wave seeming anxious to swallow us up in its wild fury. We now strayed away from the fleet and alone battled the storm.

"We shipped a heavy sea which stove all the bows in forward and swept the top deck. Immediately our first mate, Mr. Cator, the carpenter, and two men belonging to the Forty-eighth Regiment, New York, started for that point. They had hardly got to work repairing the damage done when we shipped another sea, throwing them into a heap—Mr. Cator saving his life by catching hold of the pump handle; the rest catching hold of him and such things as would make them secure until the immense body of water had rushed out as it came in. They arose from their perilous condition drenched through and in total darkness. Their lantern having been swept away, another light was secured, and with a will not to be daunted they went to work.

"But their attention was soon called to other and more important points. We shipped another sea that stove in the port gangway doors, leaving a breach through which the sea dashed at every roll of our ship, which was now laboring badly. Every man was at his post. The New York boys showed any amount of courage, and the boys from Maine and New Hampshire showed, by their exertions, that they too were on hand, and ready for duty in the hour of danger. The doors were again put up as well as they could be, and braces placed against them.

"Great credit is due the men of Company C, Forty-eighth Regiment New York State Volunteers, they being placed at these braces and other perilous points, and the next morning the noble fellows were at their posts, wet through and cold, but still anxious to do all they could. Some of them have lost their overcoats and blankets, they having used them to stop up the holes and thus keep the water from constantly dashing in upon the horses.

"Next the extra tiller broke—a solid piece of wrought iron three inches square—then the engineer reported the machinery out of order; next the rudder chain broke, leaving us in the trough of the sea, and we were now really in a pitiable condition."

The hurricane, likely a Category 1 or 2, tracked east of the Mid-Atlantic coast to New England, a vast swirl of rain, wind and high seas. At Newark and Jersey City and in New York City tides reached their highest level in more than 20 years. Modest coastal flooding occurred from Virginia to Maine, and on the Chesapeake and Delaware bays. Wharves overflowed and boats foundered at Baltimore, Alexandria and Washington, D.C.

The hurricane's fringe soaked the nation's capital. A sodden sky spoke of gathering gloom, a somber backdrop to the departure of 75-year-old Lieut. Gen. Winfield Scott. The country's Army commander, renowned hero of the War of 1812 and Mexican conflict, stepped aside for a younger general, George

McClellan. (Fighting soon became bloodier and lasted far longer than most people expected.)

"I have been up once this morning—that was at four o'clock to escort Gen. Scott to the depot," McClellan wrote. "It was pitch-dark and a pouring rain; but with most of my staff and a squadron of cavalry I saw the old man off."

He concluded, "The sight of this morning was a lesson to me which I hope not soon to forget. I saw there the end of a long, active, and ambitious life, the end of the career of the first soldier of his nation; and it was a feeble old man scarce able to walk; hardly anyone there to see him off but his successor. Should I ever become vainglorious and ambitious, remind me of that spectacle."

News of the dreadful conditions at sea reached Washington. Scott, an architect of the Anaconda Plan which helped win the war, left office concerned for the fleet. It could handle the rebels, no doubt, but to sail into the teeth of a hurricane…

The ships, in fact, fared surprisingly well. The fleet suffered only a few casualties and a day's delay as vessels regrouped.

The hurricane gave the Confederates a dubious intelligence coup when the steamer *Union* grounded near Cape Hatteras. Militia captured 73 soldiers and sailors. Inside the ship they discovered sealed orders with the message, *"In the event of your transport being separated from the fleet, you will proceed to Port Royal, S.C., and report to the quartermaster of that port."*

Richmond received word of the fleet's destination, but without an army in the vicinity the Confederates offered little opposition. Federal troops secured a valuable naval base at Port Royal (Hilton Head, S.C.) on November 7. They captured Beaufort two days later.

The easy victory buoyed Northern morale. Now, just seven months after being hauled down from Fort Sumter, the Stars and Stripes again flew over South Carolina, symbolic heart of the Confederacy. Federal troops held their gains throughout the war. The foothold became a vital naval supply and refueling station. It also served as a magnet and refuge for slaves.

Harpers Weekly, Library of Congress

A hurricane couldn't scuttle the Great Expedition. The Navy triumphed despite a battle with the elements.

1869

October

THE SAXBY GALE

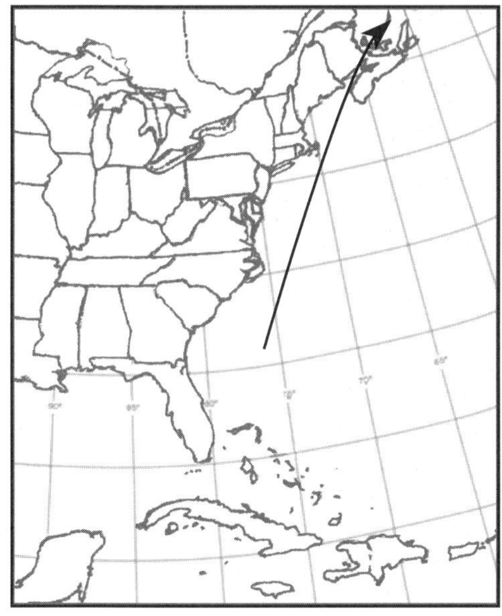

Long-range weather prediction has been a dream of forecasters since the dawn of meteorology. During October 1869, the clairvoyance of Stephen Saxby, an instructor for the Royal Navy, and Frederick Allison, an amateur meteorologist from Halifax, Canada, offered hope and fueled controversy.

Saxby theorized that the proximity and position of the sun and moon affected weather on earth. He believed that since those celestial bodies created tides on the sea, they also influenced the atmosphere.[1]

Some of Saxby's earlier forecasts seemed near the mark. Success created celebrity of sorts, particularly in Great Britain.

In November 1868, he sent a letter to the *London Standard* predicting an unparalleled coastal storm somewhere in the world 11 months hence. His reasoning: The alignment of the sun, moon and earth (a perigean spring tide—the highest of annual astronomical tides), and rare proximity of the moon to the earth's equator, would result in atmospheric turmoil leading to a superstorm. The newspaper published Saxby's dire pronouncement.

At a time when forecast offices issued one-day predictions, before any storm formed, Allison, the weather columnist for the Halifax *Evening Express,* refined and pinpointed Saxby's warning. Eastern Canada—Halifax, to be precise—would, within a week, host the main event. His letter to the *Evening Express* dated September 30, 1869, stated:

"I believe that a heavy gale will be encountered here on Tuesday next, the 5th Oct., beginning perhaps Monday night, possibly deferred as late as Tuesday night; but between those two periods it seems inevitable. At its greatest force the direction of the wind should be South West; having commenced at or near South. Should Monday, the 4th, be a warm day for the season, an additional guarantee of the coming storm will be given. Roughly speaking, the warmer it may be on the 4th, the more violent will be the succeeding storm.

"Apart from the theory of the moon's attraction, as applied to meteorology—which is disbelieved by many—the experience of any careful observer teaches him to look for a storm at next new moon; and the state of the atmosphere, and consequent weather lately, appears to be leading directly not only to this blow next week, but to a succession of gales during next month. Telegrams from points to the South West of us might give notice of the approach of this storm, and I trust this warning will not be unheeded."

The Saxby-Allison warnings caused apprehension among believers and ridicule by others. Nobody, however, was laughing on the morning of October 5.

A hurricane intensified south of Cape Hatteras on October 4 and sped toward the Canadian Maritime Provinces. Meanwhile, a cold front swept east towards the Atlantic coast. The hurricane made landfall on Cape Cod and, again, near Eastport, Maine, before moving into eastern Canada. Abundant tropical moisture collided with colder air and higher elevation. In *Early American Hurricanes,* author David Ludlum discussed the result:

[1] The current scientific view as during Saxby's day is that the position of the moon and sun affect tides but have little or no influence on weather.

The Saxby Gale caused flooding along the Schuylkill River in Reading, Pa.

Damage was widespread in eastern Pennsylvania.

"The main story of this storm for most land stations in the Middle Atlantic and New England states concerned rain, more rain than had fallen over this area in a single storm in recorded history, before or since.[2] Think of the mighty physical forces at work that could precipitate six inches of water continually in a progressive storm all the way from northern Virginia northeastward into Canada. In each of the following states one or more stations reported at least a five-inch catch: Virginia, Maryland, Pennsylvania, New Jersey, New York, Connecticut, Massachusetts, Vermont, New Hampshire, and Maine. Only coastal Delaware and Rhode Island did not give the rain-bearing clouds sufficient surface lifting to cause such downpours.

"As it turned out, the path of full hurricane blasts bypassed the Halifax region, but localities on the western shore of Nova Scotia, bordering the Bay of Fundy, as well as points in Maine and New Brunswick, suffered severely on the evening of the 4th from the combined onslaught of hurricane force winds and unprecedented tides."

Washington, Baltimore and Philadelphia—much of the Northeast—dealt with widespread flooding. The *Baltimore American*:

"From Central and Eastern Pennsylvania and New York telegrams tell one unbroken story of great floods in all the streams, and of buildings of every sort on their shores being destroyed by the torrents. Railroad travel in these localities has been entirely cut off, bridges and track being alike carried away by the waters. In the distance that it covered, the storm appears to have been one of the most disastrous that has ever happened. It will be many days before the enormous total of damages will be ascertained."

A lead story in the October 5 issue of the *Philadelphia Inquirer* began:

"The river Schuylkill has been either one extreme or the other recently. First, we have an unparalleled drought of so serious a character that the water supply of the city is greatly diminished, and but for active measures taken to meet the emergency, we would, for many weeks past, been without water entirely in some sections of the city. Following close upon the drought comes a freshet of unprecedented violence, so great a one, in fact, that bridges are carried away, factories, dwelling houses, ice houses, &c., are submerged, boats are swamped, and the river is swollen to three times its usual size, and to such an extent that Fairmount, Flat Rock, and other dams, which a few days ago were high and dry, have been completely hidden from view by the Niagara of waters that dashed and surged over them with terrific violence."

Rivers throughout eastern Pennsylvania rose to their highest levels in decades. Watercourses spilled over their banks throughout northern New Jersey, southeastern New York and eastern New England.

Hurricane-force winds and encroaching tides assaulted Maine, Nova Scotia and New Brunswick. The Category 2 hurricane killed about 100 people. Every astronomical and meteorological coincidence came together in the worst possible way, especially on the Bay of Fundy.

The bay, an arm of the Atlantic Ocean separating Nova Scotia from New Brunswick, boasts the world's greatest tidal differentials. While the confluence of astronomical factors meant a rise ranging from a few inches to a few feet elsewhere, the Bay of Fundy, with a mean range of 40-50 feet, rose an extra 12 feet. Now, the hurricane superimposed an additional, immense surge—an astronomical and meteorological combination that sent the water of Fundy up to 70.9 feet above normal low tide. The Saxby Gale produced the Saxby Tide, an event still studied today.

In the aftermath:

Allison's acclaim led to a career with the Canadian Meteorological Service.

Saxby (1804-1883) captured public attention with a prescient prediction, but interest in his notion eventually waned. He never duplicated the success of 1869.

[2] *Early American Hurricanes* was published in 1963. Hurricane Agnes (1972) likely produced more rain.

DEVELOPMENT BRINGS AN INCREASED FLOOD RISK

By the late 19th century, vast tracts of forest had disappeared from the eastern United States. Towns and cities grew, transforming groundcover to pavement and buildings. These changes increased rainfall runoff, adding to the severity of floods. The following farsighted editorial appeared in the Reading *Daily Eagle* soon after the Saxby Gale:

It is believed by intelligent observers that as a country is populated and drained by the various processes of improvement, such as clearing forests, making roads and removing deposits that check the surface drainage from rainstorms, floods become more sudden and violent. Their subsidence, for like reasons, becomes more rapid. This fact is worth the consideration of engineers and others who build bridges and construct railroads for these should be made considerably higher than the highest recorded watermark in the rivers and creeks.

Twenty years hence, when the valley of the Schuylkill will probably have double the present population, the drainage will be much more rapid and easy than it is now, and a rain fall no greater than the recent one will probably cause a more rapid and more destructive rise of the river. So it will not do, in repairing the recent damages, to take the height of the late floods as the greatest height the water can ever attain, and rebuild bridges and other structures only so as to clear this height. Millions of dollars in property might have escaped destruction after the late storm if the builders had known that floods rise higher and more rapidly as the country becomes improved.

Historical Society of Berks County

A stereoscopic view of the Saxby flood at Reading, Pa.

1876

September

THE CENTENNIAL GALE

THE PROVIDENCE UNITED METHODIST CHURCH

'Moved by the Hand of God.' September 16-17, 1876.

— North Carolina historical marker, Swan Quarter, N.C.

The Church

"Moved by the Hand of God"

SEPTEMBER 17, 1876

Providence United Methodist Church

Swan Quarter, North Carolina

"THE PLACE WHICH THE LORD THY GOD HATH CHOSEN." Deut. XII

The congregation of Providence United Methodist Church believes the event a miracle.

In 1874, members wanted to build on prime property in Swan Quarter, a village located along Pamlico Sound in northeastern North Carolina. The owner refused to sell, so they erected their church elsewhere. But there was something about the original site.

During September 16-17, 1876, on the eve of the edifice's dedication, a hurricane blew through the area. Pamlico Sound engulfed Swan Quarter, sweeping the sanctuary off its foundation. A Providence United brochure tells what transpired:

"A miracle was happening—the church was floating down the road. The church 'moved by the hand of God.' It went straight down the road to a corner and bumped into a general store owned by George V. Credle. The corner is now Oyster Creek Road and U.S. 264 Business.

"Then a curious thing happened! The building took a sharp right turn and headed down the road for about two city blocks until it reached the corner of what is now Church Street. Then it moved slightly off its straight-line course, took another turn to the left, crossed the Carawan Canal directly in front of the place where people desired the church to be, and settled exactly in the center of the Sam Sadler property, the site which had been refused."

And that's where the building remains today. The land was subsequently sold to the congregation.

Originally designated the "Methodist Episcopal Church South," it was later renamed "Providence United Methodist Church " – a tribute to what members considered divine intervention.[1]

***

The hurricane first made headlines in Puerto Rico. It slammed ashore on September 13 and inflicted tremendous damage, a monster that killed hundreds of islanders, the "San Felipe Hurricane."

The "Centennial Gale," as it was known in the United States, went from North Carolina toward the

[1] Parables based on the incident usually suggest that the stubborn land owner saw the error of his way, relented, and hastily deeded his property to the church. Recent genealogical research reveals a different tale.

Sam Sadler refused to sell, perhaps retaining the property with plans to build a dwelling for a growing family. But he died in June 1874. His wife Cora gave birth to a son on New Year's eve. She died 12 days later. The infant perished the following year. The church paid a token sum for the property during a court-approved (and community approved) auction during 1881.

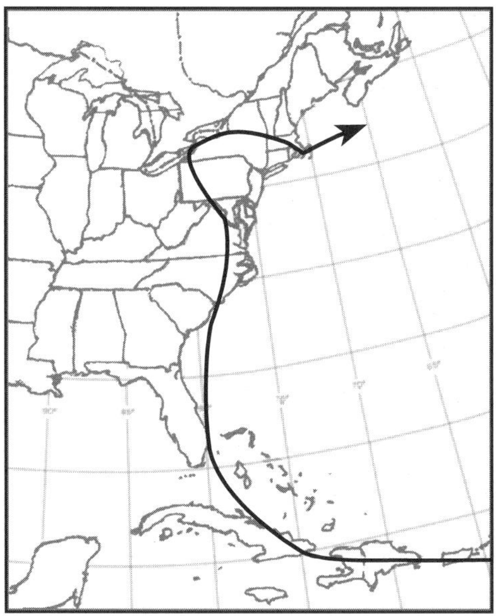

lower Great Lakes on September 17. (Its effects, particularly the reach of high winds and tidal flooding, seem comparable to those of Hurricane Isabel in 2003.)

The Norfolk, Va., Custom House and other buildings lost roofs. Nearby Cape Henry recorded a sustained wind (five-minute average) of 78 mph and 8.32 inches of rain. From the Hampton weather office:

"The late storm commenced here 8:30 p.m. on the 15th, developing into one of unprecedented violence and duration. From the evening of the 15th to 11 a.m. on the 16th, (we had) a steady light rain with a gentle wind from NE. The wind rose to a gale at 2 p.m. and continued with accelerating velocity (until it reached) the force of a hurricane.

"Great destruction among standing crops, trees and fencing has been done. The streets here are literally barricaded with fallen trees."

At Richmond, Va., the storm blew "almost a hurricane," destroying noble shade trees, damaging homes and businesses, causing much mischief in the surrounding countryside.

The *Alexandria* (Va.) *Gazette* reported a soggy, gusty passage:

"The equinoctial gale, which has been brewing for a week past, burst upon us in its full fury yesterday. At an early hour Saturday night the rain began to fall, continuing during the night and all day yesterday. The streets were all flooded, the gutters becoming miniature rivers, and the flat streets covered from curb to curb. Pitt Street had its usual torrent, and the corners of Royal, Princess, and Queen and Patrick were again overflowed.

"In the afternoon the northeast gale, which had been blowing for twenty-four hours, shifted around to the westward and blew a perfect hurricane, breaking down trees, throwing down fences and breaking several boats and small vessels loose, nearly all of which, however, were eventually recovered. Among the trees blown down was one of the oldest poplars in Christ Church yard. In the surrounding countryside the storm was very severe, the corn and apple crops being nearly entirely destroyed."

Extensive agricultural losses accompanied the gale through Maryland.

"On Sunday night we had a very hard storm all over the county," wrote Jacob Engelbrecht of Frederick, Md. "There was a general blow down of apples. People who passed the orchards yesterday morning said the ground was literally covered with apples. Most of the farmers will have to make cider."

Rough surf and high winds battered the coast. Cape May, N.J., surrendered most of its boardwalk. Gusts carried away part of the roofs on two premier hotels, Congress Hall and Stockton House.

The storm blew through eastern Pennsylvania. Shifting winds gave weather vanes a vigorous workout.

Philadelphia saw considerable minor damage. But the nation's pride and joy, the Centennial Exposition, a world's fair showcasing U.S. industrial prowess and growing might, was largely unscathed.

The *Philadelphia Inquirer* seemed prophetic when it admonished readers, "Philadelphians ought to learn wisdom by experience. 'It may be for years and it may be forever' that this portion of our Atlantic seaboard has been and will be famous for its great September gales."

***

The Centennial Gale left a lasting impression and portended future storms. A half-century lull in major Mid-Atlantic hurricane activity ended. Destructive tropical cyclones returned—an active period lasting until 1904.

1877

October

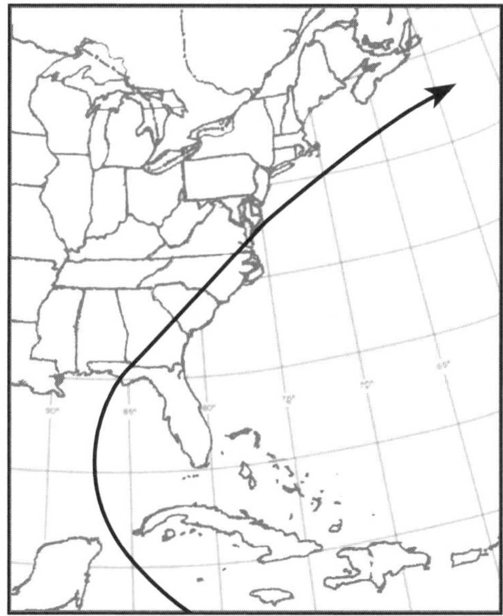

Ceaseless rain drenched much of eastern Pennsylvania during the evening of October 4. The descendants of Henrich Pennypacker headed home from a family reunion in Schwenksville. Passengers scarcely noticed the stormy weather as their excursion train rolled past Phoenixville. Instead, they told stories past and present.

Up ahead, hidden by darkness, a culvert gave way taking 60 feet of railroad bed, creating a gaping chasm. The engine and three cars leaped off the track. Thoughts of the reunion ended abruptly amid twisted metal and dead and dying passengers.

The conductor ran to Phoenixville to summon assistance. Doctors spent the night attending to more than 40 injured passengers. Seven died.

The deluge came from a hurricane that struck the Florida Panhandle and traveled up the East Coast. Torrential rain led to the wreck of the Pennypacker train and several others within a 150-mile radius.

A *Wilmington and Northern* train derailed and plunged into a ditch near Coatesville, Pa., killing the engineer.

A freight train crashed northeast of Carbondale, Pa. Authorities suspected sabotage under cover of the nasty weather. (The area was in the midst of bitter labor strife between railroad companies and workers.)

An engineer, conductor and four passengers died after the *Oswego and Philadelphia Express* hurtled into a washout at Milford, N.J. The *Daily State Gazette* of Trenton provided the following account, based on an interview with a passenger, Conrad Bennett:

"It was fearful—an awful crash. When going down the culvert the lights were extinguished and the seats were smashed to splinters. The smoking and baggage car were broken in two parts and turned upside down. The car (Bennett) was in was thrown on top of the locomotive, then into the stream, breaking the wheels and everything else into fragments. The volume of water was fiercer than was ever seen on the ocean, and no person could have stood up against it, even for a moment. He held on to the seat and people in the car were praying and screaming. The water carried out everything. He was wedged in among the seats, but managed to extricate himself and escaped through a window. He got on top of the car and then a young man with a lantern helped him get to shore. Before this, a tree was blown across the car and came near falling upon him."

New Jersey State Archives, Dept. of State

The aftermath of a bad day in U.S. railroad history. Workmen makes repairs after the wreck of the *Oswego and Philadelphia Express* in Milford, N.J.

Survivors clung to the partially submerged railroad car. A crowd gathered on the banks. With the aid of ropes, a ladder and the fallen tree they rescued stranded passengers.

Fair weather following foul brought throngs of the curious.

"Some thousands of people visited the wreck below Milford yesterday," The *Daily State Gazette* reported. "From early in the morning until late in the afternoon they came from all directions in all manner of conveyances. The churches (around Milford) were but poorly attended, and those of the surrounding country are said to have fared but little better. The crowd evinced the true American eagerness for relics of the great disaster, and such pieces as could be easily torn loose, were eagerly carried away."

Central Maryland, southeastern Pennsylvania and western New Jersey received up to 10 inches of rain. The *Oxford* (Pa.) *Press*:

"Floods in the streams did great damage to bridges, dams, mills, fencing and other property. The extent of these damages is greater than for forty years, and it will cost a large amount of money and labor to restore property to anything like its former status. The roads and fields were washed away to an unprecedented extent."

The storm retained a potent bite even after an extended overland journey. Severe flooding occurred on the Raritan River near New Brunswick, N.J. Cape May, at the southern tip of the state—east of the hurricane's track—recorded a peak gust of 68 mph. Philadelphia clocked 60 mph.

Shipwrecks littered beaches from Virginia to Long Island. The schooner *Arcturus* fought hurricane force winds on the lower Delaware Bay. Ten schooners foundered at Lewes. Gales churned waters around Long Island, claiming several ships including the steamer *Massachusetts*, which grounded on the north shore.

***

The first settlers in Virginia's Shenandoah Valley discovered a green canopy cloaking the territory. By the middle 1800s, however, primeval forest yielded to ax and plow. The Civil War wrought additional devastation. By the war's end, Union soldiers joked that even a crow would need to carry its own rations to survive a trip across the valley.

And the land wept. Soil depleted. Forests shorn for building materials and fuel. Where, now, were the trees and natural vegetation to break the force of driving rain, to temper runoff and erosion? Homesteads, indeed entire communities, brazenly occupied old floodplains.

On the night of October 4, 1877, rivers rose to claim their own. A day of moderate rain culminated in an hours-long torrent. The Shenandoah Valley suffered a natural calamity for the second time in seven years. A great inundation in September 1870 (of non-tropical origin) and the 1877 disaster came after a decades-long absence of devastating floods. Waterways in 1877 approached levels attained during 1870 but the death toll, which exceeded 100 in the earlier event, was far less. Residents learned harsh lessons when they built on land meant for water.

It was schooling administered to most sections of the Mid-Atlantic during the closing decades of the 19th century. Widespread deforestation, generations building on floodplains and a half-century since the last active hurricane cycle primed the region for disaster. Several storm-related floods devastated the Middle Atlantic states, punishing those who ignored the region's climatological history.

1878

September

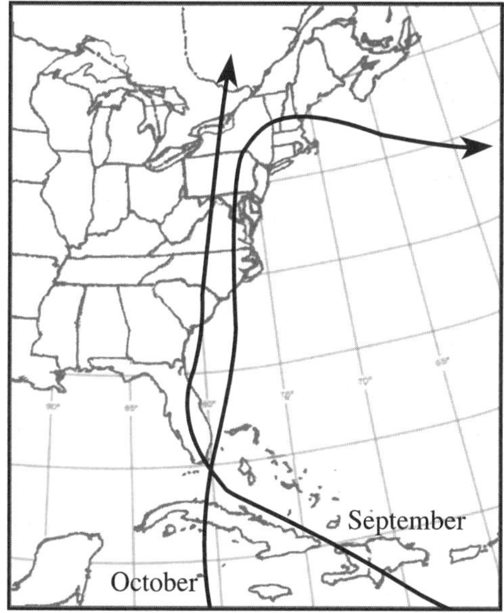

Father Benito Viñes, director of the Belen Meteorological Observatory in Havana, Cuba, the era's foremost hurricane scholar, looked toward the angry clouds hastening west. It was early September 1878. A hurricane struck the island's northeastern coast. Viñes had predicted the storm, another forecasting success, and Cubans were warned. Nevertheless, hundreds drowned. How frustrated he must have been. The padre had seen the hurricane coming. Still, so many died. Now, the foul weather pulled north, threatening Florida and beyond.

From September 8-12 the storm crawled through the southeastern United States dumping copious rain, continuing to generate flooding as it tapped the Atlantic Ocean. Remnants reached Virginia on the 12th, then accelerated northward. A new threat emerged—tornadoes.

Twisters developed in central Virginia during the afternoon of September 12. Tornadoes hit Dinwiddie County southeast of Petersburg, Nottoway County near Burkeville and Goochland County near Dover Mills, a swath of 28 miles. A furious whirlwind tore through Henrico County, several miles south of Richmond. J.E. Woodward described its startling appearance:

"About 4 o'clock p.m. there was a shower of rain; the drops were large, and fell thick and fast; but suddenly, in a breath, it stopped, and, as I remarked on its sudden stopping, I heard a sound like distant but continued thunder, or, to describe more accurately, like a great boiling in the air. I went to the window and saw approaching, at the rate of about a mile in two minutes, a fearful whirlwind. Its direction was in a straight line from southeast to northwest, the breadth of its path about 100 yards, in form round, and appeared like a dark, rolling cloud, so black that nothing could be discerned for some distance above the tops of the tallest trees; and then could be distinctly seen the whirling, boiling, twisting motion of the air. It seemed determined to tear everything in its course from the face of the earth. Houses were snatched up, trees twisted off, and all manner of vegetation mingled with muddy earth in the awful whirl, until they seemed left in the cloud that floated above."

The following account of the Henrico County tornado appeared in the *Richmond Dispatch*:

"On Saturday members of Mr. Higginbotham's family came to the city on business. They represent the storm as being far more severe than previously described in this paper. It is stated that the heavy pillars of (their) front porch were blown more than a mile away, but not a vestige of some of the other buildings could be found. The family was at dinner at the time the storm came upon them. One or two members of the family went to the front of the house to look at the singular cloud—a cloud of smoke it appeared to be—which was approaching rapidly. The sound of the wind was distinctly heard when it was a long way off, but not one member of the family imagined what it could be, although all commented on it. It seemed to them to resemble the 'blowing off' of steam from a locomotive and it grew nearer and nearer, until finally it burst upon them with great fury."

Gales swirled from the Atlantic Ocean to the lower Great Lakes. The *Richmond Dispatch* described the hurricane as bringing "one of the severest storms of wind with which our city has ever been visited." Mariners on lakes Erie and Ontario considered the blow the worst in a decade—some thought it unequaled since 1844.

Southwestern Virginia, West Virginia and western Pennsylvania had widespread and, in some places, unprecedented flooding. The New River rose "five feet higher than it was ever known to be" at Hinton, W.Va., washing away many homes.

This event was *the* Hurricane of '78 to those living in the central Appalachian region. The following month brought violent weather further east.

October

THE GREAT OCTOBER GALE

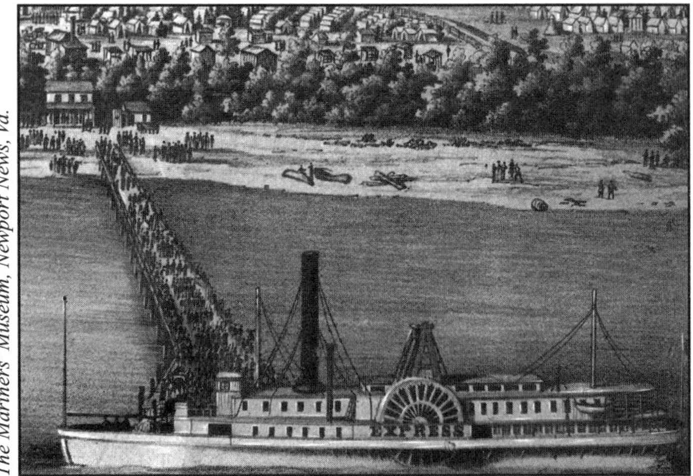

The Mariners' Museum, Newport News, Va.

The *Express* served as a transport ship during the Civil War.

Passengers boarding the Baltimore-based steamer *Express* for its regular run to Washington had little clue of a hurricane heading toward the Chesapeake Bay. City newspapers provided no information about the menace off Cape Hatteras, seemingly a world away on October 22. By next morning most would drown in one of the bay's deadliest disasters.

Captain James Barker, a veteran of steamers and the Chesapeake Bay, heard talk of the blow but wasn't too concerned. The *Express*, after all, had weathered many Chesapeake gales since its launch in 1841. The 200-foot-long double-decker—a stalwart freight and passenger vessel for the Potomac Transportation Company—seemed likely to best the elements for many more years after refurbishment in 1877.

The weather deteriorated during the evening of the 22nd. Squalls rushed inland. The hurricane charged ashore near Cape Lookout, N.C., winds screaming in excess of 100 mph.

The passenger steamers *General Barnes* and *City of Houston* were destroyed off the Outer Banks. Most onboard were rescued. Not so, for the schooner A.S. Davis.

On the night of October 22-23, the *A.S. Davis* fought a losing battle at Virginia Beach. Despite a gallant effort by the newly organized U.S. Life-Saving Service, only one crewman survived. Nineteen were lost. Frustrated at being unable to save more lives, the organization, a forerunner of the Coast Guard, agonized over its role. An investigation concluded, "The life-saving crew did their whole duty, but the tempest was so violent that human effort could avail nothing."

The hurricane raised a huge surge throughout the Chesapeake region and along the Delmarva shore. Smith and Cobb Islands, off the southeastern Virginia coast, submerged. The Chesapeake and Delaware bays had the highest tides since, at least, 1821. At Philadelphia, the Delaware River rose more than a foot above the previous standard set in 1797.

***

Captain Randolph Jones of St. Inigoes, in St. Mary's County, Md., kept a decades-long journal. On October 23, he wrote:

"A violent storm of wind and rain from 1 until 4 (a.m.). Cloudy cool northwest wind for the remainder of the day."

Two days later he inscribed another entry, circling it in black:

"This day was received the sad tidings of the loss of my wife by the wrecking and sinking of the steamer *Express* in the Chesapeake Bay, Wednesday morning October 23—last."

Mary Jones and 15 others drowned when the vessel foundered.

A hurricane seeks weakness in a ship and exploits any it finds. The *Express* was designed for the Chesapeake Bay—not for 20-foot ocean-like waves. It faced conditions seldom experienced away from the deep. The storm toyed with the *Express*. Top-heavy and cumbersome, with a bottom deck breached by a chaotic sea, the steamer capsized. James Douglass, quartermaster, told of its final hours:

"The *Express* was first struck by the storm at midnight. The gale increased in fury until, at four o'clock, it had become a furious hurricane. The steamer tried to reach the Potomac, but would not venture in, and kept on hoping to get into harbor on the east shore. Captain Barker had thrown out an anchor, but the chain parted almost as soon as it went over.

"The *Express* was going along as well as could be expected until, between 5:30 and 6 a.m., when she was in the middle of the bay, between Point No Point and Barren Island, the wind veered to the southwest, and the steamer was thrown over in less than ten minutes. She labored heavily in the trough of the sea a few minutes, entirely unmanageable, and then rolled over until her hull was bottom upward. The saloon and upper joiners' work parted from the hull as the steamer careened."

Morning's gray light disclosed a dismal sight. Survivors clung to the hull. Gradually their strength failed and each slid off. Douglass, Captain Barker and another man hugged wreckage, drifting for miles and hours, coming ashore at Barren Island on the Maryland Eastern Shore.

Barker returned to Baltimore grieving for those lost, especially for his missing son, Willie, who had joined the trip. But the teenager survived and was retrieved hours after Captain Barker. Father and son embraced on the Light Street wharf in Baltimore, a reunion said to have brought tears to the toughest salt.

***

Frank Collins, proud owner of the Hygenia House and namesake of Collins Beach, sheltered from the hurricane on his property along the upper Delaware Bay. With arduous effort he had hewn a premier resort out of Delaware swampland.

Now, Collins stared out into an angry dawn of wind and rain—and the end to his dream. A "tidal wave," as observers described a tsunami-like wall of water, roared up the Delaware Bay. It crashed ashore, according to the *Delaware Times*, "sweeping the ball room, stables, pavilion, bath houses—everything but the hotel (protected by a seawall) before it, and carrying them out of sight. The mighty tide rolled inland, submerging the country for a distance of one or two miles."

The onslaught demolished carriages, carts and wagons. Cattle perished, washed into the surrounding marsh. The wave's salty infusion altered local ecology.

In the aftermath, Collins faced daunting prospects. Heartbroken, he sold his resort months later. Despite various promotional efforts Collins Beach never recovered, dying a slow death over the next 25 years, vexed by storms.

***

The Delaware Geological Survey examined the surge that swept the Delaware Bay. Its findings are contained in a report, "The Hurricane of October 21-24, 1878," issued in 2002. The authors estimated that the "great tidal wave" slammed about 35 miles of shoreline from north of Collins Beach to south of Woodland Beach—a section where the broad expanse of Delaware Bay greatly narrows.

"The surge wave entered the Delaware Bay at about 5 a.m. with the high tide and moved northeastward along the Bay," according to the report. "Between 6:00 and 6:30 a.m., the surge mound encountered the shallow waters (less than 5-ft. deep) offshore the area of the Murderkill River entrance and built even higher. When the wave reached the shoreline it was perhaps as high as ten feet or more. It crashed onto the shore causing a great deal of damage to any nearby structures and breaking through any of the small beach-barriers along the shoreline. The marshes behind would have been flooded, and areas along the tidal stream, such as Little Creek Landing, would have seen water levels rapidly climb several feet within an hour's time. The shorelines to the south experienced flooding as well but, because of the greater width of the bay and the sheltering effect of Cape Henlopen and Cape May, did not experience the same level of surge wave."

The publication speculated on circumstances that produced the wave.

"The surge would have been unusual in the sense that it was not generated by the hurricane center making landfall (it was about 75 miles to the west), but by high winds blowing for a long period of time building upon the high tide that entered the mouth of the Delaware Bay at about 5 a.m. At the same time, winds were blowing at Cape May, New Jersey, at 84 mph from E-SE. The coincidence with a high tide that was within four tidal cycles of a perigean spring tide (the highest of astronomical tides) is perhaps the most critical factor for the storm surge wave and flooding that occurred along the Delaware Bay. ..."

The wave that wrecked Collins Beach also consumed Bombay Hook and Woodland Beach.

Delaware County Historical Society, Pa., Etching by David Scattergood

The resort of Collins Beach during the late 19th century.

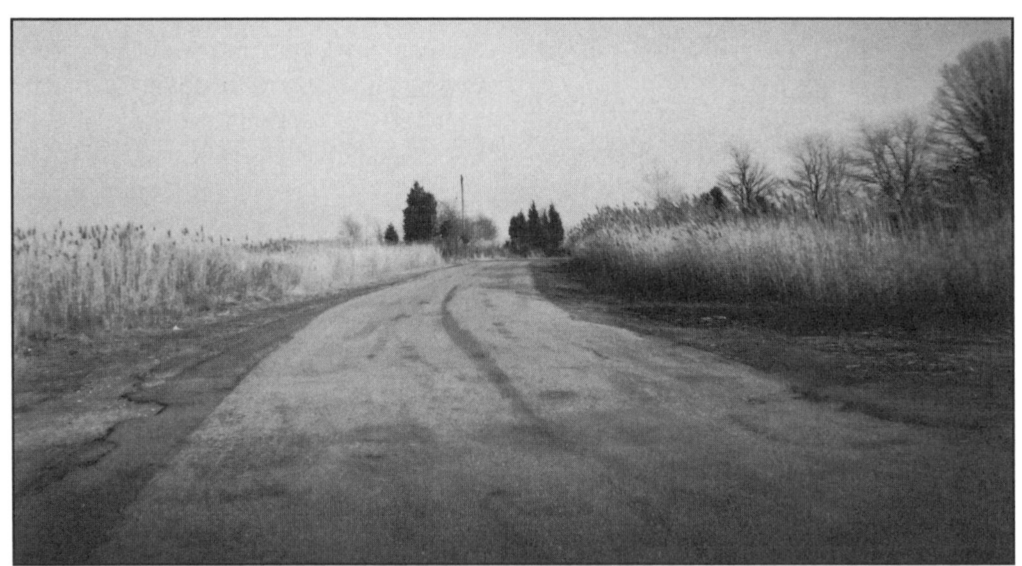

Collins Beach today.

Devastation was nearly complete along the shore. Miraculously, nobody died. The oncoming sea was initially mistaken for a rapidly approaching fog bank. From the (Del.) *Daily Gazette*:

"Bombay Hook was swept from end to end and for the past week has presented the appearance of a vast lake, the beach and banks serving as a rim to a basin to hold the water in. The only communication with the Island has been by boats. Persons on the west of the Island saw the big wave when it mounted the beach…it was not until they heard the angry roar of splashing waters that they realized the destruction in its wake, and fled for the main land."

The *Dover Delawarean* described carnage elsewhere along the bay:

"At Kitt's Hammock, the scene beggars description. All of the buildings except the main building and stable are swept away. The hotel had the weather boarding torn off and the doors and windows torn off and carried away. Much damage was done all along the coast. As far as the eye could range was a vast sea of raging water.

"Along Mispillion Creek the farmers have suffered severely in the loss of buildings, stock, corn and hay. The loss is very heavy. The Mispillion lighthouse keeper had to take to the upper story, and expected to be swept away. His chickens, cow, hogs, etc., were drowned."

Across the bay, New Jersey watermen said it was the worst storm they'd ever experienced. At least eight lives were lost to wind and tidal flooding. A vessel wrecked at the mouth of the Cohansey River and five crewmen drowned. Fortesque Island was awash. The surge carried away or severely damaged every building in the fishing enclave.

Oystermen sustained staggering losses. At least 58 boats wrecked at Port Norris, and another 33 sank or grounded at Dividing Creek. Some craft washed more than a mile inland.

Gusts of hurricane strength buffeted much of northeastern Maryland, northern Delaware, southwestern New Jersey and southeastern Pennsylvania.

The Army Signal Service weather observer in Fallston, (Harford County) Md., logged:

"The great wind from S.SE. blew at its hardest between 7 a.m. and 8 a.m. Some buildings are partly torn down and several roofs taken off. The tin roof of this house loosened up but was not torn off. Had the ground been soaked, much timber would have been prostrated, but the ground until this rain was scarcely ever dryer."

In Wilmington, Del., nearly 100 buildings lost roofs and some houses collapsed. A few churches lost steeples. A wind-fanned fire destroyed a large woolen mill in New Castle.

The hurricane is Philadelphia's most destructive windstorm. At least eight people died and hundreds were injured. The *Philadelphia Inquirer*:

"The fury of the gale cannot be described. The wind roared with the noise of artillery and moved with a prodigious force that carried down, like straws, church spires, solid walls and stately trees, and lifted off roofs as though they were of paper. Some idea of the terrific force of the gale can be gathered from the fact that the velocity of the wind, when the storm was at its height, was seventy-two miles an hour."

The Delaware Geological Survey's report on the hurricane estimated considerably higher gusts.

"… At Philadelphia, sustained high winds greater than 45 mph lasted from 5:00 a.m. to 10:00 a.m. and were greater than 60 mph for over an hour, from before 7:00 a.m. to after 8:00 a.m. Gusts during this time must have been higher. An estimate of a gust factor on modern hurricanes would be 1.5 to 2.0 times the sustained wind speed. This would suggest that winds of 90 to 120 mph were possible during the peak of the storm."

More than 700 buildings were destroyed or seriously damaged in the city. The *Inquirer* provided a partial list:

"Houses 385; depots 7; factories 19; warehouses 16; railroad offices 4; ferry houses 4; machines shops 2; vessels sunk 8; vessels damaged 22; amusement places 2; depot sheds 5; engine house 1; churches 31; mills 21; markets 7; foundries 8; hotels 5; halls 6; chemical works 2; schools 23; stores 29; slaughter houses 3; asylum 1; (covered) bridge 1."

The bridge was about 700-feet long. At the height of the storm, the passageway over the Schuylkill swayed like the "bough of a tree," and eventually, "two of the spans gave way and the remaining one (stood) like a sentinel keeping watch over his fallen comrades."

A sampling of the hurricane's blustery wrath in Pennsylvania:

Chester: Winds demolished 19 buildings. About 70 houses and shops, three churches and a meeting hall were partially or completely unroofed. At least 11 manufacturing plants were forced to close for repairs.

Lancaster: The *Reading Daily Eagle* carried this account from Lancaster: "Early yesterday morning a heavy storm passed over this place, doing a great deal of damage on the campus of Franklin and Marshall College. Trees, fences and pumps were blown over. Three chimneys on the Academy building fell about 5 o'clock. The bricks, breaking through the ceiling on the 3rd floor, fell upon the bed of two students, and unquestionably would have killed them, but fortunately they had arisen about 5 minutes before. The students at Harbaugh Hall and the Academy building could not sleep on account of the shaking of the buildings."

Pottstown: The sprawling Pottstown Iron Company nail-plate mill collapsed. Spires on two churches blew down. About 40 stables collapsed at a local racetrack. The lengthy Madison Bridge spanning the Schuylkill River crumbled after an unyielding assault.

Reading: Roofs and chimneys were frequent casualties. The wind overturned several wagons and other conveyances. In one instance, a sleigh became airborne and landed more than 100 feet away. The *Reading Times and Dispatch* reported, "Many (residents) were terror-stricken and members of families sought companionship and watched through weary hours, waiting anxiously for daylight."

Elsewhere: A church on DeKalb Street in Norristown was nearly demolished. The roof of the First Presbyterian Church peeled off in fragments. Schoolhouses in Chadds Ford and Kennett Square sustained serious damage, but no students were injured.

Newspapers throughout southeastern Pennsylvania contained long lists of residential and commercial casualties. Farmers lamented flattened crops, wrecked barns, etc. — a panorama of wind-related ruin.

In New Jersey:

Camden: At least 150 buildings lost roofs. Camden and much of southwestern New Jersey received hurricane-force gusts.

Jersey Shore: Gusts peaked at 84 mph in Cape May and 72 mph at Barnegat. Nevertheless, losses along the coast were less severe than inland.

Trenton: Many roofs took flight. Notable casualties included the Taylor Opera House, Cooper Hewett's rolling mill and the almshouse. A large tower at Roeblings wire mill blew down, as did the 60-foot wooden bell tower at the town firehouse. From the *Daily State Gazette*: "The popular greeting after the ill wind yesterday was 'Ow's yer roof?' "

***

The storm's broad center tracked between the Chesapeake Bay and Blue Ridge. In Virginia's capital, Richmond, the whirl brought, "a heavy rain and wind storm for several hours after midnight, when the wind became almost a hurricane," according to the *Richmond Dispatch*.

Washington, Baltimore and Annapolis suffered assorted, mostly minor, wind-related damage. A flood tide sloshed ashore.

The barometric pressure in Washington bottomed at 28.80 inches, at Baltimore, 28.83 inches, and in Annapolis, 28.82 inches.

At Frederick, Md., the *Daily Times* told of "a terrific gale of wind that swept over the town between one and two (a.m.), and continued with great fury for about two hours."

The hurricane turned east after leaving Pennsylvania and tracked through New England. New York City had several hours of 50-mph gales. At least 23 schooners sank off the Massachusetts coast. Portland, Maine, registered a gust of 70 mph on October 24.

***

The *Daily Local News* of West Chester, Pa., concisely detailed the wind's work:

"Word relics of the storm: torn off, unroofed, partly unroofed, razed, swept away, destroyed, blown down, scattered, flattened, leveled, uprooted, torn up, twisted off, carried away, overturned, dismantled, dashed, demolished, felled, broken off, smashed, crushed in, wrecked, devastated, succumbed, &c., &c., &c., etc."

SPIRITS IN THE WIND

The Great October Gale inspired ghost stories. The following tale appeared in the *History of St. Mary's County* (Md.) by Regina Combs Hammett:

"A St. Mary's County legend grew out of the loss of the *Express*. Jones' Wharf (later renamed Grason's), located at Capt. Randolph Jones' Cross Manor home, was one of the steamer's scheduled stops on its way up the Potomac. At the time of the disaster, Capt. Jones and some friends were sitting in the parlor of Cross Manor. They heard a knock at the front door of the mansion. Capt. Jones looked out the window and saw his wife beckon him to come to the door. He went to the door, opened it to the fury of the raging storm, and found no one there! The next day news was received that the *Express* had been lost on Chesapeake Bay. Mrs. Jones had drowned at the time Capt. Jones had seen her beckon him to the front door of Cross Manor."

***

The old Point Lookout Lighthouse is located at the confluence of the Chesapeake Bay and Potomac River. It overlooks the vicinity where the *Express* sank. Gerald Sword, a Maryland state park ranger, lived at the lighthouse for several years. He discovered that he wasn't alone. The following is an excerpt from Sword's article, "Who Goes There? Ghostly Manifestations at Point Lookout," written for the St. Mary's County Historical Society:

"... Most of my home time was spent in the kitchen area and it was there that my (ghostly) encounter took place. In mid-December 1977, at 9:15 p.m., I was sitting by the kitchen table and my 120-pound Belgian shepherd was lying on the floor between the outside door and me. What appeared to be a very violent electrical storm was fast approaching from the Virginia shore, seven miles distant. The dog was noticeably uncomfortable. He would whine, bristle his back hair and point his ears upward as if listening to something. A few minutes later I felt the sensation of being watched. Then the dog leaped toward the door.

"Upon looking out the door window, I observed a young clean-shaven white male peering through the window toward me. He had on a floppy cap, an opened dark-colored sack coat, dark hair about collar-length and dark eyes. As I lunged toward the door I focused my eyes on his and quickly pulled open the door. As the dog and I stepped through the door the man simply disappeared through the screening of the enclosed porch. Now that was different! He went right through the tiny openings and vanished.

"The dog and I continued out into the yard but found nothing. The storm passed within 15 to 20 minutes and carried with it a considerable amount of lightning and wind. As soon as the storm passed, the door on the south side of the house was heard to shut. The dog barked and we again investigated. Nothing was found. The doors were locked just as they were before the storm. The clothing worn by this strange visitor appeared to be that of post-Civil War vintage. It did not give the appearance of a military uniform. Who could this visitor have been, why did he seek out the lighthouse, and was there a relationship between him and the storm?

"Two years after the appearance of this lighthouse visitor, I was doing some research on area shipwrecks. It was during this research that a possible explanation was developed. The 200-foot long steamer *Express* broke up northeast of Point Lookout on October 23,

1878. Only 9 persons survived from the 22-man crew and 9 passengers onboard.[1] Among the victims was Joseph Haney, the Second Officer of the ship. (Haney plunged through the skylight when the ship overturned.) Haney's body apparently washed up on the shore north of the Point a few days after the tragedy and was buried there. A Baltimore newspaper reported Haney as about 25 years of age, single, and being from Baltimore. The recovered body had on a brown overcoat, blue sack coat, and was clean-shaven.

"The steamer was en route from Baltimore to the Potomac River when she was struck by the violent storm, which raged up the coast from Virginia. The ship's captain was apparently trying to get to shore near Point Lookout or round the Point into the calmer waters of the Potomac. In either case the sighting of the Point Lookout light was of importance.

"Could it have been that the mid-December visitor was Joseph Haney? The ingredients are there. A violent storm approaching from Virginia, similar clothing and physical description, the need to find the Point Lookout light, shelter just long enough for the storm to pass, a violent death and a nearby burial."

Point Lookout Lighthouse

[1] Figures on the death toll vary, but 16 seems the most likely number.

1879

August

THE GREAT TEMPEST

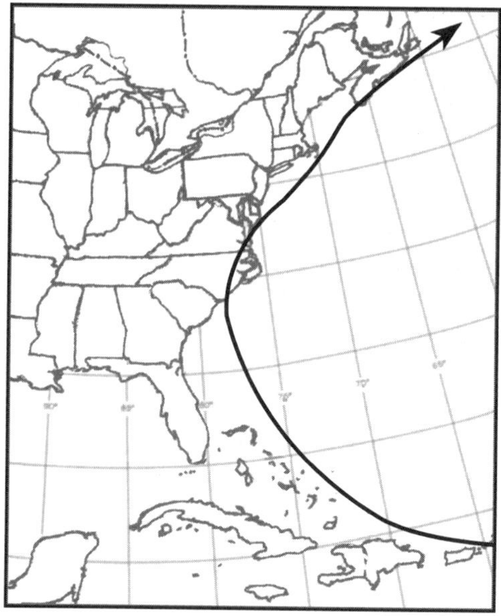

North Carolina Gov. Thomas Jarvis and his wife arrived at the Atlantic Hotel in Beaufort, N.C., during August 1879. The couple anticipated an enjoyable week at the beach capped by a reception for the state press association. They made front-page news but not in the way they imagined.

The storm that plowed through eastern North Carolina that August ranks among the century's strongest East Coast hurricanes. It made landfall near Beaufort shortly after midnight on August 18, carrying a devastating surge, routing Jarvis. He, his wife, and other guests waded through waist-deep water as the Atlantic Hotel collapsed, killing three people. The bedraggled governor left Beaufort in borrowed clothes.

The hurricane left Beaufort and destroyed every anemometer north to Cape Henry, Va. Casualties included wind instruments at Cape Lookout, Cape Hatteras, Ft. Macon, Portsmouth (N.C.), Kitty Hawk and Cape Henry. At Cape Lookout, near Beaufort, the anemometer reached 138 mph before being lost. The station observer estimated the wind peaked at 168 mph. Kitty Hawk and other sites reckoned gusts well above 100 mph.

In Portsmouth, Va., over 150 buildings were damaged. The (Norfolk) *Public Ledger* marveled at nature's might:

"Our city and section were visited this morning by the severest storm of wind and rain which has occurred for more than a score of years. The rain commenced to fall at an early hour, and as the day advanced the storm continued to increase in intensity and fury. All outdoor work was suspended, and it was dangerous for persons to pass along the streets on account of the falling trees, signs, roofs, &c. The storm attained its height between half past 11 and 12 o'clock.

"The tremendous force of the wind also backed the water up in the harbor until it reached a height which we have never seen equaled.

"It is impossible to attempt to give a list of the numerous houses which have been unroofed, and of the small buildings which have been blown down."

The rescue of the *David Dudley* became the banter of Hampton Roads mariners. The *Public Ledger*:

"In mentioning yesterday the loss of the bark *David Dudley*, we failed to state that the Captain was on shore at the time, and as his vessel was drifting over to inevitable destruction with his wife on board, he offered $200 to the Captain of a tug to take him out to his vessel, but the offer was refused. Captain Charles Salvage and the crew of the brig James Miller saved the captain's wife and the crew of the Dudley, and we desire especially to call the attention of the United States authorities to the act of these brave men. The following letter thanking Captain Salvage has been handed us for publication, and we cheerfully give it a place:

"Norfolk, VA. August 19, 1879.

Capt. Chas. Salvage, Master brig *James Miller*, of Belfast, Maine, Port of Norfolk.

Dear Captain—Permit me to take this opportunity and manner of publicly thanking you and your men in behalf of myself and wife, as well as the officers and crew of the *David Dudley*, for your heroic conduct and noble services at the climax of yesterday's tornado, by which you gallantly rescued them from imminent death, when hope was well nigh gone and assistance from any other quarter unobtainable on account of the terrific hurricane then prevailing.

Sincerely your friend,
James F. Johnson
Master of bark *David Dudley*, of Boston, Mass."

There'd be no reprieve for the *J.C. Henry*.

In all his years of sailing on the Chesapeake Bay, Captain Noah Foster had never seen anything like it. Off Gwynn's Island, Va., on the lower bay, he encountered a schooner, the *J.C. Henry*, sailing erratically. A dead woman was lashed to the rigging of the deserted ship. Who was she? What happened? Coming days solved the mystery.

The Donnelly family—Mr. Donnelly, his wife and two sons, William and Eugene—left Philadelphia on a summer cruise. The hurricane caught the group on the bay. The elder Donnelly and his boys were carried overboard. William and Eugene clung to wreckage and survived. Their father perished. Mrs. Donnelly, unable to swim, had been bound to the rigging. Nevertheless, she perished, a victim of the unrelenting elements.

The *Monthly Weather Review* noted the following bizarre occurrence as a weather station underwent a rapid pressure change upon passage of the hurricane's eye:

"At Johnsontown, eastern shore, Virginia, about 35 miles north of Cape Henry, the barometer was at its minimum between 12:30 and 1:30 p.m. The wind on that day (Aug. 18th) was heavy NE. until noon and then 'shifted' to NW. with heavy gusts. Thirty panes of glass were blown from the observer's house *outward against* the wind's direction."

The hurricane was a terror on land, a nightmare at sea. Many ships and their crews went missing. Tragedies tagged with the epitaph, "lost at sea." The *U.S. Monthly Weather Review* summarized the disaster:

"The amount of damage done by this storm can not be enumerated in detail within the limits of this Review... The damage to maritime property must have been enormous, reports already at hand show that over one hundred large vessels were shipwrecked or suffered serious injury, while the number of yachts and smaller vessels which were destroyed or seriously damaged must certainly exceed two hundred."

The hurricane continued northeast, weakening, softening the blow to the Jersey shore. Gales whipped beaches from Cape May to Sandy Hook. Cape May received 8.46 inches of rain on August 18, Atlantic City, 8.97 inches (6.72 inches in nine hours) and Sandy Hook, 6.38 inches.

1882

September

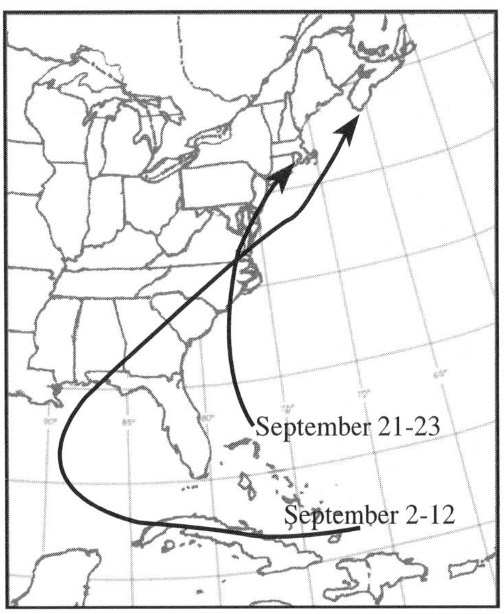

The recipe for a flood calamity: Start with days of ground-soaking showers. Bring in a huge rainmaker such as a tropical cyclone, which peaks with a deluge.

Throw in a population that encroaches on old floodplains, thus increasing runoff, ignorant of danger zones. Include a decades-long accumulation of silt in local waterways—channel sedimentation—topped by a generous helping of dead trees and other debris. Add bridges, culverts and embankments that impede or impound the flow of water—trapping material downstream and creating blockages.

These ingredients contributed to an epic flood in New Jersey during September 1882.

Trouble began when the remnants of a hurricane moved through the state on September 11-12, dumping up to 10 inches of rain. Periodic showers during the following days kept the ground waterlogged. From September 20-24, another tropical intruder pelted central and northern New Jersey with up to 18 inches of rain. The hurricane dumped the following on September 22-23:

New Jersey—Paterson 16.95" (17.90" from Sept. 21-24 and 25.98" for September), South Orange 11.00", Newark 10.72", New Brunswick 10.61", Princeton 9.18". New York City (Central Park) 10.62".

The *U.S. Monthly Weather Review* told of resulting chaos:

"New Jersey. Paterson, 24th, the streets along the river flooded, and many families were forced to take refuge in the upper portions of their dwellings. The river rose twelve feet. Many bridges were washed away and others seriously undermined. At the mills on the Passaic River, operations have been suspended owing to damage caused by high water. At Rahway, the damage is estimated at $500,000. The streets were flooded with water; eight bridges were washed away, and two others were undermined. Trains were stopped and all communication was cut off for many hours. One person was drowned, and several were injured.

"In Bound Brook, on the 24th, the water flowed through the streets of the town, and covered the counters of the stores on Main Street. Large quantities of valuable goods were ruined. At the woolen mills the water rose over the looms causing a loss of about $10,000. A bridge and a long stretch of the Lehigh Valley Railroad were washed away. The track of the New Jersey Central Railroad was three feet under water, and at the station the water was two feet deep. The canal banks gave way in several places, and the canal lock, five miles below here, was destroyed. The water was two feet and eight inches higher than the flood of 1865.

"At Jersey City and Hoboken much damage was done. The fields were completely inundated, and in many cases water covered the floors of houses, causing people to vacate their homes.

"At Elizabeth, on the 23rd, the water in the streets was knee-deep, flooding many of the houses. Barns and small buildings in some localities were floated away.

"Moorestown. From the 21st to 24th, nearly all of the mill dams in this vicinity were washed away; numerous and extensive washouts occurred on the railroad."

On September 23, rain fell in an almost continuous torrent on the state capital, Trenton. Flooding on the Delaware River and every local stream immersed much of the city. The sprawling Pennsylvania Railroad yard lay beneath eight feet of muddy effluent.

Philadelphia collected 10.09 inches on September 22-23. The *Philadelphia Inquirer* estimated that property losses in the city nearly equaled those from

Trentonia: Local History and Genealogy Collection, Trenton Public Library

The Pennsylvania Railroad yard in Trenton, N.J., during the notable flood of 1882.

THIS MAP SHOWS THE RAINFALL FOR SEPTEMBER 1882. No. 22.

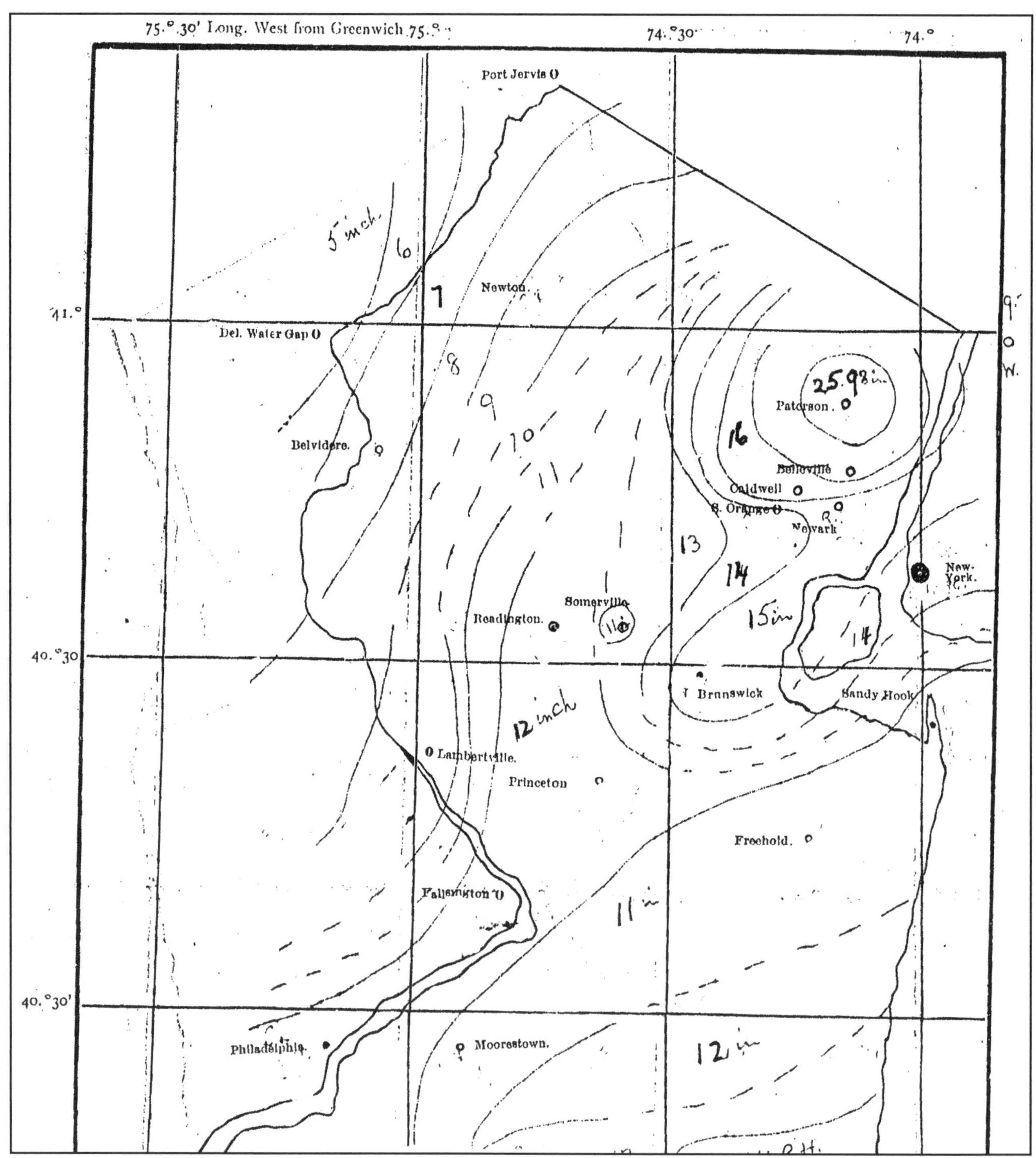

New Jersey Weather Review

THIS MAP SHOWS THE RAINFALL FOR Sept 23rd 1882. No. 23

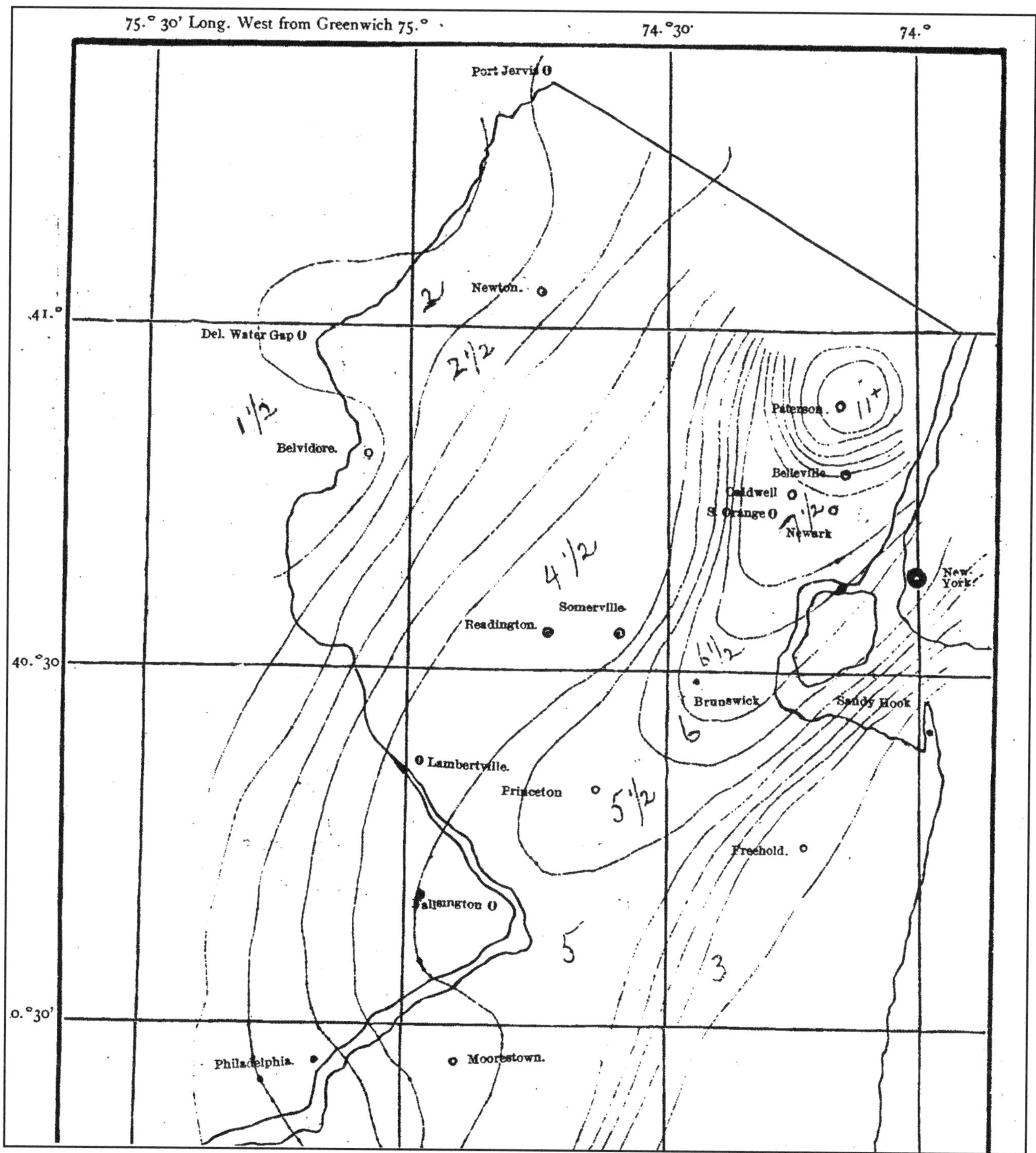

New Jersey Weather Review

the hurricane of October 1878. It reported that, "The equinoctial storm, which began last Thursday night and ended Saturday night, was the heaviest on record in this region. In some places the rainfall measured 13 inches. The floods that were caused by the rain did great damage but the loss was lessened by the absence of high winds."

The *New Jersey Weather Review* offered extensive coverage, including the following excerpt:

"One of the most memorable rain storms that has ever been recorded in the state of New Jersey occurred on Sept 20th to the 24th. (It began) on the 20th with light rains, which gradually increased until they reached an amount that has never been equaled in this state, so far as the records show, except in isolated localities. The result of these downpours was the rising of various streams, especially in Passaic, Essex, Union, Middlesex and Mercer counties until they were beyond control, when breaking all bounds, they carried destruction before them such as was never known in the state before.

"Streets were under water and navigable for small rowboats at Orange, Belleville, Paterson, Passaic, Rahway, New Brunswick, Bound Brook, Plainfield and Trenton."

The report continued:

"Property destroyed: It is impossible to enumerate by name (all) the property lost in the state of New Jersey by this storm—suffice to say that hundreds of bridges were carried away or seriously damaged and scores of dams destroyed; numbers of buildings wrecked; valuable embankments and stone retaining walls injured. Washouts on the railroad were numerous, causing detention to thousands of people—the U.S. Mails—and large quantities of freight.

"Farms were inundated and the entire season's crops destroyed. The damage to county roads is past estimating. Not only has the storm of September 20-24th done all this, but it has indirectly been the cause of much more injury. The breaking of machinery through extra strain on steam engines by loss of water-power—sickness past telling—lawsuits. All this, and much more untold, will make this storm memorable so long as the present generation lasts."

1888

August

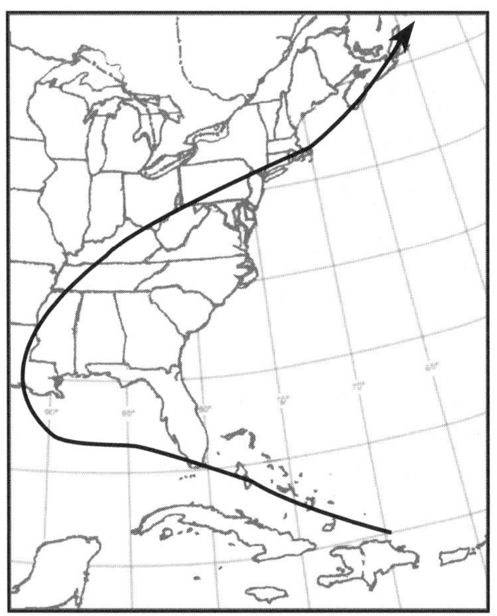

Sometimes the most spectacular feature of a dying hurricane is a tornado. A hurricane in August 1888 generated a tornado that carved an intermittent 90-mile path through Maryland and Delaware. It killed 15 people and injured scores of others.

The twister began a trail of terror after touching down in Glenn Dale, Md., north of Washington, D.C., on the afternoon of August 21. Minutes later, it demolished a church. The whirlwind remained on or near the ground for about three hours. It tracked from near Washington to beyond Wilmington, Del., paralleling a parent tropical cyclone crossing Pennsylvania.

Spiraling through the Maryland countryside, terrific winds took aim on Bowie. The monster roared through town, splintering houses and lifting a schoolhouse and church off their foundations. Moving northeast, destructive winds swirled through Anne Arundel County.

Hundreds of trees toppled at Millersville. The tornado mangled 12 homes in Jacobsville. It reached

NOAA, Department of Commerce

the Chesapeake Bay east of Baltimore, crossing the Patapsco River, tearing through North Point.

Multiple vortices formed—dark tentacles that could snare a man or wreak havoc on a ship. They gyrated off Poole's Island, narrowly missing the steamer, *Trumpeter*, and the tug, *Warrior*. Passengers marveled at a swirl of dust, shingles, fencing, corn stalks and even a woman's blue stocking. The *Baltimore Sun*:

"Four water-spouts burst over the Chesapeake Bay yesterday. The remarkable meteorological phenomenon was accompanied by tall columns of black clouds moving in rapid rotation, the bay at their bases being violently agitated and heaped up with a leaping or boiling motion, and the water being apparently carried up in large quantities. The funnel-shaped clouds seemed to descend near the mouth of the Patapsco River and pass up the bay over Poole's Island and Whorton's Point, following Elk River over Chesapeake City, and thence into Delaware. …"

Three waterspouts moved north and the other whirled east. Across the bay, at Still Pond Creek, Md., the four became two, capricious twins taking turns at mayhem. They traveled with a see-saw motion. One would touch down and destroy everything in its path. When the first lifted, the other took over.

The vortices coalesced into a single tornado and advanced east-northeast to the farming village of Still Pond. It demolished the home of William Willis. The invalid died in the wreckage.

4 p.m. Workers at the Krebs Cannery pared peaches and packed corn, unaware of impending disaster. About 40 employees occupied the main building, a two-story frame structure. They were mostly immigrants from central Europe struggling for an economic foothold.

An edgy silence preceded impact. Boom! Timbers collapsed and splinters rocketed like missiles. Hundreds of empty cans tumbled on the mass below. No chance to escape. Calamity took seconds.

From the recently installed telephone line a shrill message was sent to the Kent County seat of Chestertown, Md.: "Send all the doctors you can find to Still Pond!"

Six physicians arrived. They came too late for 10 workers, including a couple, Charles and Sophia Bearkemp, and members of the Gust family, who were found huddled in a group—husband, wife and two young sons. "They looked as though they had determined to face death together rather than separate," according to the *Kent News*.

Walter Harris has lived in Kent County for more than 80 years. He remembers stories about the Still Pond disaster starting with those of his mother.

"My mother was four years old then," Harris said. "The tornado was one of her earliest memories. An older brother made her and a younger sister stay in a closet. She said that she could feel the house shake as the storm passed.

"People who (witnessed the tornado or its effect) would always recall it and make comparisons whenever another destructive storm came along. It was one of the biggest things that happened in their lives."

The twister roiled the Sassafras River, entering Cecil County. Continuing northeast, it savaged Cecilton, razing the Methodist Episcopal Church and damaging several homes. A wheelwright shop collapsed. Chimneys and sheds became scattered bricks and lumber. Stately trees turned twisted splinters.

The tornado lifted for about 20 miles after reaching Delaware. Southeast of Newark, it resumed a murderous spree. Shattered trees marked the whirlwind's progress. By 6 p.m., a boiling mass of inky black clouds approached Wilmington.

Robert Morrison and William Wilson, on the Hares Corner road, were nearly overtaken. They leaped from their carriage, raced to a fence and clung for their lives. The men watched in amazement while the edge of the tornado passed overhead, spinning boards, trees and assorted debris. The ill wind mowed through a cornfield sucking ears out of husks.

Victims perished in their workplaces. Theodore Bruce, a blacksmith, died in his shattered Hares Corner shop. The Neblow Brothers Iron Works was wrecked as the tornado powered its way through eastern Wilmington. An employee succumbed in the rubble. Boats carrying fruit and vegetables up the Christina River sailed into the twister's path. Several capsized. Two men drowned.

The steamer *Wilmington* nearly overturned and the steamer *Brandywine* rocked furiously while horrified bystanders listened to the screams of terrified passengers. A massive plume of water marked the twister's passage. It crossed the Delaware River and lifted about two miles north of Penns Grove, N.J.

Earlier that afternoon, just after 4 p.m., another tornado struck Salem, N.J.—about 15 miles southeast of Wilmington. The Salem Brick Works was destroyed. The twister snaked northwest, lifting near the Delaware River.

***

The hurricane spawning the tornadoes struck Louisiana on August 19, the worst storm in years. New Orleans clocked 90-mph winds before the weather office's anemometer blew away.

Flooding became the primary danger west and north of a track through Tennessee, Kentucky and southeastern Ohio. The center passed Wheeling, W.Va., before crossing the length of Pennsylvania.

Rivers at Washington, Uniontown and Altoona, Pa., rose to heights unequaled in more than 50 years. Notable flooding occurred on the Youghiogheny, Allegheny and Monongahela rivers. At Reading, the Schuylkill reached its highest crest since the Saxby Gale of 1869. Central Park in New York City had 4.19 inches of rain on the 21st, an August daily record to that time.

***

Nearly all hurricane-generated tornadoes develop from "mini-supercell" thunderstorms. The cells top out at 20,000 to 30,000 feet. They produce short-lived tornadoes generally on the low end of the Fujita intensity scale. Rarely, a hurricane develops a full-blown supercell structure, a mesocyclone—as likely happened in 1888. These monsters, normally associated with the Midwest and non-tropical weather systems, soar 50,000 feet and more.

Meteorologist Eugene McCaul has researched hurricane-related twisters. Although not as lofty as full-blown supercells, they display many similar features, according to McCaul, "including wall clouds, gust fronts, tail clouds and strong, adjacent straight-line winds. They differ, however, by their relatively narrow tracks and a lack of heavy rain, hail or lightning activity."

The percentage of tropical cyclones that spin off persistent Midwestern-style supercell storms is unknown and so is the frequency, McCaul cautioned. As for the overall threat from twisters produced by hurricanes, "Additional numerical simulation studies, in conjunction with further observational work, will be needed in order to place hurricane-spawned tornadoes properly in the perspective of tornadoes in general and to improve our capability of predicting such storms."

1888-1889

Hurricanes sometimes visit the Middle Atlantic region within months of destructive nor'easters and vice-versa. Bad weather arrives in bunches.

There wasn't talk of global warming or adverse climate change in the late 1800s, but a series of weather occurrences during 1888-89 inspired profound respect for the atmosphere. Events in addition to the hurricanes of August 1888 and September 1889 included:

March 11-14, 1888: The Blizzard of '88. More than 400 people perished—200 in New York City alone. The New York metropolitan area received 20-30 inches of snow.

A low pressure system stalled south of Long Island, intensified to a fierce nor'easter, then drifted northeast and dissipated. A narrow band of tremendous snow and wind spread from the middle Chesapeake Bay and northern Virginia to central New England. The greatest snowfall, 2-4 feet, fell on central and northern New Jersey, and the Hudson and Connecticut river valleys. Drifts piled higher than 10 feet.

Mariners dubbed it the "Great White Hurricane," endless hours of icy terror. A time of hardship and suffering, numbing cold and blinding snow, howling winds and a mountainous sea. Many ships foundered. More than 100 lives were lost.

One schooner, however, proved too tough to die.

The *W.L. White* was abandoned in Delaware Bay. It blew south-southeast and reached the Gulf Stream. Currents gradually carried the vessel into Canadian waters. For months, the ghostly derelict drifted off Newfoundland. Passing ships noted its presence. The schooner then floated toward Europe. Nearly a year and more than 3,000 nautical miles later, the *W.L. White* went aground in Scotland's Outer Hebrides Islands. It arrived as a blackened hulk carrying a cargo of sea grasses and barnacles.

November 25-27, 1888: A late-season hurricane remained offshore, producing destructive wind and surf. Cape Hatteras clocked a sustained wind of 66 mph. Cape Henry registered 72 mph, and Norfolk 50 mph. A ship reported a barometric pressure of 28.96 inches near the Virginia coast. Another vessel, about 150 miles from the Delmarva Peninsula, logged 28.20 inches.

January 9, 1889: Tornadoes during the winter are extremely rare in the Mid-Atlantic, but on this day deadly winds stalked several cities.

Near Pittsburgh, hurricane-force gusts collapsed a seven-story building that was under construction, killing 15 people and injuring 49.

A tornado visited Pennsylvania's capital, Harrisburg. At 4 p.m., a "funnel-shaped cloud" churned across the Susquehanna River and plowed through the city leaving streets strewn with debris. The weather office's anemometer blew away.

Violent weather continued east. A tornado struck the Reading Silk Mill at 5:40 p.m., while hundreds of employees were at work. Winds demolished the wooden and brick factory, killing 18 workers and injuring about 100. Five employees at a neighboring paint shop died when the walls disintegrated.

Severe windstorms struck Altoona, Carlisle and York, Pa.

A tornado touched down in Camden, N.J., causing $50,000 damage.

Shortly after 7 p.m. a twister tore through Brooklyn, N.Y. It tangled with a gas storage tank causing a tremendous explosion. Moments later, the whirlwind leveled several homes in the neighborhood and unroofed a barracks at the Brooklyn Navy Yard.

April 6-7, 1889: One of the most powerful and destructive nor'easters of the 19th century took aim on the Mid-Atlantic coast. Hurricane-force winds battered Virginia Beach and the Delmarva shore. Gusts reached 75 mph in Norfolk. The *U.S. Monthly Weather Review* noted that, "The storm surpassed in violence any that have occurred in this section within the memory of man. Numerous buildings were unroofed, superstructures torn away, telegraph lines prostrated, etc."

The weather observer at Cape Henry, Va. estimated a peak gust of 120 mph after the anemometer was wrecked. Maximum wind velocities of 80 mph were reported at Cape Hatteras and Kitty Hawk, N.C. More than 40 ships foundered between Hatteras and southeastern Virginia. Gales swept inland to Richmond and Washington.

Snowfall of 6-12 inches coated the Shenandoah Valley, western Maryland and central and western Pennsylvania. "A greater accumulation than any all winter," area newspapers reported.

May 30-June 1, 1889: The Johnstown Flood. The disintegration of the South Fork dam holding Lake Conemaugh sent an immense wall of water into Johnstown, 14 miles downstream, on May 31. It crashed into the city killing 2,200 people, including Mrs. H.M. Ogle, the local Signal Service weather observer.

The Johnstown Flood resulted from persistent, slow-moving thunderstorms that bucketed the Northeast. Historic rises were commonplace along the region's great river basins, from Virginia to New York. Record crests are still the standard in some places.

July 18-19, 1889: Vicious thunderstorms raked southeastern Ohio and northwestern West Virginia. On July 18, Rockport, W.Va., (about 12 miles south of Parkersburg), collected 19 inches of rain in less than three hours to set the state's 24-hour rainfall record. Ruin spread throughout the Little Kanawha Valley. Scattered severe storms moved east to the Atlantic coast.

A tornado demolished a Reading, Pa., silk mill in January 1889. The deadly twister was one of several remarkable weather events to affect the Mid-Atlantic region during 1888-89.

1889

September

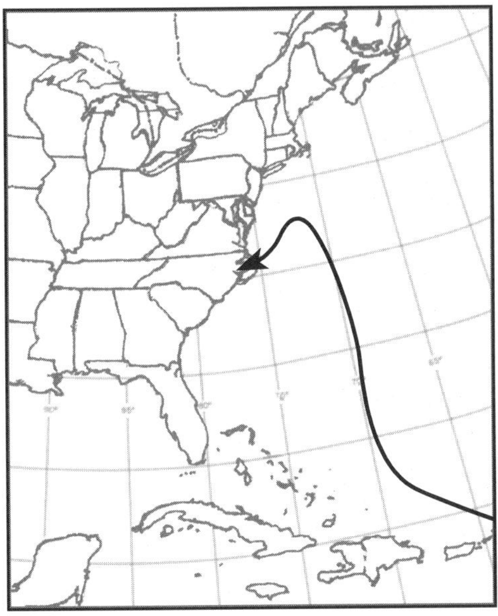

One day a big hurricane will park in the watery emptiness beyond the Mid-Atlantic shore and spin up unforgettable tides. Just like the storm of September 1889.

Priscilla Covington, then a teenager, lived in Ocean City, Md. The resort consisted of several hotels and 25 cottages. A train or ferry offered a link to the mainland.

From September 8-12, a hurricane stalled and dissipated off the Virginia coast. Prolonged easterly gales pushed the sea over barrier islands. During a 1964 interview with the *Baltimore Sun*, Covington described a fearful time for her family and others:

"We were thankful to learn that a train had been sent back to rescue us, then frightened to learn that the train could not cross the shaky trestle because the wind was heavy enough to blow over both train and trestle. Men from Berlin crept across the bridge on foot.

"Everybody evacuated Ocean City then, even the lifesavers. The men had put a handcar into service. We loaded onto it—everyone holding on to each other—and we slowly rode across the railroad trestle, the wind causing the handcar to lurch and sway with every gust. But we made it safely. We waited out the storm on the mainland. Two days later we came back to Ocean City and found sand everywhere. Things at our cottage were as we had left them—even the silver and hastily finished meal and its remains on the table were under great piles of sand, but they were otherwise undisturbed."

A hotel partially washed away. Several homes vanished. The boardwalk became debris.

The hurricane of 1889 is among Ocean City's historic storms. It also looms in the annals of other coastal communities along the Mid-Atlantic. The Jersey shore suffered tremendous damage. "Ruin and Desolation At Nearly All of the Seaside Resorts," declared the *New York Times*.

Great waves attacked coastal villages. Losses included boats, docks, pavilions, promenades and summer cottages.

Meanwhile, mariners fought an unforgiving sea. The *New York Times* described their plight:

"The arrival of every steamer and sailing craft brings fresh details from the scene of the storm's chief battle ground, the Atlantic Ocean itself. These accounts are something more than mere reiterations of the same old story of big waves, resistless winds, and decks swept clean of cargoes and crews. On the contrary, they bear testimony, unanimously, that the gale in its severest moments was something, which has seldom, if ever, been surpassed at this season on the North Atlantic coast. The height of the sea, its treachery and uncertain direction, the force of the wind, and the duration of the storm are all points which are dwelt upon by the officers of vessels in the storm as being in the very first rank and to be respected accordingly."

The *Smryna* (Del.) *Times*:

"The bark *Sorrideren* lost the second mate and steward overboard during the storm. On the 11th it picked up twelve of the crew of the Norwegian bark *Freya,* 250 miles off Cape Henry. They had been twelve hours in an open boat. On the 12th it took five men of the waterlogged schooner *Carrie Hall Lister*, Captain Howland. Monday night, in the same vicinity, the *Sorrideren* passed a vessel bottom up. Those on board the bark were unable to distinguish the name of the wrecked vessel. An abandoned four-masted schooner was also passed."

Perhaps 200 sailors died. The actual number is unknown. The U.S. Life-Saving Service, forerunner

A SCENE OF DESTRUCTION AT LOW MOOR, NEAR LONG BRANCH, DURING THE STORM.—DRAWN BY SCHELL AND HOGAN.—[SEE PAGE 762.]
Harpers Weekly

Along the Mid-Atlantic shore.

of the Coast Guard, provided stellar service. Crews at the Lewes, Henlopen and Rehoboth Beach stations in Delaware assisted 22 vessels, saving all lives.

The famous breakwater at Lewes proved a faulty haven. Capable of sheltering 40 ships, it served 100. The sea overwhelmed bulwarks, making sport of the fleet. Along a mile-long strand, from Lewes pier to Cape Henlopen Light, more than 25 craft foundered. Terrified men spent endless hours clinging to masts and rigging, sodden to the skin, serenaded by maniacal, shrieking winds.

The *U.S. Monthly Weather Review:*

"Lewes, Del.: A most destructive storm raged in this section from the 8th to the 12th. The telegraph station was washed away, the marine hospital dashed from its moorings, and the life-saving station, located forty feet above high water mark, was flooded and the foundation undermined. Humphreyville, a suburb between the town and beach (half-mile distance) was submerged, and its two hundred inhabitants fled for their lives. Thirty-one vessels are known to have been wrecked or washed ashore, and the damage to shipping is estimated at $570,000. The total number of lives lost will probably exceed forty."

Cedar, Slaughter and Bowers beaches, along the western shore of Delaware Bay, were shambles. Breakers ravaged the village of Point Pleasant, at the mouth of the Broadkiln.

Erosion sculpted the landscape. Mammoth sand dunes between Rehoboth Beach and Cape Henlopen, landmarks for as long as anyone could remember, succumbed to hungry surf.

Gales subsided by September 12. The *National Tribune*, Washington, D.C., took an optimistic view of the storm. Coastal resorts had begun to prosper and a hurricane wasn't about to thwart that.

"Millions of dollars worth of property have been destroyed, and towns and villages along the coast will require years to replace the damages, which have been inflicted by the winds and angry waves. The people are very much disheartened, but will, without doubt, with the usual American pluck, rebuild their shattered towns and come up smiling at the commencement of the coming season, and the people of the cities will again flock to the seashore."

***

The Hurricane of '89 left lifelong memories. To Covington, images at 90 were as vivid as those at 15. In 1964, she reminisced:

"I saw the big storm of 1933, and the one in 1962. These later storms caused more property damage, of course, because there were so many more buildings. But for sheer fury of the elements, I have never seen a storm wilder and more terribly beautiful than the one which came in September of 1889."

1891

October

Library of Congress

President Benjamin Harrison

The presidential yacht *Despatch*, reputedly the "largest and handsomest afloat," served chief executives from Rutherford B. Hayes to Benjamin Harrison. Three tropical cyclones combined to sink the vessel off Assateague Island, Va., on October 10.

A day earlier the *Despatch* left New York bound for Washington to take President Harrison on a naval tour. The proximity of two tropical storms and a hurricane created treacherous currents along the East Coast. Shortly after midnight, a navigational error put the *Despatch* in shallow water just south of the Maryland-Virginia border. Before the mistake could be corrected the sea intervened, grounding the yacht 100 yards from shore.

Surfmen from the Assateague Life-Saving Station rescued 79 crewmen, two dogs and a cat. Souvenir hunters gathered. The *Baltimore Sun*:

"It was a remarkable sight to see the ship roll, slow and graceful, so near the shore as she lies, listing toward the sea, apparently endeavoring with each surge to reach the shore, but old Neptune holds her in a tight grasp. Now and then, a crash is heard in the high wind and sea, a davit loosens its hold on shattered planks (and) moldings, chairs, tables, boxes, etc. spread themselves over the watery surface.

"The whole beach for over three miles is strewn with wreckage and it looks as though hundreds of people are along to observe every new object of interest which floats ashore. One man rushes down to clutch a box of cigars, another a box of candles, another a can of ham. Then here dashes a handsome chair. A large refrigerator tosses about and with one surge lands high and dry with the hinges broken."

Who knows what antiques remain buried offshore? Presidential china, silverware, and other artifacts of an elegant, bygone era... And what of items taken from the beach? Valuable heirlooms, relics from the *Despatch,* may reside in Eastern Shore attics—mementos of a trio of long-forgotten storms and a president whose ship failed to come in.

National Archives

The presidential yacht, *Despatch,* sank off Assateague Island, Va.

GUARDIANS OF THE COAST: THE U.S. LIFE-SAVING SERVICE

During the nation's first century, those on a storm-stranded ship often faced a fatal plunge into tumultuous surf. Rescue and survival were a matter of chance and the odds weren't favorable. A single wreck such as that of the *Faithful Steward* in 1785 could result in more than 100 casualties.

U.S. Rep. William Newell of New Jersey, who witnessed a disastrous stranding during 1839, proposed a coastal lifesaving organization. Congress approved an experimental effort. By 1849, eight stations operated along the Jersey shore. But the service, relying heavily on volunteers and limited funding, fell short of expectations. Still, it offered the promise of reducing deaths.

The U.S. Life-Saving Service continued Newell's initiative. Established in 1878, the agency brought organization, innovation and effectiveness to shore rescue. It established a model emulated by other nations.

Sumner Kimball (1834-1923) served as the general superintendent of the Life-Saving Service from its inception until it merged with the Revenue Cutter Service to form the Coast Guard in 1915. Throughout his long tenure, Kimball pushed for expansion. By 1891, the agency had 262 sites, most located on the East Coast. New Jersey alone boasted 42 stations between Cape May and Sandy Hook—an average of one every three miles.

A conspicuous two-story frame building topped by an observation tower and red roof served as station headquarters, boathouse and shelter. A "keeper" led a staff of six to eight members, usually local fishermen. They received meager salaries for tedious hours of watching and waiting, frequent drill and practice, beach patrols and lookouts. All in preparation for the cry, "Ship ashore!"

Crews monitored the shoreline for a stretch of three to six miles. "Surfmen," as they were known, employed a varied arsenal of rescue equipment. Surfboats rowed by a contingent of six were part of each Mid-Atlantic station. A Lyle Gun was used to shoot a line between ship and shore. The breeches buoy, life car and, less frequently, boatswain's chair might carry the imperiled to safety.

Signal flags were hoisted during the day. At night, each man carried a beach lantern and red flares. Upon discovery of a wreck, a vessel in distress, or one dangerously near shore, he ignited a flare. This alerted the lifesaving station and let those onboard know assistance would soon arrive.

Surfmen never retreated from wind and sea when lives were at risk. They went out in nature's worst to rescue strangers.

How effective was the Life-Saving Service?

The organization made shipwreck survival the norm. From 1878 to 1914, for example, surfmen responded to more than 600 incidents off the Virginia coast. Nearly 7,000 lives were endangered but only 102 lost. There'd be no more *Faithful Stewards*.

Not surprisingly, the agency's most ardent supporters were those they rescued. So it was that John Partridge, keeper of the Virginia Beach Life-Saving Station, received an appreciative letter from Peter Lopes, mate on the schooner-barge *Ocean Belle,* which sank during a hurricane in October 1903. Lopes' correspondence said, in part, how happy he was, "to see my friends, whom I never expected to see again, for which all thanks are due to you and your brave crew, who saved us from destruction by the angry seas."

He closed, "Three cheers for Captain Partridge and his crew, from one who will never forget Virginia Beach and the heroes of the Life-Saving Service."

Photograph courtesy of The Old Coast Guard Station, Virginia Beach, Va.

The U.S. Life-Saving Service protected the nation's shores. This crew is from the Dam Neck Mills station near Virginia Beach.

1893

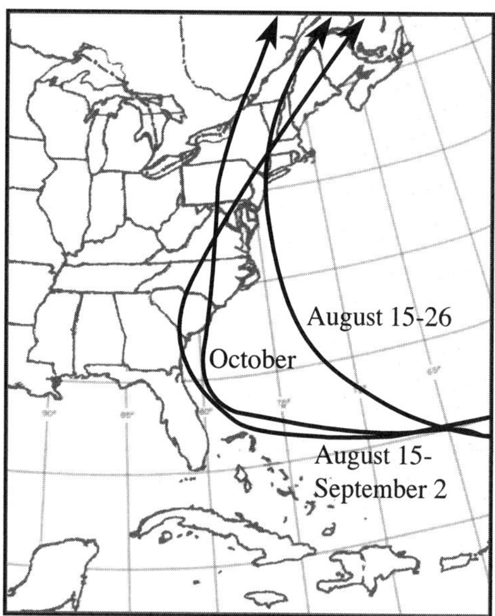

The Middle Atlantic states have rarely had a hurricane season like that of 1893. Out of a dozen North Atlantic tropical cyclones nearly half, including three major hurricanes, targeted the region.

1893 was also unforgettable in other hurricane-prone sections of the United States, particularly South Carolina and Louisiana. About 4,000 people died as a result of devastating storms. Joel Chandler Harris, a noted author of the era, wrote:

"The year of our Lord eighteen hundred and ninety-three will long be remembered as the year of storms. Inland gales rose and blew furiously southward. Cyclones rushed out of the tropics and raged northward. Hurricanes plunged through the Mexican Gulf and shook the southern region. Tornadoes crashed along the Atlantic coast, carrying death and destruction with them. The memory of the oldest inhabitant fails him when he tries to recall such another year of storms. The records show no parallel to it. And the storms themselves have wrought unprecedented destruction to life and property. ..."

August

The hurricane season got off to a late start, but during a seven-week period beginning in late August the United States would experience one of its deadliest series of weather disasters.

The Northeast labored under worsening drought even as several tropical cyclones formed that summer. By August 22, four hurricanes churned at sea, the greatest number existing simultaneously in the North Atlantic basin.

On August 24, one made landfall on Long Island. Its eyewall passed over New York City; its eye tracked slightly to the east. The barometric pressure slumped to 29.11 inches. Not since 1821 had a storm still categorized as a hurricane—albeit minimal—come so close.

Brighton Beach and Coney Island had extensive losses. "For 50 years I have lived at Coney Island and never have I seen a storm like this," said one resident.

A resort on Hog Island, near the Rockaways, was destroyed. The Hoffman House, a small hotel on Rockaway Beach, succumbed to heavy surf.

Trees tumbled throughout New York City, including many in Central Park. New Yorkers strolling through Central Park after the storm found large numbers of sparrows drowned by the rain or bruised to death by the wind. The grass at City Hall Park was also replete with them. In nearby Jersey City, residents filled pails and baskets with deceased birds.

The hurricane routed vacationers as it sideswiped the Jersey shore. In Asbury Park, the *Mary F. Kelly*, a fishing schooner, wrecked on the beach at 7th Avenue, near the boardwalk. Onlookers threw ropes toward the vessel, waded into the water and rescued four fishermen. Three others swam to shore, but four sailors drowned.

Wind claimed the roof of the Columbia Hotel at Belmar. The ocean wrecked the boardwalk. Many houses were damaged, typically a section of roofing, sheared shingles, a blown-out window or toppled chimney.

The Point Pleasant boardwalk was demolished. Denizens described it as the area's worst storm since 1821.

The hurricane stirred maritime mayhem. Storm-tossed surf sunk the tug *Panther* near Long Island, taking the lives of 17 crewmen. And the *Panther* wasn't along. From the *New York Times*:

"Reports of serious disasters at sea from the recent great storm were received today in great number, some telling sad tales of death. Indeed, it was said in maritime circles by those whose memories are long that never within their knowledge did a storm in this neighborhood wreck so many ships, and never were the wrecks more complete and never attended with a greater loss of life. Wherever there is a telegraph wire by the sea it seems there is a wreck to report."

August

SEA ISLANDS HURRICANE

"The tangled thunder of chaos shook the foundation of things. The bellowing waters of the sea leapt up and mingled with the shrieking spirits of the air. Out of the seething depths disaster sprung and out of the roaring heavens calamity fell."

— Joel Chandler Harris

The hurricane that struck eastern Georgia and South Carolina on August 27-28 is one of the deadliest to strike the United States during the 19th century. About 2,000 people died.

Shortly before midnight on August 27, it made landfall between Savannah, Ga., and Charleston, S.C. Savannah and Charleston suffered immense damage. However, few perished as the Weather Bureau had warned of the storm's approach.

Not so, for those who lived on the isolated islands off the lower South Carolina coast. The Sea Islands boasted large estates prior to the Civil War. Owners moved out during the conflict as federal troops moved in. Plantations were sub-divided and former slaves given plots. They eked out a living growing rice, cotton and other crops.

Residents lived astride a time bomb. On occasion, such as in 1893, the ocean swallowed the Sea Islands. The storm surge on the night of August 27-28 may have topped 20 feet, snaring thousands. It decimated the land. Homes washed away with fatal swiftness. Death and destitution became the event's hallmark, desperate days of precarious survival.

Federal response to natural disasters was minimal in the 19th century. South Carolina struggled to provide necessities. State officials turned to Clara Barton and the American Red Cross. The organization, which formed in 1881, mounted its first large-scale hurricane relief operation, easing the plight of Sea Islanders. Nevertheless, disease and starvation claimed additional victims.

***

The nation's worst hurricanes—the remnants of others' sorrows—often find their way to the Mid-Atlantic region. The Sea Islands Hurricane proved no exception. Diminished in strength, it traveled through Virginia, Maryland and Pennsylvania. The center passed over Richmond and Washington. A member of the Quaker community at Sandy Spring, Md., near Washington, observed:

"On the evening of the 28th and through the night, a furious windstorm prevailed, and the long-delayed rain was upon us. The morning light disclosed the havoc the gale had wrought. Noble trees were prone, branches torn and twisted, the ground covered with leaves and debris. Apples and pears lay in heaps, bruised and useless; corn was laid low and greatly damaged. The large and beautiful willow that shaded the southeast end of Norwood house was uprooted and measured its great length on the ground. But it was destined later to a useful end, as the sound logs were purchased by parties from Washington to be made into artificial legs and arms, proving in this unexpected disposal of the fine old tree the truth of the adage that 'It is an ill wind that blows nobody any good."

A tropical cyclone which tracks between the Chesapeake Bay and Blue Ridge and produces prolonged gales generates significant flooding along the bay.

"Kent County has not known a more destructive storm within the past half century," declared

The Transcript, of Chestertown, Md. "Never within the memory of the oldest citizen has the tide in the Chesapeake and the rivers reached such destructive proportions. The wind reached nearly to the velocity of a cyclone about twelve o'clock midnight, and continued very high during all of Tuesday morning."

The Chester River at Chestertown surged nine feet above mean level, six inches higher than during the Centennial Gale of 1876.

Boats navigated streets in low-lying neighborhoods of Annapolis and Baltimore. The tide rose to a level not seen in 25 years (but would be topped a few weeks later!).

The storm blew isolated gusts of hurricane force as far north as Pennsylvania. It was eastern Pennsylvania's worst hurricane since 1878.

The New Jersey coast received its second walloping in less than a week. Inland sections lost thousands of trees. Farmers experienced modest crop damage.

Even as the Middle Atlantic region licked its wounds, the tragedy further south dominated national news. Never before had a hurricane killed so many Americans.[1]

***

The Sea Islands Hurricane and subsequent hurricane disasters raise recurring issues: What are the best methods to broadcast warnings and offer protection as a major storm menaces an isolated, impoverished population? What are the most effective ways to provide relief and promote recovery?

October

American cities in 1893 featured electrical wires strung like so much spaghetti. The public pursued a love affair with the new technologies of the telephone and electric light. But harnessing electricity came with hazards. Communities discovered to their sorrow that wind, wood and wire made a volatile combination.

Howling winds rushed into the Mid-Atlantic region on October 13, as a hurricane plunged through central North Carolina, Virginia and Pennsylvania. The storm ignited scattered fires.

Brush Electrical Works of Baltimore caught fire when a downed wire made contact with wood. The neighboring city jail was made of brick. It shielded the interior from fire but offered no protection from dense, suffocating, smoke. Panic ensued among 500 inmates. They pounded doors and bars with their fists. The facility erupted into a frenzy of despair. Guards opened cell doors to allow exit into the courtyard even as inmates groped and choked in darkness. Three prisoners died and scores were sickened.

The telephone exchange of Wilkes-Barre, Pa., burned to the ground. Allentown, Pa., also wrestled with a wind-related blaze.

Reuben Bower, the lone night operator at the Pennsylvania Telephone office in Allentown, thought his ordeal over as he bested the elements and reported to work. In fact, it had just begun.

Bower had great difficulty handling the switchboard as wind-blown wires emitted sparks. Eventually, he could not extinguish flames that licked at the woodwork. Shortly after 11 p.m. the operator fled the Weightman annex, which attached to the sprawling five-story Breinig and Bachman Building on the southeast corner of 6th and Hamilton streets.

Flames coalesced and spread. They found the outside, taking wings on the gale. Adjacent buildings caught fire. Residents of Bethlehem, about four miles away, could read by the blaze's flickering light.

The Allentown Fire Department fought gallantly but at considerable disadvantage. Their finest engine was undergoing repairs. Another, the rescue hook and ladder, was out of service. After firemen arrived, water pressure failed.

The following day merchants picked through the ruins. Consumed: the telephone exchange and Breinig and Bachman clothiers. Fred Kramer's music store. Columbia Barber Shop. And the Odd Fellows library, one of the most valuable repositories in the region. It was Allentown's most destructive fire in a half century.

The hurricane raced toward Canada, battering the Northeast.

The tide at Wilmington, N.C. was the greatest in memory, making shambles of the waterfront. High

[1] A few weeks later another killer storm struck the United States. On October 1-2, the "Cheniere Caminada Hurricane," slammed coastal Louisiana, pushing a massive wall of water into low-lying bayou country, claiming 2,000 lives. At Cheniere Caminada, a fishing village opposite Grand Isle, about 50 miles south of New Orleans, more than 1,000 people died. Of Cheniere Caminada's 310 houses, only three survived. The settlement was never rebuilt.

winds and tides caused extensive losses in eastern North Carolina.

"Our people have never witnessed a storm more severe and more damaging than the one of Friday," opined the *Northern Neck News* of Warsaw, Va., in the Chesapeake Bay region.

From the *Alexandria Gazette and Virginia Advertiser*:

"The cyclone predicted to visit the southern Atlantic coast struck with all its fury last night, and moving rapidly northward and westward, carried death and destruction in its wake. The prostration of the telegraph wires south and southwest cut off the stricken section from telegraphic communication with the rest of the world. The storm, nearly reaching a hurricane in force and accompanied by a heavy, but intermitting rainfall, swept down upon this city."

Washington plunged into darkness. Poles and wires were flattened. "In this city the damage by the storm was widespread to property, but it is believed that no loss of life resulted," according to the *Washington Star*.

Hagerstown, Md., faced a lengthy cleanup.

"Washington County was visited Friday afternoon by the severest windstorm known for years," the *Herald and Torch Light* reported. "It commenced about noon and continued increasing in force with every hour until seven o'clock in the evening, when it was blowing a furious gale, with the rain pouring in torrents.

"Shade trees in the city suffered irreparable damage, many large trees being blown down, while large branches were broken and scattered about everywhere. While the heavy gale was blowing away trees, window shutters, store signs, telegraph and telephone poles, the downpour of rain was so great that the sewers were filled up and streams overflowed lowlands."

The wind peaked at 56 mph in Pittsburgh, Pa. The barometer fell to 29.17 inches. It dropped to 28.92 inches in Johnstown and 29.05 inches at Erie.

Rapid movement of the hurricane limited rainfall in most areas, but flooding affected scattered localities along the Blue Ridge. The Roanoke River invaded Roanoke, reaching a level not seen since 1858. "At midnight the river no longer looked like a river but was a vast expanse of water three-fourths of a mile in width," observed the *Roanoke Times*.

Heavy rain fell on the Shenandoah Valley. The Hawksbill River swamped Luray, Va., rising higher than the benchmark inundations during 1870 and 1877.

Gales raised a tremendous tide on the Delaware Bay and its tributaries. The Christina River at Wilmington flooded the shipyards, wharves and marshes. Wharves washed away at New Castle.

For the second time in seven weeks, the Chesapeake Bay region endured a historic storm surge. Chestertown, Md., recorded a tide eight inches higher than during August. The resort of Tolchester Beach, about 10 miles away, registered an 18-inch difference. The middle and upper Chesapeake Bay rose to levels topping the earlier event.

The Weather Bureau's forecasts proved accurate and timely. Yet, as in August, those who did not receive or heed warnings paid a terrible price. This time, tragedy centered on the Great Lakes. According to the Weather Bureau's *U.S. Monthly Weather Review,* "The total known loss on the Lakes is 13 vessels, 54 lives, and $676,000; this is the greatest loss ever known in proportion to the number of vessels out."

Buffalo, N.Y., clocked a peak wind of 61 mph. Gusts on adjacent waters reached hurricane force. Veteran mariners shook their head as they tried to recall similar ferocity. While eastern sections of Lake Erie battled flooding, the western shore had water so low that the harbor in Toledo, Ohio, closed when ships couldn't negotiate the shallows.

The Great Lakes were churned into white-streaked seas, realms of freshwater fury. From each lake came accounts of shipwrecks. Decks swept clean. Cabins stove in. Crews lost.

On Lake Erie, near Dunkirk, N.Y., the steamer *Dean Richmond* foundered with the loss of 18 crew members, including its captain, his wife and three children. A disheveled man, dazed and wandering along the shore searching for his dog, told of wild raging seas, a ship at the mercy of wind and waves, and gradual dismantling of the steamer. However, the tale lacked key details and authorities doubted whether anyone survived. They were unable to locate the 'survivor' for subsequent questioning.

There was no mystery about the fate of those onboard the steamship *Wocoken*. All hands, 14 men, died when the coal carrier foundered on Lake Erie.

Lake Superior hosted a tragedy with an odd ending. Five crewmen fled the schooner *Annie Sherwood* during the gale. They were rescued two days later, on October 16, soaked, freezing and exhausted. The schooner's captain and a seaman perished from exposure and injuries.

But the *Annie Sherwood* survived. Days later, another ship discovered the derelict floating off Caribou Island, 70 miles from where it was abandoned.

From Maryland to Maine and throughout the Great Lakes region, the storm—indeed, the 1893 hurricane season—lingered long in tales and memories.

1894

September/October

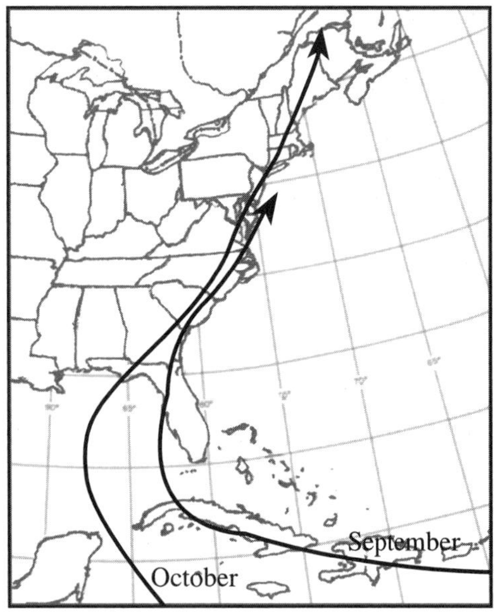

Hurricanes returned to the Mid-Atlantic region in 1894. The first impacted the coast on September 29.

The storm peaked at Cape Henry, Va., with a five-minute wind speed that averaged 80 mph and gusts greater than 90 mph. The Weather Bureau accurately predicted the hurricane, touting its accomplishment in the *U.S. Monthly Weather Review*:

"Norfolk, Va., September 30, 1894.

"Thirteen line steamers, one hundred and forty coasting vessels, and a hundred small craft obeyed warnings. Twenty coasting vessels ready to proceed to sea were held, and estimate that they were saved. ($130,000) worth of property was saved from high tides. Agents of the Old Dominion, Clyde, and Merchants and Miners' lines wish to be quoted: 'Words inadequate to express saving of life and property by your warnings.' "

A second hurricane brushed the Mid-Atlantic shore on October 10, stronger than its predecessor. In *High Winds...High Tides, A Chronicle of Maryland's Coastal Hurricanes*, Reginald Truitt wrote of the impact on the eastern Delmarva Peninsula:

"The October hurricane of 1894 was of such intensity both as to wind and tide that it became legendary in Worcester County (Md.). Oyster houses were washed away, boats were destroyed, island dwellers and beach inhabitants suffered loss of buildings and were forced to higher areas to survive. This storm's wind and rain raked the coast severely from Cape Charles to Cape Henlopen. Inland trees were felled broadly, many outbuildings were smashed and for days roads were closed. ..."

Gusts of hurricane force buffeted the New Jersey coast. They were particularly severe along the Raritan Bay and in New York City. The *New York Daily Tribune*:

"Atlantic Highlands, N.J. Oct. 10 — The storm last night was the most violent that has visited here for many years. Many small craft were destroyed and the roads washed out, trees uprooted and buildings unroofed. At 11 o'clock this morning the wind had died down and people were going along the shores examining the wreckage. So far as is known, from here to Seabright, no lives have been lost. The railroad track southward is washed away or sanded, so that train communication is temporarily stopped."

In New York City, the barometer fell to 29.25 inches and rainfall totaled 1.71 inches. Sustained winds peaked at 60 mph.

Lax building code enforcement and broadsiding gusts caused a tragedy. A factory under construction blew down on Monroe Street. Bricks and timber rained down on families asleep in an adjacent tenement. Nine people were killed and thirteen injured. The incident caused a public outcry. Critics angrily accused the city's inspection office of allowing shoddy workmanship.

The hurricane reached eastern New England and Canada, a disaster for the fishing fleet. At least 50 vessels wrecked on the Newfoundland coast and others foundered off Nova Scotia. One schooner, however, seemed determined to avoid that fate.

The *Lord Eldon*, abandoned by its crew after settling on the rocks near Halifax, Nova Scotia, blew to sea when the wind shifted. Another schooner pursued the derelict. The pair raced until evening. Treacherous conditions precluded boarding. Galloping darkness ended the pursuit. The *Lord Eldon* was last seen at dusk, feisty and independent, piloted by the wind.

1896

September

"When morning came 'the abomination of desolation' was on every side. Every hour brought some fresh revelation of destruction, and the apparent hopelessness of ever setting the face of Nature to rights again was enough to paralyze efforts in that direction."

— Annals of Sandy Spring
Sandy Spring, Md.
September 30, 1896

The summer and early fall of 1896 brought the Middle Atlantic states wild extremes: tornadoes in July, a deadly heat wave in August and a stubborn drought by September. Then came a devastating hurricane.

Farmers took delight in fitful rain and refreshing gusts on the morning of September 29. They had no idea that a menace approached with the speed of an express train.

Even as areas further north savored relief from the drought, Cedar Key, Fla., reeled from an assault by a Category 4 hurricane, complete with a mighty storm surge or "tidal wave," as residents described the onslaught of water. The town was nearly destroyed.

So began a trail of devastation lasting nearly a thousand miles, through interior sections of the East Coast to Canada. The storm retained a 50 to 75-mile-wide band of violent winds, which inflicted extensive Category 2 - Category 3 damage, and a smattering of Category 4-level losses. The whirl raced north, blasting land and buildings increasingly susceptible to windstorm ravages.

The hurricane killed at least 114 people, including 30 in the Middle Atlantic region. An estimated $7 million in property losses made it among the costliest hurricanes in U.S. history to that time.

A bulletin by the Weather Bureau summarized the hurricane's malevolent nature:

"The path of the storm across the Caribbean sea and the Gulf was not near enough to any of our stations to give any information of its violent character, only light to fresh winds being reported from that region during its passage. After it struck inland on the west Florida coast, however, and during its movement northward through the south and Middle Atlantic states it contracted in area and developed almost tornadic force, causing great destruction along its path."

At Gainesville and Jacksonville, Fla., at Brunswick and Savannah, Ga., winds caused enormous destruction. In Beaufort, S.C., the blow equaled the

Sea Islands Hurricane of 1893 but without the deadly storm surge. The Weather Bureau told of its passage through South Carolina:

"On the 29th a severe storm crossed the state from south to north, the path of the storm was from Hampton due north to Lancaster County. The wind reached velocities estimated at 75 to 100 miles per hour. The storm had a rapid progressive movement, traveling across the state in not quite 4 hours, or at the rate of about 53 miles per hour."

The blow struck savagely in the vicinity of Raleigh-Durham, N.C. The wind at Chapel Hill was "the most violent in the memory of the oldest inhabitant of the village," according to the *Raleigh News and Observer*.

A mostly rural track through North Carolina hid the storm's destructive potential, but it couldn't hide in Virginia. Richmond, the state capital, and other towns lay directly in its path.

VIRGINIA

The following headline in the *Richmond Dispatch* was indicative of the hurricane's effects along its route through the Old Dominion:

THE STORM'S DAMAGE

Havoc Wrought by the Cyclone in All Parts of the City

HOUSES UNROOFED AND WRECKED

Hardly a Block on Which There Was Not Property Injured

CUT OFF FROM THE WORLD

Telegraph Wires Nearly All Down and Railroad Trains Delayed

The hurricane is Richmond's worst windstorm. Broken windows, damaged roofs and toppled chimneys were legion. Church steeples crashed into adjacent streets and buildings. The East End suffered greatest harm.

"The East End came in as a whole for a pretty good share of the damage done," reported the *Richmond Dispatch*. "Its exposed position was in part responsible for this, but the wind seemed to play peculiar pranks, toppling over things where least expected and leaving exposed objects unharmed."

Hours of huge winds carved a path about 60 miles wide from the North Carolina border to Maryland. Nearly everywhere, it was "the worst storm in the memory of the oldest inhabitant." The following excerpts from the *Richmond Dispatch* provide a sampling of effects in Southside Virginia:

"Boydton. A tornado struck this town and vicinity with terrific force at an early hour last night, sweeping everything before it. The oldest inhabitants here say they never before experienced such a storm of wind and rain. It raged for two hours as furiously as a western cyclone. Houses were wrecked and blown down, fences were swept away, and trees were uprooted. Stables and barns were demolished, and many horses and cattle were killed or injured."

"Chase City. Last night, about 8:30 o'clock, the most furious and destructive storm ever known in this section passed through this town. The wind was from the south and west, and terrific in force and velocity. It was preceded by a heavy downpour of rain, which diminished as the windstorm increased in severity. Heavy clouds and intense darkness prevailed. There was no lightning or thunder. Around the horizon in the south was seen a long stretch of hazy brightness, which moved in an easterly direction. The appearance was like the reflected brilliancy in the sky of an immense fire. The phenomenon finally disappeared in the north about 10 o'clock."

The Weather Bureau's *Virginia Climate Report* cited the hurricane's work in central and northern sections of the Old Dominion:

BARBOURSVILLE. Terrific windstorm from the southwest, beginning at 9:30 P.M. of the 29th, became a fearful gale at 10 P.M., increasing in severity until 10:25, moderating gradually, and was almost

From the collection of Richard M. Hamrick, Jr.

Water swept through Staunton, Va., after the failure of this dam on the edge of town. The torrent wrecked part of the business district.

calm from 10:45 to 11:15 P.M., when it began again, and blew briskly all night and all day of the 30th. Great destruction was done to timber and houses.

BUCKINGHAM. Terrible windstorm on the night of the 29th. Trees and houses blown away.

GUINEA. Hurricane of 29th lasted 3 hours, and the damage to the forest was very great.

STEPHENS CITY. Storm of the 29th washed away bridges and corn crop. Many birds killed in the trees.

FREDERICKSBURG. Gale of the 29th did much damage, unroofing houses, blowing in brick walls, and destroying about 500 shade trees.

MANASSAS. From 10:45 to 11:30 of the night of the 29th wind from the southeast, thence suddenly from the southwest, played more havoc than any storm that has ever visited this section within the memory of its oldest inhabitants. Much damage to trees and houses.

QUANTICO. Continued high winds 14 hours on the 29th, recording highest about 10:30 P.M. Several houses and trees blown down.

ALEXANDRIA. At 10 P.M. of the 29th, a hurricane struck this city, and blew with increasing velocity for about two hours. Great loss of property and several lives (four wind-related deaths).

The hurricane charged through Northern Virginia. Houses and shops were unroofed at Falls Church. Windmills littered the countryside. Nearly every farm in Fairfax and Arlington counties, just outside Washington, D.C., sustained damage. Fallen trees blocked most roads.

Roofs were easy prey. The *Alexandria Gazette and Virginia Advertiser*:

"The rolling up of tin roofs from buildings alone would furnish food for vivid descriptions. It is said by those who witnessed these scenes that the huge sheets of tin sailed through the air in a manner suggestive of gigantic vampires. They would be apparently about to alight on one side of a street when they would sail upward again and fall in the opposite direction. The clatter of the tin in parting from the roofs and its fall into the streets with the roar of the wind produced a pandemonium long to be remembered. The occasional topple of a chimney and the rolling of thousands of bricks on a roof made an appalling noise."

The western sector of the hurricane had less wind but heavier rain. According to the Weather Bureau, "The rainfall in a strip of country extending from North Carolina to the southern border of Pennsylvania, probably 100 miles wide and about the same distance west of the storm center, was exceedingly heavy, 5 and 6 inches being recorded at some stations, and 3 to 4 at others."

A dam break at Staunton, Va., caused a spectacular tragedy, a calamity that made national news.

Rainfall totaling 6.73 inches fell on the night of September 29. It filled two streams that converged on Staunton's wharf district, a commercial area. Shortly after 9 p.m., men rushed through the neighborhood sounding an alarm. Shortly thereafter, a lake on the edge of town burst through an earthen dam. Within minutes, wreckage carpeted downtown Staunton and beyond. Five people died. *The Annals of Augusta*

County, Virginia, described the catastrophe this way:

"Rain fell at intervals in torrents all day; but late in the afternoon the storm seemed to have ceased. Almost half past 8 o'clock, however, it began again, and for several hours rain came down in almost solid sheets. The lower parts of the town were deluged. On the former occasions the main branch of Lewis Creek contributed little to the overflow, but on this the flood appeared to come chiefly from that quarter. Moreover, the dam at the Fair Ground and an embankment on Brew's farm, Middlebrook road, broke, and the water which had accumulated, being discharged, carried destruction in its course.

"A family of four negroes living near the stone railroad bridge on the Middlebrook road were drowned, their house having been washed away. From that bridge to the depot of the Valley Railroad was, next morning, a scene of desolation. Many buildings fell or were swept off, and from 30 to 40 horses and mules were drowned. In the midst of the storm, the electric and gaslights were extinguished, and the town was left in pitch darkness. The fire bell was rung to call people to the rescue of others who were in peril, but in the darkness and flood little could be done. As never before our people realized the meaning of the words 'the terror by night.' "

Farmers who welcomed the first drops of rain rued the last. The James, Potomac and Shenandoah rivers and many of their tributaries flooded. *The Rockingham Register:*

"The climax of high water records in the Valley of Virginia dates from the famous floods of 1870 and 1877. Strange to say, Tuesday was the 26th anniversary to the day of the flood of '70 and the appalling record of destruction by the high water of 1870 seems at this writing to have been surpassed by that of September 29, 1896.

"At the government weather station at Dale Enterprise the phenomenal fall of 6.30 inches of water in eighteen hours was recorded, and that seems to have been a fair average for this section of the Valley. For two hours Tuesday night, with the wind blowing a howling gale, the rain fell not in drops but in sheets. By midnight the smaller streams were far out of their banks, and by the middle of the day Wednesday they had swollen the rivers traversing the county to proportions hitherto unknown."

WASHINGTON, D.C.

Fury reached Washington about 10 p.m., its approach signaled by brilliant flashes of lightning against a backdrop of Egyptian darkness. The city turned shambles. Streets became a blizzard of shingles, bricks and glass. In the aftermath, newspapers struggled to report the magnitude of the event. The *Evening Star* gave up:

"At about 10 o'clock the clouds seemed to grow more dense, and there was a play of lightning that before had been absent from the disturbance. Then the wind, that had been blowing previously at the comparatively slow pace of about 30 to 35 miles an hour, began to freshen suddenly, and within a few minutes reached hurricane speed and was coming in terrific gusts that lifted tin roofs from their frames, shattered brick work, wrenched signs and awnings from their fastenings, smashed heavy plate glass windows, broke and uprooted trees, and, in short, did damage to almost every object exposed to the fury of the storm.

"Probably no detailed description of the damage done to the city and the surrounding country will ever be told, for the very greatness of it all. Summer storms of enormous violence have visited Washington and have caused great damage, and it has been possible to give in words a nearly complete record of the wreck. But today the city bears the mark of the storm in so many quarters, and the ruins are so numerous, that to enumerate them (would be) an endless task."

The Weather Bureau office recorded a five-minute average wind velocity of 68 mph, and an estimated one-minute reading of 80 mph. Gusts flirted with 100 mph. The anemometer at the Naval Observatory was lost when part of the roof bounded away.

Professor Henry A. Hazen, tasked by the Weather Bureau to investigate hurricane damage, wrote:

"On the night of September 29 there occurred the most destructive storm that ever visited Washington, and it merits special study. The weather map at 8 p.m. shows a general storm with lowest pressure, 29.30 inches, at Lynchburg, Va. The lowest pressure at Washington, 29.14 inches, occurred at 10:50 p.m. The wind velocity continued very high from 10:55 to 11:48, and at times reached 70 miles per hour. The destructive wind had a general southerly direction, but came a little from the east on the east side of the city, and from the west on the west side. In Alexandria the wind was nearly southeast."

And in Washington, "The most remarkable fact noted was that the destruction was in well-marked streaks and not universal. In hundreds of instances a well constructed roof, rafters and all, was blown off, while close by very frail structures at the same height were uninjured."

The wind could be whimsical in its power to destroy. Hazen observed, "The steeple of the New York Avenue Presbyterian Church was blown down and appeared almost as if it had been picked up, turned upside down, and dashed down on its point."

Gusts toppled a five-story brick building under construction on Pennsylvania Avenue. The wind twisted and dropped the massive roof of a streetcar garage. The roofs of the State Department and Pension Office partially peeled away. The Patent Office lost its cover entirely. The roof of President Grover Cleveland's private home in Woodley Park took flight, crashing 500 yards away.

A dormitory building under construction at Catholic University blew down. The Brookland town hall, a short distance away, was partially destroyed.

The White House grounds were defaced, a tangle of uprooted elms, sycamores, walnuts and magnolias. In an era of relaxed security, souvenir hunters chipped away—an elm planted by President Lincoln being a crowd favorite.

MARYLAND

Vicious winds blasted central Maryland. The *Annals of Sandy Spring*, a community journal, recounted hours of horror, a night when the sky screamed:

"The drought, which began in August, continued almost unbroken through September, and when the 29th dawned with a deluge of rain we all felt that we had got what we wanted," wrote a diarist from the Quaker settlement outside Washington. "We rejoiced in the downpour, even when the wind rose to half a gale at noon. At nightfall and through the evening we remarked that it was wild weather and growing worse. By 11 p.m. we had ceased to speak, while we listened to the voice of such a storm as no man now living remembers.

"For an hour and a half the world was full of a mighty, ever-growing roar, in which no separate crash of falling trees or breaking timbers could be distinguished. House shook; the whole earth seemed to tremble before the awful blast.

"From the southeast, over the course swept by the two wind storms of '93, the (hurricane) rushed, leaving ruin behind it. Towards midnight it grew less violent, and by 1:30 there was a dead calm, the sky was clear, the air soft. But for ineffaceable traces on all sides, the unspeakable awfulness of those two hours would have seemed a nightmare.

"When morning came 'the abomination of desolation' was on every side. Every hour brought some fresh revelation of destruction, and the apparent hopelessness of every setting the face of Nature to rights again was enough to paralyze efforts in that direction."

The account continued:

"When all is said and done the trees suffered the saddest and most irreparable injury. Thousands of cords of valuable timber—estimated at twenty percent of the whole amount in the region—were ruined; lawns were shorn of their most valued shade trees, and orchards were decimated, while many a noble oak and pine, cedar and maple that had been a delight to our eyes for generations, was laid low.

"Every tract of woodland illustrated the woeful and yet seemingly fantastic power of the wind—giant trees uprooted, snapped short, or twisted into fine splinters and bent like straws.

"In all directions the roads were blocked, and the telephone system was a 'hideous, tangled wreck.' Every wire was torn from its connection at the Central office by the weight of falling trees, of which there were twenty-three between Sandy Spring and Olney (about five miles)."

Bethesda Park, a popular amusement center outside Washington, D.C., was completely wrecked. It never reopened.

The *Washington Times* detailed effects in Rockville, the Montgomery County seat, about 15 miles northwest of Washington, D.C.:

"This place was nearly demolished last night by an equinoctial storm, which struck here about 10 o'clock and raged until 12:45. Many houses, churches, and magnificent shade trees were torn to pieces.

"The Episcopal Church was nearly blown to the ground. The tower was blown over on the roof of the structure, which gave way, and the large stained glass windows, which beautified the church, were broken into small pieces.

"The colored Methodist Church, a brick building, had its entire front blown off, and the Christian Church was treated in a like manner.

"The beautiful shade trees, for which the town has been famous, were utterly uprooted over the entire place. The street from Joseph Reading's drug store to the dwelling of Mr. William Veirs Bouic, Jr., is one large mass of fallen trees. The courthouse square, which has ever been the pride of this place for the beauty of its trees, was utterly stripped of them, and what remains are a few trunks without a vestige of a limb upon them."

Winds inflicted considerable harm on neighboring Gaithersburg. According to the *Washington Post*, "The severe storm of last night wrought havoc all over the western section of Montgomery County and this town seems, from current reports, to have been the most disastrously wrecked."

Several people died in the county including one man, 54-year-old Henry Sherman, who was said to have been "frightened to death." At the peak of the storm, he left his Olney home to check on the welfare of his horses. The father of three had a fatal heart attack after watching two trees blow down and the roof of his house take flight.

The hurricane showed no respect for the dead. At Ellicott City, near Baltimore, the storm uprooted an ancient cedar in the old burying ground. Cradled among its roots lay the remains of Nathaniel Ellicott, a descendant of the town's namesake.

The roots of the tree held the coffin just like the hand of a skeleton would hold an object, noted the *Baltimore Sun*. "One root, or finger, had wended its way through the coffin lid and the body of the coffin, and made an opening. Another had slipped under the coffin, forming a perfect wreath around it."

Nearly every farm in Howard, Carroll and Frederick counties sustained severe losses. The hurricane caused great fright.

"The storm of Tuesday night left its impress (in Catonsville) and heavy losses are reported in every direction," according to the *Maryland Journal*. "More than a hundred telegraph poles were blown down on the Old Frederick road. Many persons left their house for fear that they would be blown down upon them, and spent the greater part of the night walking the streets. Many sought shelter in their cellars."

The (Frederick) *Citizen* reported that, "A terrific gale swept over our city last night. There was much damage done to houses in various parts of the city. There is not a tree left in the city that has not been more or less damaged."

The *Citizen* was awe-struck by the hurricane's advance through north-central Maryland:

"Frederick County was visited on Tuesday evening last, by one of the most severe cyclonic storms in her history. Never before did such terrible blasts of wind sweep over this fertile section and leave behind a path of wreck and ruin. Several times have the flood-gates of heaven opened and torrents of water devastated the low-lying lands of the Monocacy and Potomac rivers and their branches, but our mountain-walled valley has until now been signally spared the terrors of high winds and hurricanes."

PENNSYLVANIA

The Gettysburg battlefield lost hundreds of trees felled by an enemy attacking eastern Pennsylvania.

York, Lancaster and other towns in southeastern Pennsylvania suffered tremendous property losses. Many houses were damaged—some severely. Barns blew down throughout the countryside.

Harrisburg registered a five-minute wind velocity of 72 mph. During two terrible hours, the air was filled with bricks, slate, timber and roofs. Gigantic trees, which had stood for ages, were ripped up by the roots and tossed asunder.

Four train wrecks occurred between Harrisburg and Columbia, the result of debris blown upon tracks.

In Columbia, about 40 miles southeast of Harrisburg, a railroad bridge spanning the Susquehanna River—more than a mile long and among the longest covered bridges in the United States—succumbed to mighty gusts. Repeated broadsides demolished the housing, crushing timbers and nudging the wreck off its piers.[1]

At Pottsville, according to the *Reading Eagle*, "Never before in the history of Schuylkill County did the winds blow with such great velocity as that

[1] The bridge was the third incarnation at Columbia. The first bridge opened in 1814, operating until an ice jam claimed it during February 1832. Union troops burned the second overpass on the night of June 28, 1863, in a successful attempt to discourage a Confederate drive on Harrisburg. The bridge reopened during 1869 only to be destroyed by the hurricane. A steel replacement served the Pennsylvania Railroad from 1897 to 1958. Only the piers remain.

Gettysburg National Park Commission

Hurricane-force winds toppled hundreds of trees on the Gettysburg Battlefield, including this one on Culp's Hill.

Gettysburg National Park Commission

Cross-ties. Shifting winds felled these trees in Gettysburg.

which arose at about 10 p.m., Tuesday, and continued uninterruptedly for nearly 5 hours. The wind came from the east and was accompanied by rain and in some localities, notably at Ashland, by hail. The wind finally veered, coming from the south."

The newspaper also reported:

"The storm was unusually severe in the vicinity of Lititz (Lancaster County). The Spring grounds were totally wrecked. There is scarcely a tree standing. Practically all the trees in the Moravian cemetery were blown down. A dozen barns were unroofed or demolished, causing a loss of thousands of dollars. Many tobacco farmers lost their entire crops of tobacco, which were housed in sheds that were destroyed.

"Reports from the county show that half a dozen churches and a number of school houses were badly damaged. Farmer Joseph Charles placed his market wagon close to his house last night so he could have it for this morning's market. He heard nothing of the storm, and when he looked for his wagon next morning he found that it had been blown 100 yards by the high wind and was upside down. Loss in the county, nearly $200,000."

Two men died near Reading when the casting house of the Temple Iron Furnace collapsed.

Wind blew down six houses and fire destroyed six other shanties in a miners' village near Shamokin, killing two inhabitants.

The Juniata Valley, west of the hurricane's path, experienced a destructive flood. According to a report in the *Reading Eagle*, "During the past 24 hours the rainfall has been unprecedented and the climax was reached at 2 a.m. by a cloud burst just west of (Huntingdon). This volume of water swept through the western end of town washing out streets, flooding houses, carrying away outbuildings and drowning several head of cattle. Railroads are washed out and telegraph lines crippled."

***

The hurricane brought severe weather to central and western New York. At Syracuse, it was "the severest gale ever known in this city." In Cortland, houses, barns and factories were unroofed, and electric light, telegraph and telephone wires were prostrated.

The *U.S. Weather Review* offered the following state summary:

"Notes of the cyclone of September 29th-30th: Cortland, violent wind storm, 1 to 4 a.m., buildings and trees blown down; Waverly, southeast gale on 30th, 2 a.m., blew down trees, buildings, &c.; Ithaca, large trees uprooted or broken, and buildings unroofed. Many barns demolished in vicinity; Bedford, very heavy rain night of 30th; Watertown, high south wind on the 30th, much minor damage; North Hammond, heavy gale at daylight on the 30th blowing down fences and trees. Nearly all fruit on the ground; Baldwinsville, very high wind, trees blown down, some buildings unroofed."

***

The hurricane's fringe reached Ohio putting a damper on Gov. William McKinley's presidential campaign. That fall he campaigned for the White House from Canton, delivering speeches from his front porch. Representatives from groups throughout the nation trooped to meet him.

On the day of the storm, three delegations from the east postponed their visit. Attendees who braved the elements huddled with the candidate in a meeting hall, sheltered from a pelting rain.

McKinley won the election. The tree-leveling, home-rattling hurricane was still the talk of the town when he arrived in Washington during March 1897. Hurricanes like that happened elsewhere—not in the nation's capital...

When the United States declared war on Spain in 1898, Willis Moore, chief of the Weather Bureau, met with the president. He urged the establishment of a hurricane-warning network in the West Indies. McKinley (and Congress) needed little persuasion.

"I am more afraid of a West Indian hurricane than I am of the entire Spanish navy," he told Moore. The project, forerunner of the National Hurricane Center, was soon in operation.

Hurricane rainfall totals: **Maryland**—Flintstone 4.90", Cumberland 3.91", Baltimore 1.02". **Pennsylvania**—Altoona 3.79", Somerset 3.35", West Chester 1.34", Reading .95", York .90", Harrisburg .46". **Virginia**—Woodstock 6.90", Staunton 6.73", Lynchburg 5.79", Lexington 4.73". **Washington, D.C.** .68".

October

Mid-Atlantic coastal areas received little from the tropical intruder of September, but a storm passing offshore gave shore resorts their turn on October 11-12.

The hurricane claimed the usual waterfront structures—boardwalks, concessions and bungalows. It was in a class with the hurricanes of August 1893 and October 1894, but less than the blow of September 1889.

New Jersey bore Neptune's wrath. Cape May lost a large section of its boardwalk. The Brunswick Hotel at Sea Isle City—the finest lodging in town—was destroyed. At Asbury Park, the ocean tore up a half-mile stretch of boardwalk, crashing into houses and shops.

Angry surf swept into Atlantic City. Two of the resort's three amusement piers were heavily damaged. The Iron Pier off Massachusetts Avenue was nearly destroyed after an errant schooner crashed into its pilings. Waves demolished Wenner's Wonderland, an exhibit and entertainment hall on another pier.

The storm raged along the Delaware coast. The *Luther A. Roby* grounded below Cape Henlopen.

"In the early dawn the schooner was seen driving toward the beach," reported the *New York Tribune.* "The (surfmen of the U.S. Life-Saving Service) hastened toward the spot she was heading for, but she struck before they came opposite her. Before the crew could get their apparatus into working order the vessel pounded to pieces in the heavy surf.

"The men aboard her clung to whatever pieces of wreckage they could grasp, and struggled through the whirling waters toward the beach. Three of them never reached it, but the other five, bruised and battered by the waves, were drawn ashore by the life-savers. The rescued men were taken to the Cape Henlopen Life Saving Station, where they are being cared for."

***

The popularity of seaside vacations soared in the late 1800s as Americans discovered the lure of sun, sand and surf. Railroads gave city dwellers ready access to beaches. Some came to worship their God, attending retreats or camp meetings, staying in communities like Ocean Grove or Ocean City, N.J. Others journeyed to sedate colonies for rest and relaxation. Crowds flocked to Atlantic City for fun, excitement and entertainment.

During August 1896, Atlantic City proclaimed its wooden walkway a street, legitimizing the capital "B" in "Boardwalk." The fifth version of the raised platform (one still used) rose proudly on gleaming steel girders and concrete supports. The promenade seemed to declare, "Come what may, I'm here to stay." It withstood October's gales.

Despite periodic destructive storms the mantra at the seashore remained, "Build and rebuild." To this day: Coastal resorts clean up and repair by the summer following a hurricane. A tide of tourists has always been salve for a storm tide.

A STORM TO REMEMBER...

The Charles Brewer Collection, courtesy of Peerless Rockville

Christ Episcopal Church in Rockville, Md., was nearly destroyed by the hurricane of 1896. Most buildings in Rockville and neighboring towns sustained wind damage.

The Charles Brewer Collection, courtesy of Peerless Rockville

The church, rebuilt to its pre-storm appearance, remains a city landmark.

Columbia Historic Preservation Society

Man-made marvel. The Columbia, Pa., railroad bridge spanning the Susquehanna River ranked among the longest covered bridges in the United States.

Columbia Historic Preservation Society

Natural marvel. Two hours of tremendous winds turned the bridge into a pile of splinters.

From the collection of Richard M. Hamrick, Jr.

Downtown Staunton, Va.

From the collection of Richard M. Hamrick, Jr.

A wall of water left a path of ruin.

1897

October

A tropical storm that lingered off Virginia from October 24-26, 1897, never quite gained hurricane status but still wreaked havoc along the coast. It looped at the North Carolina-Virginia border, providing 60 hours of howling gales and commensurate beach erosion to the Mid-Atlantic.

The *Peninsula Enterprise* detailed conditions at Chincoteague, Va.:

"The storm here for the past few days exceeds any in violence and length of duration in the memory of our oldest inhabitant. The distress it has occasioned and losses in property are hard to estimate. The Island was submerged by the tide in many places and houses were upturned and porches and fences blown down. At least one-third of the dwellings at one time were surrounded by water and persons in the lowlands had to seek safety in the highlands. The tide on one day was from 4 to 6 feet on our Main St., and business of all kinds was suspended."

Nobody drowned but rescues abounded. A widow and her five young children were plucked from their house after being stranded for two days. Charles Bunting, his wife and child, fled their home after it floated off its foundation. Two men adrift in a boat snared the family from rising water. The beleaguered group used a bed quilt for a sail, riding easterly winds to the mainland.

The ocean covered Cobb Island, Cedar Island and other barrier strands of the lower Delmarva Peninsula. At Wisharts Point, Wachapreague, and Metompkin Island, tides equaled those churned up by the hurricane of October 1878.

Moderate flooding surged through the Chesapeake Bay. Tides near the mouth of the James River rose five feet above normal. Solomons, Md., on the Patuxent River (about 100 miles from the ocean), was partially inundated.

***

Only a few thousand people lived along the Virginia coast in 1897, thus limiting property damage. Two decades of destructive hurricanes and nor'easters encouraged a healthy respect for the sea. A pricey lesson about the consequences of building within reach of the waves.

1899

August

SAN CIRIACO HURRICANE

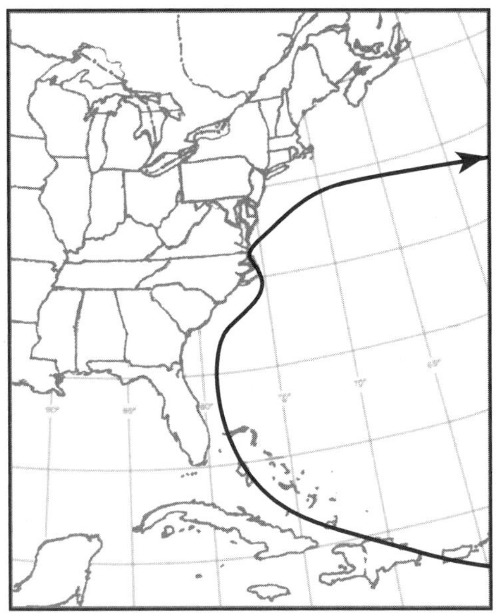

San Ciriaco. A demon with a saint's name.

Miles of beach houses cluster along the North Carolina Outer Banks. Summer crowds make the islands seem like a metropolis. Few newcomers realize that until a half-century ago the area was sparsely populated. Limited economic opportunity discouraged settlement. So did respect for hurricanes, storms like that of August 1899 — "San Ciriaco."

San Ciriaco came with an ugly history. It struck Puerto Rico on August 8, killing 3,000 people, one of the island's deadliest disasters. From August 12-16, the Category 3 hurricane crawled along the southeastern coast of the United States, about 100 miles offshore. Then it loitered over coastal North Carolina for two days.

The worst hammered beaches from Cape Lookout to Cape Hatteras and lower sections of the Outer Banks. The ocean spilled over barrier islands. More than 8 inches of rain fell in 48 hours, delivered by relentless hurricane-force gusts. S.L. Dosher, the Weather Bureau observer on Hatteras Island, detailed the storm's violent, leisurely passage:

"The wind began blowing a gale from the east the morning of the 16th, varying in velocity from 36 to 50 miles an hour, and gradually shifting to northeast by 6 p.m., with nearly stationary pressure. During the early morning of the 17th the wind increased to a hurricane and at 4 a.m. was blowing at the rate of 70 miles an hour; 10 a.m. it had increased to 84 miles; and at 1 p.m. it was blowing 93 miles an hour, with extreme velocity (gusts) of 120 to 140 miles an hour. The record of wind after about 1 p.m. was lost, but it is estimated that it blew with even greater force from about 3 p.m. to 7 p.m., and it is believed that between these hours the wind reached a regular velocity of at least 100 miles an hour.

"The barometer began to fall rapidly about 8 a.m. of the 17th, and by 8 p.m. of that date it had reached the unprecedented low reading of 28.62 inches, where it remained about an hour, when it began to rise rapidly, and by midnight it had risen nearly one-half inch. From 7:30 to 8 p.m. of the 17th there was a lull in the gale when it veered to southeast and began to blow at an estimated velocity of 60 to 70 miles, which continued until well into the morning of the 18th."

By custom, some inhabitants of the Carolina and Virginia coasts attempted to hurricane-proof their homes by accommodating the ocean. They'd include a trap door or install east and west parallel doors. Homeowners hoped that the sea would anchor their dwellings. But during San Ciriaco such tactics made little difference, particularly in southern sections of the Outer Banks. As Dosher explained:

"This hurricane was the most severe in the history of Hatteras. The scene on the 17th was wild and terrific. By 8 a.m. the entire island was covered by water from the Sound, and by 11 a.m. all the land was covered to a depth of from 4 to 10 feet. This tide swept over the island at a fearful rate carrying everything movable before it. There were not more than four houses on the island in which the tide did not rise to a depth of 1 to 4 feet, at least half the people had to abandon their homes and seek safety with those who were fortunate enough to live on the higher grounds.

"The frightened people were crowded 40 or 50 in a house. All this day the gale, the tide, and the sea continued with unabated fury. During the lull in the evening the tide ran off with great swiftness, causing a fall in the water of several feet in less than half an hour.

"Domestic stock was drowned, and it is believed that the property loss to Hatteras alone will amount to $15,000 or $20,000. The fishing industry has, for a time, been swept out of existence, and of the 13 fish-packing houses, which were situated on the water-front, 10 with all their equipment and contents were lost. A great proportion of the houses on the island were badly damaged and many families are without homes. All bridges are swept away and roadways are piled high with wreckage. All telegraph and telephone lines are down."

Dosher continued, "The damage to the instruments and property of the Weather Bureau office was considerable, the anemometer being carried away before the storm attained its maximum strength, and the rain gage was swept away the morning of the 17th."

His conclusion: "The people of this locality had ample warning of this storm, yet such preparations as could be made were of little avail in a storm of this character."

The Weather Bureau opined: "Only the fact that the coast is sparsely settled prevented an enormous loss of life. Some lives were lost, as far as known, however, probably less than 25."

More people would have perished had it not been for Rasmus Midgett of the U.S. Life-Saving Service. Early on August 18, the surfman came upon the wrecked barkentine *Priscilla*. Midgett waded into the ocean and individually assisted seven men to shore. He climbed onboard the vessel and carried three others to safety, negotiating massive breakers. His heroics earned the organization's paramount honor, the Gold Life-Saving Medal.

***

The hurricane reached the Atlantic near the North Carolina-Virginia border and churned out to sea. Upper sections of the Outer Banks fared better than further south. Along the Delmarva Peninsula and Jersey shore, the storm amounted to little more than a respectable nor'easter. So close, yet, so far.

***

San Ciriaco was a calamity for southern sections of the Outer Banks. Diamond City, a village of 500 and North Carolina's only whaling community, became a ghost town. The nearly destitute inhabitants moved to the mainland, beaten by repeated hurricanes.

HURRICANES
1900s

1903

September

*reakish Vagabond Hurricane*. That's what the *Atlantic City Daily Press* dubbed the storm of September 16-17. It struck the southeastern coast of New Jersey, becoming the only tropical cyclone of the 20th century to make initial landfall in the Garden State.

The lack of wholesale devastation dismayed some reporters who flocked to ground zero, Atlantic City, bent on covering a disaster. The *Atlantic City Daily Press*:

"Mayor (Franklin) Stoy made a tour of the Boardwalk yesterday to note the damage done by the storm and when he reached City Hall later, he was in a humor to speak rather brusquely about those reporters who had sent wild stories to the metropolitan papers about the damage that had been done by the vagabond hurricane. His Honor remarked that it was really a miracle how this resort escaped so easily with such a big blow. That not a life was lost could hardly be imagined. He smiled when told of how a Philadelphia newspaperman had come in the city on the afternoon train, all excited, wanting to get a list of the killed and wounded, and then blurted out, 'What's Mayor Stoy going to do, send a public appeal all over the country for assistance?' The mayor thought this was a good joke, for when the first train arrived in the afternoon Atlantic City people were calmly lining up along Atlantic Avenue to see the Sons of Veterans parade.

"Another newspaperman from New York came down in a flurry and said, 'Well, our paper will guarantee to raise a fund of $200,000 to help out the sufferers. Let's get photographs of the hotels and piers that have been blown down or washed away.'

"When they investigated and found that the only damage done was the blowing down of a number of pavilions on the Boardwalk, many of which should have been torn down some years ago, and that a few roofs were off, the special correspondents quietly kicked themselves, as the saying goes, and took the first train home there to give a less lurid report of what they found 'in the devastated district.' "

Gusts of near-hurricane force swept the shore from Virginia to western Long Island. The highest winds weren't clustered around the storm's center. Rather, they were localized. Rainfall totaled about 4 inches along the south Jersey shore. Less than 2 inches fell elsewhere.

Frequent gusts of 50-60 mph overturned wagons on the Brooklyn Bridge and sent workmen scampering from New York's new Williamsburg Bridge. President Theodore Roosevelt witnessed the sinking of the harbor tug *James Kay* as he sailed down the East River on his executive yacht, which sought shelter at the Brooklyn Navy Yard. Class adjourned early for 900 students at the West Brighton School on Staten Island when the building's roof took flight.

Further south, the *Democratic Messenger* (Snow Hill) reported that winds rather than waves caused trouble in Ocean City, Md.:

"At Ocean City, almost every building was damaged. The roof was blown from the big bathing pavilions of Gilbert B. Cropper and also from the pavilions of J.D. Rayne. The Rayne Hotel suffered considerably. The Atlantic Casino's upper porch was torn away, as was also a part of the roof of the new casino building. The Mount Pleasant sun parlor was demolished. The Colonial Hotel was partly unroofed, and a part of the upper porch railing was blown into the house, frightening the inmates."

On the eve of flight and radio, technologies that would save countless lives at sea, mariners coped with storms as they always had. They could discern when one was brewing, but size, duration and intensity were unknown. Surprise, too often, meant disaster. The hurricane of September 1903, with its singular track, proved no exception.

The yacht *Red Dragon* foundered near Atlantic City and five people drowned. Several sailors died when the schooner *Hattie A. Marsh* wrecked on the Delaware coast near Lewes. Gusts at Lewes peaked at 80 mph.

Freakish Vagabond Hurricane. It may have been a vagabond to Atlantic City, but freakish behavior occurred at Fort Monroe, Va. The *Washington Star* included the following peculiarity:

"The rain storm that broke with great fury over Old Point Comfort last night was accompanied by a downpour of small birds such as have never been seen in this section before.

"The wind blew furiously as the tail end of the southern storm broke over the reservation, and from its encircling grasp as its strength departed fell this flock of half-feathered birds that had evidently been caught up in the tropics and borne on the stronger winds of the pitiless gale.

"As the late dancers left the Chamberlain Hotel they slipped and slided over the battered birds that burst with the force of (impact) on the pavement.

"At the residences in the fort, occupants were startled by the striking of the birds against the windows and thought the English sparrows that abound were drawn by the lights from the violence of the storm and inky blackness of the night. These birds, however, are about the size of a wren and are not fully feathered."

October

"Toms River (N.J.) – A most remarkable storm began last Thursday, the 8th, and lasted till Tuesday morning, the 13th. It was remarkable for its duration, for its almost unheard of rainfall, for the damage from freshets and floods, and also from winds, tides and high seas on the coast."

— Fred G. Bunnell
U.S. Cooperative Weather Observer

Residents of New Jersey who witnessed the hurricane-related flood of 1882 thought they'd never see the like again. They were wrong. On October 10-11, 1903, a hurricane stalled and dissipated south of New England, pumping tropical moisture toward a waiting cold front. Then a rainstorm from the Great Lakes fused with the dissipating tropical system, resulting in catastrophic flooding.

A wet summer put the region at risk. The hurricane in September and frequent showers during early October ensured saturated ground.

Downpours fell periodically from October 8-11, peaking on the 9th. Storm totals included: Paterson, N.J. 15.10", Newark, N.J. 11.58" and New York City (Central Park) 11.17". (New York City measured its greatest daily rainfall, 8.01", on October 9.)

The Passaic River crested at a record level in northern New Jersey, leaving a swath of unbroken destruction. The U.S. Geological Survey reported:

"The Passaic River overflowed its banks on October 8, 1903, and remained in flood until October 19. Between these dates there occurred the greatest and most destructive flood ever known along this stream. Ordinarily the channel of the lower Passaic at full bank carries about 2,000 cubic feet of water per second, but at the height of this flood it carried about 35,700 cubic feet per second."

The report also included, "The destruction along several stretches of the valley was almost complete. Nearly all the dams failed, and every bridge across the river, with one exception, was carried away. Some small villages were swept bare, and the damages to realty value and personal property were excessive.

"It was only by strenuous measures that the dam impounding the waters of Tuxedo Lake was saved. If this had failed the destruction along the entire course of the river, even to the cities in the lower valley, would have been enormously increased."

Rainfall in the Passaic River basin averaged 12 inches, with isolated totals exceeding 15 inches. Rivers feeding the Passaic—the Ramapo, Pompton, Wanaque, Pequannock, Rockaway and Saddle—had a "100-year flood." Many dam failures added to the devastation.

Floodwaters overwhelmed Ramapo, N.J., (locally the event is known as "The Great Ramapo Valley Flood"). Sloatsburg, N.Y., was nearly washed away. A dam at Cranberry Pond in Arden, N.Y., burst, destroying several villages. Another dam, at the Ludlum Steel and Iron Company, failed at Pompton Lakes, N.J. The 200-acre reservoir engulfed Pompton Plains.

Flooding in Paterson, N.J., encompassed more than 10 miles of city streets. Most bridges spanning the Passaic River in Passaic, Essex and Bergen counties were destroyed.

Newspapers cited woes throughout the area: lives lost; railroad tracks and bridges gone; telegraph, telephone and power lines crippled; thousands of people made homeless.

The event left an indelible impression on residents of the Delaware River Valley. Few floods have wrought greater property damage. Folks in the vicinity of Manunkachunk and Belvidere, N.J., would remember it as "The Pumpkin Flood." The Delaware carried away the ripened crop, blanketing the river.

The Weather Bureau's *Monthly Weather Review* detailed conditions along the Delaware River and its tributaries:

"Reports from Scranton stated that as a result of the heavy rainfall the Lackawanna Valley has one of the worst floods in its history, the waters of the Lackawanna River rising six to seven feet higher than they had ever before.

"At Easton, the Delaware was higher then ever before, and a 600-foot railway bridge was washed away.

"Along the upper Delaware scarcely a whole bridge remained standing. At least six of the nine between Trenton and Phillipsburg were entirely swept away, and the others badly damaged.

"At Trenton the Pennsylvania Railroad was blocked for twelve hours on account of the water covering the tracks at a low point. The damage by the flood in that city amounted to $150,000. Fortunately no lives were lost, but 100 families along the riverfront were driven from their homes, and so rapidly did the water invade the houses of the occupants that they narrowly escaped drowning, saving none of their effects.

"At Burlington, N.J., never since its settlement had that vicinity been swept by such a flood as submerged four-fifths of the city and surrounding country for miles. The tide in the Delaware, rushing along like a millrace, was constantly carrying down houses, barns, chicken coops and small craft of all descriptions, and bodies of drowned animals. The southern section of the city was covered with from two to six feet of water, and rowboats landed passengers at the railroad station in the very center of the town."

Philadelphia had flooding from rainfall and tide. The Delaware River surged five feet above mean high water, impeding drainage.

Courtesy of the Trenton Public Library

Trenton, N.J.

Tragedy followed in the wake of the flood. Days later, 17 men died and 33 were injured when their fog enshrouded train collided with another while en route to Washington Crossing on the Delaware River. The laborers had been sent to repair a flood-damaged bridge.

Rainfall in southeastern Virginia and on the Delmarva Peninsula caused few problems. Seaside flooding was the story here and to a lesser extent along the Jersey shore.

The hurricane of October 1903 ranks among the worst for Ocean City, Md. Most residents left prior to the storm, fleeing across a tenuous rail link to the mainland.

"It was a wonderful sight Saturday to see people fleeing from the island," said Charles Sees, a visitor from Baltimore. "A load of women and children would be placed on a flat car or hand car and the men would push them across the long trestle, waves tossing the spray over them at times so as to hide them from sight."

From the *Baltimore Sun*:

"Wreckage is strewn from one end of the beach to the other. Bureaus, bedsteads, tables, chairs and every kind of furniture could be seen floating around in the water. Near Congress Hall (hotel) a handsome piano was standing on end almost half buried in the sand, and the other half reared in the air, the surf breaking against it at every wave."

The Windsor Hotel collapsed. Neighboring Congress Hall was severely damaged. Summer cottages on the northern end of Ocean City suffered modest losses, but the south side was devastated.

"The saddest feature of the storm is the fact that so many of the persons who lost their all are the poorest of the town and will feel the blow most keenly," noted the *Democratic Messenger* of Snow Hill, Md. "The lower portion of the place is inhabited principally by fishermen, and in most cases they had nothing but their boats and household goods, and these, of course, are destroyed."

Chincoteague, Va., and neighboring Assateague Island were battered. The *Democratic Messenger*:

"The storm that broke upon this island Thursday at 4 p.m., and which raged without intermission and with unexampled fury ceased Sunday night.

"Chincoteague has been wrecked fore and aft. All the houses, or nearly all those built on the bay side of the street, extending for five miles, have been submerged or swept by wind and wave. Singular to relate, no loss of life had been reported, but what is the fate of the unfortunate cabin dwellers in the wake of the torrent that broke in from the sea over Assateague Island and of the life-saving station on Assateague beach, no one knows at this writing.

The article went on, "The present storm recalls the tidal wave, which well-nigh destroyed the island on September 3, 1821. Chincoteague was then swept by a wave, which rolled over from the sea to the bay."

The average five-minute wind speed at Cape Henry, Va., peaked at 74 mph on October 10. The tide in Norfolk rose 9 feet above mean low tide, among the higher levels of the 20th century.

Wrecks littered the Mid-Atlantic coast. For example, from Kill Devil Hills, N.C., to Virginia Beach, a distance of 50 miles, five vessels went ashore.

Treacherous conditions kept the U.S. Life-Saving Service busy.

Surfmen at Assateague Beach saved eight fishermen after the group's shelter was swept away by high water.

The Life-Saving staff at Wachapreague, Va., abandoned their flooded station. While rowing to the mainland, they assisted several fishermen marooned in a disintegrating oyster shanty.

At False Cape, near Virginia Beach, surfmen carried nine women and seven children to safety. Members of the Dam Neck Mills station evacuated eight members of the stricken *Nellie W. Howlett.*

The coal barge *Ocean Belle* grounded off Virginia Beach. Walter Capps won the service's highest honor, the Gold Lifesaving Medal, after he rescued two members of the vessel. The citation read, in part:

"Capps had been sent out from the station on patrol and had proceeded only about a half-mile when he discovered the wreckage of the barge. Shortly thereafter, he saw a man struggling in the surf. He immediately rushed in, dragged him ashore, placed him in the lee of a sand hill, and started to the station for aid.

"He had gone about a mile when he discovered another man, apparently dead, 100 yards out in the surf. Although the undertaking involved extreme peril, Capps immediately divested himself of his outer clothing and unhesitatingly plunged into the rescue. Just as the man passed into the 'inner break,' he seized him and turned for the beach. The heavy sea, however, knocked him down. With the man unable to help himself, it was with great difficulty that Capps was able to raise and haul him ashore to a safe place on the beach. He then applied the Service method of resuscitation and in twenty minutes the man (was) sufficiently revived to sit up."

The storm's breath was felt south to the North Carolina Outer Banks. At Kitty Hawk, two young men, Wilbur and Orville Wright, fought cabin fever as the inclement weather delayed their air current experiments. Soon, they'd attempt to defy gravity in their newfangled flying machine. Wilbur wrote to aviation pioneer Octave Chanute:

"The upper surface of the new machine is completed. It is far ahead of anything we have built before. The lower surface is about half done. It will probably be nearly Nov. 1st before we are ready for trial, especially if we have some nice soaring weather. On Saturday, Oct. 3rd, we had some nice gliding, the wind being a little too light for soaring, only 6 to 7 meters; however, we increased our record to 43 seconds and made quite a large number about 30 seconds. We have had no suitable winds since, as the last round of north winds ranged from 30 to 75 miles and was accompanied by four days of constant rain. A cyclone is supposed to have gotten becalmed off the coast near here and could not get away sooner. The natives report it the worst storm within many years. We had no trouble except the annoyance and a little delay."

On December 17, the Wright brothers made the first successful airplane flight.

Hurricane rainfall totals (Oct. 8-9): **Delaware**—Seaford 3.73", Newark 3.55", Milford 3.45". **Maryland**—Princess Anne 4.00", Cambridge 3.11", Chestertown 3.07". **New Jersey**—Paterson 15.00", Newark 11.58", South Orange 10.10", Perth Amboy 10.00", Atlantic City 9.75", Newton 8.30", Asbury Park 6.82", Trenton 6.09". **New York**—New York City 10.04", Port Jervis 9.41". **Pennsylvania**—Milford 9.78", Lansdale 6.68", Doylestown 6.50", Philadelphia 6.17", Scranton 4.72", Reading 3.50".

B. UNDAMAGED BRIDGE ACROSS PASSAIC RIVER AFTER PARTIAL SUBSIDENCE OF FLOOD.

B. THE WRECK OF A HOTEL IN PATERSON, N. J.

NORTHERN NEW JERSEY MAY SEE ANOTHER *FLOOD OF 1903*

After the disaster of 1903, the U.S. Geological Survey concluded, "In view of actual events, the fact must be emphasized that in adopting measures to prevent floods the margin of safety must be extremely wide. The extraordinary rainfall of those three October days cannot with assurance be accepted as the maximum."

What would a similar (or greater) rainstorm mean today for the populous Passaic River basin?

Expect major damage and disruption, says Clark Gilman, a floodplain management engineer for New Jersey. He cautions, however, that any dollar estimate would be a guess. Changes since 1903 have had mixed impacts.

Several reservoirs supply the region's water. Late summer or early fall, the most likely time for a tropical cyclone, coincides with the lowest annual water levels. The reservoirs could effectively retain some excess. Although not specifically aimed at flood control, Gilman estimates such containment would reduce flooding by at least 10 percent. And if reservoirs were significantly drawn down prior to a storm, reduction would be greater.

Development has increased runoff—a definite negative for flood control. Studies suggest that if ground water and rainfall were similar, the flood of 1903 would be one-third greater today.

"The damage centers would change," Gilman commented, "There would be more destruction along upper tributary streams and less in the central and lower Passaic basin."

Population growth and related development continue in northern New Jersey. The areas at greatest risk, according to Gilman: the upper Rockaway River ("Our biggest problem right now."), the Saddle River and its tributaries, particularly in Bergen County, and the Ramapo near the New Jersey and New York border.

Efforts to stave off disaster include the enactment of developmental regulations, conservation easements and buy-outs of property owners. Some Corps of Engineers and local containment projects are in place. There have been discussions, proposals and studies concerning a regional flood control strategy but, as of 2006, no comprehensive plan exists.

U.S. Geological Survey

Dam break at Pompton Lakes, N.J.

1904

September

Delaware usually escapes the brunt of hurricanes but not during 1904. Winds gusted to 100 mph at Lewes on September 14, the highest in the Middle Atlantic region during passage of a coast-hugging storm. The town's Harbor of Refuge turned anything but for the many ships anchored there. The sea left a tumbled mass of splintered timber, broken spars and twisted rigging.

Squalls blasted interior sections of the Delmarva Peninsula. Weather observer T.E. Keenan of Cambridge, Md., reported:

"A severe wind and rain struck here at 1 a.m. (on the 15th), doing much damage, uprooting many large trees, by which many chimneys, dormer windows, and parts of shingle roofs were torn off, some metal roofs blown off; but the most damage was to boat property, no person hurt. The rainfall during the night was 1.57 inches; during the previous day 3.45 inches fell, making the total 5.03 inches."

Southeastern Pennsylvania and sections of New Jersey received more than 5 inches of rain on September 14-15. Friesburg, N.J., tallied 10 inches. The weather office in Philadelphia recorded 2.05 inches in 40 minutes on the 14th.

The *U.S. Monthly Climate Review* noted that in Baltimore, "street cars, vehicles, and other varnished surfaces such as doors, which were exposed to the rain, were observed subsequent to the storm to be thickly covered with spots, or patches, of a white deposit or encrustation. This phenomena was reported to be most marked on cars that were out during the early morning hours of the 15th."

***

Decades of frequent, destructive Mid-Atlantic hurricanes ended in 1904. Activity remained sporadic until 1933, the start of a period that again made the region, "Hurricane Alley."

1915

August

August 3 began as another in a spate of rainy days for Erie, Pa. A vigorous tropical storm moving up the East Coast interacted with low pressure over the Great Lakes. The combination resulted in tragedy.

Rain fell on Erie throughout the afternoon, filling streams and reservoirs. That evening, thunderstorms dumped several inches within hours. Placid Millcreek turned raging river.

Millcreek Valley offered many obstructions that were ideal for the creation of artificial dams. Blockages formed at culverts and bridges before giving way like dominoes. A ribbon of ruin coursed through Erie. Residential and industrial sections along Millcreek were devastated. Despite warning and evacuations, 29 people died.

Looters swarmed in. A carnival-like atmosphere prevailed at the Quinn and Neumer warehouse as barrels of whiskey washed free and were hurriedly hauled away. "Not even the most watchful guard set by the officers of Company G, nor the naval militia could prevent it," said the *Erie Dispatch*.

Close behind the plunderers came hordes of sightseers, invading victims' homes and mingling with overwhelmed emergency workers. They came by the thousands to gawk and snap photographs.

"Between 30,000 and 40,000 people yesterday traversed the stricken district and about every fifth one carried a camera," the *Dispatch* reported. "At those spots where particular property damage was done, or where those actuated by more humane motives were burrowing in the heaps of twisted timbers for the dead, scores of cameras clicked and snapped continually. When one photographer gave up a place of vantage to seek another, someone else assumed the vacated station."

They had plenty to record. Mountains of debris. Cars nesting in treetops. The remains of 400 wrecked buildings.

Debris dams are a danger in any flood, especially in urban areas. They form and disintegrate without warning. In Erie, burst accumulations carried downstream sweeping away or crushing those in their path. A sudden surge took the lives of a fireman and the city's fire chief.

The fire department, led by Chief John McMahon, quickly responded when the flood began. They performed numerous rescues. McMahon, washed away twice, emerged from the froth and resumed work. He and four comrades had just finished evacuating a residence when a rush of water destroyed the dwelling.

"Save yourselves!" the chief shouted as the group fought to stay afloat. They flailed for several blocks. Three men survived, but John Donovan drowned after saving McMahon. He became the first Erie fireman to die on duty. McMahon developed complications from his injuries and succumbed 17 days later.

(After the disaster of 1915, the city resolved that Millcreek would never take another life. Visitors unfamiliar with Erie would be hard-pressed to find the stream today even if they were standing over it. Most of Millcreek is piped underground.)

Erie captured national headlines, but the twin storms thrashed the entire Northeast.

Runoff inundated low-lying sections of Richmond, Va. The state capital suffered its second flash flood in two days. Water from hillsides funneled into Shockoe Bottom, a district of shops and warehouses along the James River. The flow caused devastation (a calamity repeated during Hurricane Gaston in 2004).

A tornado descended on Petersburg, Va., before traveling northwest for five miles. It demolished hundreds of trees at Poplar Grove National Cemetery.

Another twister struck Milford, Va., overturning a

Erie County Historical Society and Museums, Erie, Pa.

After the flood of Aug. 3rd, 1915, between 12th and 13th on French St., Erie, Pa.

Dozens died when floodwaters created and burst through debris dams.

Erie County Historical Society and Museums, Erie, Pa.

"No Man's Trolley"

Cleaning the Streets after the Flood of Aug. 3rd, 1915, Erie, Pa.

railroad station and wrecking several buildings.

The *Alexandria* (Va.) *Gazette* reported the loss of countless birds:

"The storm of last Tuesday night, which extended over a large area, drowned many thousands of English sparrows. A resident of our suburbs gathered a bushel basket of the dead birds yesterday morning. Thousands were killed in Baltimore, Washington, Pennsylvania, New York, Delaware and other places. They were washed from nests and drowned by the heavy rains and cloudbursts."

In Annapolis, Md., winds peaked near midnight on August 3 and continued unabated for several hours. The blow, said to be the worst in years, damaged or destroyed chimneys, roofs and trees. One family had to chop a way out their front door.

Storm surge washed into the city. Enough fish were found on streets and lawns near Spa Creek to supply breakfast for the entire neighborhood.

A tornado roared through Easton, Md. It left a calling card of toppled tombstones after plowing through a cemetery.

A cloudburst swamped city streets and flooded hundreds of basements in Cumberland, Md.

Streams in southeastern Pennsylvania rose to levels not attained since the Johnstown Flood of 1889. A correspondent for the West Chester *Daily Local News* wrote:

"At Lenape yesterday all sorts of things were noticed afloat. There were a couple of good-sized cabins, several outhouses, one baby coach, tubs, a washboard, wood horse and many other articles which had been loose about yards affected by the rising water. On pieces of timber were perched muskrats, rats, mice, snakes and many other living things. Several ducks also went down the stream."

The storm blew through New Jersey early on August 4. Long Branch clocked a gust of 78 mph and Sandy Hook had 54 mph. More than 5 inches of rain fell on some locations. Flash flooding submerged sections of Metuchen, New Brunswick and Elizabeth. A dam at Scotch Plains burst, sending water through Plainfield. Passaic, Essex and Union counties were among the hardest hit in the Garden State.

The tropical storm passed directly over New York City, a swirl of foul weather that dissipated over Connecticut and Massachusetts. The *New York Times* told of effects in the metropolitan area, where eight people died:

"The two-headed storm reached the height of its violence in New York about 9 o'clock in the morning, when the wind blew sixty-four miles an hour and rain fell in sheets. Between 7 and 10 o'clock the average wind velocity was sixty miles and the rainfall for the six hours ending with this period was 2.19 inches.

"There was much damage in Hoboken, Bayonne, and other Jersey towns near New York. In Atlantic Highlands many persons, driven from their homes by the water, fled in boats and were not able to return to their homes until afternoon.

"Staten Island, because of its exposed condition, was laid waste in many places. More than 2,000 new trees planted between St. George and New Brighton were blown down, and the best trees surrounding residences of New Brighton were also destroyed."

ANNAPOLIS, MARYLAND

Maryland State Archives

A storm surge invades the historic city.

Maryland State Archives

Low-lying neighborhoods were inundated.

1923

October

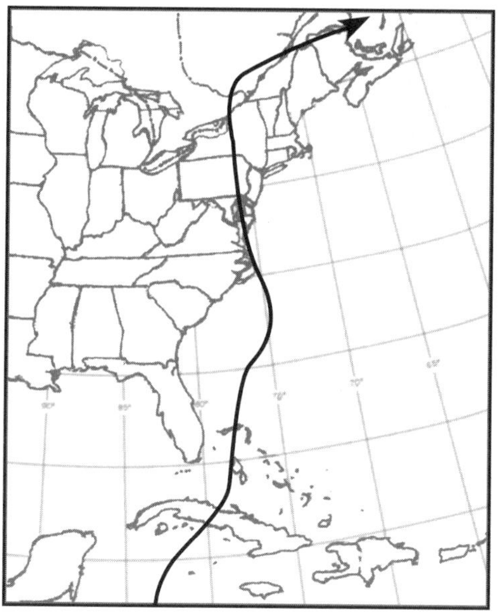

Hurricanes transport warm air to northern latitudes. Some travel considerable distances to do so, but rarely do they traverse the hemisphere like a tropical cyclone during October 1923. It journeyed thousands of miles from the rain forests of Central America to the gates of the Arctic.

A disturbance formed near Panama on October 14 and soon became a tropical storm. After nine days, the storm reached the Chesapeake Bay. It brought gales and modest coastal flooding. Cape Henry registered a sustained wind of 56 mph. Atlantic City reported a gust of 82 mph.

Winds gusted to 54 mph in New York City. Rainfall totaled 3.92 inches in Central Park.

The storm provided an early snowfall to part of the southern Appalachian Mountains. Accumulations included: **North Carolina**—Mount Mitchell 8", Asheville 3". **Tennessee**—Johnson City 5". **Virginia**—Wise 7", Dante 7", Wytheville 2", Marion 2". **West Virginia**—Bluefield 7".

The system became extratropical and tracked through Canada. It was last charted off the southern coast of Greenland, approaching the Arctic Circle.

1925

December

That's right, *December*. During the opening days of December 1925 a hurricane made its way up the East Coast, the latest tropical cyclone to strike the United States.

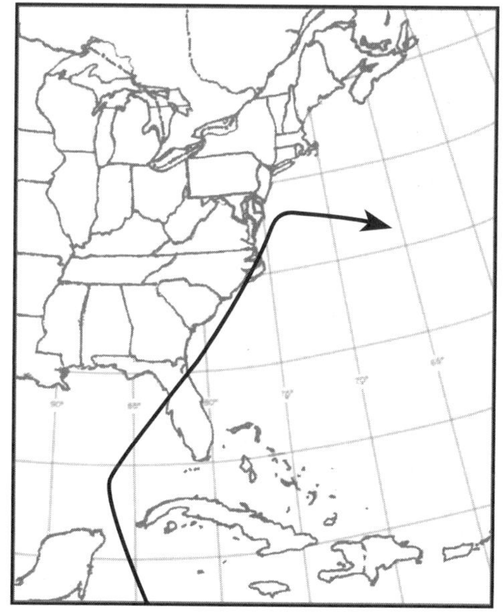

It briefly became a hurricane prior to landfall near Sarasota, Fla., on November 30. The system crossed Florida into the Atlantic Ocean and again intensified to a hurricane on December 1. It weakened to a tropical storm before reaching North Carolina and Virginia on December 2-3.

About 2-3 inches of rain fell as far inland as Richmond and Fredericksburg, Va. Frolicsome gales along the coast lasted two days, churning up minor to moderate flooding. Cape Henry clocked a peak five-minute wind speed of 60 mph. Atlantic City recorded 64 mph, with a gust of 70 mph.

Beach erosion plagued the Mid-Atlantic. The *U.S. Monthly Weather Review* described conditions in New Jersey:

"The one outstanding weather event of December was the occurrence of a tropical storm which moved from the southern coast of the Atlantic seaboard to a position off the New Jersey shore on the afternoon of the 3rd. Gales driving long-continued rain did considerable damage along the waterfront of the entire Jersey coast. Bulkheads, boardwalks, and other structures were washed out or otherwise seriously damaged by the combined forces of wind and wave. Great holes were washed in some of the noted resort beaches, and great combers in some instances overtopped the barriers and swept into town and building. Some lives were lost due to the storm, and there was considerable loss and delay to navigation."

The report chided mariners:

"Enumeration of marine and other losses is necessarily incomplete, but they were quite severe, due, largely, to the fact that shipping throws caution to the winds, as it were, after the last of October, resting upon the Utopian belief that the end of that month marks the close of tropical cyclone activity in these latitudes."

Hurricane rainfall totals (Dec. 2-3): **Delaware**—Millsboro 2.35", Dover 1.00". **Maryland**—La Plata 2.13", Easton 2.06", Salisbury 1.66", Baltimore .98". **New Jersey**—Atlantic City 2.35". **Virginia**—Langley Field 3.61", Warsaw 3.10", Williamsburg 3.05", Richmond 2.27", Fredericksburg 2.23", Charlottesville 1.65".

Photograph courtesy of the Norfolk Public Library

December surprise. Hurricane-tossed surf floods Ocean View, Va.

1928

August

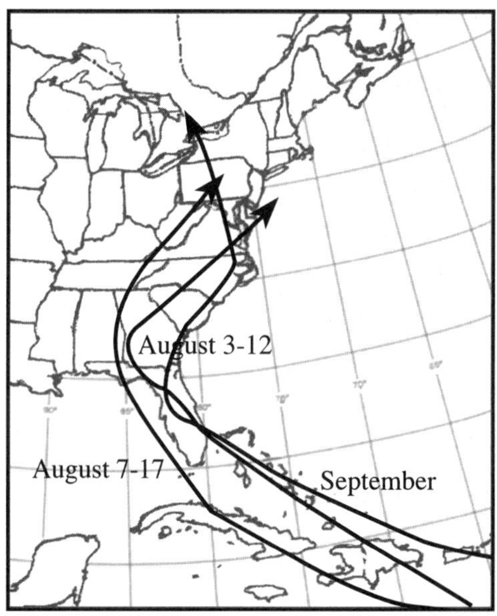

Months in the nation's capital rarely come soggier than August 1928. Two tropical storms doused Washington, D.C., contributing to the city's wettest August. Monthly rainfall totaled 14.41 inches, including a 24-hour deluge of 7.31 inches on August 11-12.[1]

The remnants of a hurricane supplied the rain. The disturbance tracked through southeastern Virginia and the Chesapeake Bay. At Cheltenham, Md., near Washington, 12.76 inches of rain fell in 30 hours.

A second tropical storm passed through West Virginia and western Pennsylvania on August 16-17. Rain again drenched much of the Mid-Atlantic region, disrupting travel, swamping countless basements and making life difficult, especially for farmers. The Virginia Department of Agriculture assessed crop losses in the Old Dominion:

"While it is impossible to make an accurate estimate at this time of the damage suffered by Virginia farmers from the storms of the past week, it can be safely stated that they have never experienced such a heavy loss from storms, and the total will run into the millions of dollars when the damage to crops, livestock, soil, fences and buildings is considered."

An editorial in the August 18 edition of the *Richmond Times* opened:

"During the past week the South, in the breaking of the torrid (heat) wave which swept for weeks over the greater part of the country, has been subjected to such a continuation of terrific storms as it has suffered few times in all its history. Here and there were cyclonic outbursts bringing in their wake swift and sudden destruction. However, the principal damage has been wrought through steady, almost unprecedented, downpours of rain which resulted in rivers and smaller streams rising to such an extent as to dislodge bridges, break dams, halt highway and railroad traffic, destroy crops and imperil, even take, human life."

The editorial concluded:

"Nor will the rain and the cyclonic winds be without their valuable lessons. The greater portion of this loss, perhaps, has been unavoidable. It merely demonstrated again the futility of man, no matter how far he has climbed toward the highest peak of civilization, against the lashing fury of the elements. Providence has not yet taught him how to guard against such disasters. Much of the loss, however, could have been obviated if man's knowledge of building and of precautions against severe storms had been employed to the utmost. In the rebuilding of the devastated sections of the South nothing will be left undone which will assure against such disasters in the future."

[1] It is Washington's second wettest month on record, runner-up to September 1934 when 17.45 inches fell. The period between 1928 and 1934 was one of precipitation extremes. Washington suffered its severest drought between the wet years of 1928 and 1934. Rainfall only totaled 21.66 inches during 1930. (The city's annual average is 39 inches.)

Hurricane rainfall totals (Aug. 11-12): **Delaware**—Dover 8.78", Wilmington 2.92". **Maryland**—Cheltenham 12.76", Annapolis 10.21", Millington 9.20", Rock Hall 8.85", Baltimore 4.35", Frederick 1.67". **New Jersey**—Cape May 4.67", Atlantic City 4.51", New Brunswick 1.52". **Pennsylvania**—Philadelphia 1.44". **Virginia**—Quantico 9.12", Lynchburg 7.68", Richmond 4.43", Fredericksburg 4.40", Charlottesville 3.31". **Washington, D.C.** 8.67".

Rainfall totals (August 1928): **Delaware**—Dover 13.62, Wilmington 8.16. **Maryland**—Cheltenham 18.68, Annapolis 14.30", Rock Hall 13.51", Baltimore 9.70", Frederick 6.64". **New Jersey**— Atlantic City 6.20", New Brunswick 5.87" Cape May 5.46". **Pennsylvania**—Philadelphia 5.47". **Virginia**—Quantico 15.27", Lynchburg 14.87", Fredericksburg 12.08", Charlottesville 11.97" Richmond 8.05". **Washington, D.C.** 14.41".

September

THE GREAT LAKE OKEECHOBEE HURRICANE

The Herbert Hoover levee towers over sprawling Lake Okeechobee, Fla. With an average depth of 10 feet, Okeechobee hardly seems worthy of such respect. Therein lies a tale of one of the nation's deadliest natural disasters.

On September 16, 1928, a Category 4 hurricane blasted ashore near Palm Beach. Winds in excess of 150 mph piled up Okeechobee's waters. That night the lake broke through earthen dikes and rolled through surrounding farmland. About 2,000 people drowned.

Survivors struggled with grief and destitution. The dead were located during the following days, weeks and years. Most victims were buried in a mass grave at Port Mayaca Cemetery, on Okeechobee's eastern shore. A monument is inscribed, "In Memoriam: To the 1600 pioneers in this mass burial who gave their lives in the 1928 hurricane so that the Glades might be as we know it today."

Earlier, the storm devastated Puerto Rico. The "Second San Felipe Hurricane," as it's remembered, struck on September 13, killing 400 people and making more than 200,000 residents homeless.

After leaving Florida, the hurricane tracked north. From September 17-20, it played tag with land and sea, jogging up the East Coast before dissipating near Lake Ontario. Both Cape Henry and Atlantic City recorded a (five-minute) average wind speed of 72 mph. Southeastern Virginia received 4-7 inches of rain.

Moderate flooding occurred on the Chesapeake Bay and Mid-Atlantic coast, particularly along the Jersey shore. Gales brought down many trees and caused widespread mischief. The *Atlantic City Press*:

"Avalon reported water running two feet deep in the streets, with residents using rowboats to go from house to house. Bridges were under water and the town was isolated for several hours. Heavy seas swept over the beaches at Wildwood, and at Cape May a large section of the boardwalk was washed away, windows were shattered and a number of buildings sustained serious structural damage.

"Damage to houses (from high winds) was reported from Merchantville, Audubon, Burlington and Haddon Heights, while several orchards were reported damaged in sections around Hammonton and Moorestown."

As the remnants reached Canada, pressure rose, winds subsided and rain diminished. The hurricane went out in a breeze even as its doings in Florida stunned a nation.

***

The hurricane of 1928 remains a cautionary lesson on the power of nature. A monument in hard-hit Belle Glade, near the southeastern shore of Lake Okeechobee, dramatizes that horror—lest we forget. A sculpture of a terrified family fleeing an approaching menace tops the memorial. A couple's arms are raised in a futile gesture to shield themselves and their children. Etched in the pedestal below are monstrous waves sweeping across the land, devouring homes and everything else. The scene is inscribed, "Belle Glade 1928."

1933

August

CHESAPEAKE AND POTOMAC HURRICANE

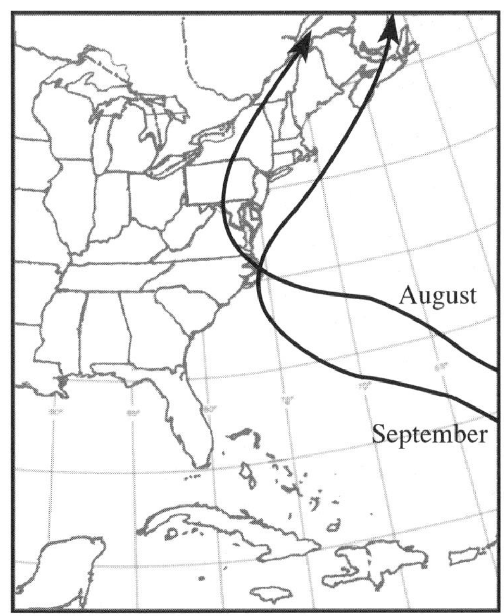

The windstorm crept toward New Jersey's southeastern coast on the afternoon of August 20. Boats plied the sea beneath an overcast sky and sultry summer calm. No hint of an impending calamity.

Suddenly, a gale struck. Many vessels sank. The Coast Guard rescued over 200 people but a dozen drowned.

Newspapers described the event as a "freak storm," "dry northeaster," or "dry gale." —Nature's surprise. No rain fell. The wind was actually a gust front, a forerunner to powerful thunderstorms beyond the horizon. That evening, 2.25 inches of rain fell within an hour at Atlantic City, part of 8.12 inches that doused the resort on August 20-21.

The squall heralded a hurricane south of Bermuda, a blow destined to become one of the Mid-Atlantic's most destructive natural disasters. Flooding encompassed a greater geographic area of the region than in any 20th century hurricane except Agnes (1972).

High pressure anchored over New England steered the storm toward North Carolina's Outer Banks and into the Middle Atlantic states. Its rare track ensured days of high winds and a vast domain of treacherous ocean. Passengers and crew of the cruise liner *Madison* could testify to that.

On the morning of August 23, the *Madison*, about 25 miles off Virginia Beach, was struck by several 70-foot waves. They destroyed a large section of the forward cabin. When seamen Lycurgus Lawrence and Edward Corbett went to check the damage and secure a dangling lifeboat, additional mountains of water washed them overboard. Shortly thereafter, the *Madison* sent an SOS. A Coast Guard escort guided the ship into Norfolk.

The Category 2 hurricane made landfall near Nags Head on August 23 and quickly tracked through southeastern Virginia.

"While hurricane velocities were not actually recorded at any Weather Bureau station," the agency said, "it seems quite probable that along the coast between the Delaware Breakwater (Lewes) and Cape Hatteras winds may have reached the lower limits of hurricane force for short intervals."

Winds gusted to 88 mph at Norfolk Naval Air Station. They gusted to 75 mph in downtown Norfolk. The barometer bottomed at 28.68 inches.

Norfolk, drenched by nearly 7 inches of rain and awash from the highest tide of the 20th century, resembled an American Venice. Boaters navigated the business district. Fish frolicked among homes, shops and offices.

The Chesapeake Bay swamped Willoughby Spit, situated on a sandy peninsula created by past hurricanes. Nearly every house was seriously damaged or wrecked. Hundreds of families were displaced.

The ocean mauled Virginia Beach, surging through shops and leaving cars half buried in sand along Atlantic Avenue, the resort's main thoroughfare.

Ocean City, Md., received a useful inlet as the sea carved a passageway through the southern edge of town. (Shifting sands are not necessarily harmful. The Ocean City Inlet remains a boon to the local economy. Sport fishing and pleasure boats shelter in a protected bay and enjoy convenient access to the sea.)

Forecasters knew the hurricane would affect the Mid-Atlantic coast but underestimated its impact on the interior. Heavier than expected rainfall produced far-flung regional flooding. An unforgettable storm surge encroached on tidal sections.

The Chesapeake Bay trapped a relentless Atlantic and rose to historic levels. After covering every marsh and mudflat, ocean-like surf invaded places people called home. Water covered most islands in the bay and on its tributaries. Bridges submerged. Islanders escaped by boat or were marooned on upper floors of their homes, on rooftops or in trees. Wreckage carpeted every shore: wharves, docks and sea walls. Boats.

Lester Trott remembers the plight of his father's 50-foot cabin cruiser, moored on St. Patrick's Creek in St. Mary's County, Md. The hurricane launched the craft, depositing it more than a quarter-mile from its berth.

"Here she was, sitting in this corn field," Trott said. "They hadn't harvested the corn yet and there was one little opening where she came in. Corn grew all around her. Even in the opening the stalks had started to grow back. I wondered, 'How in the world did she get here?'

"You couldn't get equipment in to (float) the boat. It was a soft field, soaked from the rain. So what they did was cut two loblolly pine trees, skin them, and put them under the vessel. Then they took oxen and pulled the boat back into the creek."

Many craft were left to fields and forests, forgotten calling cards from the hurricane of '33.

The resorts of the Chesapeake Bay region were wrecked by hammering surf.

Chesapeake Beach, Md., located along the middle bay, had been conceived as a rival to Atlantic City and Coney Island. It never attained that distinction. Nevertheless, the village thrived during the early 20th century. A railroad connection made it a convenient excursion from Washington, D.C. Steamboats brought visitors from Baltimore. A boardwalk, ballroom and assorted amusements catered to guests. Fishing, picnicking and camping were popular diversions.

The hurricane proved devastating. Chesapeake Beach's half-mile steamboat pier, featuring a miniature railway that provided a link between steamships and shore, was heavily damaged. The bay swallowed the town's promenade, made sport of an amusement park and shattered concession stands. At neighboring North Beach, 70 summer cottages were damaged or demolished.

Colonial Beach, Va., on the lower Potomac River, suffered substantial losses. Freeland Mason remembers the wild scene.

"The waves were like those you'd expect at the ocean—just amazing," Mason said. "We had never seen anything like that."

He recalled the commotion as men fought to save their boats. And his mother's heartbreak as magnificent trees at her inn succumbed to wind and erosion.

"One by one the trees went down," said Mason. "My mother couldn't stand the loss and left for her parents. She couldn't bear to watch."

Wallace Berry observed the storm from the Colonial Beach Hotel. The teenager worked the night shift, but there'd be no rest on August 23.

"I couldn't sleep that day," Berry said. "Everybody, once they got up, began looking. The storm came up the bay and the waves gathered momentum. After a while, they looked like ocean waves, just rolling ashore.

"It reached its height about midday and began receding in the afternoon. By nightfall the river and weather were back to normal. The storm came in with a roar and left leaving silence."

He reflected on Colonial Beach of a bygone era:

"It was a vacation land," Berry said. "Back then, you didn't have fast transportation like you have today. People that lived in Washington, mostly government people, would save their money and go to the beaches close by like Colonial Beach. Maybe Rehoboth. Maybe Virginia Beach. But Colonial Beach was quite a spot."

The resort prospered in the summer of 1933 thanks, in part, to the end of Prohibition. Maryland made alcoholic beverages legal. Virginia hesitated. Entrepreneurs built three "beer piers," taking advantage of a legal loophole dating back to the 1600s. Maryland owned the Potomac River by right of colonial charter. Patrons strolled past a prominently marked state line as they went to enjoy brew and musical entertainment.

Wallace Berry

The Potomac demolished the piers. Berry recalled the angst of one musician.

"He had a lot of equipment stored in a building out on the longest pier. He was one frustrated person when the building in which he stored his instruments, which meant much money to him, went down into the river."

Cases of beer also slid into the Potomac. After the storm, adventurous swimmers dove for the suds, savoring their rewards in the river lest they violate Virginia law.

Berry watched the waterfront turn wreckage: A pavilion with its arcades. The Palm Garden, which housed a bowling alley, dance hall and skating rink. Concession stands. The next morning…

"The sun was out and it was a shame," Berry said. "You looked at the waterfront and all you saw were planks, boards and debris. People tried to salvage what they could."

Mr. Moore, who sold nickel bags of peanuts and popcorn, and Mr. Farris, the saltwater taffy man, as well as other vendors—familiar faces of summer. They lost their concessions. Some never returned.

Colonial Beach recovered despite the carnage. Other communities weren't as fortunate. The hurricane dealt a sledgehammer blow to an area in decline. During the 1920s and 1930s growing popularity of the automobile cut business for Chesapeake Bay steamers. Vacationers from Baltimore and Washington increasingly chose the seashore over close-in destinations.

The hurricane hastened a death knell for the historic resort of Piney Point, Md.

Piney Point, on the lower Potomac River, served as a summer getaway for several presidents from James Monroe to Theodore Roosevelt. During 1820, President Monroe established the first "summer White House" in the hamlet. Notable 19th century statesmen such as Daniel Webster, John Calhoun and Henry Clay vacationed there. Theodore Roosevelt was a frequent visitor early in the 20th century.

Guests chose Piney Point for its invigorating climate and scenic vista. The storm heavily damaged Tolson's Hotel, a premier establishment, and made shambles of the waterfront. After the Hurricane of '33, fewer vacationers flocked to Piney Point, and business steadily declined.

Some men became heroes during the storm—Robert Hedrick among them. He took a rowboat from house to house at Piney Point, warning residents to seek higher ground. The teenager found a woman and her children stranded at one home. There wasn't enough room in the boat for everyone so Hedrick tied a rope around his waist, jumped overboard and swam the craft to safety.

Kendall Morgan and Zeke Briscoe braved the surf to row 23 people at Tolson's Hotel to higher ground.

Thomas Steinise, keeper of the Seven Foot Knoll Lighthouse at the mouth of the Patapsco River near Baltimore, rescued five members of the tug *Point Breeze* as the vessel foundered in 15-foot seas. Steinhise individually ferried the men to safety in his motorboat even as the chaotic waves threatened to sink him.

Captain Charles Ridgell shuttled dozens of residents to safety in the vicinity of Point Lookout-Scotland Beach, Md. He maneuvered his powerboat through turbulent water and assorted debris.

The hurricane of 1933 left memories throughout the Chesapeake Bay region.

A historic storm surge piled into Baltimore. Light and Pratt streets vanished beneath the onrush. Water engulfed much of historic Fells Point.

The Chesapeake Bay inundated the waterfront of Annapolis, where sustained winds reached 65 mph. Docks at the Naval Academy were mangled. Practically all the school's training boats sank.

Bayside farms were ravaged, including the property of Walter Harris in Kent County, Md.

"The storm ruined our steamboat wharf," he said. "It took the wharf agent's house and moved it about 250 feet." An orchard wasn't spared. "So much fruit was blown off the trees in the midst of the peach harvest."

The Potomac River washed into Alexandria and Washington, swamping waterfront warehouses and factories. The barometer fell to 28.94 inches in the nation's capital as the storm tracked through. Gusts peaked at 58 mph.

Ruinous tides weren't the only threat. Rainfall of 6-12 inches caused tremendous destruction in eastern Virginia and Maryland. Delaware, southeastern Pennsylvania, central and northern New Jersey and southeastern New York also had abundant flooding.

Every creek and river of the central and northern Delmarva Peninsula went on a spree. High tides impeded drainage.

Salisbury, Md., struggled to contain the Wicomico River. An army of workmen dug a ditch to divert the Wicomico away from the business district. Nevertheless, Salisbury suffered heavy losses.

Engineers at Laurel, Del., dynamited a section of a dam to relieve pressure and prevent even greater flooding in town.

The hurricane severed ground communications throughout the Eastern Shore, adding to concern, especially outside the region. Sporadic radio traffic fueled wild rumors. A broadcast out of Laurel declared, "Salisbury is in a serious condition and practically wiped out!" Stories grew until reports suggested thousands of people had drowned.

Actually, 'thousands' numbered fewer than a dozen. Most inhabitants were never seriously threatened. They took the event in stride.

Marvin Smith remembers that newspapers never arrived for his Federalsburg, Md., paper route. He joined others to gawk at the flood and have a good time.

Main Street became main entertainment. The owner of a local printing company comically maneuvered his bicycle through receding water. One man converted a washtub into a canoe. Others took to more conventional craft. Some, like Smith, enjoyed a swim.

Baltimore received 7.62 inches of rain and Washington, 6.39 inches, on August 23, their wettest day on record.

The rain produced multiple disasters, including a train wreck outside Washington, in Cheverly, Md.

Shortly before 4 a.m. on August 24, the *Crescent Limited*, en route from New York to New Orleans, derailed after a flood-weakened bridge buckled on the eastern branch of the Anacostia River. An engine and nine cars careened off the track, killing the engineer and fireman while injuring 13 passengers. A sleeper car partially submerged. Panicked passengers scrambled out the windows, groping their way to shore.

Flooding plagued the highlands of northeastern New Jersey and southeastern New York. Rivers crested at their highest levels in decades.

Large sections along the Lehigh, Schuylkill and lower Susquehanna rivers of Pennsylvania were evacuated. The Lehigh Valley had its worst flood since 1902.

The Eastwick section in southwestern Philadelphia became a lake 5 to 10 feet deep, encompassing 10 square miles. Several hundred people sought shelter with the Red Cross.

York, Pa., collected 8.48 inches of rain on August 22-23 and more than 13 inches during the storm. Normally placid Cordorus Creek drove 3,000 people from their homes as it crested 15 inches higher than ever before. Only the roofs of houses remained visible in some neighborhoods. Flooding claimed 47 bridges in York County.

The sun reappeared on August 24. The weather was delightful, as if to make amends for the previous tantrum. But at least 47 people had died and the Middle Atlantic states faced a massive cleanup, a daunting recovery.

***

The Chesapeake and Potomac Hurricane impacted the livelihoods of more residents in the Mid-Atlantic than any other storm except, perhaps, Hurricane Agnes in 1972. It struck during the Great Depression, when earning a living was challenging enough.

Consider the plight of the farmer: His crops lost on the eve of harvest. Orchards harvested by the wind. Livestock drowned.

Or the fisherman: His boat wrecked. Nets and traps lost. A lifetime of work and savings gone within hours.

And the merchant: The farmer and fisherman were vital customers.

They faced a dismal winter.

Less-prosperous communities went the way of Piney Point. Age-old settlements faded. Wharves at smaller ports throughout the Chesapeake region were destroyed and never rebuilt. Their economic lifeline, the steamship, stopped calling.

Difficulties reached beyond the Chesapeake. Factories in eastern Pennsylvania had clustered on rivers since the early 19th century. Flooding savaged the industrialized region. Most business owners (and residents) lacked flood insurance. Many firms closed for repairs. Some shuttered forever.

***

For Wallace Berry, the hurricane symbolizes a divide between the "good old days" and the modern era. He returned to Colonial Beach on the eve of the 60th anniversary. Berry spent the night at a Days Inn overlooking the Potomac River, former site of the Colonial Beach Hotel.

"It meant a lot to me," he said. "I would have returned for the 50th anniversary, but I was working. I went back to reminisce about those times and the storm. If I'm around, I might go back for the 75th anniversary."

Hurricane rainfall totals (Aug. 21-24): **Delaware**—Bridgeville 13.24", Milford 8.78", Dover 8.47", Wilmington 7.44". **Maryland**—Baltimore 10.98", Snow Hill 10.80", Salisbury 10.12", Annapolis 9.92", Easton 7.34", Solomons Island 7.48", Frederick 7.06", Cambridge 6.25". **New Jersey**—Atlantic City 10.91", Port Norris 7.85", Asbury Park 4.11" Trenton 3.85", New Brunswick 3.80". **Pennsylvania**—York 13.82", West Chester 7.63", Allentown 6.79", Bethlehem 6.04", Harrisburg 6.58", Lancaster 6.15", Philadelphia 5.66", Reading 4.22". **Virginia**—Norfolk 8.16", Williamsburg 7.66", Fredericksburg 4.04", Richmond 3.36". **Washington, D.C.** 7.96".

HURRICANE ODDS AND ENDS

- The 1933 hurricane season was the busiest on record in the North Atlantic basin until the 27 tropical cyclones of 2005. There were 9 hurricanes and 12 tropical storms, a total of 21 tropical cyclones.

- As the tide receded in Norfolk, an assortment of aquatic life was stranded in the streets. Meanwhile, goldfish escaped from the courthouse fountain.

- A police officer in Portsmouth, Va., directed traffic while sporting a bathing suit.

- Rosa Le Darieux had a unique view of the hurricane, at least for a time. During the summer of 1933, Le Darieux was a "flagpole sitter," as those pursuing the national craze were called. She maintained residence on a 55-foot-high platform at Ocean View Park, near the mouth of the Chesapeake Bay. The stunt began on July 1 and was to continue until Labor Day. Firemen brought down a protesting Le Darieux in the midst of the storm.

- A flood tide engulfed cemeteries in some Chesapeake Bay communities, raising coffins and sending them adrift.

- The tide carried a house off its foundation on St. George Island, Md. When the water subsided, according to local lore, hogs were discovered sleeping in the owner's bed.

- Mounds of oysters washed up on St. George Island. One pile was about 50-feet long, 10-feet-wide and 5-feet high. Countless oysters, clams and fish washed ashore throughout the Chesapeake Bay region.

- During the hurricane, a tornado swept in from the sea and descended on Wildwood, N.J. The twister tore through the resort, inflicting additional damage.

- In *High Winds...High Tides, A Chronicle of Maryland's Coastal Hurricanes*, Reginald Truitt wrote, "Maryland Seasiders could fairly well foretell approaching severe storms by the mood of the sea and especially by the roar of the swells breaking on the beach six or seven miles away. Such a roar was heard two days in advance of the 1933 storm in Snow Hill and Berlin, the former some eight air miles distant."

- An immense flock of blackbirds attracted considerable attention as it flew over Allentown, Pa., prior to the storm. The parade extended for several miles. Perhaps there's truth to folklore suggesting birds sense an oncoming tempest. Consider the mariner's proverb: "The glass (barometer) is down, the gulls flocked along the shore, the clouds low'ring fast, soon the wind will roar."

- Joseph Duckworth, a mail pilot for *Eastern Air Transport*, arrived at Washington's Hoover Airport just before conditions closed the facility. Seeing the gathering clouds, he may have wondered what it would be like to fly into the storm's mysterious center. Duckworth found out a decade later when he became the first man to intentionally fly into the eye of a hurricane.

- A Louisiana heron found its way to New York. The bird was observed in Steeplechase Park on Coney Island. (Hurricanes sometimes provide a bonanza for bird-watchers. The birds get trapped in the eye and are carried along in their airy cage. Vagabonds often flock to ships or find refuge in distant lands. A hurricane's northeast quadrant is best for locating exotic birds.)

• While there were many individual acts of selflessness, groups also participated. Military and civilians worked feverishly, successfully bolstering a dam at Lake Denmark near Picatinny Arsenal, N.J. The lake endangered the homes of thousands of residents.

• Allen Butler, a 15-year-old Boy Scout from Belleville, N.J., discovered that fame is fleeting. Butler was hailed a hero after he stopped a commuter train from crashing into storm-tossed wreckage blocking the track. Days later, when he reenacted his feat for newsreel cameras, the uninformed engineer wasn't amused. "Listen," thundered the trainman, "I don't care who you are. If I ever catch you fooling around this track again, I'll have the cops on you!"

• Startled onlookers watched the Statue of Liberty's torch go dark during the evening of August 23, after lightning struck the plant providing electricity. (The torch had last gone out in early 1929.)

• 1933 began a period of increased Mid-Atlantic hurricane activity that lasted until 1961.

September

On September 16, a powerful hurricane made landfall along the North Carolina coast. Barometric pressure dipped to 28.25 inches at Cape Hatteras and gusts exceeded 100 mph. Up to 13 inches of rain pelted the area.

It was the most severe hurricane at Cape Hatteras since 1899, and the worst in northern sections of the Outer Banks since 1879. The blow killed 21 people. The Red Cross calculated that 1,166 buildings were destroyed and 7,244 damaged in eastern North Carolina.

The Virginia coast sustained less damage than in August. Winds peaked at 65 mph at Cape Henry and 56 mph in Norfolk. From the September 1933 issue of the Weather Bureau's *Climatological Data Report for Virginia*:

"The only storm of the month was a tropical hurricane touching the North Carolina and Virginia coasts on the 15th and 16th, with damage in Virginia limited practically to the southeast coast. High winds disrupted traffic in Hampton Roads, uprooted hundreds of trees, damaged roofs, broke many display windows, disrupted power lines and put out of commission more than 2,000 telephones.

"Water flooded many fields of spinach, kale, cabbage and collards; and rendered impassable many roads in Gloucester County and several highways between Norfolk, Suffolk and Virginia Beach in addition to blocking streets in Norfolk and smaller coastal towns. High waves damaged roads, bridges, cottages, jetties, and seawalls along the beaches, materially changing the lines of many of the beaches themselves."

The hurricane veered northeast, sparing the upper Delmarva Peninsula and New Jersey high winds but dumping considerable rain, particularly in the New York metropolitan area. Central Park had 7.27 inches from September 14-17.

***

The cruise liner *Morro Castle* tangled with the hurricane as it sailed from Havana, Cuba, to New York City. The ship lost radio contact for two days while battling mountainous seas and 100-mph winds off the Outer Banks.

Captain Robert Wilmott spent many hours on the bridge, safely bringing the *Morro Castle* to port.

Grateful passengers voted a resolution of thanks and raised a purse for the crew. Wilmott received a watch inscribed, "In recognition of superb seamanship through a most perilous hurricane—Sept. 13-18, '33."

But the following year brought a different tale...

AUGUST 23, 1933
SURF BATTERS OCEAN VIEW, VIRGINIA

Photograph courtesy of the Norfolk Public Library

Photograph courtesy of the Norfolk Public Library

Photograph courtesy of the Norfolk Public Library

Norfolk, Va.

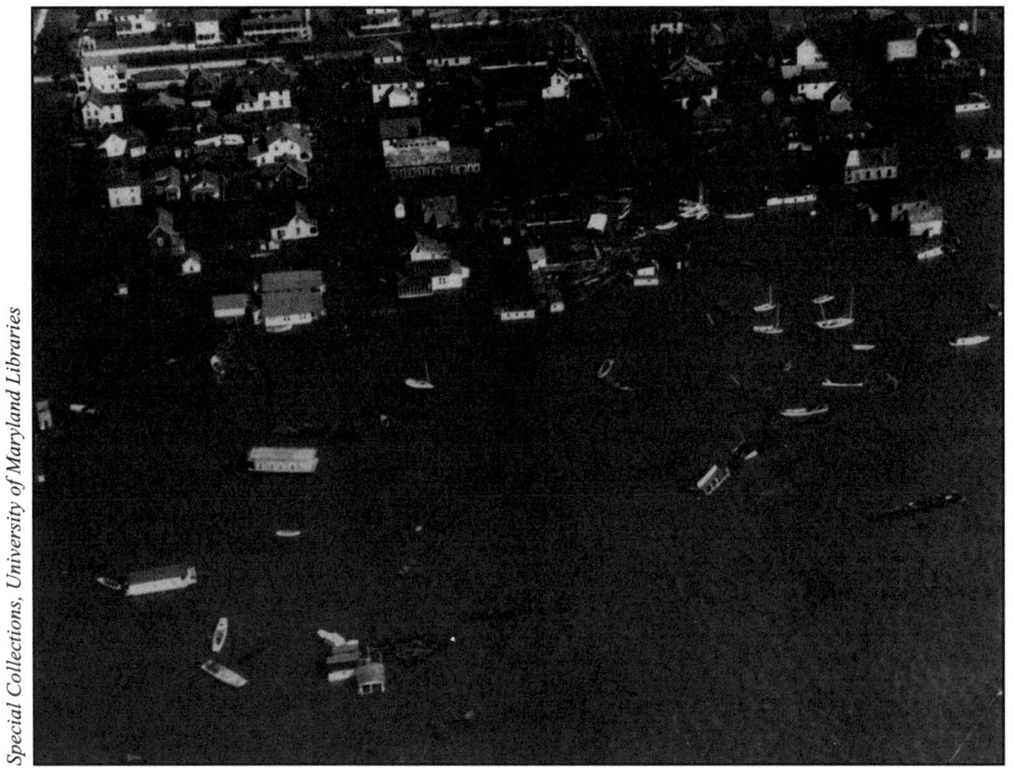

Special Collections, University of Maryland Libraries

Ocean City, Md. (bayside view) The hurricane created a valuable inlet.

Special Collections, University of Maryland Libraries

Thousands of boats sank or were driven ashore throughout the Chesapeake Bay region, including this craft in Annapolis, Md.

Chesapeake Beach Railway Museum

Chesapeake Beach, Md., would long remember the hurricane of August 1933. The resort's popular ballroom and waterfront promenade succumbed to the storm.

Chesapeake Beach Railway Museum

Chesapeake Beach

Special Collections, University of Maryland Libraries

The partial collapse of a railroad bridge led to a deadly train derailment outside Washington, D.C.

Special Collections, University of Maryland Libraries

Baltimore, Md. Winds toppled trees and power lines causing widespread outages.

Special Collections, University of Maryland Libraries

Laurel, Del.

Historical Society of Berks County

Reading, Pa.

York County Heritage Trust

York, Pa.

1934

September

MORRO CASTLE STORM

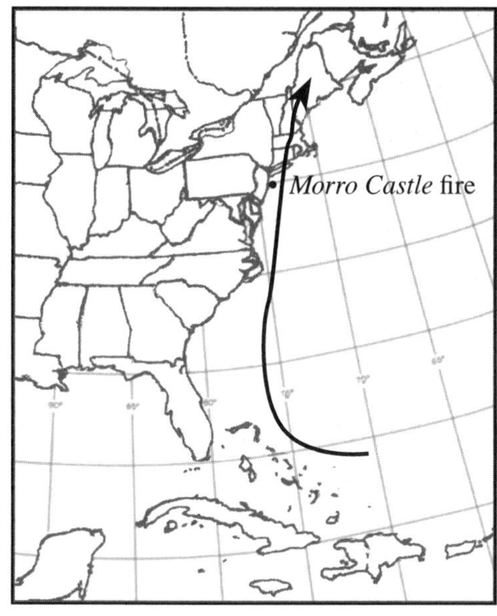

What began in ice ended with fire.

The luxury liner *Titanic*, thought unsinkable, foundered in 1912 after striking an iceberg. More than 1,500 people died because there were too few lifeboats. Subsequently, passenger ships were required to carry an adequate supply.

By the mid-1930s, the American public embraced cruise vacationing as never before. Complacency—a sense of invulnerability—returned. Innocence ended off the New Jersey coast on September 8, 1934. A fire gutted the *Morro Castle* even as a hurricane hindered rescue operations. The tragedy claimed 134 lives. An astonished public asked, "What went wrong?"

***

Pride of the Havana Fleet, the *Cuban Ferryboat* and *Honeymooner Liner* were monikers attached to the *Morro Castle* after its launch in 1930. The Ward Line touted it as "the safest cruise ship afloat."

Gleaming lifeboats hung on davits like so many ornaments. Each carried up to 70 people, enough total capacity for everyone on board. The *Titanic* tragedy ensured that. However, crew members received little or no training in their use. Lifeboat drills were perfunctory if held at all.

Multiple layers of paint and varnish, along with ornate and extensive woodwork made the *Morro Castle* luxurious. They also fueled an inferno.

The floating resort made roundtrips between New York and Havana. It offered passengers a chance to shed the shackles of constraint and Prohibition once outside the U.S. territorial limit. Merrymaking began shortly after departure and continued until the wee hours before return.

Prohibition ended by 1934, but the fun continued. Singles looking for a mate. Honeymooners. Families, retirees, sober charter groups. All signed on. There were businessmen, émigrés and government agents, too.

Passengers were unaware that the *Morro Castle* smuggled arms to the Cuban government. Crates marked "Sporting Goods" became staples in its hold, cargo eagerly awaited in Havana.

Cuba grappled with political turmoil and sporadic violence. The ornate wooden portal to the Palacio Presidencial seemed like a revolving door after the resignation of President Gerardo Machado in early 1933. Factions vied for attention and power. The *Morro Castle* became a symbol of what some groups considered Yankee imperialism. Shadowy rumors of impending sabotage surrounded its visits.

Dissent simmered and occasionally boiled over in September 1934. Shortly before the ship's arrival, student demonstrators clashed with police. While the *Morro Castle* was in port, a dockside gun battle fought between rival labor factions left one man dead.

Politics was one thing; a disgruntled crew another. The smiling façade of the steward, waiter and mess boy often hid unhappy employees. Low wages, long hours, poor living conditions and growing mistrust between officers and their charges fed simmering resentment. With such conflict, who thought of lifeboat drills?

***

Passengers gathered for a gala farewell dinner on September 7. Outside, off the Jersey shore, wind, occasional rain and fog swept the deck. A hurricane located 300 miles south, off the North Carolina coast, pursued the vessel.

The hour grew late and Captain Robert Willmott didn't appear. Cruise director Robert Smith walked to a microphone. "I have sad news," he began.

Willmott had died in his cabin. Doctors claimed he succumbed to a heart attack. However, subsequent events created suspicion of foul play.

The first officer, William Warms, took command. Thank goodness the ship would be in New York by morning, he thought.

The *Morro Castle* never reached port.

Shortly before 3 a.m., late-night revelers smelled smoke. A crewman located a fire in the writing room closet. He opened the door and a dragon lashed out.

Initially regarded as minor and easily extinguishable, the blaze spread throughout the ship within a half hour. The *Morro Castle* sent an SOS message at 3:18 a.m. By then, it was a floating torch.

Alarms rang. Crew members raced through smoky passageways. "Fire! Get Up! Get Out!" They banged on pots and pans. Whistles blew. Reveille sounded.

Passengers, half-asleep, dazed and confused, negotiated their way toward exits. The fire fed on walls, ceilings and wiring. It traveled through ventilation shafts, false ceilings and hallways. Lights went out. The blaze flared into those fleeing, igniting some, adding to terror.

The crowd stumbled outside, many clutching or awkwardly strapping on life jackets. They waited for direction that never came.

The fire control panel on the bridge flashed a mass of red lights. The whistle of a dying ship tolled above the din.

A night watchman at the Belmar Fishing Club thought he saw the first rays of the sun. A Coast Guard observer figured the glow a rising moon. But it was raining and three hours before dawn. A ship burned at sea.

***

As the *Morro Castle* flamed, the Jersey shore slept. Soon, a call-out alerted emergency workers. Phones began ringing and doors banging. Headlights raced through the night. Men who had trained to save, at most, a few people imperiled by the sea were tasked with rescuing hundreds. They tackled a challenge almost beyond belief.

***

The *Morro Castle* briefly sped up in a desperate attempt to reach the comparative shelter of Sandy Hook Bay, about 20 miles away. The dash had an unintended effect. Dismayed passengers watched brisk northeast winds fan the fire like a bellows. Burning strips of paint peeled off the hull and soared through the air. Flames leaped from portholes. Captain Warms cut the engines. The *Morro Castle* drifted.

Efforts to contain the blaze proved futile. Fire doors weren't closed. Few crewmen knew how to use firefighting equipment. Water pressure faltered. Flames raged out of control.

Cruise director Smith attempted to bring order. Few listened. Confusion turned to panic.

A blur of images: Father Raymond Egan (who survived), the right side of his face burnt, leading groups in prayer before they jumped. Crewmen heaving buoyant objects overboard to give those without life jackets a chance to survive.

Passengers demanded lifeboats but found few. Fire consumed or blocked access to several, and the ship's employees commandeered others. Bitter survivors charged that crewmen left them behind.

Shortly after 6 a.m. the first lifeboat reached the beach at Spring Lake. Seven seamen and three passengers disembarked from a craft with the capacity for 70. Eban Abbott, the ship's chief engineer, fled in a half-empty boat. Fewer than 100 people made it to shore in lifeboats. Nearly all were employees.[1]

Passengers leaped into the sea—individually, groups, couples holding hands. Depending on the deck, they jumped 20 or 30 feet. Those reluctant to leave were shoved over the railing. Nobody could remain on the ship and live.

Once in the water survivors settled into troughs, kicking and paddling to avoid regularly dunkings. Many grew exhausted, surrendering to the deep.

A surfboat from the Coast Guard station at Sea Girt approached the *Morro Castle*. Warren Moulton, at the engine controls, brought the craft to within several hundred yards of the stricken liner. Suddenly, a crowd converged. "Help!" implored a frantic chorus.

[1] While many crew members fled, others fought the fire and provided assistance. They attempted to get passengers to safety at risk to their lives. Of the 134 people who died, 40 were *Morro Castle* employees.

There were too many begging assistance. They threatened to swamp the surfboat. Moulton turned toward shore, only able to retrieve two.

Lights flickered from the distant shore, but the ocean remained dark. As a result of the storm, nearly all fishing and pleasure craft remained in port.

***

A diverse flotilla converged on the *Morro Castle* at daybreak. Coast Guard vessels, fishing boats and tugs. Passenger liners and freighters. There was little coordination. They engaged in a hit-and-miss search, hampered by high seas, brisk winds and steady rain. Smaller craft battled mountainous surf, struggling to see beyond the next swell. Oar boats turned back.

Gov. Harry Moore, at his summer residence in Sea Girt, was awaken and told of the disaster. He became increasingly frustrated with the chaotic rescue effort. Moore had his personal pilot fly him to the scene. The reconnaissance quickly became a lifesaving mission. From the cockpit of an Army biplane, Moore dangled a red flag to guide searchers toward those treading water. He helped rescued four people.

"It was a sight I shall never forget," the governor said. "One man in particular impressed me with the thin line that may be drawn between life and death.

"He was struggling feebly, partly submerged, when he heard our plane and looked upward. I waved to him. A small boat was passing not twenty feet away, but could not see him because of the high waves that obscured their view. I spotted him for them and saw him safely taken onboard."

Rescue operations ended by early afternoon. Among ships performing yeoman duty: The liner *Monarch of Bermuda* brought in 71 people and the fishing boat *Paramount* hauled out 67. The freighters *City of Savannah* and *Andrea H. Luckenbach* secured 65 and 26, respectively. Some passengers swam to shore, including a couple that made it to Sea Girt clinging to a life preserver.

***

The storm made landfall on central Long Island during the evening of September 8. The weather office in New York City reported a peak gust of 65 mph and 4.92 inches of rain. Mitchell Field, in western Long Island, had a gust of 67 mph.

Sandy Hook, N.J., reported a peak gust of 65 mph. About 5 inches of rain fell on neighboring Long Branch. In southeastern New Jersey, Pleasantville, near Atlantic City, collected 6.56 inches.

Two seamen drowned and three were rescued after a tugboat overturned in New York Bay. One man died after rough seas sunk his sailboat near Northport, Long Island. Three crewmen perished when the schooner *Neshaminy* capsized off Brigantine, N.J.

Steamship Historical Society of America Collection, University of Baltimore

The Coast Guard cutter *Tampa* waits to take the *Morro Castle* under tow.

***

Captain Warms was among the last to leave the *Morro Castle,* having taken refuge with several staff members in the bow at the furthest point forward. He boarded the Coast Guard cutter *Tampa*, which took the burning hulk in tow. The *Tampa* began hauling the *Morro Castle* to a secure berth in New York harbor but nature intervened—gales snapped the towline. Warms watched his charge drift toward Asbury Park.

Tom Burley, an announcer for radio station WCAP, was reading the latest disaster bulletins from a studio located in Asbury Park's Convention Hall. About 6:30 p.m., he glanced out a seaward window. "Oh my God!" Burley exclaimed. "The *Morro Castle*'s here!"

During the following month more than a half-million sightseers converged on the storied wreck.

***

Warms, Chief Engineer Abbott and Ward Line vice president Henry Cabaud were indicted. On January 25, 1936, after a trial lasting 11 weeks, a jury convicted Warms, Abbott and Cabaud of willful negligence. Warms was sentenced to two years in prison and Abbott to four years. Cabaud was fined $5,000 and given a one-year suspended sentence. The Ward Line paid Cabaud's fine. The ship's officers appealed the ruling to the U.S. Court of Appeals.

On April 7, 1937, the court set aside the verdict. Justices lauded Warm's dedication to the *Morro Castle* stating, "he maintained the highest traditions of the sea by staying on his vessel until the bridge had burnt under him and no one else remained on board."

After the trial, Warms said, "It's hard for a jury to understand the conditions which confronted me. Having no knowledge or experience of the way of the sea, the jury probably didn't comprehend what it means to suddenly battle against a raging sea, the worst storm for years along the Atlantic Coast, and a fire which was sweeping the vessel."

He returned to sea captaining a Ward Line freighter.

***

Congress enacted regulations to ensure better fire protection on passenger ships. Lifeboat emergency drills became mandatory.

There were investigations by state and federal agencies. The following excerpt is from a report issued by a Senate panel:

"There existed no organization for concerted, unified action in cases of emergency.

"Leadership and direction of the crew were sadly conspicuous by their absence.

"No material improvements can take the place of well-instructed, disciplined, and properly organized crew personnel. While a poor ship may be operated safely by a well-disciplined crew, the best ship can easily come to grief with a poor crew."

***

Nobody was ever charged with arson or murder. Investigators ruled the blaze an act of God. But skepticism lingers. Spontaneous combustion, Cuban political intrigue or sabotage by a disgruntled employee? Take your pick. Each theory has supporters. Perhaps, the truth has yet to be told.

© Colesco 1934
S.S. MORRO CASTLE ASHORE AT ASBURY PK. N.J.

New Jersey State Archives, Dept. of State

Steamship Historical Society of America Collection, University of Baltimore

At Asbury Park, N.J., legions of sightseers converged on the beach.

1935

September

GREAT LABOR DAY HURRICANE

The Great Labor Day Hurricane of 1935 is the most intense to strike the United States. It devastated the upper Florida Keys. It killed 400 people.

But the hurricane's rampage didn't end in Florida. Older residents of the middle Chesapeake Bay region and Delmarva Peninsula remember it as the "Flood of 1935."

On September 1, the storm left the Bahamas as a minimal hurricane, seemingly of modest threat. The next day—less than 200 miles later—it arrived in the Keys, pouncing on the vulnerable island chain.

The storm deepened explosively—a process that still baffles meteorologists and gives forecasters fits. The central pressure plunged to an ultra-low 26.35 inches, the lowest ever in the United States. Winds gusted up to 200 mph along a 30-mile section, from near Tavernier on the east to Vaca Keys on the west.

Hundreds of unemployed World War I veterans had found government work there building the Overseas Highway (U.S. 1), an engineering feat designed to link Miami with Key West. Work camps consisted of tents and shacks located at ocean's edge. They were no match for a strong gale. Now, a Category 5 hurricane bore down.

Those near the compact eye endured utmost violence. Less than 100 miles away, however, at Miami and Key West, the blow seemed little more than the rustling of palm leaves.

A train was sent from Miami to bring out veterans and other residents. One delay after another slowed progress. Finding a crew was difficult on Labor Day weekend. Evacuation didn't seem urgent—officials thought the storm a marginal hurricane.

The train began its return as the worst arrived. A monumental surge struck, an avalanche of ocean. It swept railcars into the sand. Meanwhile, veterans camps were decimated.

Utter destruction and shattered communications slowed news of the catastrophe. A belated relief effort began.

The hurricane tracked over the Everglades and churned through the eastern Gulf of Mexico. It made landfall again near Cedar Key in northern Florida. Winds rapidly diminished as the storm sped over

National Archives

Death train. Sent to the Florida Keys to evacuate residents, a storm wave swept it off the tracks.

land. Ominously, the area of circulation and rainfall increased. Flooding and tornadoes became primary threats when it reached the Mid-Atlantic from September 4-6.

***

The firehouse siren in Federalsburg, Md., wailed shortly before dawn on September 6, 1935. Marshyhope Creek, an extension of the Nanticoke River, lapped at Main Street in the Eastern Shore town.

"It came up very quickly," said Anita Richardson. "Nobody expected it. Everybody kept thinking the water would start going down. Instead, it kept rising."

Downtown transformed into a beehive of activity as home and shop owners hurried to save their possessions. They rushed as a creek turned river. Flooding routed about 1,000 people, more than half of Federalsburg's population. Marshyhope Creek crested at 17.4 feet, 5 feet higher than ever before or since.

The post office, movie theater and shops merged with Marshyhope. Debris floated down Main Street. A rooster dodged the municipality's sole traffic light while perched on a chicken coop. Concrete burial vaults from a funeral home drifted on the current, battering buildings and destroying the ornate railing on the town bridge.

Federalsburg Historical Society

Telephone operators Reba Pusey (r) and Molly Wheatley (l) became heroines during the disaster.

Edward Nuttle's general store stayed open throughout the crisis, even as water lay siege. His son, Enoch Nuttle, stood behind the counter wearing hip boots selling food to customers attired in similar gear. Rescue workers from neighboring towns, including a contingent of watermen from Secretary, were among the patrons. The watermen did splendid work, evacuating many marooned families.

Charles Carpenter, whose own home was flooded, joined the rescue effort. Carpenter, pastor of Union Methodist Episcopal Church, took time for a special mission. A member of his congregation, Marvin Smith, laughed as he recalled:

"There's a story that the preacher swam down the aisle in our church to rescue the Bible off the pulpit. That was a stunt. He could have waded up the aisle."

Smith continued, "The following year he went into the Army and later was selected as the first chief chaplain of the Air Force."

Telephone operators Molly Wheatley and Reba Pusey became heroines.

The flood engulfed the Federalsburg telephone office, located on the second floor of a brick building on Main Street. Wheatley struggled to arrive early on September 6. She got within a hundred yards.

"I had to take off my shoes and wade the rest of the way, sometimes waist deep, but I finally got to the exchange, soaked and barefooted," Wheatley said. Pusey, not scheduled to work, also waded in.

In 1935, telephone calls went to a central station. Operators manually connected the exchange through a switchboard. No operator, no call.

The women stayed on the job for two days. Water besieged the building. Linemen brought baskets of food, hauled up by improvised pulley. There'd be no repeat of August 1933 when telephone outages led to wild rumors.

The operators handled countless calls, soothing anxious callers, alerting people to evacuate and assisting in the dispatch of aid. At one point, they peered out a window and saw two men clinging precariously to the awning of a drugstore. In another instance, two men overturned in a canoe outside the telephone office. All survived thanks to the women's intervention.

Gov. Harry Nice toured Federalsburg soon after the flood. He vowed to seek financial aid and met with

Federalsburg Historical Society

Federalsburg, Md. (north)

Federalsburg Historical Society

Federalsburg (south)

victims—little comfort to the displaced. The disaster left inconsolable heartbreak.

"We returned after the flood but, at first, couldn't stay," said Anita Richardson. "Everything was a mess. It was awful. My parents brought a garden hose and hosed everything down. You had to scrub and clean and clean some more."

Much of the furniture had been carried upstairs away from the water. However, the loss of a piano put an end to Richardson's lessons. Her parents' businesses (poultry feed and supplies/furniture and wallpaper) were swamped, the contents a total loss.

"I can't imagine losing two businesses, having two children to raise, and having to start over," she said. "They must have been devastated but they didn't want us to know. They picked up and went on."

Her father, R.D. Segars, eventually prospered in the Delmarva poultry industry. Richardson's mother never reopened her furniture and wallpaper shop.

"My father would buy furniture from estate sales when he'd travel to Philadelphia on business," Richardson said. "My mother would have wonderful things to sell. Everybody was always waiting to see what she'd have in her store. She had a really nice place and enjoyed it. But I guess after going through all that—to go back into business again—it was prohibitive."

No lives were lost in Federalsburg. Residents blamed the flood on several factors: dams that failed upstream at Smithville and other places, a railroad embankment in town that impounded and impeded the flow of water, and a large increase in agricultural drainage ditches dug in the decade before the flood.

The primary cause, however, was the incredible rainfall. Easton, for example, recorded 1.85 inches of rain on September 4. Then, when the land could hold no more, 14.78 inches fell during the next two days. Totals in the Marshyhope basin ranged from 10 to more than 16 inches.

Large sections of Virginia, Maryland and Delaware dealt with disaster.

Dam failures on the Eastern Shore contributed to the loss of roads and bridges. Incessant rain turned fields into lakes.

A freight train plunged down a culvert near Felton, Del., killing three crewmen.

Students in Cambridge, Md., were displaced when the town's high school burned down.

St. Mary's County, Md., on the western shore of the Chesapeake Bay, and counties in the adjacent Northern Neck region of Virginia reported most roads closed and many communities swamped.

The James River surged through central Virginia. In Scottsville, on the middle James, four feet of water covered downtown. At Richmond, the river crested at 25.5 feet, above a 9-foot flood stage.

From the Weather Bureau: "The total rainfall for the 5th and 6th averaged 6.5 inches for the entire (James River) basin, but the rain was considerably heavier east of the Blue Ridge; in fact the river did not reach flood stage at or above Lynchburg. It is quite unusual for the river to reach such high stages at Columbia and Richmond, and yet remain below flood in its upper reaches."

Gales lashed the lower two-thirds of the Chesapeake Bay and the coast. At Windmill Point, Va., (near the mouth of the Rappahannock River), the tugboat *Fanny May* sunk. Its 10-member crew was rescued.

The hurricane launched a swarm of tornadoes.

A squall passed through Washington, D.C., on the afternoon of September 4. Multiple tornadoes touched down east of the city. They passed through Naylor, Dunkirk, Jewell and Fair Haven, Md., wrecking homes, barns and outbuildings. The cyclones took an intermittent 40-mile path across the Chesapeake Bay and Eastern Shore.

At Naylor, a tornado resembled "a ball of smoke." Near Croom, a pigpen with six squealing hogs was lifted and safely deposited 200 feet away.

The twisters dissipated by evening. They returned the next day.

Around 10 a.m., a tornado swept through Pittsylvania County near Danville, Va. It lifted for a time before touching down in Prince Edward and Cumberland counties. The storm killed three people in the vicinity of Farmville and damaged Hampden-Sydney College.

Just before 4 p.m., a whirlwind tore through Hampton Roads, Va., zigzagging through western Norfolk, Craney Island and Willoughby Spit. It killed three people and caused considerable property damage, tearing up houses along a track the width of a football field. As the tornado churned across the Elizabeth River, the area was doused with a downpour said to have a salty taste.

A tornado struck Waverly, in southeastern Virginia, tracking about a mile. Other twisters descended on Gloucester and Middlesex counties near the mouth of the Rappahannock River, demolishing homes at

Deltaville and Woods Crossroads. During the evening, a tornado—perhaps a continuation of earlier storms in Virginia—journeyed for 10 miles across northwestern Somerset County, Md., from Dames Quarter through Mount Vernon and over the Wicomico River to Whitehaven, hacking forest and fields.

***

The disturbance intensified after finding the Atlantic, a process that likely began over southeastern Virginia. It regained hurricane strength within hours. By September 10, the Great Labor Day Hurricane dissipated, a broad area of low pressure over the North Atlantic Ocean near Greenland.[1]

***

A national furor raged over treatment of the veterans, the bungled rescue effort and the failure of the Weather Bureau to warn those in the hurricane's path. A Congressional investigation followed. In the end, the controversy led to additional funding for hurricane research and a more comprehensive warning system. Hurricane forecast centers were bolstered in Jacksonville, Fla., New Orleans, La., and San Juan, Puerto Rico. The Jacksonville office eventually relocated to Miami and evolved into the National Hurricane Center.

***

At Islamorada, Fla., on lower Matecumbe Key, an expansive memorial hewn out of coral pays tribute to victims of the Labor Day Hurricane. A thousand miles away another remembrance—albeit modest—graces an exterior wall of Federalsburg's city hall. A solitary white brick inlaid among red bricks denotes the high water mark of the flood of 1935, one of the Delmarva Peninsula's worst natural disasters.

Hurricane rainfall (Sept. 4-6—nearly all fell within 50 hours): **Delaware**—Bridgeville 12.60", Milford 11.89", Dover 10.07", Wilmington 6.76". **Maryland**—Easton 16.63", Salisbury 12.10", Princess Anne 12.10", Solomons 11.39", Annapolis 7.05", Baltimore 5.68", Snow Hill 5.60", Frederick 3.12". **New Jersey**—Atlantic City 13.31", Northfield 11.86", Hammonton 7.89", New Brunswick 4.64". **Pennsylvania**—Philadelphia 7.14", West Chester 5.43". **Virginia**—Tappahannock 12.24", Dahlgren 11.85", Fredericksburg 8.13", Richmond 7.41", Lynchburg 6.99", Charlottesville 6.05", Farmville 3.77", Norfolk 3.20". **Washington D.C.** 6.70".

[1] The Labor Day Hurricane, as well as more recent tropical cyclones such as Camille (1969), Agnes (1972) and Gaston (2004), seemed to strengthen while their center of circulation was still over land. Each unleashed prolific rainfall during the process.

DIARY FROM GROUND ZERO

A SURVIVOR AND THE GREAT LABOR DAY HURRICANE

James E. Duane Jr., a volunteer observer for the Weather Bureau, logged passage of the storm. Duane maintained a fishing camp on Long Key, Fla., directly in the hurricane's path. The eye passed over, a calm haven surrounded by winds gusting at more than 175 mph. The following are excerpts from Duane's weather journal:

September 2:

2 p.m. Barometer falling; heavy sea swell and a high tide; heavy rain squalls continued. Wind from N. or NNE., force 6 (30 mph).

3 p.m. Ocean swells have changed; this change noted: large waves are rolling in from SE., somewhat against winds which are still in N. or NE.

4 p.m. Wind still N., increasing to force 9 (50 mph). Barometer dropping 0.01 every 5 minutes. Rain continued.

5 p.m. Wind N., hurricane force. Swells from SE.

6 p.m. Barometer 28.04; still falling. Heavy rains. Wind still N., hurricane force and increasing. Water rising on north side of island.

6:45 p.m. Barometer 27.90. Wind backing to NW., increasing; plenty of flying timbers and heavy timber, too—seemed it made no difference as to weight and size. A beam 6 by 8 inches, about 18-feet-long, was blown from north side of camp, about 300 yards, through observer's house, wrecking it and nearly striking 3 persons. Water 3 feet from top of railroad grade, or about 16-feet deep.

7 p.m. We were now located in main lodge building of camp; flying timbers had begun to wreck this lodge, and it was shaking with every blast. Water had now reached level of railway on north side of camp. (Note –This was water rapidly piled up from the shallow expanse of Florida Bay, under the drive of northerly hurricane winds.)

9 p.m. No sign of the storm letting up. Barometer still falling very fast.

9:20 p.m. Barometer 27.22 inches; wind abated. We now heard other noises than the wind and knew the center of the storm was over us. We made for the last and only cottage that I think can or will stand the blow due to arrive shortly. All hands, 20 in number, gather in this cottage. During this lull the sky is clear to northward, stars shining brightly and a very light breeze continued; no flat calm. About the middle of the lull, which lasted a timed 55 minutes, the sea began to lift up, it seemed, and rise very fast; this from ocean side of camp. I put my flashlight out on the sea and could see walls of water, which seemed many feet high. I had to race fast to regain entrance of cottage, but water caught me waist deep although I was only about 60 feet from the doorway. Water lifted cottage from its foundation and it floated away.

10:10 p.m. Barometer now 27.02 inches; wind beginning to blow from SSW.

10:15 p.m. The first blast from SSW, full force. House now breaking up—wind seemed stronger than any time during the storm. I glanced at barometer, which read 26.98 inches, dropped it in water and was blown outside into sea; got hung up in broken fronds of coconut tree and hung on for dear life. I was then struck by some object and knocked unconscious.

September 3:

2:25 a.m. I became conscious in a tree and found I was lodged about 20 feet above ground. All water had disappeared from the island; the cottage had been blown back on the island, from whence the sea receded and left it with all people safe.

THE FEDERALSBURG FLOOD

Jean Jefferson, a Federalsburg, Md., teenager, penned this verse in the aftermath of the disaster:

"I say what place is this?
I can't quite tell as yet—
Federalsburg?"
O little damp—
I mean, the streets seem wet,
And phew! Good Lord, what odors!
An awful musty smell,
Just like the place's been buried,
Don't like its looks too well.
The piles and piles of rubbish
What do these people do?
A window pane, a waffle iron,
A chair and one old shoe,
And here, before this drug store
Gosh! They're throwin' stock away.
Cosmetics, cameras, bottled drugs,
An' books an' soap—I say!
That grocer's chuck'in out his food
Why cans and cans of stuff,
And bread and meat—oh well—
I guess he's had about enough.
That's funny white stuff spread around
It looks like lime to me.
The houses all are emptied out,
What could the idea be?
I never have seen such a town
Entirely caked in mud.
What could have happened? Maybe—
Why—
My gosh! They've had a flood.

A TWISTER VISITS HAMPDEN-SYDNEY COLLEGE

The following article appeared in the October 1935 issue of *The Record*, a publication of the Hampden-Sydney Alumni Association:

TORNADO NOTES

At 1:15 P.M. September 5th, first sounding like a distant whistling and very quickly like a great roar, there came from the southeast a tornado, up in the air and looking like a funnel, and moving with a rapidity that would have made the fastest aeroplane seem slow.

Beneath the tornado, as it approached Hampden-Sydney, there was a hard wind, sufficient to blow down a few trees here and there, but not large ones. When the funnel reached the space around the Administration Building it dropped to the ground, wrenched the great old red oak, which has stood guard over the Administration Building and the College Shop and which was probably a vigorous young tree when Hampden-Sydney was founded (1776), threw it instantly to the ground, between the College Shop and the Administration Building. At the same time the tornado played all around Dr. Wilson's (dean of students) residence, but fortunately did not strike it. It took a large old oak at the corner of Wilson's garage, and without touching the garage threw the tree completely over the fence into the College Church Cemetery.

At the same time it blew down an immense red oak just inside the cemetery, and wrenched up by the roots several goodly cedars that were keeping guard over the graves; it half-opened a few graves, blew tombstones around like marbles, and broke several of them. At the same time it took most of the roof from the Administration Building, lifted parts of it up in the air, and took these along, dropping them around Mrs. Lacy's and in Death Valley.

Andrew Johnson's filling station to the north was torn to pieces, and a few small trees were blown up by the roots. The tornado then jumped about two miles and destroyed "Willington," the home built by Major James Morton, of the War of the Revolution. It then continued its girations (sic) towards the northeast killing two people about three miles northeast of Farmville.

Just as the tornado reached Hampden-Sydney a smaller one came in from the west but did no damage except to a big cedar just north of the Memorial Gate. All the trees fell towards the west, except a part of this big cedar, which was torn off and thrown across the street into the church yard on the east.

Not a leaf was disturbed in the church yard, or at the manse, or at Dr. Booker's residence.

The red oak, standing guard over the Administration Building and the College Shop measured twenty feet, nine and a half inches, in circumference one foot from the ground, and a little over fourteen feet, ten inches, nine feet from the ground. The big oak at the cemetery, near Dr. Wilson's residence, measured nine feet, nine inches, in circumference, six feet from the ground.

Close to the northeast corner of the Administration Building was a large post-oak. It was wrenched up by the roots and scraped the north wall of the building. Some of the limbs scraped a north window, and two or three windowpanes were broken. Other big oaks close by were hardly touched.

The unanimous wish at Hampden-Sydney is that Florida will keep her tornadoes, hurricanes, cyclones and other disturbing things in her territory. "The Hill" prides itself on the quiet and calm, which characterize the college community. We resent this uninvited visitor!

An ancient oak toppled during the tornado at Hampden-Sydney College.

1936

September

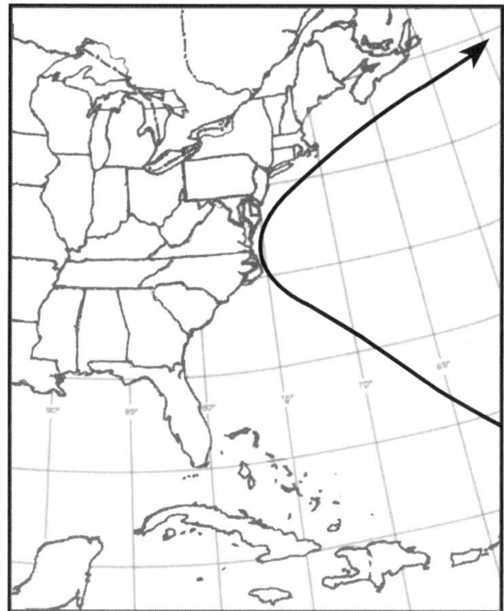

The Time: The 21st century. *The Place:* The lower Chesapeake Bay. A major hurricane makes landfall, bringing enormous devastation.

Although that hasn't happened during the past 400 years, a hurricane in September 1936 came perilously close. The Category 2 storm approached Virginia on September 17. It veered away on the 18th after coming within 25 miles of Virginia Beach. The Weather Bureau's Norfolk office:

"The tropical hurricane that visited the Tidewater area on September 17-18, on its journey up the coast, can be characterized as the worst storm ever experienced in this section, and only the intensive system of warnings by the Weather Bureau, and the splendid cooperation of the general public, and municipal, state, and national forces, saved it from being a major catastrophe."

The hurricane almost ruined Norfolk's bicentennial anniversary. Storm surge flooding inundated the business district and high winds caused various mischief. The tide peaked at 9.3 ft. above normal at Sewells Point, near downtown, the second highest rise of the century (only inches less than during the hurricane of August 1933).

Cape Henry clocked a five-minute average wind speed of 84 mph before the anemometer cups failed.

Gusts of hurricane force brought down power lines and trees throughout southeastern Virginia and the Delmarva Peninsula. Residents of Chincoteague Island, Va., thought the winds more severe than the gales of August 1933. The storm was less destructive, however, as excessive tides lasted for one day rather than several.

The boardwalk at Ocean City, Md., was partially destroyed and the sea surged through adjacent streets. Anywhere the ocean went piles of sand followed.

***

Around noon on September 18, three men rose from the surf and crawled ashore near Lewes, Del.

"The *Long Island* down—crew lost!" gasped Richard McQuillan. He, his cousin Harry, and Delmar George, son of the *Long Island's* captain, spent six hours clinging to a hatch cover. The men thought they were the sole survivors from a crew of 42.

The *Long Island* trawled off the New Jersey coast for menhaden, a fish used for animal feed and fertilizer. With foul weather approaching on September 17, the steamer made for Lewes. Trouble began shortly before daybreak on the 18th as the boat neared the mouth of the Delaware Bay. A huge wave caught the vessel broadside, hurling fishermen from their bunks.

The craft bobbed like a toy. The sea sent water across the deck. Those onboard labored at the pumps in a desperate effort to free the hold of water. Everyone strapped on life jackets. The cargo shifted; the vessel became unmanageable.

Weather conditions deteriorated. The Coast Guard Station in Cape May received an SOS from the *Long Island*: "Taking on water and unable to last." The message was relayed to the Lewes Coast Guard Station, closer to the vessel, but high winds and a rough sea precluded search and rescue.

Suddenly, radio contact ceased. The *Long Island* sank. Some men sought the Delaware shore. Others took refuge aboard an auxiliary boat. Seven crew members drowned.

The tragedy garnered national attention. Headlines proclaimed that there were only three survivors.

Special Collections, University of Maryland Libraries

Downtown Norfolk, Va.

Photograph courtesy of the Norfolk Public Library

Sea Bright, N.J. Beachfront property along sections of the Mid-Atlantic coast suffered during the hurricane.

Early the next morning, Harry Derrickson, commander of the Lewes Coast Guard station, noticed Old Glory fluttering above a supposedly abandoned coal barge. He discovered a miracle. Occupants of the barge, 32 refugees from the *Long Island*, sought sanctuary when their escape craft began to founder. Unable to contact the mainland, they hoisted a flag at dawn and awaited rescue.

Upon returning to shore, crewmen read their own obituaries.

The Mariners' Museum, Newport News, Va.

The *Long Island*. Most crewmen, given up for dead, survived.

A RISING OCEAN CREATES GHOST TOWNS

Which barrier strand will become the next Hog Island?

A relentless sea has devoured much of the sandy, pine-covered rise, located off the Virginia coast. Hog Island occupies a fraction of the acreage that greeted settlers during the 1600s.

The ocean has risen about a foot in the past century. The Environmental Protection Agency predicts an additional rise of a foot by 2050, and possibly as soon as 2025—a level ensuring more Hog Islands.

The strand once boasted more than 80 buildings and an internationally famous hunting lodge. Guests during the late 1800s included President Grover Cleveland. The island had a population of 300 when fierce hurricanes swept through in 1933 and 1936.

"After a powerful hurricane in 1936, the second in three years, the residents realized they were fighting a losing battle against erosion," said Bruce Hayden, professor of environmental sciences at the University of Virginia. "The land they were on was melting away like butter on a hot day. They packed their belongings, jacked their houses onto barges, and floated their lives back to the mainland. The community disappeared overnight. If you went looking for where Broadwater (Hog Island's only town) was, you'd have to look in the sea."

Other settlements along the Mid-Atlantic shore share Hog Island's fate. Neighboring Parramore, Cobb and Smith islands are among them. Inhabitants claimed roots going back hundreds of years. They live on the mainland today. Also gone are the New Jersey communities at Tuckers Island and South Cape May.

Tuckers Island consists of a sandbar located off the southern tip of Long Beach Island—no evidence of an illustrious past. The strand hosted New Jersey's first beach resort in the early 19th century. It included a town, Sea Haven; two hotels; more than 70 cottages, and a lighthouse. The latter succumbed to erosion in 1927. By the mid-1940s, the island was deserted.

South Cape May, on the southern tip of New Jersey, incorporated in 1894. The borough had lofty plans, but hurricanes plagued development from the start. Buyers remained sporadic. "Look at an old planning map and you'll see streets that never were," said Jim Campbell, historian for the Cape May Historical Society.

"It's well under water today," said Bob Fite, a member of the Cape May Historical Society. "My uncle owned a lot of property there. They had Spanish-style single-family homes. They had a mayor and council. The erosion was horrendous."

South Cape May included 50 dwellings. After the hurricane of 1936 and an even more severe blow in 1944, the borough disbanded. Remaining homes were either moved or claimed by the sea. The area is now a nature preserve.

The Chesapeake Bay region suffers persistent erosion. Numerous islands have disappeared, including many that boasted habitation. A sampling:

Poplar Island, in the upper Chesapeake Bay, covered more than 1,000 acres during the mid-18th century. President Franklin Roosevelt made it one of his retreats during the 1930s and 1940s. Crucial World War II strategy sessions were held there. Only five acres remained by 2000. (The Army Corps of Engineers is replenishing Poplar Island with muck dredged from Baltimore Harbor. The agency plans to create a wildlife refuge.)

Holland Island, Md., in the central Chesapeake Bay, had 300 residents during the early 20th century. It included a church, schoolhouse, post office and several shops. Only a few desolate acres are left.

Sharps Island, at the mouth of the Choptank River, consisted of 600 acres in the early 19th century but has been a sandbar for the past half-century. The island was home to a small farming and fishing community. All that remains is the decrepit Sharps Island Lighthouse, seemingly fated to disappear like its namesake.

A rising sea, powerful storms and a propensity to build along waters' edge will, no doubt, displace other settlements by the bay and Atlantic coast.

Watermen say that on a sunny day they can see tombstones through shallow water. Nobody lives on Hog Island anymore.

Special Collections, University of Maryland Libraries

The mayor's house in South Cape May, N.J., after the hurricane of 1936. Relentless erosion and repeated hurricanes claimed the borough.

1938

September

GREAT NEW ENGLAND HURRICANE

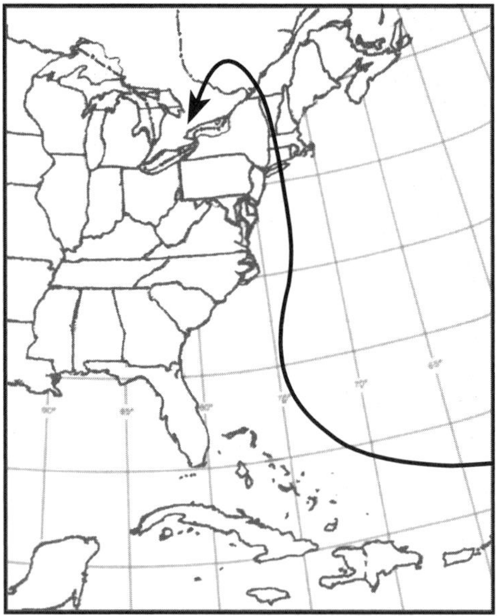

Denizens of the New Jersey shore knew that a monster prowled at sea. Towering waves churned by winds far greater than the gales lashing their homes gave clue to a menace targeting New England. On September 21, the hurricane burst with rare fury on an unsuspecting populace killing more than 600 people. It ranks as New England's deadliest natural disaster.

A day earlier the storm turned north, sparing Florida. Forecasters predicted it would remain offshore. The hurricane had another idea.

It traveled at an astonishing 60 mph, so fast that the media dubbed the whirl the "Long Island Express." New England hadn't experienced a major hurricane since 1869 and nothing like this since 1815.

The hurricane struck eastern Long Island, coming ashore about 50 miles east of New York City. Sustained winds blew at 120 mph. An avalanche of ocean smashed beaches, in the eye and east. The worst came from a breaker survivors described as a "tidal wave." According to the Weather Bureau:

"As the storm approached, approximately at right angles to the Long Island, Connecticut and Rhode Island shores just before mid-afternoon, it heaped up a storm-driven wave which overflowed great portions of the shore from Fire Island, off Long Island, well up to the heads of Narragansett and Buzzards Bays, into Gardiners Bay, and the mouths of the Thames and Connecticut Rivers. In several instances the wave destroyed the old shoreline by washing away the barrier beaches, which had captured salt ponds behind them.

"This wave was the most tragic factor of the storm. It destroyed thousands of shoreline properties of substantial as well as weaker structures, and upwards of seven hundred lives were lost. The railroad along the eastern Connecticut shore was wrecked, and in connection with railroad washouts from rains in Massachusetts, there was no rail transportation between New York and Boston for something like a week.

"As a general observation, the storm wave was approximately 14 feet above mean tide. Reports range from 12 to 25 feet above mean low water. The high water levels were reported as: Point Judith 18 feet, Fairhaven 25 feet, Pocasset 20 feet, and Nobska Point 15 feet. At Fall River 'the water came up rapidly in a great surge,' the crest being estimated as '18 feet above normal.'

"Reports of damage indicate 1,700 injured severely; 9,300 families suffered property losses; summer dwellings destroyed 7,000; other dwellings 1,900; boats destroyed 2,600; barns 2,400; and other types of buildings 7,400. The total loss expressed in dollars is probably more than three hundred million."

Beaches disappeared and homes crumbled when the storm wave struck. Inhabitants struggled for life. Providence, the capital of Rhode Island, and other towns along Narragansett Bay experienced unprecedented flooding as the bay funneled the onrushing sea.

Hurricane-force gusts carried hundreds of miles inland, as far north as the Canadian border.

At Providence, winds topped 95 mph before destroying the anemometer.

The Blue Hill Observatory near Boston (elevation 640 ft.) registered a sustained wind of 121 mph. The anemometer was not intended to measure gusts. "We took numerous readings and established a peak gust of 186 miles per hour, with a margin of error of 30 or 40 miles per hour," said observer John Conover.

New Hampshire had its most destructive windstorm. Gusts of 75-100 mph were commonplace. Many homes and businesses sustained minor to major wind-related damage.

Heavy rainfall deluged sections near the path of the hurricane. Flooding was disastrous in Connecticut, Vermont, New Hampshire and Massachusetts.

Lighter rain fell well east of the hurricane's track. Providence, for example, recorded just .10 during the hour of highest wind and only .17 for the entire storm.

Further south, coastal communities from North Carolina to Delaware sustained modest losses. Gusts peaked at near-hurricane force in some places. Gales extended about 50 miles inland.

The hurricane pounded the Jersey shore.

Atlantic City had a sustained wind of 61 mph, the highest in the state. A 300-foot section of the bridge connecting Brigantine Island and Atlantic City collapsed minutes after a passenger bus crossed.

H.N. Steele, commander of the Toms River Coast Guard station at Seaside Park, described the hurricane as the worst he'd seen since 1889. Foaming breakers were visible from three miles inland.

Boardwalks at Manasquan and Point Pleasant were splintered. "Never in the history of the shore had a storm done so much damage in such a record time," declared the *Ocean County Leader*.

The sea peaked with an enormous, 25-30 foot, greenish wave.

Long Branch had a top gust of 56 mph. The barometric pressure tumbled to 28.71 inches in nearby Sandy Hook as the hurricane passed about 60 miles offshore.

Gales swept the state. More than four inches of rain fell on most sections. This followed days of showers and resulted in notable flooding. The worst occurred along the Raritan River in central New Jersey.

Thousands of trees toppled. Essex County alone reported the loss of at least 2,000.

Despite nature's assault, New Jersey escaped the fate of its northern neighbors. At grievous cost, New England developed a storm-savvy population. That knowledge paid dividends as more hurricanes were on the way.

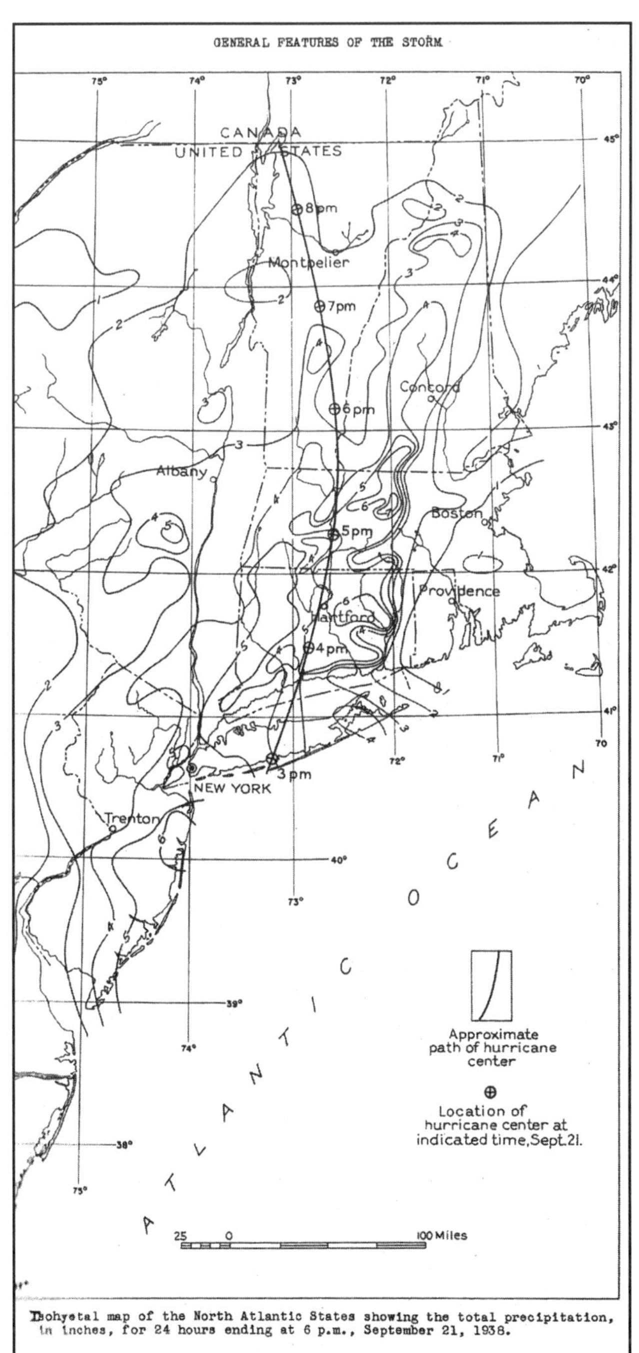

Isohyetal map of the North Atlantic States showing the total precipitation, in inches, for 24 hours ending at 6 p.m., September 21, 1938.

1939

August

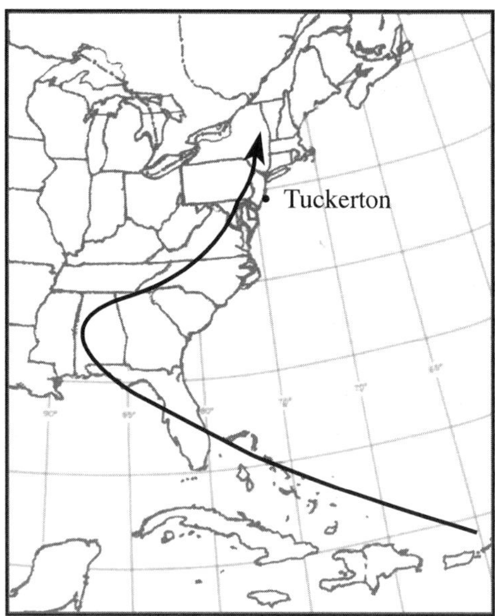

August 19-20. When the weather observer in Tuckerton, N.J., examined the rain gauge on August 20, he was amazed. Rainfall totaled 14.81 inches, New Jersey's new 24-hour rainfall record at an official weather station. Unofficial totals in the vicinity ranged as high as 18 inches.

The remnants of a hurricane that struck the Gulf Coast days earlier provided the deluge. The storm lingered over Alabama before tracking northeast.

Chatsworth, about 20 miles northwest of Tuckerton, reported rainfall of 13.50 inches. Undermined tracks derailed the *Blue Comet* near Chatsworth during the afternoon of the 19th. The train, traveling from Atlantic City to New York, careened into a cranberry bog, injuring 17 passengers.

Flooding plagued sections of southern New Jersey and northern Delaware. But excessive rainfall wasn't the only threat to the Mid-Atlantic. The hurricane spawned a deadly tornado along the western shore of the lower Chesapeake Bay during the early morning of August 19.

The twister gyrated north-northwest, tracking about 15 miles. Winds destroyed the post office at Fleeton, Va. The tornado spun through the fishing village of Reedville leaving uprooted trees, wrecked homes and downed power lines. A man drowned when his boat capsized in the Great Wicomico River.

It crossed the mouth of the Potomac River, continuing a rampage through eastern St. Mary's County, Md. Three people were injured in Scotland, a two-story house disintegrated at Dameron, and a woman died in the ruins of her home on St. Jerome's Creek.

***

After widespread drought and the great Midwestern dust storms of the early and middle 1930s, some pundits predicted a Sahara over large sections of the United States. By decade's end, they fretted about a potential Amazon, at least in New Jersey. The record-setting deluge of August 1939 was surpassed the following year. At that time, the New Jersey State Water Policy Commission opined, "This (rain) is comparable to the heavy rains of 1934, 1938, and that over a smaller area in 1939. Prior to 1934 no such heavy precipitation had occurred in South Jersey for at least 50 years and a change in climate appears to be taking place."[1]

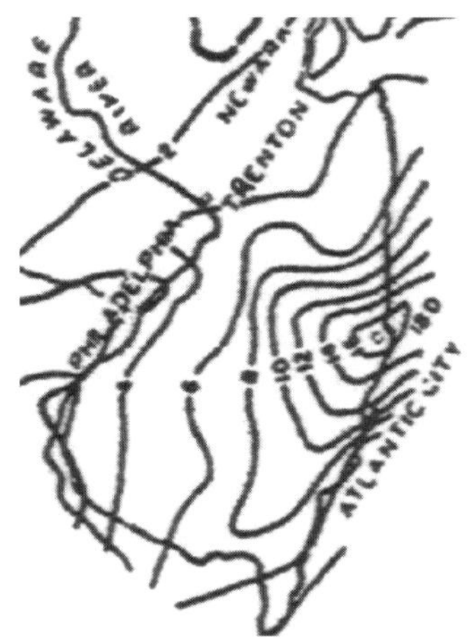

Rainfall Map
(Source: U.S. Weather Bureau)

[1] Climate tends to be cyclical. New Jersey again fell under the grip of a drought during the early to middle 1950s. The dry spell was broken by hurricanes Connie and Diane in 1955. By the early to middle 1960s, the state again suffered drought.

1940

August

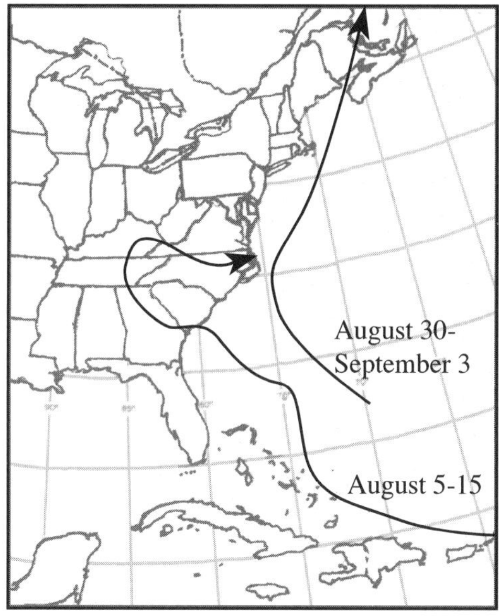

Hurricane-related flood events continued during 1940. August brought a disaster to Virginia. The following month opened with an incredible cloudburst in southwestern New Jersey.

From August 13-15, a hurricane carved a serpentine route through the Appalachians. Rainfall averaged 10 inches in northwestern North Carolina and southwestern Virginia. Record crests occurred along the Yadkin River in North Carolina, and the Clinch, New, Roanoke and Dan rivers in Virginia.

The southern tier of the Old Dominion experienced extensive flooding. Among the hardest-hit towns:

Altavista: The Roanoke River rose to 40.1 ft., exceeding a flood stage of 18 ft. (The rise was phenomenal—far above the next highest crest of 27.4 ft., which occurred in November 1985.)

Danville: The Dan River crested at 20.5 ft., its highest level in 50 years.

Farmville: The Buffalo and Appomattox rivers isolated the town's 3,000 residents. Water swept through homes and businesses. Farmville received 9.22 inches of rain on August 14-15.

Emporia/Petersburg/South Boston/Franklin: Emporia battled the Meherrin River while Petersburg struggled with the Appomattox. Emporia lost its water plant and over 100 families were displaced. All highways into North Carolina were closed between South Boston and Suffolk. At South Boston, the Dan River crested at 31.8 ft. (flood stage 25 ft.), its greatest on record to that time. A rare flood on the Blackwater River inundated downtown Franklin.

Galax: Hundreds of residents left as Chestnut Creek expanded to several times normal. Water rose to the roofs of houses. Boats did yeoman service. Landslides and the extensive loss of bridges blocked highways in the mountainous region. The state health department rushed in doctors to help immunize against typhoid fever.

Radford: Heavy rainfall upstream produced the town's worst flood. The New River rose to a record 36-ft. crest (flood stage 14 ft.). Several hundred people were driven from their homes.

Richmond: Virginia's capital endured a major flood. The James River crested at 23.3 ft. (flood stage 9 ft.).

Roanoke: More than 13 inches of rain fell on nearby mountains from August 14-17. Roanoke collected 9.45 inches. The Roanoke River rose to 18.3 ft. (flood stage 10 ft.), its highest level since 1907.

Waynesboro: Water reached to the windows of automobiles in the business district as the South River breached sandbag dikes. The river crested at 13.4 ft. (flood stage 9.5 ft.).

Rainfall totals in Virginia (Aug. 14-17): Clarksville 14.63", Kenbridge 12.75", Emporia 10.44", Bedford 9.64", Lynchburg 7.99", Martinsville 7.73", Richmond 7.63", Radford 6.33", Danville 5.83", Staunton 5.01", Charlottesville 5.01".

September

September 1. The day the dams failed in southwestern New Jersey. They faltered by the dozens—topped, bypassed and washed out. Rainfall lasting about eight hours totaled more than 22 inches.

A day earlier, severe thunderstorms raked Virginia, Maryland and Pennsylvania. A Pennsylvania Central Airlines DC-3 transport en route from Washington to Pittsburgh crashed near Lovettsville, Va. It was the deadliest commercial airplane disaster in United States aviation to that time; 25 people died, including U.S. Sen. Ernest Lundeen from Minnesota.

The weather caused flash flooding in Frederick, Md., about 30 miles northeast of Lovettsville. It was the city's worst inundation in decades.

Thunderstorms stalled on September 1, blocked by a hurricane tracking about 150 miles off the Mid-Atlantic coast. Shore areas remained in a nearly rain-free corridor sandwiched between downpours.

Precipitation on the central and northern Delmarva Peninsula totaled 2-4 inches. Rainfall in southwestern New Jersey bucketed down. The Soil Conservation Service gauge in Ewan recorded an unofficial state 24-hour rainfall record, 22.4 inches. [1]

The cloudburst centered on the New Jersey counties of Salem, Gloucester, Burlington, Camden and Cumberland. Rainfall averaged 12 inches. Much of it cascaded during eight hours beginning 2 a.m. on September 1. The towns of Wenonah, Mantua and Bridgeton collected 18, 15 and 10 ¾ inches, respectively. Four people drowned.

A report by the New Jersey State Water Policy Commission stated:

"The storm centered over the headwaters of those streams which drain west and south into the Delaware River. In this area there are many small dams at present not under the control of the State Water Policy Commission, and many old mill dams antedating state laws on stream regulation. A high proportion of these structures had either inadequate spillways, or were sadly in need of repair, with the result that when the high water reached them, the dam embankments failed.

"The failure of these smaller dams superimposed rapidly moving flood crests on the already swollen streams causing many of the larger dams downstream to fail in succession, producing an ever-increasing flood. Many of these larger dams also were out of repair or had spillways too small for this unprecedented flood, even without the failure of the smaller dams.

"The majority of the bridges, both railroad and highway, in the area had openings too small for the passage of these excessive stream flows. This resulted in increased flood heights above the structures and when the bridges, or more frequently, the fills adjacent to the bridges failed, the effects were similar to the breaking of the dams."

In addition, hurricane-driven tides on the Delaware Bay impeded the drainage of many waterways.

Ten dams failed along Oldmans, Salem and Alloways creeks. Dams were breached at Grenloch and Blackwater, near Camden, forcing out many residents. Water reached the rooftops of some homes.

Cohansey Creek rose 10 feet above normal. It destroyed three bridges at Bridgeton after a dam burst upstream at Seeleys Pond.

Workmen piled sandbags against Union Lake dam at Millville. The weakening structure threatened to unleash its contents on hundreds of homes.

Rancocas Creek spread ruin through sections of Mount Holly and Medford. A Medford fireman was treated for multiple bites after seeking refuge in a tree occupied by terrified rats.

Mantua Creek washed through 80 houses at Mantua.

So the flooding went throughout southwestern New Jersey.

[1] The Philadelphia Navy Yard—20 miles north of Ewan—received 4.10 inches. One can only imagine the magnitude of the disaster had Philadelphia received 22 inches of rain.

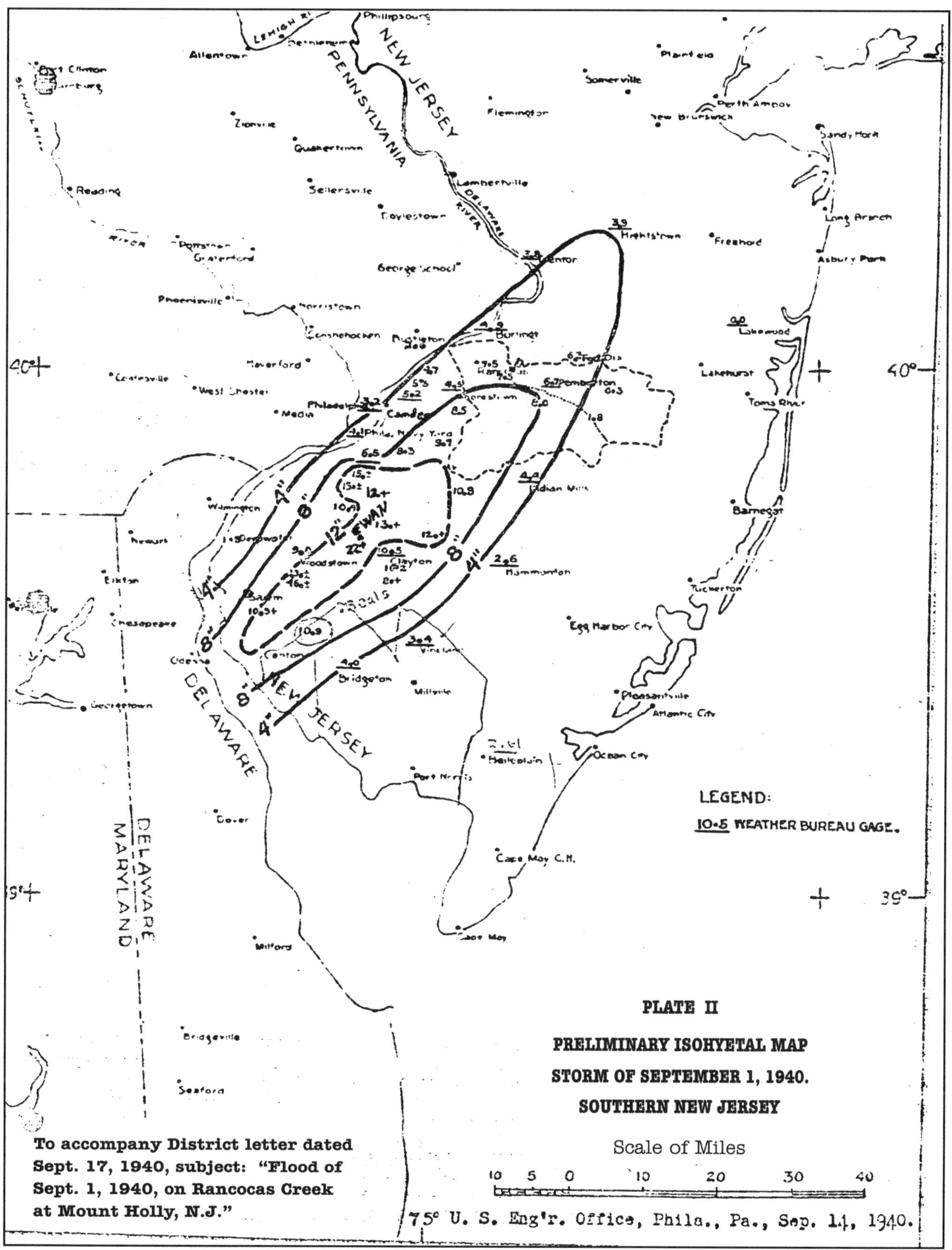

PLATE II

PRELIMINARY ISOHYETAL MAP
STORM OF SEPTEMBER 1, 1940.
SOUTHERN NEW JERSEY

To accompany District letter dated Sept. 17, 1940, subject: "Flood of Sept. 1, 1940, on Rancocas Creek at Mount Holly, N.J."

***

The Garden State is home to thousands of minor, often nameless, dams—the kind that failed in 1940. Normally they pose little risk and, as such, they're subject to less stringent safety and inspection regulations than major structures. But when small dams fail en masse, they magnify a flood disaster.[2]

Dams in southwestern New Jersey failed after 22 inches of rain drowned the area. The Mary Elmer Dam in Bridgeton was among the casualties.

[2] Deteriorating dams are a hazard in most states. The American Society of Civil Engineers gave the nation's dams a marginal grade of "D" in "The 2003 Progress Report for America's Infrastructure." The organization estimates that $10.1 billion is needed by 2015 to address all critical non-federal dams (structures that pose a risk to human life should they fail). The estimated costs for the Middle Atlantic States include (in millions): New Jersey $103.8; Virginia $147.2; Pennsylvania $646.2; Maryland $64.6; Delaware $3.7.

1942

October

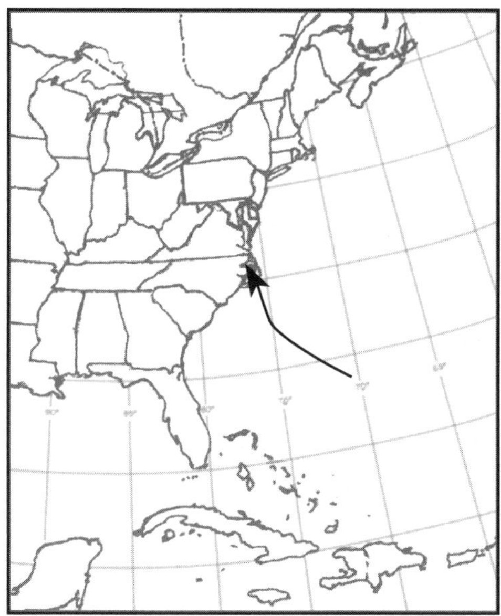

William Beck, a former mayor of Fredericksburg, Va., jokes about his family connection to the city's worst flood—the inundation of October 1942.

"My mother said that she decided to marry my father when she saw him in his little rowboat rescuing people from their second-story windows."

Imagine a river's greatest rise and add to it. That was the flood of 1942.

A tropical storm made landfall in North Carolina on October 12 before stalling and dissipating over Virginia. High pressure anchored in New England blocked its progress. Interaction of the two systems set up a moist flow resulting in frequent showers. The hardest-hit areas included central and northern Virginia, western Maryland and eastern West Virginia.

Five days of periodic downpours produced prolific flooding. Rainfall from October 13-17 totaled 8-16 inches throughout much of northern Virginia. Fredericksburg collected 11.02 inches during October 14-16, including 6.17 inches on the 16th. The city, indeed much of the countryside, faced a disaster.

"That's the flood everybody talks about," Beck said. "There are a lot of stories."

The Chatham Bridge in downtown Fredericksburg was completed in 1941, built at a height based on the highest floods of record (1889 and 1937). At nearly 40 feet above the Rappahannock River, it was thought untouchable. However, the river crested at 42.6 feet on October 17, exceeding an 18-ft. flood stage, drowning the bridge.

Highways became impassable. Rail traffic halted. Hundreds of families in Fredericksburg and neighboring Falmouth fled their homes. The Rappahannock River covered much of downtown Fredericksburg in mud.

Federal soldiers were called in to maintain order. They patrolled city streets for the first time since the Civil War.

Mary Washington College was quarantined. Students were restricted to campus until they could receive typhoid inoculations (as did thousands of residents). The Fredericksburg Rescue Squad evacuated about 90 women.

Blanche Moran lived on Hanover Street, beyond the reach of the Rappahannock River. Life during the flood was tough, but not too difficult to help a neighbor in need.

"We were high and dry but had no electricity for a while, and water was contaminated," Moran said. "We had to have typhoid shots, and we had to burn oil lamps. I remember a friend of my mother's lived down below the railroad and they were flooded that way from Hazel Run. She was so upset and nervous. She came to the house and my mother had a pot of soup on cooking. She said, 'Oh, that smells so good.' She stayed with us that night because we weren't flooded out and she had lost a lot of her clothing and furniture because her house had flooded. I remember years later she talked about (that night) and said, 'I never tasted anything so good in my life as that soup.' I said, 'It was just because you were upset and nervous. That's why.' "

Floodwaters breached a canal, which turned neighborhoods into lakes.

"People wondered how they could be flooded even though they were far from the river," said Gordon Shelton, a lifelong resident of Fredericksburg. "The canal acted as a conduit."

Water drained slowly as the flow clashed with a tributary below Fredericksburg, Hazel Run, and oncoming tides surging up the Rappahannock.

Shelton, then 17, remembers the flood's effects.

Historic Fredericksburg Foundation

The Chatham Bridge in Fredericksburg, Va., was built in 1941 and thought safe from flooding. The Rappahannock River proved the experts wrong.

Historic Fredericksburg Foundation

"It coated the world with mud," he said. "You'd go into a basement years later—I ran an electrical contracting business for 30 years—and there'd be dried mud all over the place. I suspect you'd find it today in some buildings.

"A lot of basements had to be pumped out. One man told me that he was sitting upstairs in front of a fire and heard knocking coming from the floor. He couldn't figure out what the heck was going on. He started to his basement but only went down two or three steps before reaching water. Firewood had floated to the ceiling and was making the noise.

"After the floodwaters went down, everywhere I looked I saw white. Downtown, on Sophia Street. Lime (used as a disinfectant). "

Raging water created other hazards. Fuel storage tanks floated on the Rappahannock and periodically exploded. Booming eruptions spewed massive plumes of fire. Smoke obscured day. The night blazed red. Police and military cordoned off part of Fredericksburg for fear flames would ignite adjacent neighborhoods.

Fires were contained without a holocaust. A special chemical squad, rushed by police escort from Norfolk, extinguished the blazes and kept damage to a minimum.

Flooding devastated much of northwestern Virginia. Big Meadows in Shenandoah National Park received 12.30 inches of rain during a 24-hour period on October 14-15 and about 19 inches for the entire storm. Front Royal, Va., reported 17.6 inches. A survey by the Weather Bureau indicated that the greatest total, 25 inches, fell six miles north of Front Royal.

Many communities along the Rappahannock, Shenandoah and Potomac rivers count the inundation of '42 among their worst. For decades, the event was simply known as, "The Flood."

The Shenandoah River crested at an unprecedented level. Millville, W.Va., recorded 32.40 ft. (flood stage 13.5 ft.). The Shenandoah reached a height of 50 feet at aptly named Riverton, Va., 28 ft. above flood stage and 12 ft. beyond the previous high water mark. Nearby Front Royal sustained tremendous damage.

Various tributaries, which under normal conditions scarcely deserved the term 'run' or 'creek,' carved paths of devastation. Harrisonburg, Va., for example, had large property losses when Blacks Run cut a course through the city.

At Cumberland, Md., the Potomac River left streets under 3 ½ feet of water. Downtown Hancock, Md., drew 8 feet. Near Williamsport, Md., the Potomac expanded to four miles in width—about 20 times normal. The Potomac River peaked at 17.7 ft. in Washington (flood stage 7 ft.), still the modern record.

The flood ranks among the Mid-Atlantic's big disasters. More than 60 years later it still holds records at many gauging sites along the Potomac, Shenandoah and Rappahannock rivers.

***

Big floods in 1889 and 1937 were Fredericksburg standards until 1942. Nothing has eclipsed the Flood of 1942 although Hurricane Agnes, in 1972, came close. Could Fredericksburg see worse?

Yes, says Beck. "There's been considerable land-clearing and development upstream. During recent years, we've seen an increase in the number of minor floods. It's only a matter of time before we have a flood greater than that of 1942."

Fredericksburg, like many older communities, is built along a waterway. Its location has been a blessing and a curse. Downtown is part of a floodplain. As such, the area is dangerously vulnerable. Although the city follows federal floodplain management guidelines, it has no major control projects. Home and business owners who can afford flood insurance may purchase a policy. However, 'protection' mainly consists of hoping the Big One never comes.

When hope clashes with recurring hurricane patterns, history usually prevails.

Tropical storm rainfall totals (Oct.13-17): **Maryland**—Frostburg 8.39", Cumberland 6.47", Baltimore 5.41", Frederick 5.41". **Virginia**—Riverton 16.79", Winchester 13.41", Fredericksburg 12.57", Luray 10.65", Manassas 8.34", Charlottesville 7.93", Vienna 7.66", Culpepper 6.96". **Washington, D.C.** 6.27".

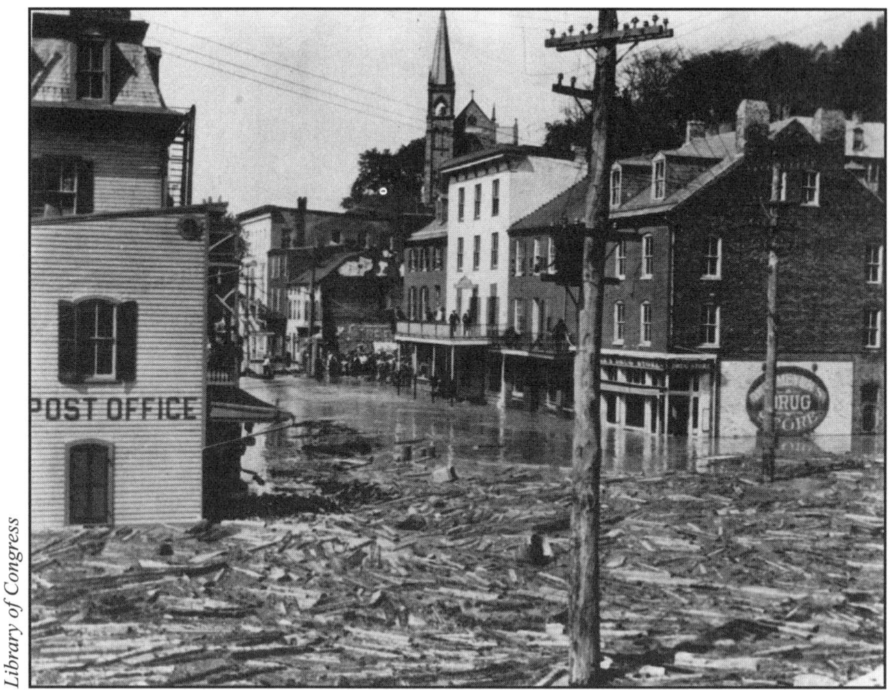

Library of Congress

Harpers Ferry, W. Va.

Copyright Washington Post; Reprinted by permission of the D.C. Public Library

Georgetown waterfront,Washington, D.C.

FREDERICKSBURG RESIDENT URGES FLOOD AWARENESS

Gordon Shelton

When Gordon Shelton stands next to an enlarged map of the Rappahannock River basin, when he launches into the cause and scope of the great flood of October 1942—and warns of a coming calamity—the Fredericksburg native speaks from experience.

Shelton's family escaped the worst, but he remembers a ravaged business district and residential neighborhoods. He remembers the hardship that followed. Retired after 24 years on the city council, including three terms as vice-mayor, Shelton recognizes Fredericksburg's increased vulnerability after years of development. The small town of his youth is now a bedroom community to Washington, with population growth to match.

The Army Corps of Engineers conducted a study of the Rappahannock basin during the 1960s. It predicted that in the future the river could exceed the 1942 rise by 10-15 feet. "And that report is stale," Shelton warns.

A flood equaling the rise of 1942 would destroy more property today. It would also deliver a blow to Fredericksburg's commercial battle with strip malls that have sprouted outside town, near Interstate 95.

Decades ago, the Corps of Engineers proposed a project that would have reduced potential flooding in Fredericksburg. That plan met opposition and died. Shelton regrets its demise.

Years later, he sponsored a resolution requiring property owners to inform buyers of the flood history of their parcel. It was defeated, a decision that rankles him.

"Not disclosing that information benefits a seller, but how about the poor soul that's buying it?" Shelton asks. "Do you think real estate agents are going to tell them? Do you think they're going to parade pictures in front of them?"

Shelton's given more talks on the flood than he cares to count. For years, he exhibited photographs. Not everyone appreciated those efforts—like when the pictures were displayed in a downtown store.

"I had a bunch of people come to me and give me a hard time," Shelton said. "They said, 'What are you trying to do here?'

"I'd tell them, 'This is River City. It was River City when I was born in '25 and it's still River City. You may be able to do a few things and satisfy yourself to some degree. But the bottom line is that nature's going to win."

Shelton's flood awareness effort has been frustrating.

"Every so often I'll find someone who wants to do something and they'll pursue it for a while, then lose interest," he said. "I've had an uphill struggle, but the big flood is coming again. We can close our eyes all we want, but it's coming."

He wonders who will carry on his struggle. Who will remember the Flood of '42?

Memories of friends and neighbors numbed, confused, frightened, despairing.

"You had terrible sights," Shelton recalls. "There was much misery, much misery."

Photograph by Gordon Shelton

Fredericksburg.

1944

September

THE GREAT ATLANTIC HURRICANE

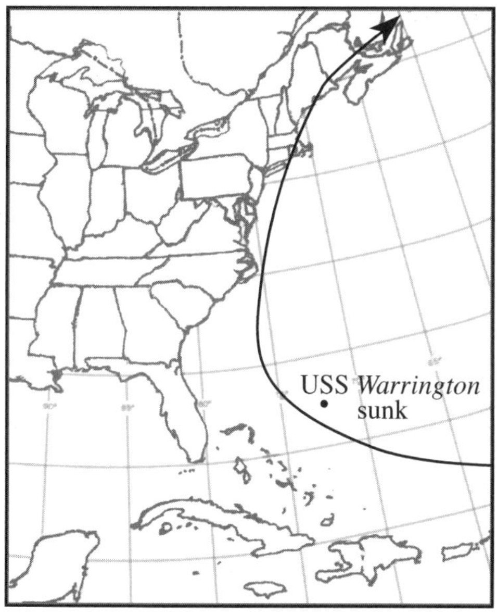

The Great Atlantic Hurricane. That's what the Weather Bureau named the menace approaching the East Coast during September 1944. Forecasters wanted the public to know that this was no ordinary hurricane.

The monster roiled the seas off the Eastern Seaboard from September 12-15. It capsized the destroyer USS *Warrington*, with the loss of 248 men, and a minesweeper, *YMS-409*. It sank two Coast Guard cutters, the *Bedloe* and *Jackson,* off North Carolina's Outer Banks. A total of 47 crewmen drowned. The ships' 31 survivors were rescued after more than 50 harrowing hours on rafts.

The hurricane also destroyed the *Vineyard Sound Lightship* off Cape Cod. Its 12-member crew sent a last garbled message: "Our anchor has holed us." Divers later discovered that one of the vessel's anchors had ripped through the hull.

On September 14, the hurricane swept by the Mid-Atlantic coast and into New England. Cape Hatteras had a record low barometric pressure of 27.97 inches as the eye passed offshore. Sustained winds of 100 mph pounded the North Carolina Outer Banks.

Patrick Michaels, Virginia's state climatologist, believes, "given the intensity of the hurricane, and assuming that the center was around 15 miles out to sea (as it passed Hatteras), a lowest pressure of 27.50 inches would seem reasonable, making the storm a high Category 4 or low 5. If this storm had been some 50 to 100 miles further west, it would likely have been the most severe (Mid-Atlantic) storm of the last 200 years."

If the storm had traveled 50 miles further west, it would have left unforgettable devastation from eastern North Carolina to Canada. Cities along its route—Norfolk and New York—would have experienced unprecedented winds. As it was, Cape Henry, Va., clocked 134 mph—a record for the Middle Atlantic region—with an estimated gust of 150 mph.[1]

The Weather Bureau office in Norfolk reported:

"The Atlantic hurricane of mid-September reached Norfolk on the 14th. The lowest pressure recorded at the city office was 29.11 inches and occurred at 11:45 a.m. EST. The maximum (5 minute) wind velocity was 56 mph from the NW between 11:50 a.m. and 11:55 a.m., and the fastest mile recorded was at the rate of 73 miles per hour. No gust recorder is located at this office, but it is estimated that wind gusts as high as 90 mph occurred at frequent intervals."

---

[1] Cape Henry's 134 mph wind was unique to that observation site. It might have been caused by "spin-up vortices," a concentrated area of significantly higher winds contained within a hurricane eyewall. Generally ranging in width from several feet to a few hundred yards, the phenomenon was identified by the tornado expert, Theodore Fujita. Fujita inspected damage patterns left by Hurricane Andrew in 1992 and observed pockets of intense destruction surrounded by areas of considerably less damage.

The hurricane passed about 40 miles off shore. Anemometers in coastal Virginia registered sustained winds of minimal hurricane force, well below that of Cape Henry. The anemometer at Cape Henry is located 90 feet above the ground, while most weather stations set their wind-recording devices at about one-third that height. The difference in wind speed seems the result of higher elevation and additional factors.

Gales and heavy rain extended west to the Blue Ridge Mountains. Despite the storm's huge circulation, damage in Virginia remained slight except along the coast.

Rehoboth Beach Historical Society

The *Thomas Tracy* in Rehoboth Beach, Del.

The whirl moved briskly toward Long Island. Boardwalks were demolished at Virginia Beach, in Ocean City, Md., and at Delaware's coastal resorts. The freighter *Thomas Tracy* grounded at Rehoboth Beach.

Forecasters warned residents of the Delmarva coast to expect a storm wave. None appeared. It struck further north. A dome of water surged out of the eye and leapt on shore.

At Cape May, N.J., the assault of wind and sea peaked with what newspapers described as a "40-foot tidal wave." The rush of water came during the late afternoon, carrying away large sections of the boardwalk and Convention Hall. Tom Hand recalls:

"The hurricane lasted from approximately 10 a.m. to 5 p.m. Short-lived, but for sheer force plus the storm surge that September 14, it was incredible.

New Jersey State Archives, Dept. of State

Cape May lost its boardwalk (left).

"I was on the second floor of our home on Stockton Avenue, one block from the ocean, and it was a sight I'll never forget. The boardwalk smashed like matchsticks. Destruction of homes. Destruction of the fishing pier.

"The Great Atlantic Hurricane of 1944: 'Only' several hours, but incredibly destructive. By 6 p.m. it was a beautiful late summer day. Amazing."

A sudden surge invaded the lower Delaware Bay. It struck fishing villages, wrecking homes and carrying workboats into woodland and meadows.

Minutes of terror doomed South Cape May on the lower tip of the Garden State. Mountainous surf wrecked most buildings. The borough, established in 1894, disbanded months after the storm.

Three massive waves accompanied the hurricane along the Jersey shore. More than 100 bungalows washed away on the five-mile strand between Sea Isle City and Strathmere. Avalon lost a municipal pier and boardwalk. Margate's boardwalk became kindling.

Two hours of destructive winds in Atlantic City peaked with gusts greater than 100 mph. The barometer slumped to 28.73 inches.

Huge waves struck the resort around 6 p.m. as the edge of the eye passed 35 miles away. They destroyed or mangled most of the Boardwalk. They smashed shops, hotels and houses. Cars were strewn like toys. Heavy debris, including entire sections of the Boardwalk, floated for blocks. The oncoming sea wrecked the Garden and Heinz piers.

Two people died and 121 were injured. Governor Walter Edge sent an urgent telegram to the state's congressional delegation imploring federal aid for the stricken resort. It said, in part, "The entire Atlantic City Boardwalk is almost completely demolished so it is impossible to provide facilities for the thousands of patients in the armed forces convalescing there. Other communities have suffered comparable damage."

Robert Levy will never forget that day.

"I've been through quite a few storms, but that was the worst," said Levy. He left work and drove toward his home, located a block from the ocean near Absecon Inlet. A powerful gust sheared the canvas roof off his Ford convertible. Concerned for the safety of his wife and daughter, he negotiated the final six blocks by walking, wading and swimming.

"It was blowing like hell. I watched a tree fall and take down power lines," Levy said. "They fell about

30 feet from me. I thought the wires were live and I was done for. It scared the heck out of me."

He arrived home and found his family had taken refuge in the upper level of the apartment building.

"There was a 25-foot section of boardwalk complete with a railing on the front steps," Levy said. "I ended up with about two feet of water in my apartment. There were sand crabs and seaweed everywhere. What a mess!

New Jersey State Archives, Dept. of State

Harvey Cedars.

"We had just bought a living room set and saved it by propping the furniture up on kitchen chairs and tables. But we lost bedding and almost everything else. It was tough."

On Long Beach Island, north of Atlantic City, the sea swept completely across portions of the southern section. It then withdrew, causing additional damage. Five people drowned. The ocean damaged or destroyed hundreds of homes.

The north Jersey shore suffered one of its worst storms. The savage Atlantic destroyed dozens of summer homes at East Keansburg and Port Monmouth on Raritan Bay. Villages from Sea Girt to Long Branch lost boardwalks, houses and shops.

The *New York Times* reported that in Asbury Park, "A series of three tidal waves swept over the beachfront, carrying everything in front of them. The waves were said to be nearly fifty feet high. A 50-foot section of the boardwalk in Asbury Park was lifted by the heavy seas and dumped a block and a half inland, with railings and light standards still attached."

An assessment of the disaster by the *Shore and Beach Journal*:

"It appears that New Jersey received the major share of damage along the North Atlantic Coast and it will be some months before normal conditions return.

"Observers reported that three 'large' waves came ashore, then quickly receded. Scientists will be studying the reports for years to come, but it seems that the most practical opinion was voiced by a porter at the Union Station in Atlantic City, who said: 'Only God could have pulled the ocean in here so far and dragged it out so fast.' "

The Jersey shore was whipped by sustained winds of 75-90 mph, with higher gusts. Western New Jersey had peak gusts of 50-60 mph. New York City had a record 99-mph gust at the weather office.[2]

Rainfall from September 12-15 totaled 11.40 inches at Rahway, N.J., and 11.62 inches in neighboring Elizabeth. However, most sections of the Garden State measured less than 5 inches.

The hurricane made landfall on eastern Long Island. It weakened prior to dashing ashore, arriving as a strong Category 2. The center reached the coast near low tide. Damage was considerably less than during the hurricane of 1938. Lessons learned from the earlier event and heeded warnings kept casualties remarkably low. Although 390 people died in the hurricane, only 46 perished on land.

***

Technological developments provided meteorologists an incisive look into a hurricane's anatomy.

Radar operators at Fort Monmouth and Lakehurst Naval Station, N.J., and the Massachusetts Institute of Technology Radiation Laboratory observed circular spiraling cloud bands. The spirals caused a stir; forecasters viewed the structure of a hurricane as never before. They recognized radar as a tool for storm observation and research.

The hurricane marked the beginning of organized air reconnaissance missions into tropical cyclones. A new unit, the forerunner of today's Hurricane Hunters, began operation.

***

Atlantic City's Garden Pier is a sobering reminder of the day the big waves crashed ashore. Rusting steel girders and crumbling concrete pilings supported a

[2] The anemometer was located at a height of 450 feet above street level. (Hurricane winds increase about 10 mph every 100 feet above the ground.)

1,000-foot section that straddled land and sea. The site once featured the B.F. Keith Theatre and a large ballroom. Noted performers such as comedian Ray Bolger, crooner Rudy Vallee and magician Harry Houdini dazzled audiences. Now the legacy of wind and wave holds sway.

During October 2003 the mayor of Atlantic City, Lorenzo Langford, proposed that the pier be rebuilt and serve as the location for a museum and educational facility on man-made terrorism, the "National Homeland Technology Center." An ironic twist to a long-standing exhibit on natural terrorism.

THE GREAT ATLANTIC HURRICANE SINKS A NAVY DESTROYER

247 Men Lost in Shark-infested Waters

National Archives

The *Warrington* off Virginia weeks before the hurricane.

The Navy destroyer USS *Warrington* challenged the Japanese and Germans, earning two battle stars, but the Great Atlantic Hurricane proved its deadliest nemesis. On September 13, 1944, en route to the Caribbean, about 400 miles east of Jacksonville, Fla., the *Warrington* sailed into what was, at least, a Category 3 hurricane. Its final hours are described in the *Dictionary of American Naval Fighting Ships*:

"Two days out of Norfolk, along the Florida coast, the (*Hyades* and *Warrington*) encountered heavy weather. In the afternoon, *Warrington* received word that she was steaming directly into a hurricane. Later that evening, the storm forced the destroyer to heave to while *Hyades* continued on her way alone. Keeping wind and sea on her port bow, *Warrington* rode relatively well through most of the night. Wind and seas, however, continued to build during the early morning hours of the 13th. *Warrington* began to lose headway and, as a result, started to ship water through the vents to her engineering spaces.

"The water rushing into her vents caused a loss of electrical power which set off a chain reaction. Her main engines lost power, and her steering engine and mechanism went out.

She wallowed there in the trough of the swells—continuing to ship water. She regained headway briefly and turned upwind, while her radiomen desperately, but fruitlessly, tried to raise the *Hyades*. Finally, she resorted to a plain-language distress call to any ship or shore station. By noon on the 13th, it was apparent that *Warrington*'s crewmen could not win the struggle to save their ship. By 1250, her crew had left *Warrington*; and she went down almost immediately. A prolonged search by (several Navy vessels) rescued only 5 officers and 68 men of the destroyer's 20 officers and 301 men. *Warrington*'s name was struck from the Navy list on 23 September 1944."

For two agonizing days, no other vessel knew what had happened. Most men left the *Warrington* alive. During the next 48 hours, most died.

Those who fled the ship endured a nightmare. Sailors drowned or succumbed to injuries. Some died from saltwater poisoning. A few were lost to hungry sharks. In *The Dragon's Breath, Hurricane At Sea*, author Robert Dawes, Jr., told of the attacks:

"For some unknown reason, the sharks seem to have been fairly selective. Some survivors never saw any, but others say there were many around. At least two survivors claim they drove curious sharks away with blows of their fists (perhaps the sharks were small). On the other hand, Torpedoman Lawrence Allphin saw a shark attack a man next to him on a raft. He states that he saw a ten or twelve-foot shark approaching his raft, so he drew up his legs, and, as the shark went by, he kicked it with all his strength. The shark, undeterred by the kick, went by and seized the man next to Allphin at about waist level. It took him down so fast he made no outcry, but only looked terribly surprised and somewhat indignant."

On Friday, September 15, the *Hyades,* searching for the *Warrington*, discovered a raft carrying eight men. Only then did the Navy learn of the *Warrington*'s fate.

A Navy court of inquiry found human error partially to blame. The main factor, however, was that the *Warrington* sailed into the most violent sector of a vicious hurricane.

The lesson didn't travel far. In December 1944, a Pacific typhoon provided a deadlier encounter. The Third Fleet sailed into the teeth of the storm while about 500 miles east of the Philippines. Once again, sailors perished by drowning, exposure and shark attacks. This time, the death toll reached 790. This time, three destroyers were lost.

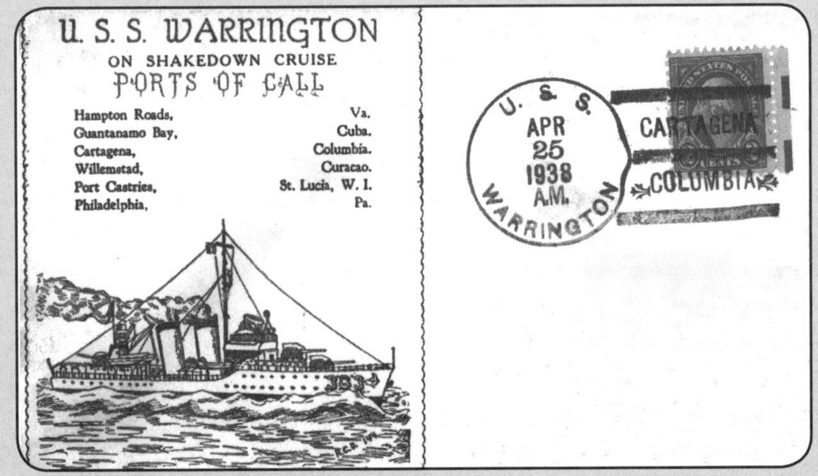

The course taken during the hurricane was eerily similar to the Warrington's shakedown cruise.

A VIEW FROM THE SKY...

AIRMEN MAKE PIONEERING FLIGHT INTO A HURRICANE

Floyd Wood, Harry Wexler (later the Weather Bureau's director of research) and Frank Record flew out of Bolling Field in Washington to study the hurricane of September 1944. While previous flights had reconnoitered the monster, they undertook the first research mission into a hurricane. The men encountered the storm's edge over the lower Chesapeake Bay. Wexler described its appearance as a "sharp black wall of rain sloping westward with height."

Wood flew at 3,000 feet, near the base of dense clouds. "The waves in the Chesapeake Bay were enormous," he said. "A freighter plowing through the bay was being swept from bow to stern by huge waves which at times appeared to engulf the whole vessel at once." And, Wood surmised, if the aircraft had been forced down, "neither life rafts, 'Mae Wests,' or any other life-saving device would have saved us from drowning."

They flew out over the Atlantic and through the eyewall. "At 5,000 feet," said Wood, "I cut the power. The clouds thinned and through a thin mist we could see the sun. We were just at the edge of the hurricane's eye."

At a press conference, Wood described the turbulence near the eye as "just like going up in an elevator." Winds aloft were lighter than expected. The pilot believed that his effort had proven that a well-built plane could survive a mighty hurricane. "I have no hesitation about going out again," he concluded.

An article in the September 27, 1944, issue of *War Times* provided flight details:

OFFICERS FLY INTO HURRICANE TO STUDY WEATHER THEORIES

None the worse for their experience, a trio of officers of the Weather Division, Army Air Force, knocked previous theories concerning hurricanes into a cocked hat when they deliberately flew a Douglas Havoc from Bolling Field into the midst of last week's roaring hurricane out in the Atlantic.

Col. Floyd B. Wood, Deputy Chief of the Air Forces Weather Division; Maj. Harry Wexler, research meteorologist, and Lieut. Frank Record, also of the Weather Division, were the trio that flew out to the big storm to "see what they could see."

They saw plenty, according to Major Wexler, who told a War Times reporter they experienced a big surprise right off the bat! It seems up until now, those who know about such things, always had the idea there was considerable turbulence associated with the swirling winds of a hurricane. The trio flew into the storm at right angles, having obtained their bearings at Langley Field, and fully expected to be bounced all over the sky. Actually, however, they found the winds to be "somewhat stable."

In addition, they found that instead of encountering strong "up winds" as expected, actually it was just the opposite, as Col. Wood, the pilot, had to "gun" the engine quite a bit to maintain his altitude of 3,000 feet.

As they drew nearer the center of the storm, or, as the weathermen call it, the "eye," instead of finding "down winds" always believed to be the case heretofore, they found themselves kicked upstairs suddenly to 5,000 feet! This was all very disconcerting.

Maj. Wexler was graduated from Massachusetts Institute of Technology in 1934, where he specialized in the study of weather, or meteorology. He is one of the few meteorologists trained in the "Norway technique." This system was devised by Norway when cut off from the outside world during the World War.

Was the flight a planned affair? Well, not exactly. It was almost on the spur of the moment, and anyway, it was Col. Wood's day off!

It was amusing about Lieut. Record's selection. When news of the intended flight got around the weather office, the clamor to go along as the third passenger was so great that it was decided by drawing straws among the other officers of the section. Lieut. Record won.

"We probably would have found more turbulent weather had we gone on through the center of the storm and got into the other side," Wood said. "Usually, and we noted it to be true in this case, thunderstorms accompany the southeast section of such storms. Had we encountered that, we would probably have been bounced around quite a bit. We found one theory to be correct, too, and that was near the center of the hurricane all was apparent calm, and we could see the sun through the clouds." (Wood) added that there were winds 125 mph encountered, and some gusts probably higher, but there was no way to tell that exactly. Visibility was nil most of the time, and besides, it was "raining like hell."

Col. Wood stated he had flown through many thunderstorms with turbulence much greater than that experienced with this flight, but he fully intended to turn about if too strong turbulence was felt. The lack of crosscurrents, which, in thunderstorms can tear the wings off a plane, was quite a surprise to him, too.

The Colonel has been flying for the Army since 1929, when he won his wings as an aviation cadet. He is an overseas veteran of the Southern Pacific area, and has been Deputy Chief of the Weather Division since his return to the States.

Maj. Wexler entered the Department of Commerce as weather expert following his graduation from M.I.T. He was loaned to the University of Chicago later for a tour of duty as a teacher. Then he taught from October 1940, to November 1941, at one of the five schools opened for civilian and army students over the country. Following Pearl Harbor he donned the uniform and taught meteorology at the largest school of its kind at Grand Rapids, Michigan, until September 1943, when he was assigned to his present post as Research Executive AAF.Hq., Weather Division.

A VIEW FROM THE BEACH...

EYEWITNESS TO A "TIDAL WAVE" AT ATLANTIC CITY

Allen "Boo" Pergament

The afternoon of September 14, 1944, began like a holiday for Allen "Boo" Pergament. He and his classmates left school at noon after being told to prepare for a hurricane.

Pergament lived on the ground floor in an apartment building that overlooked the northern section of the Atlantic City Boardwalk. Those were heady days for a boy of 12. The military took up residence in the city's hotels. Even Convention Hall, home to the Miss America pageant, had become "Camp Boardwalk." Something always seemed to be happening. The prospect of a hurricane seemed tame by comparison.

"They told us there was a hurricane on the way, but it didn't mean anything," said Pergament. "We had experienced northeast storms and were not afraid of them. Besides, it was a gorgeous day with a blue sky and not a cloud in sight."

That changed by late afternoon. Dark clouds raced in, the surf grew dangerous and the wind howled. Water seeped into the apartment. Pergament, his mother and an elderly neighbor began picking objects off the floor.

"When I heard my dad (and brother) who were upstairs at the time call down," said Pergament, "I opened the front door and ran up the steps with everyone following me," he said. "The water outside was about two feet deep. Had we stayed there much longer, who knows what might have happened."

Occupants of the three-story building retreated to the top floor. By 6 p.m., "Everyone huddled together and tried to stay occupied," Pergament said. "The men played cards and the women fretted."

Then came the stuff of nightmares.

"There was a girl my age," Pergament said. "The young lady and I went to a back room to look out a window, which we were warned not to do. After clearing the window—it was damp with condensation—we peered out and looked toward a lighthouse a short distance away. This was about a 75-foot-high lighthouse, a steel-framed structure that had a red and green light constantly revolving around. It sat on a concrete platform on a small jetty on the ocean side of the Boardwalk.

"Beyond the lighthouse—I would estimate about 100 feet further out—I vividly remember seeing this huge mountain of water that appeared to be about three-quarters up to the top of the lighthouse (about 50-60 feet). The wave came crashing down with a thunderous movement and reached the Boardwalk in a second. It picked the entire Boardwalk off its concrete supports as far as I could see in either direction, tossed it over backwards, and crushed it like you'd crush toothpicks.

"I didn't watch any longer. I was so awfully frightened by that sight, seeing the power of that huge mountain of water doing such devastation, that I jumped from the window, got into a corner of the room and stood frozen until my father pulled me away from there.

"During the time we remained in the building the water swept through the lower floor and through the street. It reached the second floor. The house shook with every wave. You'd have a lull and then another wave would hit. The place would vibrate. We didn't know the severity of what was coming, but it seemed like a wave would eventually make the house fall down."

The building survived but the family lost their possessions, returning to a home layered with several feet of sand. The storm also destroyed a furnished apartment they'd rented out. Pergament found a heavy cedar chest filled with soggy clothes on his bed and a 30-gallon water heater— "I have no idea where that came from!"

The youth lived with relatives for several months before moving into the third-floor apartment that served as shelter during the hurricane.

"In all my life, nothing has given me more respect for the power of wind and water than that storm," said the lifelong resident of the Jersey shore, who now lives in Margate.

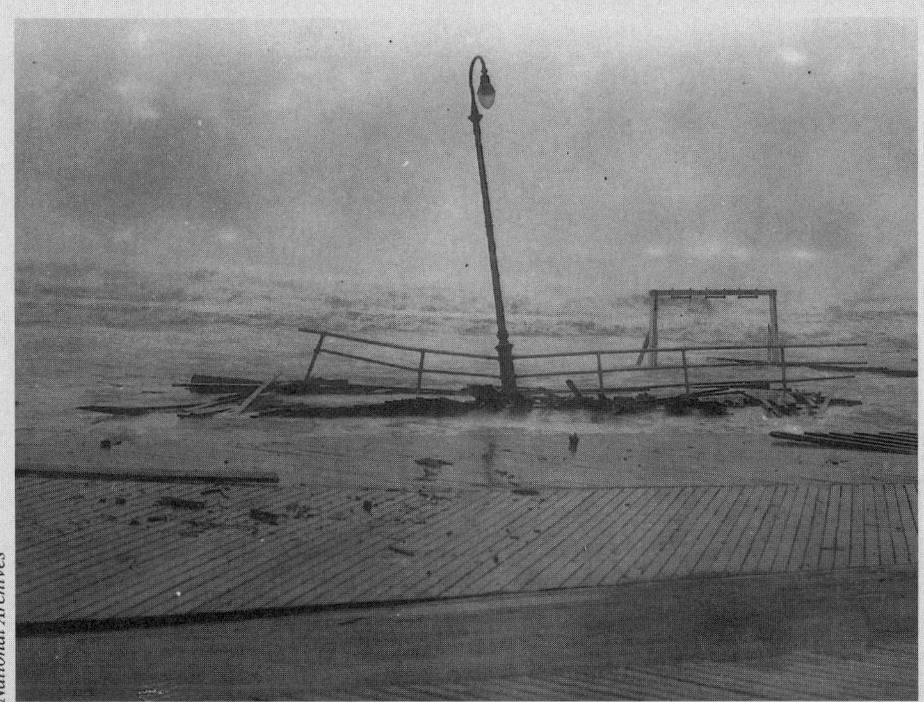

National Archives

The ocean engulfed Atlantic City's beach shortly before the big waves.

Collection of Allen Pergament

"(The wave) picked the entire Boardwalk off its concrete supports as far as I could see in either direction, tossed it over backwards, and crushed it like you'd crush toothpicks." — Allen "Boo" Pergament

National Archives

Within minutes, a series of huge waves left massive destruction along the Atlantic City waterfront.

ATLANTIC CITY, NEW JERSEY
SEPTEMBER 14, 1944

Collection of Allen Pergament

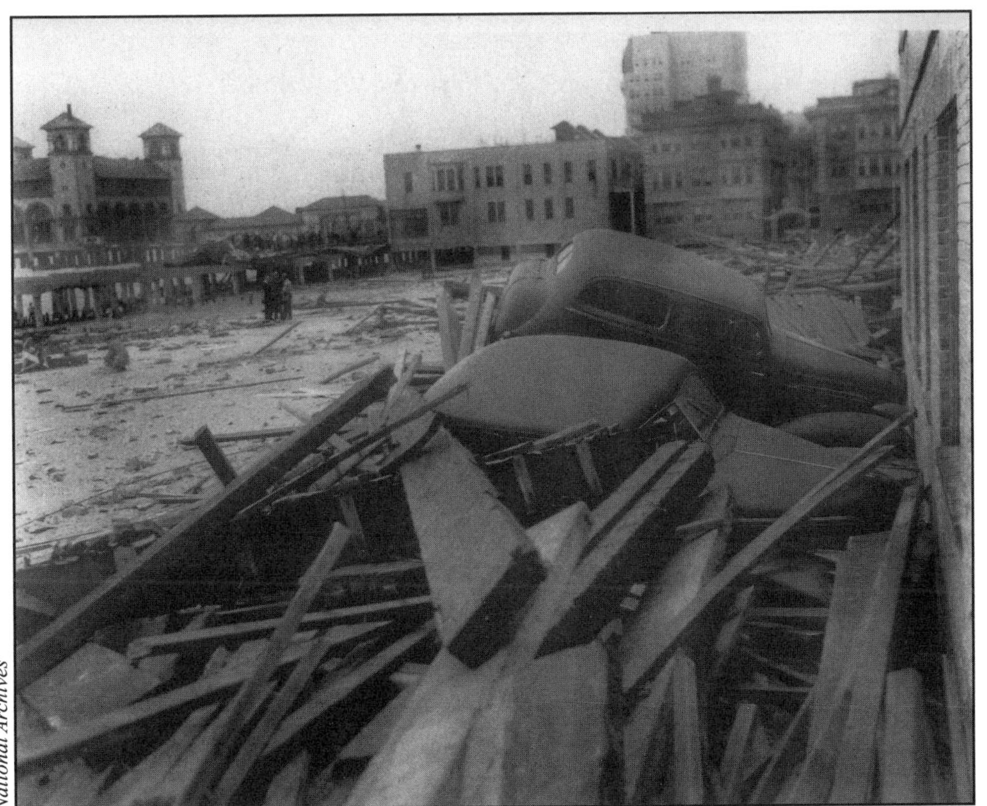

National Archives

National Archives

National Archives

National Archives

National Archives

The hurricane destroyed Heinz Pier.

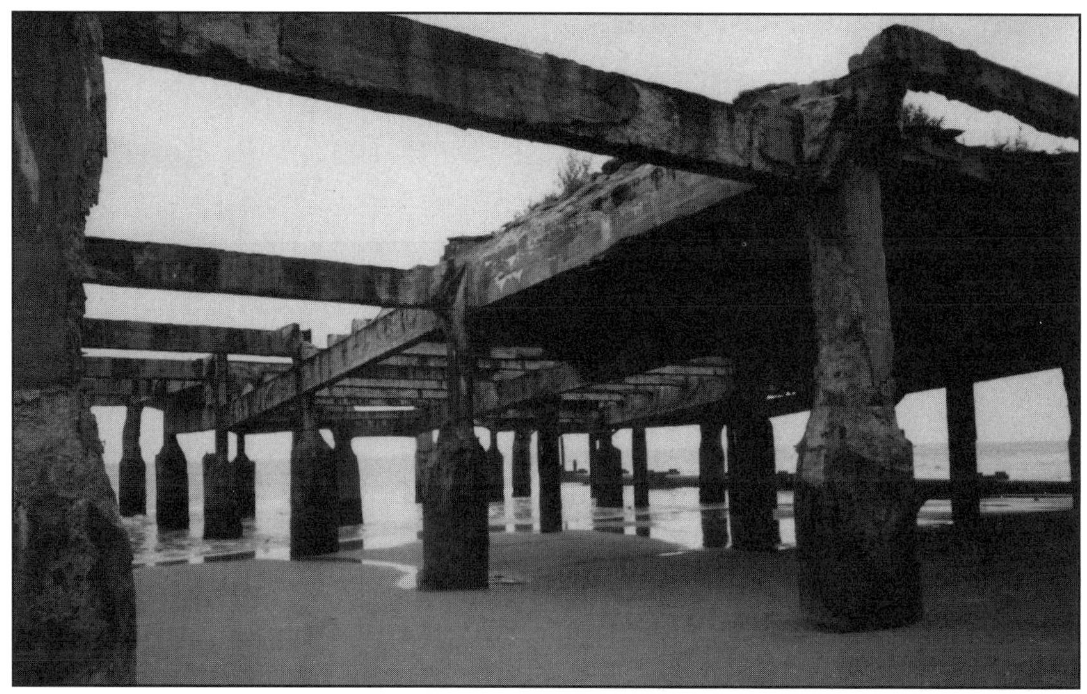

The ghostly ruins of the Garden Pier remain a sobering reminder of an unforgettable day.

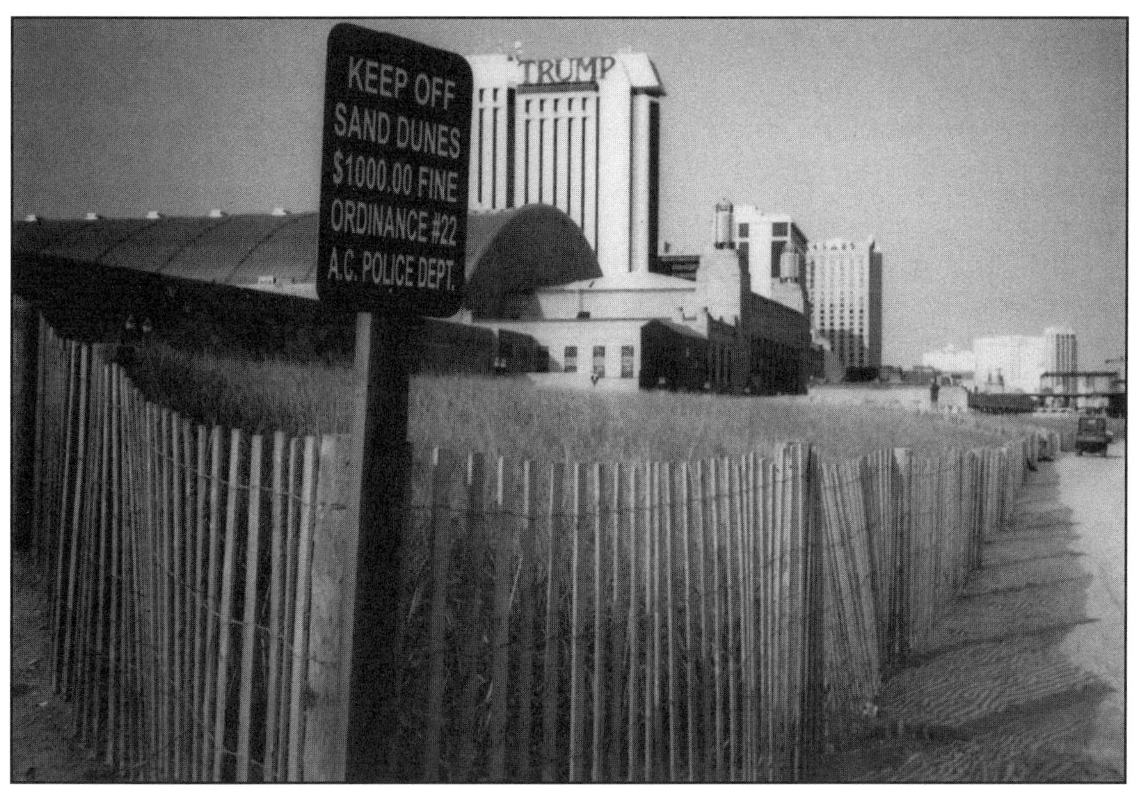

Atlantic City today. Dune protection is taken seriously and *will* be tested.

1945/1949/1952/1953

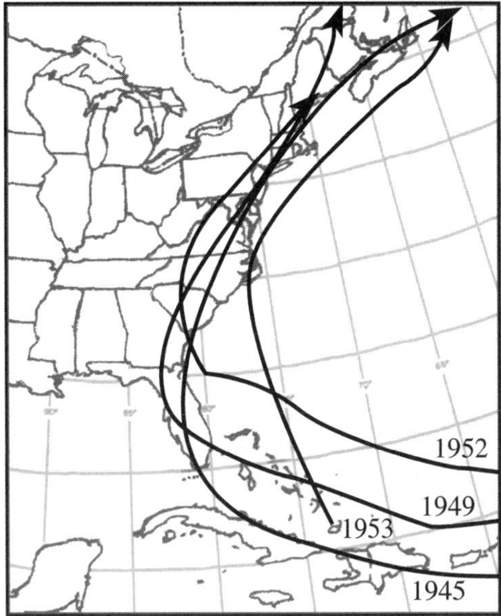

Hurricanes during 1945, 1949, 1952 and 1953 tracked through the Middle Atlantic states as medium-strength remnant systems. Each followed a classic trail with typical effects, bringing several inches of rain and gale-force winds to areas east of the Appalachian Mountains.

***

On September 15, 1945, a Category 4 hurricane struck southern Florida. It followed an inland route up the East Coast. Remnants reached Virginia on the 18th and brought minor to moderate flooding. The system contributed to the state's second wettest September since 1871, exceeded only by September 1944.

***

A Category 3 hurricane came ashore at Palm Beach, Fla., on August 26, 1949. On August 28 it spawned a tornado in southeastern Virginia that wrecked several homes in Wakefield. Gales caused minor but widespread damage to crops, trees and power lines in eastern sections of the Mid-Atlantic.

This was the second tropical cyclone to visit the Old Dominion during 1949. In June, a depression tracked from the Georgia coast into central Virginia before dissipating. A moist flow against the eastern slopes of the Blue Ridge generated downpours over the southern Shenandoah Valley and Potomac Highlands. More than 10 inches of rain fell in three days, with up to 8 inches in 24 hours on June 17-18. The heaviest showers pelted Augusta, Rockingham and Rockbridge counties causing flash flooding and mudslides.

***

Hurricane Able made landfall in South Carolina early on August 31, 1952, eventually churning through Virginia, Maryland and Pennsylvania.

Winds gusted to 63 mph in Washington, D.C. Rainfall totaled 3.49 inches. Flash flooding caused severe losses in neighboring sections of Maryland, particularly in Bladensburg and Brentwood.

Shortly before midnight on August 31, a tornado followed an intermittent track through the southern and northwestern suburbs of Washington. The twister descended on Franconia, Va., destroying one house and damaging several others. Downed trees and splintered trunks marked several other touchdowns as the whirlwind skipped through Fairfax and Arlington counties, Va. Violent winds damaged several homes in Potomac, Md.

Able caused a pre-dawn flash flood in historic Ellicott City, Md., on September 1. A cloudburst and subsequent stream blockage detoured Tiber Creek through Main Street. Water invaded shops and homes. About two-dozen cars were carried away and demolished. It was the town's worst flood since 1869.

***

Hurricanes were frequent visitors to the Mid-Atlantic during the 1950s. In 1953, Barbara took its turn.

The hurricane developed over the Bahamas on August 11-12, and came ashore in North Carolina on August 13. Barbara brought gusts of 80-90 mph to the Outer Banks. Gusts of 75 to 85 mph whipped the Virginia coast. Norfolk Airport had a sustained wind of 63 mph and a peak gust of 76 mph. Portsmouth recorded 9.30 inches of rain on August 13-14 and Norfolk gathered 6.28 inches.

Two deaths were associated with the hurricane, including a man in Wrightsville Beach, N.C., who drowned when swept off a pier, and a Chesapeake, Va., police officer, Talbot Barrow, who was electrocuted by a submerged power line.

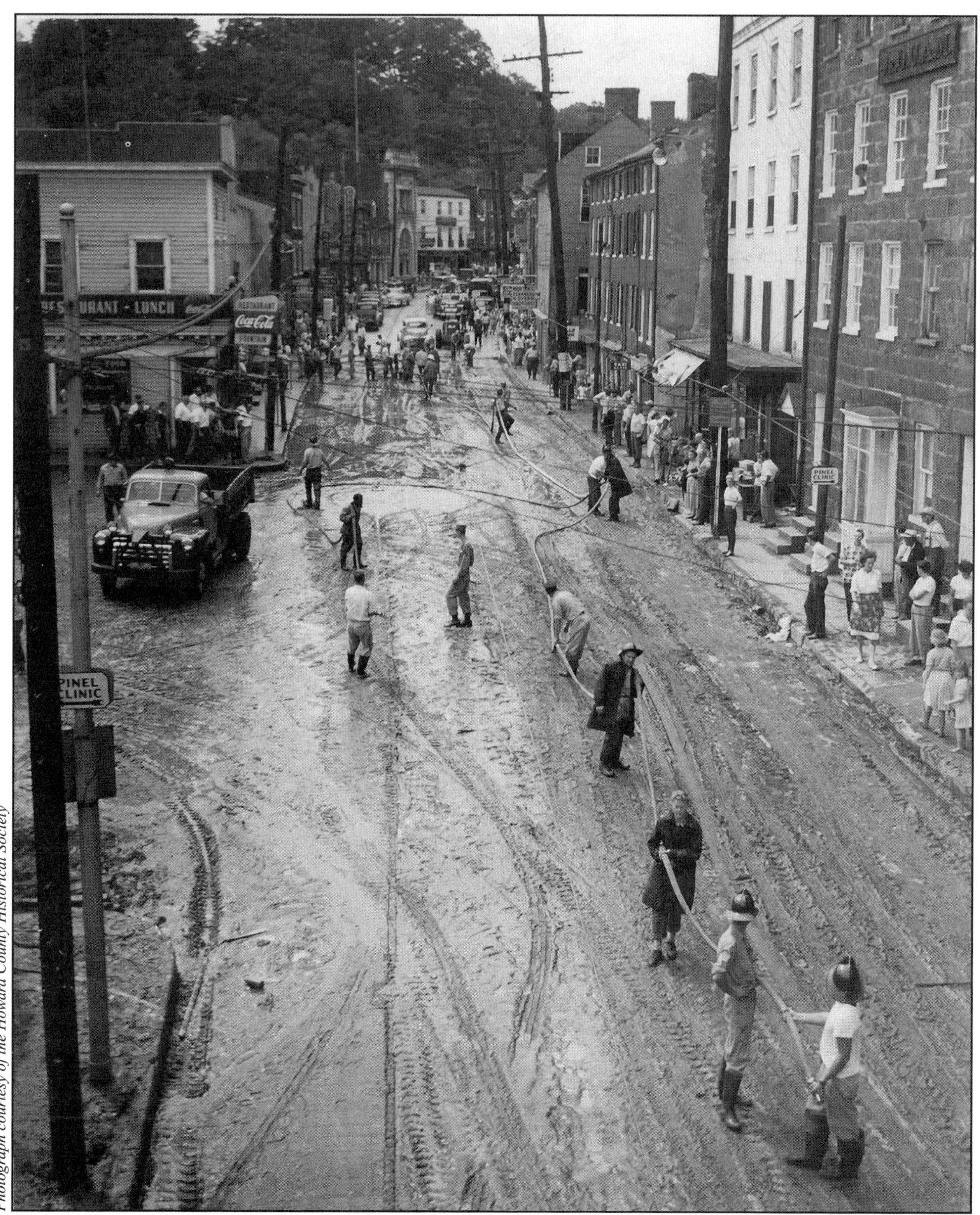

Photograph courtesy of the Howard County Historical Society

Ellicott City, Md., firemen hose down the streets after the flash flood of September 1, 1952.

1954

October

HAZEL

Grady Norton, who Floridians dubbed "Mr. Hurricane," was told by his doctor to take it easy. But during October 1954 Hurricane Hazel barreled through the eastern Caribbean. Norton, in charge of the hurricane forecast office in Miami, couldn't take it easy. He couldn't ignore the big one, putting in long hours as Hazel strengthened.

During the previous two decades Norton made Miami the hub for hurricane prediction. He is considered the first, albeit unofficial, director of the National Hurricane Center. Colleagues were amazed at his uncanny ability to figure out where storms would go. This intuition was shared with the public through radio and print.

Accuracy and a folksy style won him fans. His obsession killed him.

Norton had a stroke and died during the evening of October 9. Hours later, Hazel veered north.

NORTH CAROLINA

"We have looked for your house on the beach but never did find it and believe that it may no longer exist. If we have the site located correctly the house must be completely gone."

— Letter from an insurance claims adjuster

Hazel powered ashore on the South Carolina-North Carolina border at 9 a.m. on October 15. Sustained winds roared to 140 mph, gusts to 160 mph. The barometer dived to 27.70 inches, making Hazel a strong Category 4 hurricane.

At Long Beach, N.C., near landfall, the hurricane destroyed 352 of 357 buildings. At Robinson Beach, all 72 cottages were lost. Hazel wrecked 138 out of 150 shops and dwellings at Holden Beach.

After killing nearly 1,000 Haitians Hazel continued the count, leaving 19 dead in the Carolinas. The hurricane claimed 80 lives in the United States.

Among the debris littering North Carolina beaches were green coconuts, pieces of bamboo and large tropical clams weighing up to eight pounds. A beachcomber found a mahogany bowl. Upon closer examination he noticed the inscription, "Made in Haiti."

VIRGINIA

The Fredericksburg city council thought it found a solution to the terrible drought plaguing the area. At a special session on the morning of October 15, 1954, officials unanimously passed the following resolution:

"Whereas, the water supply of the City of Fredericksburg is critically low and a condition has arisen that imperils the health, welfare, trade, commerce and industries of the City and its inhabitants;

"Now, therefore, be it resolved that the Council appropriate $3,500.00 for the employment of W.E. Howell Associates Inc., for cloud seeding operations.

"Be it further resolved that the City Manager with consent and advice of the Water Committee of the Council hereby is authorized to enter into a contract with W.E. Howell Associates Inc., for cloud seeding operations."

"I've heard people joke about that," said former Fredericksburg mayor William Beck. "When we have a drought, someone will say, 'Let's get a rainmaker like they did before Hurricane Hazel.' "

That night, more than 10 inches of rain fell upstream in the Rappahannock River basin. Fredericksburg declared the drought emergency ended.

***

Hazel's gusty passage through the Old Dominion took less than four hours but left memories lasting a lifetime.

Gusts of the now extratropical storm exceeded hurricane force throughout the eastern half of Virginia. The Red Cross estimated that 17,000 homes in the state received severe wind-related damage.

From Emporia to Crewe in south-central Virginia (a distance of 50 miles), nearly every tobacco barn or stripping shed blew down. One woman was killed near Emporia when a warehouse wall collapsed. The front of the Greenville County Courthouse needed extensive repairs after a department store's roof catapulted into it.

Norfolk had a top sustained wind of 78 mph, with a peak gust estimated at over 100 mph—the maximum limit of the anemometer. (When installed, nobody thought a greater capability would be needed!) Gusts occasionally exceeded 100 mph between 2:45 p.m. and 4:30 p.m. Only a trace of rain fell.

Langley Air Force Base caught a gust of 96 mph before its anemometer failed. Virginia Beach clocked 85 mph. Gusts closer to Hazel's path topped out at 100-115 mph.

Suffolk recorded the state's highest gust on a reliable instrument, 108 mph, even as Hazel tracked 100 miles west. The blow demolished a large Planters Peanut warehouse.

William Barnes of Accomack County and J.G. Raiford of Southhampton County died when the roofs of their chicken houses blew off as they attempted to secure them.

Hazel overturned two tractor-trailer trucks near Charlottesville. Winds gusted to 80 mph in Gordonsville, and the barometer bottomed at 28.74 inches as the storm center passed about 20 miles to the east. At Blackstone, about 50 miles southwest of Richmond, the barometer tumbled to 28.71 inches. Winds toppled Radio WKLV's 150-foot transmission tower.

Richmond clocked a sustained wind of 68 mph and a gust of 79 mph. The barometer sank to a record low 28.75 inches. More than 50 houses lost roofs. Plate glass windows, assorted debris and trees littered downtown.

Lynchburg, about 40 miles west of Hazel's center, registered a peak gust of 56 mph and 4.98 inches of rain. Outlying areas reported gusts of 65-70 mph.

Rain softened the ground, enabling gales to bring down thousands of trees. Orchards in the Shenandoah Valley were swept clean, an involuntary apple harvest. Power outages caused large losses for turkey growers and others dependent on electricity.

The hurricane's huge winds, massive circulation and inland track churned up Chesapeake Bay region flooding that rivaled the hurricane of August 1933. Harry Rollins of Colonial Beach, Va., still marvels at the rise along the lower Potomac River.

"Hazel took my brother's boat and floated it a block-and-a-half leaving it in the middle of a highway," Rollins said. "My father's boat was tied to a pear tree about eight feet above the normal river level. She drew about three or four feet of water!"

Edna Edmondson drove from college in North Carolina to Colonial Beach. She saw plenty of Hazel's work along the way. But the worst awaited journey's end.

"Downtown looked like a disaster area, with piers destroyed, the beach eroded and the boardwalk washed away," she recalled. "There were lots of trees down and houses damaged, with shingles lying all over the place. Everyone seemed kind of shocked. They couldn't believe what happened."

Gaming brought Colonial Beach prosperity after World War II. Slots were illegal in the Old Dominion but lawful in Maryland. Casino piers were built over the Potomac River, part of Maryland by right of colonial charter, conveniently extending the vice to Virginians. Colonial Beach was touted as "Las Vegas on the Potomac."

Now, the storm threatened the casinos. Julian Caruthers, 20, spent the day driving around town in his "almost-new" 1953 Chevy, assisting residents trying to save their property. He watched the destruction of Colonial Beach's waterfront even as he aided the owner of the Jackpot Casino.

Julian Caruthers circa Hurricane Hazel

"I was helping board up the back windows when a big wave hit," said Caruthers. "The water came over our heads, soaking us. The facility survived but with a lot of damage."

Hazel consumed the Little Steel Amusement Pier and its casino. Employees attempted to salvage slot machines. The devices couldn't be legally carried into Virginia. Workers rigged a pulley system and saved nearly all the equipment by hauling it to a stronger, sturdier pier.

Proceeds were carried into Virginia. With banks closed, protection of the cash became paramount. Caruthers recalled that an employee, Sonny Lemons, "sat in a pickup truck with a shotgun guarding the money they took off the pier. There must have been $10,000."

On a neighboring pier, the staff of the Little Reno casino stacked boxes of beer and whisky for hasty transport and sent cash registers to storage. The Little Reno, which boasted the largest neon "R" in the United States and 400 slot machines, was at the mercy of the storm.

"If the wind hadn't shifted, the river might have destroyed it," Caruthers said.

The Weather Bureau detailed losses along inland tidal waterways of Virginia and Maryland:

"Marine damage ran high. Crab potters were almost put out of business with losses as high as 80-percent of their pots. A second and also costly effect developed as a result of losses of pound net equipment. Oyster beds in the rivers were seriously damaged by being covered with silt or carried away and the industry generally forced to rely largely on shell stock from the small, undamaged, areas.

"In addition to the sinking of the tug 'Indian,' there were many small craft sunk or driven ashore. Piers were demolished and private docks swept away in the Tidewater rivers."

Hazel affected the entire state. Areas to the west of the hurricane's track saw less wind but extensive flash flooding. Rainfall along the Blue Ridge tallied 5-10 inches.

Richard McClintock hasn't forgotten the torrential downpours and tremendous winds.

"My parents chose the day of Hazel to drive from Charlottesville (Va.) to Charlotte (N.C.)," he said. "There were trees falling everywhere. We had a Ford station wagon with wooden side panels—a 'woody.' I remember the rain coming into the car—not through the windows but through the wood paneling!"

WASHINGTON, D.C.

Hazel targeted the nation's capital with record force. National Airport clocked a sustained wind of 78 mph and a gust of 98 mph. Weather observers scrambled to safety after a broadside shattered an office window. Tremendous winds were the hurricane's outstanding feature.

The storm provided 1.73 inches of rain. However, only .06 inches fell during the height of the storm, between 4 p.m. and 6 p.m. The barometer plunged to 28.80 inches.

Extreme weather inspired a lifetime of meteorological interest for many people, including Keith Allen. He watched wide-eyed as nature turned terror.

"I saw a large dumpster blown over and nearly fall on a man as he scrambled to get out of the way," said Allen, who now coordinates the Verizon telephone weather recording for the Washington metropolitan area. "I saw a woman thrown down by the wind and taken away in an ambulance.

"Hazel didn't have much rain, but boy did the wind howl. You could feel it shake the apartment building.

"When it was over, Washington looked like a war zone. Trees down and debris everywhere. Electricity was off for two or three days. I think the utility company said it was the largest power outage in its history."

The loss of various utilities created inconvenience and more. Wendy Garner recalled the plight of her parents.

"My dad and mom, Frank and Ruth Mittleman, had just bought a mom and pop business at the corner of Georgia Avenue and Kennedy Street called Kennedy Korner," Garner said. "It was one of the traditional long narrow buildings with a counter and grill in the middle, groceries and deli in the back, and newspapers and magazines in the front. My parents spent everything they had to purchase the store. Hazel hit a week or two after they opened, and there was a grill full of food when the power went off. It nearly did them in, but they worked hard and managed to recover."

MARYLAND

Hazel's exceptional forward speed spread destructive winds hundreds of miles inland. Hurricane-force winds punished eastern and central sections of Maryland. Terrific gusts turned deadly.

Wade Bloodsworth was killed near Salisbury when crushed by windblown debris. Howard Ward died when a brick wall blew down on him while inspecting his Salisbury skating rink. Near Denton, Henry Blazejak, Jr., and his mother, Emma, perished when the chicken house roof they were attempting to secure blew away.

Wind gusts of 80-100 mph destroyed countless chicken houses. Hazel devastated the poultry industry, an economic mainstay of the Eastern Shore.

About one-third of the state lost electricity, with the Eastern Shore hardest hit. Trees blew into wires. Utility poles were leveled by gusts. High winds and sparse rain caused salt spray to accumulate on the insulators of power lines. Current arced across the insulators at a Vienna, Md., substation, triggering short-circuits that darkened thousands of homes.

A quirk of the storm: An empty boxcar took an eight-mile wind-powered journey from Sudlersville to Millington before derailing. It rolled through Millington at an estimated 35 mph.

John Swaine Jr., a cooperative weather observer from Royal Oak, on Maryland's Eastern Shore, wrote: "The hurricane on the 15th blew down many trees and many chicken houses and a few barns. It also started moving roofs on houses. Salt water covered many fields as the tide came about five feet above normal. Wind reached 108 mph at Oxford and 104 mph at Easton. Both readings taken on an anemometer."

And on Swaine's farm: "We had a low-lying area where the water (from the Chesapeake Bay) sat for some time. Crops wouldn't grow there for years."

Gusts of more than 100 mph swept Southern Maryland. Patuxent River Air Station recorded the state's highest hurricane-related gust, 112 mph. The following accounts from St. Mary's County in Southern Maryland attest to Hazel's fury:

Floyd Abell (Hollywood): "My father worked for the Highway Department. When he got home he said, 'It's getting rough out there, trees and wires down all over the place.' This was a big, strong guy who would never admit to being afraid. But he was. I saw fear in his eyes."

Frank Davis (La Plata): "I worked as a lineman for the telephone company when Hazel came through.

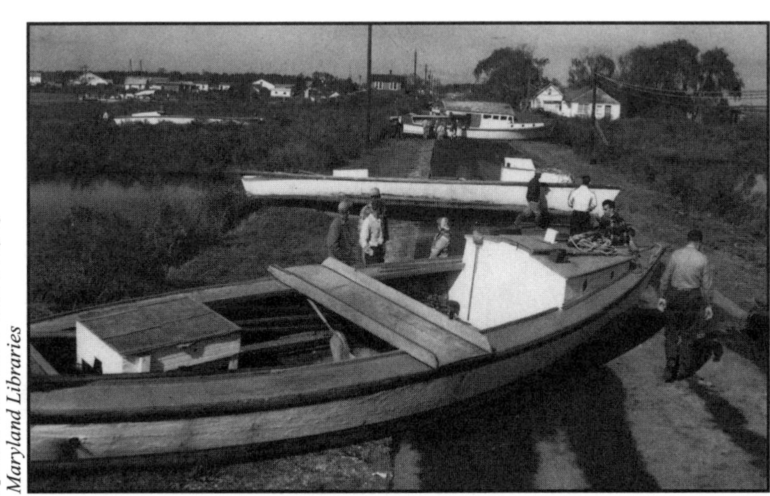

Special Collections University of Maryland Libraries

Kent Island, Md.

That day I was climbing poles (in La Plata) to test the lines. Everything was swaying—not a good feeling. I was thinking, 'I'm going to get killed if I stay up here.' I got down and stayed down. The next morning those same poles were lying in the road."

Ruth Hill (Leonardtown): "I remember the winds. They were absolutely devastating. Just to see the trees blow down... One of our neighbors lost a barn and the wind damaged the shingles on our house. Being a child, it seemed all the more powerful to me."

Hazel wrote the last chapter to Tolson's Hotel at Piney Point, an age-old landmark converted to rental units after World War II. Gusts in excess of 100 mph blasted the building, turning it to shambles.

Julius Tolson, son of the owner, was a student at the University of Maryland. Shortly after the hurricane he telephoned his father and asked how the property fared.

"Hazel scalped us," the elder Tolson said, without giving details.

When Julius returned home, he found the roof of the former hotel completely torn off. Also lost: two guest cottages and most trees. A powerful storm surge on the Potomac River left the waterfront strewn with debris.

Hazel collapsed about 250 tobacco barns in St. Mary's County. In neighboring Charles County, 96 barns were destroyed or seriously damaged within an eight-mile radius of Hughesville. Calvert County lost 100 barns.

Winds gusted to 90 mph in Annapolis. The Naval Academy lost the *Vamarie*, a noted 72-foot racing ketch.

There were losses that couldn't be measured monetarily. Hazel claimed prized trees, venerable sentinels, local landmarks.

Two-thirds of the 350-year-old "Liberty Tree" was blown down on the St. Johns College campus in Annapolis. Under the tulip poplar's shading branches, patriots had listened to firebrands espouse a break from Britain during the tumultuous days of 1775.

The nation's largest basket oak, a 400-year-old giant, fell at St. Paul's Church in Kent County, on the Maryland Eastern Shore. In adjacent Queen Anne's County, the wind snapped Maryland's tallest loblolly pine, a 98-foot champion. The state's loftiest ailanthus toppled in Talbot County.

Heavy rainfall caused extensive flash flooding in western Maryland. More than 300 residents of Kitzmiller, on the upper Potomac River, fled their homes. Oakland, in Garrett County, had a rare flood when Wilson Creek spilled over its banks.

A U.S. Geological Survey report underscored stark contrasts—dangerously low reservoirs followed by prodigious flooding.

"Floods, record high at some stations in western Maryland with less than 10 years of data and exceeded only by those of March 1924 in the upper reaches of the Potomac River, occurred as a result of the passage of hurricane 'Hazel' and accompanying rainfall of more than 5 inches in 12 hours."

DELAWARE

Delaware caught little rain, but what wind!

Wilmington measured a gust of 98 mph even as Hazel tracked 100 miles to the west. Rainfall totaled .27 inch.

Gusts up to 72 mph tore part of the roof off a hotel and damaged other buildings in Rehoboth Beach. Lewes clocked a gust of 75 mph before the anemometer blew away. The National Guard Armory in Dover was demolished by high winds. Utility companies estimated that 80 percent of their customers lost power.

Five people perished in Delaware, including two men in the Dover area. John Hullneck died when a chicken house collapsed. George Haggerty was crushed to death when wind demolished a cinderblock garage

The *Delaware State News* (Dover) on Hazel: "It was a harrowing, horrible experience. It was nature on a rampage—unleashing all its terrible might, making every human cringe in helplessness. There was nothing that could halt the frightful devastation. It was something you will never forget—and something you don't want to ever happen again."

NEW JERSEY

Hazel was the third hurricane to affect the state in 1954.

Hurricane Carol caused minor to moderate damage along the shore while en route to New England during August. There it killed 60 people, injured more than 1,000, and caused about $460 million in damage. Hurricane Edna provided a glancing blow to the Garden State in mid-September but, like Carol, saved its worst for New England.

Hazel, on the other hand, wrought considerable mischief in the Garden State. Winds felled trees and power lines. Gusts of hurricane or near-hurricane force caused widespread, mostly minor, structural damage. Millville, in rural southwestern New Jersey, had a state high gust of 86 mph. In downtown Bridgeton, winds sheared the roof off an office building, hurling it 200 feet. Farmers received little drought relief as rainfall in the state generally amounted to less than an inch.

Hazel assisted a group of Somerville homebuyers in central New Jersey. They claimed that their nearly finished houses were poorly constructed. The builder argued otherwise. Winds settled the issue, taking the roof off a finished model and leaving its sides sagging.

PENNSYLVANIA

The Weather Bureau's assessment of Hazel in eastern Pennsylvania:

"Major damage was spotty, but more or less general. Rail traffic was delayed or halted by downed trees, wires and poles. Many highways were blocked by fallen trees and downed wires. Ships and small craft were torn loose from their moorings in the Delaware River. Wind damage could have been greater from falling trees, but for the fact that the ground below the surface layer was still fairly dry and firm when the winds were strongest, thus providing better anchorage for the root systems."

Peak gusts included: Philadelphia International Airport 94 mph, Reading 86 mph, Allentown 82 mph, Harrisburg 80 mph.

Winds aloft were considerably higher than those on the ground, a characteristic of hurricanes. This posed a hazard for lofty transmission towers. Station WIBG went off the air when a pair of 250-foot aerials collapsed near Norristown.

The *Doylestown Daily Intelligencer's* staff produced a commemorative 150th anniversary edition the old-fashioned way. Newsmen worked by candlelight and kerosene lamps. Their effort maintained a perfect 150-year record of publication.

Winds made sport of television aerials throughout eastern Pennsylvania, sent slate and shingles flying, shattered windows, toppled chimneys—and occasionally launched a roof.

James Weber helped tie a neighbor's roof down, but it still took flight. The Lancaster County resident remembers "slate flying everywhere" and having to lean into the wind to walk. He rigged up a "crude wind instrument" only to see it blow away. Weber made the following notation in his weather log:

"The worst hurricane ever to hit Lancaster County. The center moved up the Susquehanna River Valley around 7 PM Fri., Oct. 15. Between 6 + 8 PM sustained winds of 60 to 70 mph were recorded. Peak gusts of 85 mph were reached. During that period the barometer fell rapidly to 28.98 inches."

Record 80-degree temperatures preceding Hazel gave way to autumn chill. Many sections of Pennsylvania had frost on the morning of October 17. Residents shivered in darkened homes as they waited for restoration of electricity.

Areas east of Hazel received little rainfall. Philadelphia, for example, only had .43 inches. Torrential rain fell to the west. Flooding inundated the Allegheny and Monongahela basins and 13 people drowned.

The storm dumped 4.6 inches in Uniontown, sending Coal Lick Run and Redstone Creek sweeping into the municipality. Destructive flooding ravaged Turtle Creek, Butler, Zelienople and Harmony. West Newton, Connellsville and Confluence watched the Youghiogheny River top the benchmark flood of March 1936. Somerset County in southwestern Pennsylvania received up to 7 inches of rain. Five people died in flash flooding.

***

Since 1933, hurricanes had spared Pennsylvania. Starting with Hazel, a trio of destructive storms struck within 10 months. And for the third time in 76 years (1878, 1896, 1954), a tropical cyclone tore through eastern Pennsylvania bringing an extended swath of hurricane-force winds.

NEW YORK

The Weather Bureau office in New York City reported a gust of 113 mph, breaking the previous mark of 99 mph set during the Great Atlantic Hurricane of 1944.[1] LaGuardia Airport had a peak gust of 66 mph.

[1] The anemometer was located 450 feet above street level (compared to a standard height of about 30 feet).

Hazel embraced the entire state. Buffalo attained a gust of 83 mph. Syracuse Airport reported a gust of 80 mph. Broome County Airport (elevation 590 ft.) near Binghamton had 94 mph. Winds toppled a 491-foot television tower south of Elmira.

CANADA

The storm raced into Canada at 50 mph. Moisture from Lake Ontario fueled prodigious downpours. Within hours, more than 8 inches fell on Toronto.

Residential development in the Toronto area encroached on old floodplains. Flooding from Hazel killed 81 people and left more than 1,800 families homeless in the metropolitan area. The Humber River west of the city obliterated Raymore Drive, drowning 32 residents.

The storm swept through northern Quebec and Labrador. It tracked across the North Atlantic Ocean, dissipating over Scandinavia.

***

Hurricane Hazel is remembered at Capt' Billy's Crab House and Restaurant in Popes Creek, Md. Snapshots of storm damage are on display. The owner, Billy Robertson, was 24 then. He had recently opened the crab house and business seemed promising. Then came Hazel.

A destructive surge swept the lower Potomac River, accompanied by ferocious winds. The restaurant was nearly destroyed. Robertson reopened after hauling his fishing boat out of the dining room, replacing a wall and making other extensive repairs.

Captain Billy died a few years ago. The photographs remain.

"He wanted people to take storms seriously and wanted customers to know what he went through to continue the restaurant," says his daughter, Celene Graves. "They're staying up as long as I'm around."

Hurricane Hazel rainfall totals: **Delaware**—Georgetown .52, Dover .32, Lewes .31. **Maryland**—Frostburg 5.27", Cumberland 4.03", Hagerstown 1.83", Rockville 1.35", Baltimore 1.28", Frederick 1.23", Salisbury .54", Cambridge .50". **New Jersey**—Trenton .32", Newark .31", Atlantic City .13". **Pennsylvania**—McConnellsburg 5.69", Breezewood 5.25", Somerset 4.97", Chambersburg 3.20", Harrisburg 1.57", Lancaster 1.18", Reading 1.03", Allentown .89", Philadelphia .63". **Virginia**—Big Meadows 10.71", Roanoke 6.88", Martinsville 6.40", Harrisonburg 6.34", Danville 5.61", Luray 5.35", Lexington 5.33", Staunton 5.00", Lynchburg 4.98", Norfolk .63".

HURRICANE HAZEL'S FURY AT COLONIAL BEACH, VA., ALONG THE LOWER POTOMAC RIVER

Photograph by Julian Caruthers

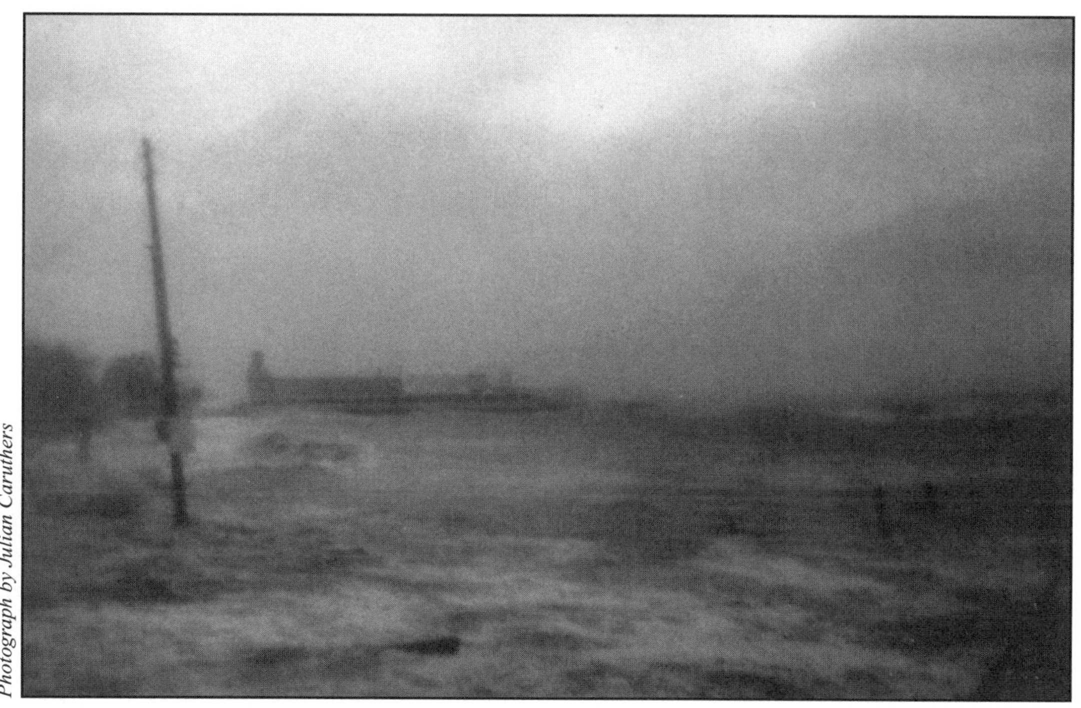

Photograph by Julian Caruthers

Photograph by Julian Caruthers

Photograph courtesy of the Colonial Beach Historical Society

Delaware Public Archives, Dover, Del.

Wilmington, Del.

Delaware Public Archives, Dover, Del.

National Guard Armory, Dover, Del.

Chester County Historical Society

West Chester, Pa.

Seneca Falls, N.Y. Hurricane-force gusts battered upstate New York.

Photograph by Jim Campbell

Ardmore, Pa., near Philadelphia. Gusts approached 100 mph in southeastern Pennsylvania.

ONE MAN'S BATTLE WITH HURRICANE HAZEL

FROM THE LOGBOOK OF THE BARRACUDA...

Mike McKenney

Mike McKenney invested three years of heart and effort to build a 38-foot cabin cruiser, Barracuda. He wasn't about to lose the boat to Hurricane Hazel without one heck of a fight. McKenney arrived at the Colonial Beach, Va., Yacht Club around noon on October 15, 1954. Three friends joined him. They boarded the vessel, moored on Monroe Creek—an appendage of the lower Potomac River. Strong winds prevented removal from its slip. Rising water threatened to dash the craft on the dock and pilings. The following are excerpts from the Barracuda's logbook:

Friday October 15, 1954 (about 1 p.m.) Hurricane Hazel romping around. Water very rough. Waves breaking on front of beach about ten feet high. Barometer 29.50. *Barracuda* pitching very badly. Wind from stern. We doubled the lines on the stern—portside—the pile on the starboard side amidships is our problem. The boat is riding on it and if the water gets much higher, it will do damage to the hull.

A few boat owners came by. None stayed. Survival of their vessels became a matter of chance. "There was one boat named, 'Skipper,'" McKenney recalls. "Nobody got aboard. Nobody did anything to help it. Still, it came through the storm and nothing happened."

Friday October 15 (about 4:30 p.m.) The barometer has been dropping steadily. It is down to 29.00 inches. We thought of moving the boat from the slip but did not believe it possible to do, so we gave up that idea!

McKenney watched helplessly as other boats and assorted debris narrowly missed the Barracuda. Waves rocked the boat relentlessly. A large pile driver bore down but at the last minute was diverted by its owner. "If that pile driver had struck us, it would have been over," McKenney said. Wind and waves increased.

Friday October 15 (about 5 p.m.) The boat is certainly in a state of disruption—lines everywhere. We decided that we had done all we could with the storm increasing and darkness coming on in a short while—that we should try to get ashore and hope for the best. We were all getting exhausted. Water was waist deep (in the parking lot by the yacht club). It was going to be very difficult to get off—we would tie a line around ourselves and to each other. Life jackets were broken out and we put them on.

Fortunately, a workboat came by and took the group to safety. The wind eventually shifted to the west-southwest and blew its hardest. Nearby, the Dahlgren Naval base reported a gust of 108 mph. "That's the only time in my boating career (50 years) that I've ever gotten off a boat with a life jacket on," McKenney says. "It was rough."

Friday October 15 (early evening) We were getting off so fast that we almost forgot to turn off the engine. It was a sickening feeling to leave our *Barracuda* to the mercy of the wind and waves—to battle nature for its life—but, after all, human assistance seems to have its limits.

The Barracuda survived, but many boats did not. At least 27 foundered in the immediate vicinity. McKenney and company returned the next day.

Saturday October 16 (afternoon) Damage is extensive—quite a few boats sunk and also a number ashore. We arrived at the club about 1 p.m. and got a rowboat and went out to the *Barracuda*. On board at 1:35 p.m. Barometer 30.04—a very nice day—sun bright—some clouds. We set about restoring the boat to a little order. All the dry lines were stowed and a heavy anchor was put away. Wet lines and fenders were put on the cabin top to dry. After we got the boat shipshape we went out the slip and up the creek to take some movies and snapshots of the destruction.

Sunk—*Moonglo*, Mill's boat, *Hazel D*, *Mamba*, *Dismal Seepage*, another at Stanford's. Beached—*Little Heron*, *PeeWee*, a large boat near Parker's, and a small boat at Lunsford's upper wharf. Also, smaller boats *Reno* and *Bibo*. Numerous boats damaged.

Navigation will be somewhat dangerous because of underwater obstructions. The navigational aids suffered untold damage. The entrance lights for Monroe and Maddox Creeks are damaged and extinguished.

Barracuda

1955

August

CONNIE

"This bulletin just in: Hurricane Connie has sunk the Chesapeake Bay schooner Levin J. Marvel..."

Lester Trott heard that broadcast during the evening of August 12, 1955. The news had a personal sting.

From 1946 until the early 1950s, Trott served as publicist for the Annapolis, Md., company that offered windjammer cruises on the *Marvel* and its sister ship, *Edwin and Maud*. Although no longer with the enterprise—it had new owners—he mourned for the lost vessel and 14 passengers who drowned.

"I wondered how so many lives could have been lost," Trott says. "I also wondered how a boat in the *Marvel*'s condition could be out in a storm."

An unlikely end for a vessel of humble origin.

The *Marvel* was built in 1891 to haul fertilizer and lumber, one of a small fleet of "Chesapeake Bay rams," enlarged workboats. The refurbished freight hauler became a windjammer ship during 1946. Herman Knust, owner of the *Marvel*, conceived of a "dude cruise," as he called it, the nautical equivalent of a western dude ranch. Customers took excursions to various Chesapeake Bay ports. They assisted with some of the sailing functions and got an up-close view of others.

Knust's idea proved successful. He eventually retired to a farm in Virginia and sold his company, including the *Edwin and Maud*. The entrepreneur then sought to sell the *Marvel*, which had been retired because of safety concerns. Knust told Trott, "If you like her, we'll work something out."

Trott knew the business and loved the bay. He went to inspect the schooner.

"I got up four in the morning and went to Salisbury—she was laying up on the Wicomico River—and when I got there and saw (her decrepit shape) I said, 'Oh my God, what is this?' I went through the ship and was disgusted, really, because the interior had begun to rot. And she had a hogged (broken) keel. I got so downhearted I didn't know what to do.

"I looked up the old captain who was the *Marvel*'s caretaker. He was a typical Eastern Shoreman and wouldn't say much at first. I did most all the talking. He mumbled now and then. Finally, I asked, 'Captain, has anything happened since the *Marvel*'s been down here?' He said, 'Son, we almost lost her a few months ago. I had a hard time keeping the water out. It was coming in faster than I could get it out of her.'

"I said, 'Captain, it's floating again. What did you do?' He said, '...there ain't nothing like Wicomico mud to seal the seams.' I thought, 'Oh my God, the seams are open. Mud is in the seams. I might not be able to get this thing away from the dock.' I told the Captain, 'Thank you. Goodbye.'"

Where Trott saw an ugly duckling, John Meckling envisioned a swan. With repairs and remodeling the

Photograph courtesy of Lester Trott

The *Levin J. Marvel* was based in Annapolis, Md.

125-foot *Marvel* could be his way out of a humdrum job in Altoona, Pa. Largely a self-taught skipper, he launched a cruise company in 1954—low in budget, high in hope.

Business prospered. What the *Marvel* lacked in luxury it made up for in jaunty camaraderie, hearty meals and fantastic scenery.

There were problems, too. Early on, the vessel sprang a leak and beached while en route to Baltimore for repairs. It reached a shipyard after given a temporary patch. But shortly thereafter, the schooner ran aground in the Choptank River.

In September 1954, the Coast Guard office in Baltimore ordered *Marvel* cruises stopped pending a formal inspection. Meckling successfully appealed, arguing that at 183 tons the windjammer fell short of the 700-ton minimum requirement for checking commercial passenger vessels.

***

Hurricane Connie was a vague threat when the schooner left Annapolis on Monday, August 8. Meckling and three crewmen accompanied 23 passengers. Throughout the week, the storm moved closer.

The Chesapeake Bay enjoyed deceptively gorgeous weather on Thursday even as Connie's rain bands reached North Carolina. Near Cambridge, Md., passengers enjoyed a refreshing swim in the Choptank River or lounged on deck. That night they watched the sparkling Milky Way.

Forecasters weren't sure what the hurricane would do. They debated whether it would curve northeast and remain over the ocean or come inland and travel up the bay.

Connie chose the latter. It made landfall on Friday, August 12, striking Cape Lookout, N. C., as a minimal hurricane. The storm retained a sprawling circulation. Spiral arms stretched 300 miles north to the Chesapeake Bay.

On Friday, Meckling battled the elements. Squalls brought gusts of 50 mph. Winds seldom dropped below 25 mph. Whitecaps heaved water on deck.

By early afternoon, Meckling anchored in Herring Bay. He was 20 miles south of Annapolis and sanctuary.

Passengers ate a light lunch. Each strapped on a life jacket. Few seemed worried.

The weather deteriorated. A two-masted schooner, the *LaForrest L. Simmons*, sank several miles away. Its crew escaped in a lifeboat.

The *Marvel* had none. And the bay poured in. Portholes couldn't be sealed because of rust, rot and lack of maintenance. Passengers used pillows and blankets in a frantic effort to plug leaks. Men labored with an emergency hand pump, waist deep in water, after mechanical pumps failed. Water kept rising in the *Marvel*, the vessel riding lower, taking on more and becoming increasingly unstable—a death spiral. At 2:40 p.m., the ship capsized when a gust of wind caught it broadside.

Passengers drowned after being trapped or struck by debris as the *Marvel* broke up. Or they succumbed to waves, exposure and panic.

Meckling radioed a call for assistance earlier, a transmission authorities could not decipher. Now, more than two-dozen people were in the water, nearly a mile offshore, with nobody aware of their predicament. About two hours later, a woman made it to shore and alerted authorities.

Meckling struggled in the water for more than an hour before finding refuge in a duck blind about 200 yards from shore. He and five others signaled passers-by. Billy MacWilliams and George Kellam of North Beach, who heard of the sinking and rushed over "to lend a hand," borrowed a skiff, ventured into the fierce surf and ferried everyone to safety.

An investigation by the Coast Guard found fault with Meckling, citing a lack of sailing experience, a disregard of storm warnings and failure to maintain the *Marvel* in a safe condition. A grand jury indicted him for negligence, misconduct and manslaughter. He was acquitted of the latter but found guilty on the other charges, receiving a suspended sentence and probation.

The tragedy led to federal legislation mandating inspection and safety regulations for nearly every cruise or charter vessel.

Meckling left Annapolis. Years later, he'd find success in a land-based business. He kept a painting of the *Levin J. Marvel* on his office wall.

Trott never owned a cruise business. However, he spent decades sailing pleasure boats, exploring nooks and crannies of the bay, gathering fond memories.

Trott views the tragedy as a cautionary tale to those who would short-change safety standards and take the Chesapeake Bay lightly. Its placid nature can

Maryland State Archives

Connie's gales over saturated ground toppled trees throughout central Maryland.

Special Collections, University of Maryland Libraries

be deceptive, highly changeable. He recalls an incident from his days as an instructor at the Annapolis Sailing School.

"A group of 10 or 15 centerboard sailboats were racing at the mouth of the Severn River," Trott said. "It had been a beautiful day, but I could see a squall coming. I said to my students, 'This is going to be a lesson for you. Watch those boats.'

"They were sailing beautifully, but the squall kept coming as rapidly as could be conceived down the Severn. As the boats left the windward shore and moved out to open water, gusts struck them one after the other, flipping them over like ducks in a shooting gallery. Bip. Bip. Bip. Not every boat went down. Some had good sailors who could handle the situation. But those who weren't use to that sort of thing were being knocked over before they could even react to it."

***

Hurricane Connie lashed the eastern half of the Mid-Atlantic region with peak gusts over 50 mph. A top gust of 70 mph at Ocean City, Md., and 67 mph at Philadelphia Airport, were the highest winds recorded beyond North Carolina.

Many places experienced strongest gusts well before Connie's nearest approach. Washington, D.C., for example, clocked gusts of 58 mph at 5:22 p.m., and 54 mph at 10:54 p.m., on August 12, yet the center didn't pass the city until 8 a.m. on the 13th. Connie's remnant eye grazed Norfolk, Va., and Baltimore, Md., but Baltimore (150 miles further north), had a gust of 58 mph versus only 52 mph at Norfolk.

Most hurricanes traversing the Middle Atlantic region dump heaviest rain in the northwestern quadrant (when they track north). Connie didn't discriminate. The storm dumped 5-10 inches within 100 miles of its track. Richmond, Va., recorded its greatest daily rainfall on August 12, 8.79 inches.

The Baltimore metropolitan area suffered disastrous flooding. The northern branch of the Patapsco River and other area waterways climbed to record crests.

Prolonged gale-force winds across the Chesapeake Bay created tidal flooding. According to the Weather Bureau, "On the western shore of the bay, storm surge heights were several inches higher than those of 'Hazel' last year but on the eastern shore tides were a few inches lower than those of 'Hazel.' "

***

As Connie tracked through western Pennsylvania, barometric pressure rose, rain subsided and whisper replaced roar. It died a quiet death near the Canadian border.

The storm rainfall followed 1-3 inches dropped by a non-tropical weather system on August 7-8. The initial showers were welcome relief to a parched land. Then came Connie. In the aftermath, Mid-Atlantic residents mopped up. Meanwhile, Hurricane Diane approached.

Hurricane Connie rainfall totals (August 12-13): **Delaware**—Georgetown 6.36", Lewes 5.51", Dover 5.07". **Maryland**—Cambridge 9.21", Solomons 9.16", Towson 8.88", Easton 8.88", Baltimore 7.95", Annapolis 6.92", Salisbury 6.78", Frederick 5.91". **New Jersey**—New Brunswick 7.00", Newark 5.32", Trenton 5.03". **New York City**—LaGuardia Airport 12.20" (fell within 38 hours). **Pennsylvania**—Bethlehem 6.41", Reading 6.40", Stroudsburg 6.27", Philadelphia 5.44", Lancaster 4.97". **Virginia**—Richmond 8.85" (8.79" on August 12), Warsaw 8.71", Williamsburg 7.02", Fredericksburg 6.09", Norfolk 3.82". **Washington, D.C.** 6.60".

August

DIANE

Analomink, in northeastern Pennsylvania. August 18, 1955. Evening.

About 30 vacationers, mostly women and children, trudged to a lodge, seemingly safe from Brodhead Creek. Fueled by incessant rain from Hurricane Diane, it began inundating the bungalows of what was unofficially "Camp Davis," a retreat sponsored by Baptist minister Leon Davis.

On any other night the building would have offered protection, but Brodhead Creek crested at 30 feet, more than doubling its previous record. Much of the rise occurred within 15 minutes as the torrent blasted through debris blockages.

Campers retreated to the attic—a time of prayers and hymns. The building disintegrated shortly before midnight. Nancy Johnson recalled:

"I grabbed for floating wood and held on until I crashed into a big tree—which I climbed as quickly as possible although I had never climbed a tree before.

"I held on for what amounted to nine hours, although it appeared like nine years of darkness inter-washed with roaring water. Screams rang out all around me."

By morning, Brodhead Creek claimed 37 of the 46 people at Camp Davis, including most who sought sanctuary in the lodge.

***

Who could have known that Diane would kill 200 people when it made landfall in North Carolina as a minimal hurricane? Who could have predicted that it would become the first "billion-dollar hurricane?" Forecasters wrote the storm off as it traveled through Virginia. The public relaxed even as a killer stirred.

Winds gusted to 62 mph in Roanoke, Va., and 56 mph in Lynchburg as Diane traveled near those cities. But rain was the menace. Moisture streamed toward the Blue Ridge. As it lifted and cooled, precipitation increased.

Diane produced the most destructive flood in the Shenandoah Valley and along the Potomac River since 1942. Streams and rivers immersed roads and drowned bridges. A Trailways bus driver detouring through the Mt. Jackson area stopped his vehicle before each bridge and had passengers walk across—high water made the structures' suspect. Then the busman drove across, not willing to risk any life but his.

Meteorologists thought the deluge a last gasp and missed its meaning. Diane combined with a stationary front and mountains to produce furious downpours. The heights of the Blue Ridge (2,000-4,000 ft.) were similar to terrain north of the hurricane's track as it turned east-northeast through Pennsylvania and New Jersey. Copious moisture continued toward higher ground and bumped up against a stationary front.

During the night of August 18-19, rainfall totaling 10-20 inches dumped on the Pocono, Catskill and Berkshire mountains. Every river born in these watersheds reached record or near-record levels, devastating highly populated valleys.

Few towns were ravaged like the Stroudsburgs in eastern Pennsylvania. Sitting astride Brodhead Creek, Stroudsburg (pop. 6,500) and East Stroudsburg (pop. 7,500) lost their single connecting bridge as the stream, now nearly 1,000 feet wide, attacked residential and commercial areas. Dozens of people drowned.

The Stroudsburgs hadn't had a major flood since the hurricane of October 1903. Most residents couldn't conceive of malevolence from placid Brodhead Creek.

Complacency... Firemen had built a recreation hall/civil defense headquarters on the Brodhead Creek floodplain. Bingo players crowded the hall as Diane's rain swept the night. The games came to an end, and most participants went home. Four women remained, waiting for a ride. Three drowned when a wall of water blasted through.

Helen Brown, who lived in Stroudsburg, documented the storm through a collection of slides. They form the basis of a videotape produced by the Monroe County Historical Society. The following are excerpts from Brown's narration:

"I had an apartment in my niece's home. My niece and her two sons lived on 9th Street. They got out by wading in water up to their waist."

"My clothes were carried away (and some items recovered). I paid $75 to have them cleaned but the smell of sewer mud was so bad that I had to give them away. Some of my clothes were stolen. Fortunately, the thieves missed my jewelry box."

"A big problem after the flood was sewer rats invading our homes. I killed a very large one in the kitchen with a hot shovel. All the homes had to be fumigated and the rats were exterminated."

"It didn't matter if you lived in a house made of brick or stone or wood. If it was in the path of the water, it was wiped out."

A sampling of Diane's work in Pennsylvania and New Jersey:

PENNSYLVANIA

Allentown-Bethlehem: More than 15,000 people were temporarily out of work after the Lehigh River crippled 15 industrial plants. Widespread residential damage occurred at Lehighton and Freemansburg. The Lehigh River at Bethlehem crested at 25.9 ft., exceeding a 16-ft. flood stage and the previous high-water mark of 25.6 ft.

Cresco: A Delaware, Lackawanna and Western Railroad train became marooned in the Poconos at Cresco. Helicopters airlifted 235 passengers. (In a region where nearly every bridge was knocked out and most highways closed, helicopters—new to flood rescue—proved invaluable.)

Delaware River Valley: A pilot reported that water in Yardley, Fort Washington and New Hope, Pa., reached the top of telephone poles. Residents of Raubsville and Riegelsville, Pa., Carpentersville and Stockton, N.J.—or anyone living along the Delaware River—still remember Diane.

Easton, Pa.-Phillipsburg, N.J.: The Delaware River crested at a phenomenal 43.7 ft. in Easton (flood stage 22 ft.), besting the previous record of 38.3 ft. (1903). The rise resulted in a large-scale evacuation.

Scranton: Diane devastated this city of 120,000. Mayor James Hanlon declared a state of emergency, which lasted five days. He ordered all factories, business offices and stores closed.

The Southside Flats and Little England residential neighborhoods were devastated. One of the city's main bridges collapsed.

Scranton lost its municipal water supply. For days, residents lined up at water tankers supplied by the Army.

Hawley: The Lackawaxen River reached a record height. Hawley, built along the confluence of two waterways, sustained huge losses.

Tamaqua: The town flooded for the first time in 25 years as Wabash Creek merged with the Little Schuylkill River. Wreckage marked anywhere the water reached. National Guardsmen patrolled streets here and in other stricken municipalities.

NEW JERSEY

Branchville: A dam containing Stony Brook burst, sending a rush of water through town. Trees and automobiles acted like battering rams, adding to the devastation.

Lambertville: More than 200 families had their homes damaged or destroyed in this town of 4,500. New Hope, Pa., across the Delaware River, suffered proportionately heavier losses.

Princeton: An off-duty police officer, Billie Ellis, and two teenagers drowned. Ellis attempted to rescue the boys after their canoe overturned in the Millstone River at Lake Carnegie Dam.

Trenton: The Delaware River spread into the state capital. The river crested above the benchmark flood of 1903.

Elsewhere: Three river systems, the Delaware, Raritan and Passaic, inundated northern sections of the state. Flooding was particularly severe along the south branch of the Raritan.

Sussex, Mercer, Hunterdon and Warren counties were designated disaster areas. Belvidere, the Warren County seat, located on the Delaware River, suffered extensive damage. The Delaware crested at 28.4 ft. (flood stage 20 ft.), nearly equaling the record 28.6 ft., which occurred in 1903. About 200 families were evacuated in Oakland as the rising Ramapo River inundated sections of the town.

Diane focused on northwestern New Jersey and along the Delaware River. Rainfall totaled less than 3 inches in the southern two-thirds of the state.

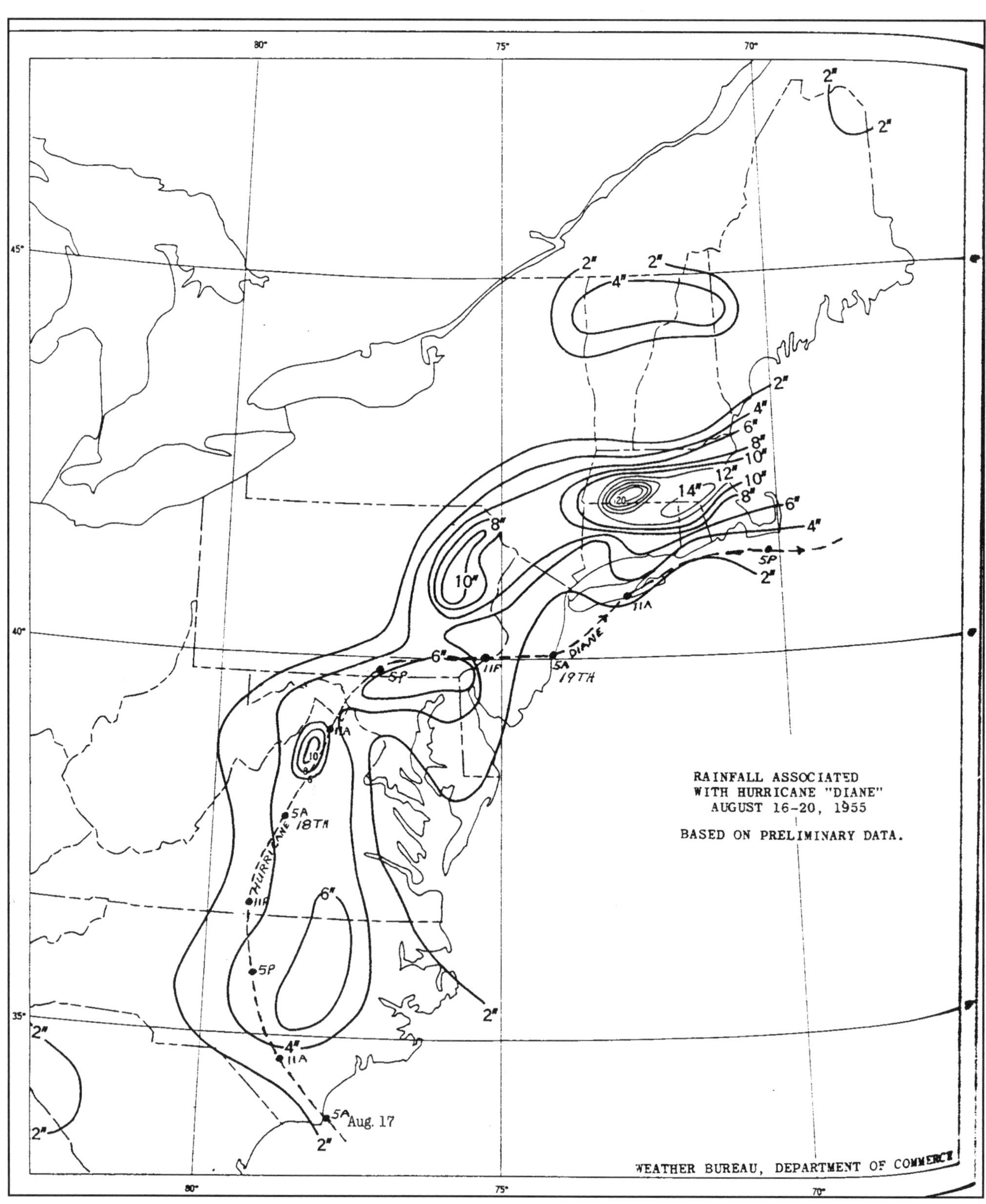
RAINFALL ASSOCIATED
WITH HURRICANE "DIANE"
AUGUST 16-20, 1955
BASED ON PRELIMINARY DATA.
WEATHER BUREAU, DEPARTMENT OF COMMERCE
Aug. 17
HURRICANE
DIANE
18TH
19TH

***

Summer camps are a mainstay of the Pocono Mountains. About 10,000 youngsters converged on the region in time for Diane. Although most were never in danger—cabin fever being the greatest menace—some required a hasty evacuation.

A large-scale rescue operation took place on three islands in the Delaware River between Erwinna, Pa., and Frenchtown, N.J. Flooding threatened several hundred boys and girls attending scout camps. Occupants of one island left by boat. But the powerful current precluded a nautical evacuation of the other two. Authorities sought helicopters. The challenge: Where to find a fleet in a hurry during a time when helicopters were still a rarity?

They scoured the region, finally assembling a group of "whirlybirds," including some just off the assembly line and others from regional military bases. The last evacuees waded through waist-deep water to reach a landing site. Everyone escaped.

Given the magnitude of the disaster and fearing an epidemic, Gov. George Leader ordered the closure of all summer camps in the Poconos. Operation Kid-Lift, coordinated by the state police and civil defense, ensured campers a safe and orderly trip home.

***

August 19, "Black Friday," brought New England one of its greatest natural disasters. Diane killed more than 80 people (70 in Connecticut alone) and injured 5,000. Flooding in sections of New York, Connecticut, Massachusetts and Rhode Island rivaled or exceeded that in the Poconos. The 18.15 inches of rain that fell on Westfield, Mass., and 12.77 inches measured in Burlington, Conn., on August 18-19, set respective state 24-hour rainfall records.

Downpours caused unprecedented flooding in Columbia, Dutchess, Orange, Sullivan and Ulster counties in southeastern New York.

Every river in Connecticut crested at a destructive, if not historic, level. Damage was extreme at Torrington, Ansonia, Derby and in Winsted, Naugatuck and Waterbury. At least 15 people died in Waterbury. In Putnam, hundreds of magnesium barrels from a flooded plant exploded as they bobbed through the municipality. Gov. Abraham Ribicoff pledged, "We will emerge from the flood disaster a finer state, a greater state."

Massachusetts shared Diane's excess. Towns such as Westfield (pop. 20,000) could only be reached by helicopters or amphibious vehicles. Water covered 40 percent of Worcester (pop. 195,000).

Rhode Island felt Diane's soggy lash. Woonsocket, R.I. (pop. 50,000) was hardest hit. Water topped a dam on Mill River, and then burst the Horseshoe Dam on Blackstone River. The surge reached the tops of streetlights. The Blackstone River, normally 70 feet across, embraced more than a mile.

***

On Saturday, August 20, the sun rose over panoramas of muddy mayhem throughout the Northeast. Pastoral valleys were chasms of ruin, homes now tombs. More than 100,000 people routed by flooding sought public shelter or took refuge elsewhere. Cities lacked utilities and other necessities.

Amid calls for a special session of Congress, President Dwight Eisenhower met with the governors of Pennsylvania, New Jersey, New York, Connecticut, Massachusetts and Rhode Island. He broadcast this message to the nation:

"In my opinion, everybody within the sound of my voice will sleep better tonight if he turns in everything he can spare to meet this great disaster that has happened to our fellow Americans.

"This is a chance where each of us can rise to an emergency and prove that the American people regardless of governments, regardless of the limitations on them, can meet an emergency and do it well."

Relief agencies rushed assistance. They faced a challenge poignantly described by the American Red Cross:

"The all-pervading tragedy against which thousands (of rescue workers) rose so valiantly must be sketched in some detail for a full realization of their courage. The towns and cities in which they worked had little semblance of ordinary life. No lights, no water, no telephones. Many were cut in two by raging rivers, with all bridges either gone or far under water. No one knew how many lives the rampaging waters had claimed. Families were separated. In many places police, fire or ham radio provided the only communication between isolated sections; others had no communication at all, either with others inside town or with the outside world. Countless rescues were made by helicopters, boat and improvised breeches buoy."

The Northeast went from drought to flood in less than 10 days. Workmen in Trenton piled sandbags to protect government buildings from the rising Delaware. Earlier, legislators debated emergency relief for dwindling reservoirs and suffering farmers. Now, New Jersey Gov. Robert Meyner declared that flooding had wrought the worst natural disaster in state history.

***

Raymond Winfield heard about the Camp Davis tragedy while at his Rutherford, N.J., home. Winfield's wife, Edna, and his children, 8-year-old Rowan and 11-year-old Karen, were missing. He rushed to Analomink and joined searchers.

They soon recovered the bodies of Edna and Rowan. However, Karen couldn't be located. After the search wound down, Winfield pursued a solitary quest. Through the waning days of summer, during autumn chill, until late November. Finally, worsening weather sent him home. Five years later a farmer plowing his field came across Karen's remains. Two boys have never been found.

Hurricane Diane rainfall totals: **Maryland** (Aug. 17-18)—Frostburg 4.31", Baltimore 3.58". **New Jersey** (Aug. 18-19)—Sussex 8.10", Newton 7.64", Branchville 7.41", Phillipsburg 6.01", Paterson 4.88", Flemington 4.72", New Brunswick 2.41", Cape May .31", Atlantic City .19". **Pennsylvania** (Aug. 18-19)—Hawley 10.28", Matamoras 8.22", Stroudsburg 6.15", Scranton 4.58", Allentown 3.34", Philadelphia 3.11". **Virginia** (Aug. 17-18)—Big Meadows (Shenandoah National Park) 11.45", Luray 10.32", Culpepper 5.58", Natural Bridge 4.79", Charlottesville 4.77", Richmond 3.39".

EFFECT OF A RUMOR IN A DISASTER-STRICKEN COMMUNITY

A rumor of a dam break created mass panic in Port Jervis, N.Y., during the troubled days following Hurricane Diane. It happened when the rain seemed endless and rivers rose higher than anyone thought possible.

Flooding from Diane inundated large sections of the Delaware River community of 9,000, located near the tri-state border of New York, Pennsylvania and New Jersey. Even as water receded on Saturday, August 20, residents remained fearful about the immense Lake Wallenpaupack Dam, about 45 miles upstream.

A planned but poorly publicized water release may have been responsible for subsequent events. A study commissioned by the U.S. Civil Defense Administration, *The Effects of a Threatening Rumor on a Disaster-Stricken Community*, analyzed a panic that sent about 3,000 inhabitants of Port Jervis on a wild scramble for higher ground. According to the report:

"At about 10:30 PM Saturday night, a stranger ran into a restaurant in Sparrowbush (upstream from Port Jervis) and told the owner that the Wallenpaupack Dam had broken. He added that firemen in a community up the river were evacuating everyone. The restaurant owner's telephone was out of commission because of the flood. He went with three other men to the highway and began to stop cars to warn them of the impending danger."

They stopped the captain of the Sparrowbush Fire Department. He sent a message to fire companies throughout the area suggesting that the dam *might have broken*. However, the transmission was misunderstood. It became, "Emergency…the Wallenpaupack Dam *has* broken!"

Residents of previously flooded sections of Port Jervis heard the warning as they stood by fire trucks pumping out their basements. Various emergency vehicles spread the alarm. In Matamoras, Pa., across the Delaware River, a firehouse siren began wailing.

A civil defense official recalled, "The rumor, which spread like wildfire throughout the city, in both high and low sections, caused our citizens to begin fleeing. Before (the report) could be halted, most of the city was on the move. People dressed in only night clothing rushed from their homes and to their cars, some taking a suitcase of belongings along. Others fled with just the clothing they had on."

They waited for a rush of water that never came. Wallenpaupack Dam remained intact, a fact confirmed by beleaguered Port Jervis officials, who attempted to defuse the rumor. From the Civil Defense Administration report:

"The city's Fire Department, with loudspeakers blaring, went about the city attempting to calm the populace and telling them the reports were untrue and to return to their homes. Ralph Frederick of the *Union Gazette* staff, and a representative of Station WDLC, put that station on the air after midnight and repeated the story that the rumor was untrue for countless minutes on the air."

WDLC sought wording for a message that would calm the public. All references to a dam, water or flood were edited out for fear that someone tuning in during the middle of the broadcast might hear one of those trigger words, listen no further, and panic. The final version went: "Ladies and gentlemen. It is only a rumor—it is not true. There is no need for anyone to be up on mountains or high places. It would be best if you returned home and did not spread the rumor."

The Civil Defense reported:

"Gradually the truth began to dawn on those who fled. They returned, but not until after they had created one of the greatest near-disasters in the history of the city. The actions of some could have resulted in a worse catastrophe than the flood itself."

During August 1955 it came to this: If you lived in a flood-prone valley and thought the creek was rising, you got out of the way. Questions could wait.

September

IONE

The region continued as a hurricane magnet. Just a month after Diane, Ione (eye-own) approached storm-weary denizens. Hazel. Connie. Diane. Three disastrous hurricanes in less than a year! Now Ione loomed—a tropical menace that threatened to bring winds like Hazel and rain like Diane. Fear peaked on September 19 as the storm made landfall near Morehead City, N.C. It aimed at Richmond, Va., and Washington, D.C.

"90 MPH Winds Due To Lash City Tonight," proclaimed a banner headline in the (Washington) *Evening Star*. Residents braced for the worst.

Surface weather features appeared similar to those on the eve of Hazel. Forecasters thought Ione would follow a like path. But on the afternoon of September 19 the hurricane slowed while nearing landfall, seemingly undecided on direction.

It clipped North Carolina before suddenly veering out to sea. Eastern sections of the state saw unprecedented flooding.

The cooperative weather station at Maysville measured 48.9 inches between August 11 (Connie) and September 19 (Ione). About one-third fell during Ione.

Heavy rain drenched southeastern and central Virginia, but waterways stayed tame.

Ione's departure closed the Mid-Atlantic's 1955 hurricane season.

HURRICANE DIANE'S AFTERMATH IN THE VICINITY OF THE STROUDSBURGS, PENNSYLVANIA

Special Collections, University of Maryland Libraries

Monroe County Historical Association

Monroe County Historical Association

Diane destroyed the Canadensis Bridge north of Stroudsburg.

DIANE ATTACKS BRIDGES ALONG THE DELAWARE RIVER

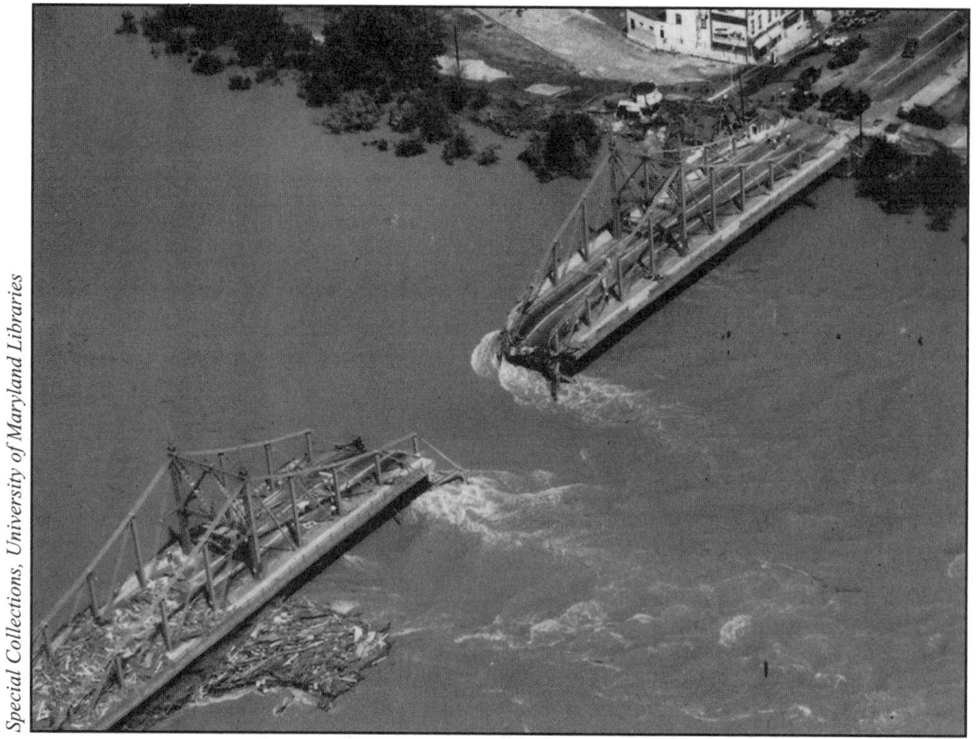

Special Collections, University of Maryland Libraries

Easton, Pa./Phillipsburg, N.J.

New Jersey State Archives, Dept. of State

End of an era. The covered bridge at Portland, Pa., and Columbia, N.J., was the last of its kind to span the Delaware River.

1957

June

AUDREY

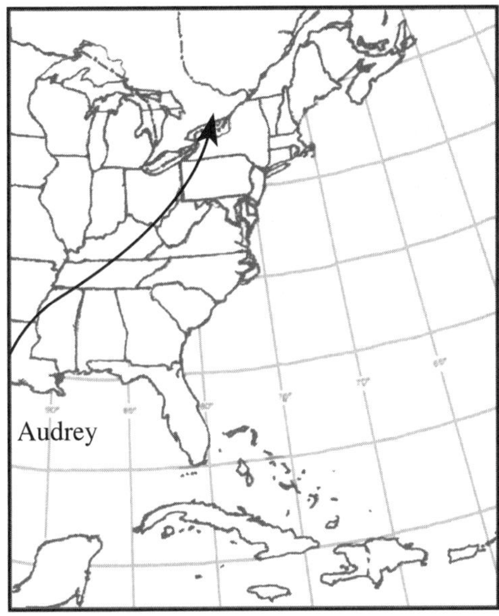

Western sections of the Middle Atlantic region aren't immune to hurricanes. Remnant systems have brought high winds, flooding and tornadoes. Few, however, have been as potent as Hurricane Audrey in 1957.

Audrey, arguably the most intense hurricane to strike the United States during June, came ashore along the Louisiana/Texas border shortly after dawn on June 27. It explosively deepened and sped up prior to landfall, surprising many residents unaware of the sudden changes. Punishing winds and the storm surge claimed more than 400 lives, most in Cameron Parish, La.

The hurricane savaged a 50-mile section of coastline. Sustained winds topped 110 mph. Survivors reported that Audrey brought a "tidal wave," leveling everything in its path.

Audrey lost strength and tropical characteristics while tracking northeast over land. It became extratropical in northern Mississippi on June 28, merging with a low pressure system the next day. Barometric pressure rose from 28.33 inches at landfall to more than 29.00 inches in the Tennessee Valley. Then, surprisingly, the storm deepened. Barometric pressure plummeted, bottoming at 28.70 inches on June 29 as it entered eastern Canada.

In a tropical cyclone's concentrated eyewall, such intensity produces highly destructive winds. With the extratropical system's sprawling circulation, the drop meant greater atmospheric instability and scattered severe weather.

Audrey's 22 tornadoes were a hurricane-related record to that time. One slammed Elkins, W. Va., destroying several buildings and uprooting numerous trees.

Severe thunderstorms marked the remnants' passage through Pennsylvania. Allentown had a gust of 75 mph as a squall raced through. Patrons attending a drive-in theater at Beaver Falls in northwestern Pennsylvania watched the screen topple after a hurricane-force blast. Pittsburgh registered a gust of 65 mph.

Although only 2-3 inches of rain fell on the western slopes of the Appalachians, up to 10 inches swamped sections of eastern Illinois and central Indiana. Tropical moisture clashed with an advancing cold front. Flooding displaced thousands of people.

Strong thunderstorms caused widespread, mostly minor, property damage and power outages in the Mid-Atlantic region and western New England. At Norfolk and Richmond, in Washington and New York City, swift lines of storms brought 50-60 mph gusts, intense lightning and brief, torrential downpours. A gust of 100 mph buffeted Jamestown in western New York.

From the lowlands of Louisiana to the farmlands of Illinois, and east to the Atlantic Ocean, Audrey earned a retired name.

1959

September

GRACIE

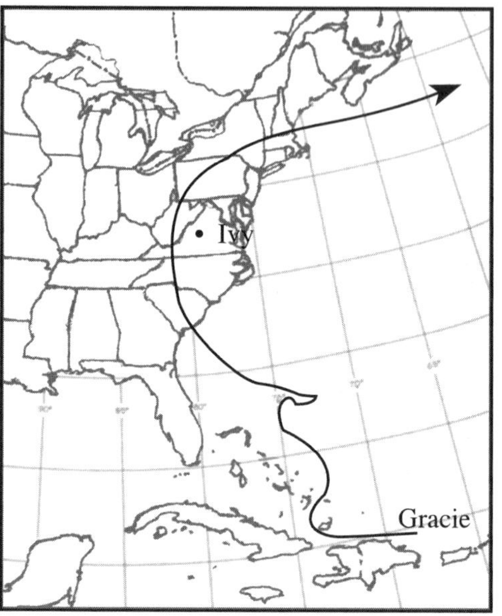

Hurricane Gracie slammed South Carolina on September 29. It tracked through the southern and central Appalachians delivering heavy rain. Then...

September 30. 4:30 p.m. Just south of Ivy, Va., west of Charlottesville.

The Morris family sheltered from a terrific squall in their two-story frame house. A tornado approached with a sound like a freight train. It demolished the residence, hurling occupants in all directions. Within moments, 10 people died. A neighbor, Lilly Bruce, also perished.

The tornado was the second to visit the neighborhood that day. Earlier, a twister moved through a different section of Ivy uprooting large trees, damaging buildings and flattening utility poles along a five-mile swath.

The Ivy tornadoes were part of an outbreak. A tornado swept southeast of Charlottesville traveling through Fluvanna County shortly before 6 p.m. It passed near Palmyra and through Cunningham, destroying several houses and a church.

A funnel touched down south of Charlottesville and skipped north into Greene County. The Blue Ridge School at St. George suffered extensive damage. Robert Morris, a maintenance worker, was killed when his workshop disintegrated. The whirlwind blew vehicles, including tractor-trailer trucks, off bustling U.S. 29 and injured nine people.

***

Forecasters can't predict how many tornadoes a hurricane will spawn or where they will strike. Twisters are a threat away from the ocean. Gracie traveled hundreds of miles over land. A single tornado, far from the sea, accounted for nearly all deaths.

1960

September

DONNA

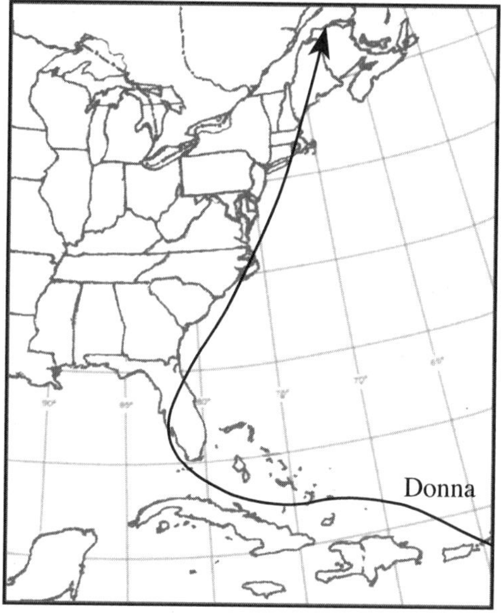

On August 29, 1960, an Air France jet en route from Paris with 63 people onboard made two passes at the airfield in Dakar, Senegal, on the western coast of Africa. A thunderstorm made visibility difficult. The plane soared over the Atlantic for a third landing attempt. It never returned. "Pancaked" is how investigators described the aircraft's demise, the victim of a fierce downdraft.

The lethal thunderstorm joined others. Circulation formed. Two days later, forecasters discovered a tropical storm south of the Cape Verde Islands. They named it "Donna."

The storm became a hurricane on September 1, strengthening during a long journey through tropical pastures. It roared through the Caribbean mauling one island after another. Along Donna's murderous route: Antigua, St. Barts, St. Maarten and Anguilla. Then Puerto Rico, Cuba, the Bahamas.

Forecasters now faced a dilemma. High pressure blocked the hurricane from swinging northeast and moving safely away from the United States. Would the menace continue west and attack Florida? Or would it head north and invade New England?

Donna did both in a big way. It became the first tropical cyclone to bring hurricane-force winds along the entire East Coast from Florida to Maine.

The monster tracked across the middle Keys on September 9-10, reached the Gulf of Mexico, then curved inland at Fort Myers. It emerged over the Atlantic Ocean southeast of Jacksonville.

Donna was the most violent storm to strike the Keys since the Great Labor Day Hurricane of 1935. Winds gusted to 170 mph. An astounded observer at Tavernier watched the anemometer needle remain stuck against the 120 mph mark—the maximum it could reach—for 45 minutes. Barometric pressure tumbled to 27.46 inches in the Florida Straits, the sixth lowest on record from a hurricane striking the United States. Pressure dipped to 27.97 inches at Naples and 28.08 inches at Fort Myers, where winds gusted over 100 mph.

Donna rushed northeast from Florida, making landfall near Cape Fear, N.C., early on September 12. Sustained winds were estimated at 115 mph. The greatest damage occurred in the vicinity of Morehead City and Beaufort. As the storm crossed interior sections of eastern North Carolina, barometric pressure in the eye remained between 28.30 inches and 28.55 inches, and winds gusted to more than 100 mph. Damage in southeastern North Carolina was said to equal that from Hurricane Hazel. Further north, along the Outer Banks, losses were greater from Donna, which passed much closer.

The Middle Atlantic states battened down for an assault of wind, rain and sea. Decades of severe hurricanes made the public experts in the drill: stock up on non-perishable food and drinking water, secure property and follow the terrible progress of yet another tropical invader.

Sustained winds peaked at 73 mph at Norfolk International Airport and gusted to 89 mph at Virginia Beach. They were accompanied by minimum barometric pressure readings of 28.64 inches and 28.51 inches, respectively. An observer on the Chesapeake Lightship, 17 miles offshore, estimated a peak gust of 138 mph. From the Norfolk office of the Weather Bureau:

"The highest winds in the area were well up in the hurricane-force range. Cape Henry reported gusts to 91 mph, from WNW at 7:14 a.m., however, reports were heard of gusts up to 120 mph aboard a vessel moored at the Army base piers. Extensive damage ravaged trees, boats and utility lines and at least three deaths can be attributed to the hurricane in the Hampton Roads area. Communications and power were not restored to many sections for four days or more."

Donna's elongated eye passed over the Delmarva shore providing a brief respite. Hurricane-force gusts battered the coast from Virginia to New Jersey. Ocean City, Md., recorded 85 mph before the anemometer became disabled. Cape Henlopen, Del., clocked 74 mph. Salisbury, Md., about 30 miles inland, caught a gust of 83 mph. Gales and rainfall of 3-8 inches extended west to the Blue Ridge and eastern Pennsylvania.

Donna ranks among the United States' major hurricanes. As a result of excellent warnings, casualties remained low. Despite high winds, flooding rains and raging tides, only nine people died in New Jersey.

Authorities reported many narrow escapes. There are always those who tempt fate: Surfers looking for the perfect hurricane-generated wave. Stick-it-out types who ignore evacuation orders. The curious who travel to water's edge and gawk at a mesmerizing sea.

Clark Gilman, a flood plain management engineer for New Jersey—then a college student—remembers riding with a police officer in the seaside town of Lavallette.

"There was a woman standing on the boardwalk taking photographs from a dangerous location," Gilman recalls. "I went up and nicely asked her to leave. She told me, in so many words, to mind my own business.

"I went back to the cruiser and told the officer what she said. He got on the public address system and in his loudest voice shouted, 'LADY, get off the (expletive) boardwalk, NOW!' "

The woman hurriedly complied. "A minute later—no more than two—a wave came in and the section where she had stood was gone," Gilman said. "I think we proved our point."

Would-be heroism had its down side.

"We went up to one of the oceanfront houses and noticed somebody was inside," Gilman said. "A fire was going, the lights were on and, as it turned out, rags were stuffed under the door to keep water out. We went in and told the residents they had to evacuate.

"No more than a second or two after we pushed our way in, leaving the door open, a wave came through and rolled across the living room floor and into the fireplace. There was hissing, steam and smoke. I don't know whether they evacuated or not, but we hastily left. They weren't very happy with us."

The Jersey shore experienced a brief period of light breezes and sunshine as Donna's eye clipped the coast. Bob Levy, a lifelong resident of Atlantic City, then a teenager, watched in awe.

"I remember going out and it was real calm. It was beautiful. I remember my father saying, 'Stay (inside) this isn't over yet.' All of a sudden, it began again. You could hear the wind pick up and see clouds returning. But there had been an opening. There was a dead spot. That's the only time I remember something like that happening."

Long Branch, N.J., had a gust of 79 mph and a barometric pressure of 28.56 inches, typical of the Jersey shore. Heavy rain fell throughout the state.

Donna struck Long Island as a Category 2 hurricane and Connecticut as a Category 1. Its wide, elliptical eye extended over much of Long Island, a distance of more than 90 miles.

LaGuardia Airport in New York City had a peak gust of 93 mph. Gusts in the metropolitan area generally flirted with hurricane force. Rainfall totaled 3-6 inches. The barometer dipped to 28.65 inches. A record tide six feet above normal surged ashore from Raritan Bay, N.J., to New York City. Losses were heavy along the Raritan Bay, in northeastern Monmouth County and on Staten Island.

Donna's final act seemed one of atonement. The hurricane brought desperately needed rain to the Maritime Provinces of Canada, which had endured a summer-long drought. Firefighters rejoiced as downpours doused stubborn forest fires.

Hurricane Donna rainfall totals (Sept.12): **Delaware**—Vernon 7.26", Milford 7.23", Dover 6.33", Wilmington 5.62", Lewes 4.72". **Maryland**—Denton 8.29", Cambridge 6.59", Chestertown 4.40", Snow Hill 4.34". **New Jersey**—Seabrook 8.50", Freehold 5.19", New Brunswick 4.47", Plainfield 4.20", Atlantic City 3.06". **Pennsylvania**—Marcus Hook 5.62", Terre Hill (Lancaster County) 5.06", Philadelphia 4.60", Allentown 2.60". **Virginia**—Williamsburg 5.93", Norfolk 5.22", Newport News 4.40", Fredericksburg 3.79", Alexandria 3.42", Charlottesville 1.72", Richmond 1.63".

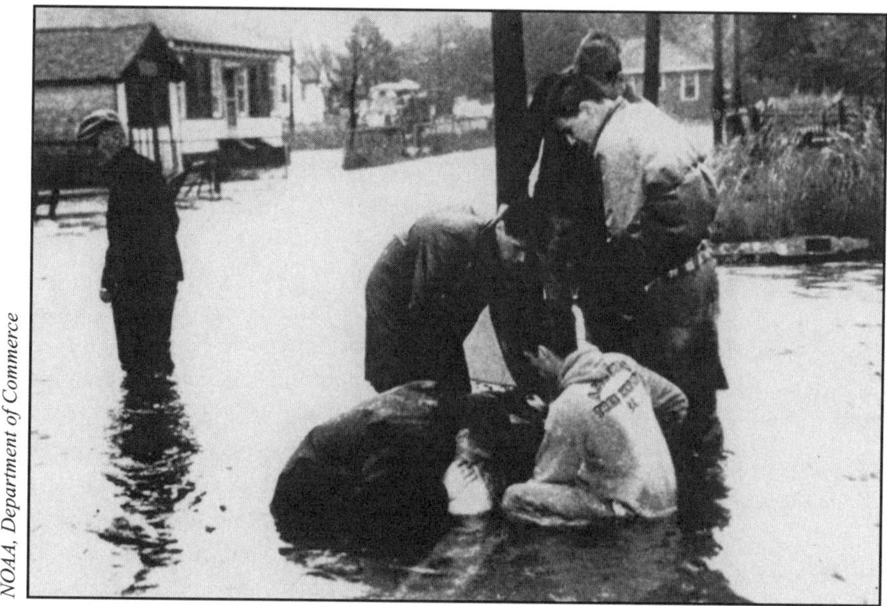

NOAA, Department of Commerce

Rescuers administer mouth-to-mouth resuscitation to a flood victim of Hurricane Donna. The storm sent 10-foot tides through three of New York's boroughs.

American Red Cross

Record tides invaded New York City.

1961

September

ESTHER

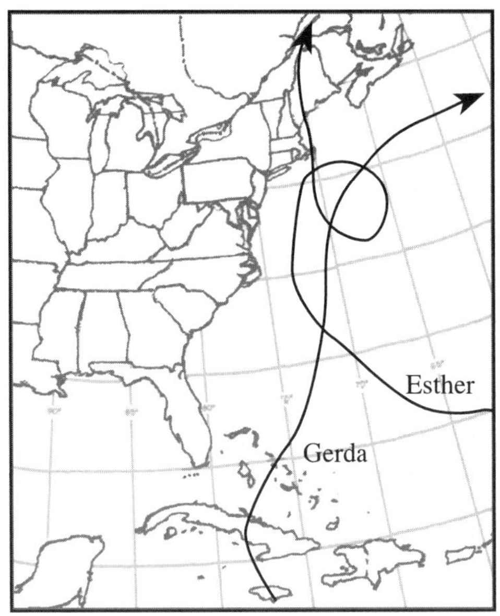

The Space Age embraced hurricane observation during the early 1960s. In 1960, the TIROS I weather satellite made history by transmitting images of a hurricane. Then, on September 10, 1961, TIROS III became the initial satellite to spot the birth of a tropical storm, a whirl soon named "Esther."

The hurricane was involved with several firsts. It's the only known tropical cyclone to make a clockwise loop off the Mid-Atlantic coast before striking New England. And Esther became the earliest target of a hurricane modification project.

Weakening a hurricane? The experiment captured national attention.

On September 16-17, while over the Atlantic Ocean midway between Puerto Rico and Bermuda, Esther received the opening salvo of what became an ongoing research and hurricane modification program, *Project Stormfury*. Aircraft from the Weather Bureau, Navy and Air Force bombarded Esther's eye with silver iodide in an effort to induce weakening. There was scant evidence of any change in strength.

The hurricane peaked north of Puerto Rico on September 17, swirling winds of 150 mph. Barometric pressure fell to 27.37 inches.

Esther weakened to a Category 1 storm off the Mid-Atlantic coast and meandered south of New England from September 21-25. High pressure blocking the hurricane prevented a breakout. Hurricane-strength gusts were limited to the tip of eastern Long Island. Montauk Point recorded a gust of 92 mph.

Nassau and Suffolk counties on Long Island received the brunt of periodic gales. About 280,000 homes lost power. Tides surged up to six feet above normal. Still, the storm caused less damage than anticipated.

Gales and needed rain spread into eastern New Jersey. Atlantic City and Newark each had sustained winds of 46 mph, with gusts of 69 mph and 62 mph, respectively. Point Pleasant had a gust of 73 mph. Days of brisk easterly winds and the autumnal equinox caused moderate flooding along the Jersey shore.

A month later, Hurricane Gerda churned up high seas. The storm stayed well offshore but slow movement from October 20-25, easterly winds, and astronomical factors combined to create a second round of coastal flooding and significant erosion along the Mid-Atlantic coast.

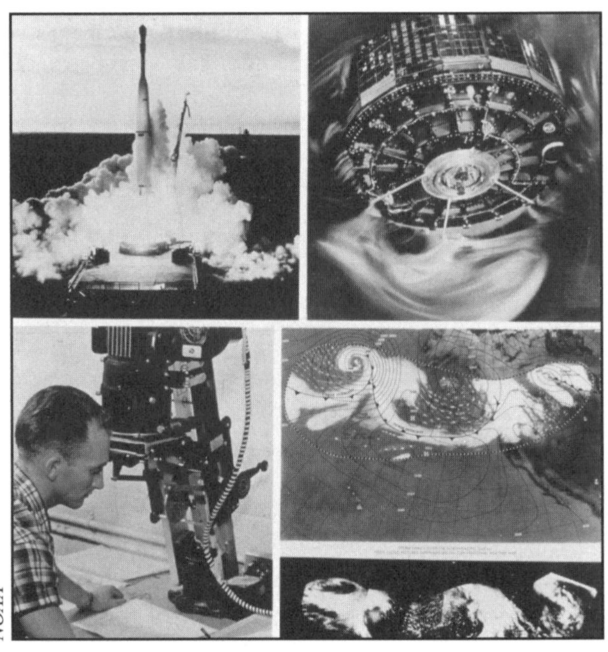

NOAA

TIROS I images of North Pacific storm system on May 19-20, 1960. TIROS I launch on upper left; TIROS I satellite on upper right; processing images on lower left.

PROJECT STORMFURY AIMED TO MODIFY HURRICANES

Can hurricanes be tamed?

That question, indeed the idea of altering climate to serve the public good, created considerable speculation after World War II. There was growing optimism that scientists might control weather. The following item, for example, appeared in the February 1951 issue of *Weatherwise Magazine*:

"On January 11th, a bill to set up a weather control commission was introduced into the Connecticut general assembly by Representative William A. Ward of Clinton. Authority would be vested in the state water commission to institute research and to issue licenses for rainmaking projects."

Frustrated by decades of devastating hurricanes, residents of the East Coast wondered what could be done to control them. The Weather Bureau and military were listening. After an experimental effort to weaken Hurricane Esther, they initiated *Project Stormfury.* The program, a joint venture of the Weather Bureau, Navy and National Science Foundation, formally began in 1962.

Hurricane modification involved seeding the inner edge of a hurricane's eyewall with silver iodide. This would, in theory, dissipate the clouds nearest the center of the storm, expand the eye, increase barometric pressure and weaken the winds—in other words, take some bite out of the beast.

Candidates for seeding had to be hundreds of miles from land. The program targeted the following Atlantic hurricanes: Beulah (August 1963), Debbie (August 1969) and Ginger (October 1971). Each decreased in strength soon after seeding but quickly regained their former intensity.

The key question never answered during two decades of *Stormfury*: Were the changes part of a natural process or had they been induced?

The program lingered into the early 1980s, but no Atlantic system was seeded after Ginger. Doubt and growing skepticism doomed the experiment. Results were deemed inconclusive. Not enough was known about the internal mechanisms of hurricanes to determine lasting effect. A growing number of researchers thought the premise behind hurricane seeding was theoretically flawed.

Meteorologists have since learned that dynamics in the eyewall continuously change. Concentric eyewall replacement cycles are an integral process of major hurricanes. A new wall forms outside the inner eyewall, gains prominence and cuts off inflow to the latter causing its disintegration. Fluctuations in wind strength accompany the changes. *Stormfury* unintentionally attempted to duplicate a natural process.

Scientific uncertainties, the difficulty of finding hurricanes that met increasingly stringent search criteria, and limited funding brought *Stormfury* to an end. The effort achieved a better understanding of tropical cyclones. But hurricane modification proved elusive.

Through it all, officials feared a public outcry if a destructive hurricane struck land after being targeted. Indeed, a short-lived forerunner, *Project Cirrus,* created a furor when a seeded hurricane surprised forecasters by turning west and striking the Georgia coast during October 1947. The ghost of *Cirrus* always haunted *Stormfury*.

1964

August/September

CLEO AND DORA

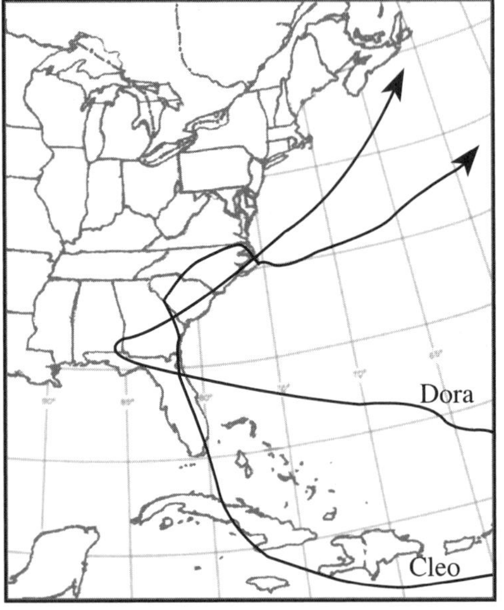

Various ocean-going hurricanes have affected Norfolk, Va., but an inland storm provided its most prodigious rainfall.

Hurricane Cleo struck Miami, Fla., on August 27. The storm crawled through the Carolinas on August 31 and September 1. Days of sporadic showers in coastal Virginia became torrents. An intensifying Cleo dallied for several hours along the North Carolina-Virginia border, then sped out to sea. Moisture clashed with a slow-moving cold front.

Much of southeastern Virginia recorded daily and 24-hour rainfall records. Norfolk collected 11.40 inches in 20 hours on Aug. 31-Sept.1. The Back Bay National Wildlife Refuge, about 20 miles southeast of Norfolk, gathered 14.09 inches. Virginia Beach garnered its heaviest 24-hour rainfall, 13.70 inches.

Just 13 days after Cleo, Hurricane Dora struck the northeastern coast of Florida. It produced disastrous flooding in the Panhandle region, Georgia and the Carolinas. Remnants drenched southeastern Virginia with another 3-6 inches of rain. As a result of the two hurricanes, Norfolk had its wettest September, 12.26 inches.

***

While the southeastern United States dealt with too much rain, the Northeast struggled with too little. From 1961 to 1966, extreme drought plagued the Mid-Atlantic region and New England. New Jersey, among the hardest-hit states, had its longest and most severe dry spell. During the late summer of 1964, denizens could only look south and hope while facing stringent water restrictions and ever-dwindling reservoirs.

1967

September

DORIA

Hurricane Doria gave the Northeast a scare during September 1967 when it threatened to directly strike the Mid-Atlantic coast and plunge inland.

A disturbance intensified to a tropical storm off the southeastern United States on September 9. It soon moved out to sea while continuing to strengthen, seemingly of little concern to the East Coast. However, high pressure anchored over the New England states steered the hurricane west, from September 13-16. Red and black-checkered flags were hoisted along the Delmarva Peninsula and Jersey shore.

Doria approached the Mid-Atlantic region with nearly the same strength, speed and direction as the infamous hurricane of August 1933. Fortunately, it was compact. Coastal flooding remained minimal and onshore winds never exceeded gale force.

Forecasters couldn't determine where the whirl would go next — "capricious," "erratic," and "fickle" were some of the nicer adjectives used to describe its singular track. They thought the storm might retain 100-mph winds until landfall in Maryland, Delaware or New Jersey. Doria would then swing through Pennsylvania and New York.

Instead, the hurricane turned south on September 16 and weakened. Gusts of near-hurricane strength were recorded at a few locations along the central Delmarva coast. Doria diminished to a tropical storm while off Virginia and gradually dissipated.

1969

August

CAMILLE

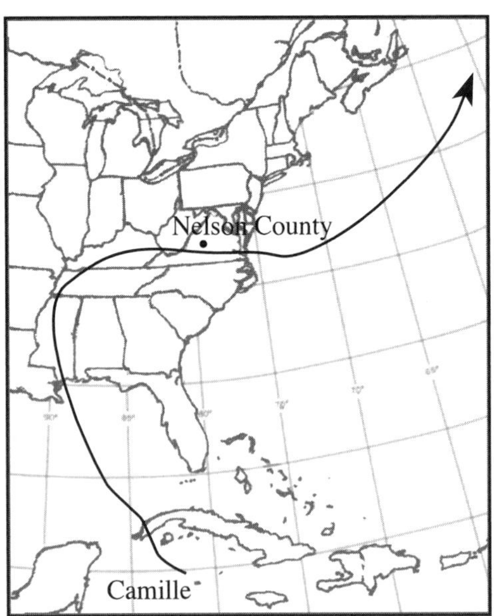

Hurricane Camille.

The name conjures up dread images of wind and wave along the central Gulf Coast. On August 17, it blasted the area with gusts of 200 mph and generated an immense storm surge. A minimum central pressure of 26.85 inches made Camille the second strongest hurricane to strike the United States, runner-up to the Great Labor Day Hurricane of 1935. It claimed about 140 lives in Mississippi, Louisiana and Alabama. It left 200,000 people homeless.

But Camille wasn't finished.

In Nelson County, Va., as well as other sections of the state, memories of Camille are of flood, mud and death. By sunrise on August 20, 1969, the hurricane dealt the Old Dominion its deadliest natural disaster.

Nelson County and Hurricane Camille are forever linked because of five terrible hours. Between 10 p.m. on August 19 and 3 a.m. on August 20, the rural enclave of 12,000 residents received most of a rainfall that likely exceeded 30 inches on local mountainsides. At least 151 people perished in Virginia—most in Nelson County— more than the number of confirmed dead along the Gulf Coast.

***

Camille should have died a quiet death after clobbering Mississippi. It plunged inland doing the things a sputtering tropical cyclone usually does. Rainfall decreased, subsiding to a modest 2-4 inches. Forecasters downgraded the system to a tropical depression when it reached Kentucky.

But Camille played possum. Then it threw a tantrum while traversing the Appalachian Mountains. The Weather Bureau predicted 2-3 inches of rain for rural Nelson County, about 30 miles southwest of Charlottesville, Va. Instead, the area received an epic cloudburst.

Turbulent clouds portending trouble converged on the county around sunset on August 19. Showers began, gently at first, clattering on rooftops—good sleeping weather. Rain intensified, becoming torrential around 10 p.m. As the storm progressed, inky streaks of intense precipitation were highlighted against a backdrop of almost constant lightning—natural strobe lights. The downpour became deafening.

A spokesman for the Weather Bureau said, "The devil himself couldn't have put together a more unlikely series of freakish events with such perfect timing to produce such a concentrated torrential rainfall. The maximum verified amount of rain reported, 27 inches, is close to the maximum amount of rainfall theoretically possible in this part of the world in an 8-hour period."

The Weather Bureau concluded that Camille produced a greater than once-in-a-thousand-year event.[1]

Timing may have played a role, according to Paul Chaston, a meteorologist and author of the book, *Hurricanes!*

[1] It was, perhaps, a millennium event for Nelson County but not necessarily the Middle Atlantic states. The region boasts some of the most intense short-term downpours on earth. Unionville, in north central Maryland, collected 1.23 inches of rain in one minute on July 4, 1956, a world record. Guinea, in central Virginia, about 10 miles south of Fredericksburg, earned a planetary record with 9.25 inches of rain in 40 minutes on August 24, 1906. A cloudburst at Smethport, in northwestern Pennsylvania, deposited 30.6 inches of rain in six hours on July 18, 1942, and a total of 34.5 inches. A thunderstorm dumped 10.1 inches of rain in two hours, and a total of 12.44 inches, on Leonardtown in Southern Maryland on the night of July 22-23, 1969.

"Some of the heaviest rains associated with a hurricane occur from one to a few days after landfall with the rain becoming more intense at night and less intense during the daytime. These storms 'breathe in' at night and 'breathe out' during the day. More research is needed to yield the definitive reasons why the upward motion of air and moisture convergence increase toward the center of the low at night when it is inland."

Patrick Michaels, the Virginia state climatologist, described the synoptic and geographic conditions that tragically coalesced:

"The same feature that turned Camille to the east was also pushing a modest cold front through the Midwest. Because the airstream Camille was embedded in was slower moving than the front, the front eventually caught up with Camille's moisture core over central Virginia.

"The denser air behind the cold front undercut Camille's tropical air mass and, in the process of lifting it, doubled the amount of rainfall that had occurred in Kentucky. In addition, Camille's remnant circulation was now able to draw moisture from the Gulf Stream, which it focused towards the central Virginia mountains. Finally, the mountains themselves mechanically lifted the entire moisture complex further aloft and, in the areas of maximum relief, redoubled the enhancement resulting from the cold front.

"A relatively confined area about 100 miles long and 25 miles wide, stretching from Allegheny to Fluvanna counties, experienced 12-hour rainfalls generally in excess of 10 inches. Certified totals ranged up to 27.35 inches at Massies Mill (elevation 600 ft.), near the junction of the Tye and Piney rivers, and an unofficial measurement showed 31 inches fell in five hours."[2]

All cascading downhill. Nelson County garnered the most intense rainfall for a five-hour period since the National Weather Service began keeping records in 1870. Some localities averaged more than five inches of rain per hour. (Perspective: Most observers would consider one inch an hour as heavy.) Creeks transformed into rivers. Mountainsides turned to mush.

"What could people do?" asks Clifford Wood, who directed the county's rescue effort. "What would you do if you knew 30 inches of rain was on the way? When you hear the word 'flood', you think 'higher ground.' But mountain slides caused many of the casualties."

To make matters worse, the deluge fell as residents slept. By the time they realized what was happening, rising streams and accumulated debris prevented escape.

Water destroyed in many ways. Creeks rose to unbelievable, murderous levels. Mountainsides slid into valleys, tumbled muck leveling and submerging all. Through the hills and valleys came cries, shrieks, pleas for help. "Help!!!"

They resonated through the pounding rain.

What could one do? To attempt rescue would likely require rescue, or worse. Where those snared by the water, mud or debris were going—who could tell? God help 'em.

The full story will never be told. No description can do that night justice. Each survivor endured a unique ordeal.

Along the Tye River, on Davis Creek, at the Rockfish River—along every waterway in the county—residents awoke to a nightmare. They waited helplessly, trapped in darkened homes immersed by a wild, unrelenting current. How high would the water rise? How much punishment could one's abode withstand?

Dwellings resisted the onrush for a time before disintegrating. Or they'd become waterborne en route to oblivion.

Nearly every house was destroyed and 22 people died at Massies Mill (pop. 100) as the Tye River engulfed a narrow valley. Along Davis Creek, about five miles north of the Nelson County seat, Lovingston, 52 people drowned, more than half the valley's inhabitants. The normally inches-deep Davis Creek crested at 50 feet near Woods Mill.

"Although the word 'flood' is frequently used

[2] Gathering reliable rainfall totals proved challenging. A team from the Weather Bureau searched the region to find unobstructed containers known to be empty prior to the storm. They measured 11 inches of rain in a washtub. An ice cream freezer yielded over 13 inches. The greatest verified total, 27 inches, came from a barrel used to burn trash.

(Surveyors faced difficult conditions, thus limiting their investigation. Unconfirmed reports from remote areas suggested that the total storm rainfall on local mountain peaks, particularly those in the vicinity of Davis Creek, exceeded 30 inches and might have been as much as 46 inches.)

to identify the Nelson Disaster, most of the deaths resulted not from drowning but from crushing and massive injuries," wrote Jerry Simpson in the book, *Torn Land*. "The earthslides off the mountains, great conglomerations of trees, boulders, and mud, were the primary cause of death and damage. Those who died in the areas of Tyro, Massies Mill, Norwood, and Rockfish River mostly drowned. Practically all the others died of injuries. These were sudden and overwhelming injuries, and death probably came, in most instances, quickly. Very few persons were found injured after the storm. 'They were either dead or healthy,' a rescue worker said."

Mountains as high as 4,000 feet loom over western and northern Nelson County. A report by the U.S. Geological Survey described how Hurricane Camille induced landslides and debris flows:

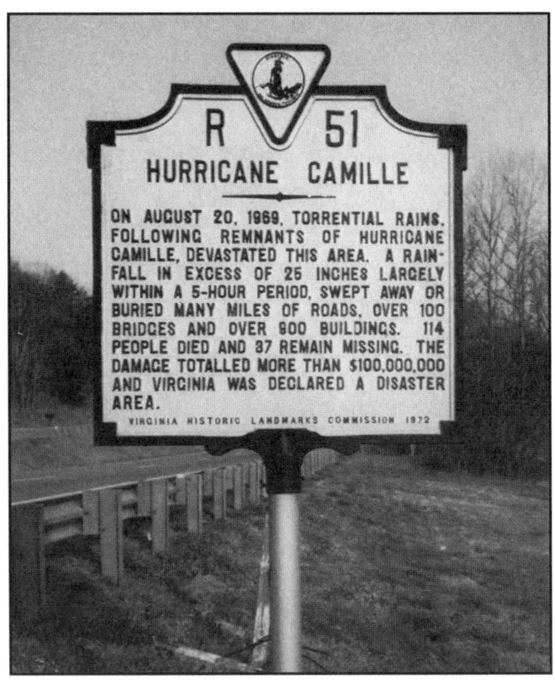

"On the eastern slopes of the Blue Ridge, the soil is underlain directly by rather impervious igneous and metamorphic rocks. In places, the sudden introduction of large amounts of water quickly saturated the soil, increasing the weight of the soil layer, decreasing the cohesive shear strength of the soil, and lubricating the layer. The result is that under the force of gravity a whole section of a mountainside suddenly gave way and slid down, aided by the steep slope angle. All the vegetation, including large trees and much of the soil, was stripped away in scars that in many places exposed bedrock."

Rugged terrain, disruption of communications, impassable roads and demolished bridges made rapid assistance difficult if not impossible. The sound of helicopters became hauntingly familiar and indispensable during the days following Camille.

Flooding plagued much of central Virginia as rivers nourished by the mountains of Nelson County went berserk. The Rivanna, Maury and Jackson rivers attained record crests. The middle James River spread out for more than a mile along part of its route.

Villages along the South River in Rockbridge County, west of Nelson County, were devastated. Vesuvius. Midvale. Cornwall. A family of eight perished in Cornwall.

At Buena Vista, the Maury River rose to an unprecedented 31.2 ft. (flood stage 17 ft.). Factories submerged, houses were ripped from their foundations and vehicles swirled through downtown. More than half of Buena Vista's 6,000 residents were driven from their homes. The business district became muddy shambles.

The Maury and James rivers combined to inundate Glasgow, routing about one-quarter of its population, invading neighborhoods thought immune to flooding. The Red Cross reported that 125 houses were damaged or destroyed. Two families—eight people—took refuge in a barn just north of Glasgow. The Maury River destroyed the building, carrying the group downstream. Only a 7-year-old girl survived.

The James River crested at 26 ft. at Lynchburg, its highest level since 1877.

More than 10 inches of rain fell on Scottsville, about 15 miles south of Charlottesville. Fire sirens blew about 1:30 a.m. on the 20th to alert residents to a flash flood. Two creeks roared through part of the town. Later that day the James River rolled through, wrecking most businesses and many homes, putting a damper on the village's 225th anniversary celebration. The water crested at 30.5 feet, eclipsing a 17-ft. flood stage.

The James rose to 28.6 ft. at Richmond (flood stage 9 ft.), its highest level in nearly 200 years. City employees and volunteers heaved countless sandbags on dikes protecting the city. The levee held. Nevertheless, floodwaters surged through sewers to swamp the old Shockoe Bottom district.

Camille dumped 10-15 inches of rain on sections of Albemarle, Fluvanna and Louisa counties, east-southeast of Charlottesville. Those counties and nearby Caroline, Hanover and King William counties tallied enormous losses.

The town of Louisa, about 25 miles east of Charlottesville, received 11.18 inches of rain on August 19-20. The deluge caused a dam break at 500 acre Lake Louisa. A 20-foot wall of water surged into the North Anna River, swamping vast acreage of farmland, drowning hundreds of cattle and blocking major highways.

Photograph courtesy of NOAA, Department of Commerce

Richmond, Va.

The storm churned the lower and middle Chesapeake Bay with 50-60 mph gusts. Worcester, Somerset, Wicomico, Dorchester, St. Mary's and Calvert counties in Maryland, and Sussex County, Del., reported 3-6 inches of rain and isolated flooding.

Camille reached the Atlantic Ocean early on August 20. It rapidly strengthened from a depression to vigorous tropical storm. (That process that may have begun over Virginia.) The remnants merged with a frontal system off Cape Race, Newfoundland, on August 22 and lost tropical characteristics.

The Buena Vista Lions Club presents an annual Citizens Award to an individual who makes an outstanding contribution to the town. In March 1970 the chapter broke with tradition by recognizing the "community-at-large." A plaque outside the Buena Vista municipal building recalls the honor. It's inscribed:

TO THE CITIZENS OF BUENA VISTA AND THEIR GOOD FRIENDS FROM FAR AND NEAR, IN GRATEFUL RECOGNITION OF THEIR COLLECTIVE EFFORTS AND ACHIEVEMENTS IN THE REBUILDING OF BUENA VISTA FOLLOWING THE FLOOD WHICH CAME IN THE WAKE OF HURRICANE CAMILLE ON AUGUST 20TH 1969.

THIS PLAQUE EXPRESSES APPRECIATION FOR THE LABORS, MONEYS, SERVICES, SUPPLIES, EQUIPMENT, LEADERSHIP, AND THE SPIRIT OF COOPERATION WHICH WERE EXTENDED BY INDIVIDUALS, ORGANIZATIONS, AGENCIES, AND COMPANIES; BOTH LOCAL AND THROUGHOUT THE NATION; TO RELIEVE THE FLOOD DEVASTATION AND TO RESTORE ORDER TO OUR CITY. IN UNITY LIES OUR STRENGTH.

NELSON COUNTY FOUND LEADERS IN ITS HOUR OF NEED

Clifford Wood (far right) with other officials during the crisis.

Life works in strange ways.

Clifford Wood, who had never held public office, volunteered as a write-in candidate for Nelson County supervisor during the final days of the 1968 campaign. He won. Shortly thereafter, his colleagues on the board chose him vice-chairman. Then came Camille.

A year before the hurricane, Nelson County sheriff William Whitehead attended a civil defense workshop at the University of Virginia. It focused on handling the aftermath of a nuclear attack but was applicable to natural disasters.

The seminar ended with a crisis simulation exercise. Whitehead grew impatient. He had been sheriff since 1960 and thought he knew a thing or two about disaster response. Yet, his solutions didn't satisfy instructors.

"What would you do if this didn't work out?" they asked. "What would you do if that didn't work out?" "What if?" "What then?"

"I told them they were crazy," Whitehead said. "Nothing like that is ever going to happen. Well, Camille made the exercise look like a piker."

***

Wood became a county supervisor almost by accident. The unopposed incumbent had died weeks before the election. Wood felt it a civic obligation to step in. The farmer invested $100 to notify voters of his availability.

"In my election campaign," said Wood, "the $100 was the cost of printing my letter to constituents. It simply stated that I would serve if elected. It included a sample ballot to explain how to write my name in. It was my only expense. I had no party affiliation. I won easily since no one else was interested in the position."

Wood heard the weather forecast as Camille approached and, frankly, it didn't sound ominous. The dying remnants were expected to drop some rain on his farm in Wingina, on the eastern fringe of Nelson County. The corn crop was nearing harvest. A little rain wouldn't hurt.

He beheld a stunning sight the next morning. The James River submerged his field. The water was crimson—an indication that a deluge had fallen and mingled with the Piedmont red clay of northwestern Nelson County.

A flood on the James River normally takes a day or two to reach Wood's property. This took hours.

Camille dropped about 4 inches of rain on his farm. However, less than 20 miles to the northwest it dumped more than 25 inches.

Wood attempted a telephone call but the line was out of service. A neighbor arrived and said that nearby Howardsville (pop. 300) had flooded. Boats were urgently needed. Wood and two cousins hitched up an 11-foot skiff and proceeded to the beleaguered village. In the book, *Torn Land*, he recounted:

"We could see that Howardsville had washed away.

"We could see a couple on a rooftop. Apparently the husband had chopped his way out of the attic and had gotten out on the roof. I asked them if there was anyone else (in a nearby house) and they said yes, 'Mother lives down there and I told her to go upstairs.'

"We paddled down that far and met this real sweet old lady. We told her who we were and why we were there. She said she didn't think she would leave; she had decided to go upstairs. She thought she would be all right, and she didn't like boats anyway.

"We tried to impress on her what a *good* boat we had, and how *well-trained* we were at handling this boat, and I ended up claiming kin with her, and everything else. And we *were* related, in some sort of way. We talked about the church meetings and so forth. We spent about 30 minutes just talking to her, and finally she agreed to come out with us, and she was just as calm as she could be in the boat. She got her medicine and her handbag and so on, and we paddled back up and picked up her son and his wife.

"His wife was upset. She told me in the boat that she had just gotten word from Mississippi or Louisiana, some kin folks had called to tell her that they were all right down there, that they had escaped the hurricane and she was so pleased to know this, and now look what was happening to her! And what she seemed most upset about were two things: one was the color television set, this was what was on her mind just then, and the pictures of all of her children—this was what upset her more than anything, the loss of these pictures."

Wood left Howardsville and returned to Wingina. He received a report of casualties in Norwood, near the confluence of the James and Tye rivers, about five miles away.

"Two families had disappeared," Wood said. "A man, his wife and three children, and an elderly couple.

"Their houses were slightly elevated and the water first went around the homes separating their occupants from safety. In a situation like that, your natural inclination is to hang on to your house.

"They were swept away at daybreak. People saw them floating down the river yelling for help. The houses struck a railroad bridge and disintegrated.

"Had we known what happened at Massies Mill we could have reached those people before daylight and gotten them out easily or warned them. But we just didn't know. There was no telephone system, the roads were inundated, and everybody was cut off on their own little island."

Wood's uncle, a resident of Buckingham County, forever remembered August 20 as the day the James River flowed backward. He lived about three miles upstream from where the Tye River empties into the James.

"He said that he came on his porch around 6 a.m. and saw the James flowing in the wrong direction," said Wood. "It was flowing back toward Lynchburg and covered with logs. He said that it stayed like that for a while, and then stood still for a time before it returned to a normal direction. Can you imagine?"

The stupendous volume of water on the Tye River caused it to spread out at its juncture with the James, seemingly reversing the James' flow for several miles and hours.

While in Wingina, Wood met a utility repair crew supervisor who told him that several people had drowned in Lovingston, the county seat. "I thought, 'That's unbelievable. Something horrific must have happened.' Lovingston doesn't have a stream, hardly. It has a stream that in wet weather will run and in dry weather doesn't."

Wood drove to Lovingston, taking a circuitous route. Arriving at noon, he dodged beef carcasses left after the destruction of the town's supermarket. A house lay on the median strip north of the village, the casualty of a mudslide along the county's main thoroughfare, U.S. 29. Nearly every road out of town was impassable. In fact, five major washouts and 30 landslides blocked the 47-mile section of U.S. 29 between Amherst and Charlottesville.

Wood and several other officials drove north along U.S. 29 until debris blocked their way. Dazed survivors told them that many inhabitants of Davis Creek, just ahead, were missing. The group returned to Lovingston.

Hunter Mawyer, chairman of the board of supervisors, was marooned in his home. He delegated disaster response to Wood.

It was important, Wood emphasized, that representatives of Nelson County rather than outsiders lead the emergency operation. "Someone had to take charge and be the leader. It fell on me."

Nelson County had no formal natural disaster response guidelines. In 1969, few Virginia counties did. The men leading the operation winged it using prior military training and common sense. They winged it with a citizenry willing to fight back. They winged it with a magnificent outpouring of support from people throughout the nation.

***

Sheriff Whitehead spent the evening of August 19 at the county courthouse in Lovingston monitoring state primary election results. He left for his Roseland home shortly after 9 p.m., turning on windshield wipers to sweep away a gentle rain. Showers turned heavy around 10 p.m. During the next five hours about 27 inches of rain fell at Massies Mill, just two miles away.

Shortly after 10 p.m., Whitehead received a telephone call from a deputy, Ron Woods. Woods, also fire marshal for the Piney River Volunteer Fire Department, had taken a truck to pump out a basement. The effort ended when a wall collapsed and muck and water gushed in. Woods battled blinding rain and flooded roads while returning to the firehouse.

Whitehead offered to drive to Piney River. Woods urged him to stay home. The five-mile route would be treacherous, if not impossible. Conversation ended. The telephone remained silent. Unknown to Whitehead, a slide on a nearby mountain knocked out service.

"It had been a long day and I was tired," Whitehead said. "Sometime between 11:30 and 12, I decided to go to bed. By that time, we started to get lightning. It came in brilliant flashes. It would light everything up like day. Down beneath the rain clouds there were almost continuous flashes. You could get around without a light.

"I went to bed, but my wife was deathly afraid of electrical storms. I dozed off and went to sleep. My wife couldn't sleep. Finally, she woke me up a little after midnight. She said, 'I thought you told me that there wasn't going to be any hurricane.' I said, 'That's right. I talked to the Weather Bureau and they said that the hurricane-force winds were gone, but we'd get some rain.' She said, 'I'd wish you'd listen. Listen to the wind blowing out there.'

"I listened and I could hear roaring. I couldn't understand it. There wasn't supposed to be hurricane winds. I got up and went to the window.

"You could hear this roaring, but the leaves of the trees were hanging straight down," Whitehead said. "There wasn't a breath of air stirring. However, it was like the trees were under a waterfall. You couldn't see any grass, just water. The yard slopes down and normally water quickly runs off. But the rain was falling faster than it could run off, so it was covering the grass, a continuous stream several inches deep.

Whitehead looked closer and shuddered.

"I stuck my head out the window and looked toward the creek. It was almost up to my swimming pool (about 30 feet above normal). It was a torrent of water going like a runaway freight train, with waves four or five feet high and white-capped. I told my wife to get dressed and wake the children."

He stepped outside and went to a neighboring house on the top of the hill, his mother's residence. Whitehead tried to rouse her, but deafening rain challenged all efforts. "I had to hold my hand over my mouth and nose to be able to breathe. It was like being under a waterfall."

The door parted. Whitehead described what he'd observed.

"She told me that she'd seen worse and not to be concerned about it—'Go back to bed.' I said, 'Mother, you've never seen anything like this! Nothing like this has ever happened before!' "

Whitehead drove to Route 151 but didn't travel far. The road was blocked in each direction. As he returned home, the lights of a pickup truck stabbed through a curtain of rain.

Two friends, Wilson White and Frank "Tinker" Bryant, Jr., came looking for him. A slide on a tributary of Hat Creek claimed Bryant's house. His wife and three daughters were missing. The sheriff learned what happened.

"A dam formed 200 to 300 yards above his house," Whitehead said. "It broke and a 30-foot wall of water and debris slammed into his house knocking it off its foundation and sweeping it downstream.

"He and his wife were downstairs and the three girls were sleeping upstairs. The house started to move. Tinker grabbed his wife by the hand and they tried to go up the steps to where the girls were. The water swirled through and ripped off part of the house. It jerked her away from him, washing them and the girls away.

"He said that he was under water, swimming, struggling and trying to get a breath. He thought his lungs were going to pop. He had just about given up, was ready to swallow water and die. About that time Tinker came to the surface and gasped for air. He grabbed a tree and held on. That saved his life."

"Help find my family!" Bryant told Whitehead.

Rain slackened shortly after 3 a.m. The sheriff organized a search party but their effort proved futile. (The bodies were discovered days later.) Receding waters later that morning revealed wrecked houses, the flotsam of everyday living, and the dead.

Whitehead made radio contact with the regional civil defense office. But the channel was jammed with emergency traffic; his message misunderstood. He was told not to worry, that floodwaters on the James River wouldn't affect Nelson County for a day or two. Officials had no clue about conditions on the Tye or Rockfish rivers, or at Davis Creek, where more than 50 people died.

Ed Tinsley

Road interrupted. Along U.S. 29.

***

When Lloyd Thomas, a state police lieutenant, reported for duty late on August 19, he expected an uneventful shift. By early on the 20th, however, flooding and landslides left him stranded in Lovingston. His radio became a vital link to the outside world.

Thomas witnessed the fantastic that night. He stopped outside Lovingston to assist a truck driver stalled in high water along U.S. 29.

"While I was sitting there working with this tractor-trailer, a bolt of lightning struck a house trailer about 100 feet from our location and it just blazed up like a large match had been struck, and it was completely destroyed," Thomas told a Congressional panel investigating the disaster. "While sitting there, the lightning was such that it would light things up almost as bright as day, and I observed, right in front of us, a home sliding down off the mountain, and it slid right down into the highway and lodged there, and remained there for several days after this problem arose."

The Virginia Office of Civil Defense heard of the flood from Thomas. It dispatched Jim Tribble to assess the situation. He flew to Lovingston by helicopter on the afternoon of August 20 and met with Wood. Their partnership proved critical in the days ahead. Tribble relayed Wood's disaster declaration to Richmond. The immediate task: form an organization to deal with the crisis.

An aerial survey provided an eye-opener. The scene defied comprehension. The mind couldn't accept it. The impossible had happened.

"The county was a mess, an absolute mess," Wood said.

Landmarks were gone. A canyon of mud and debris marked Davis Creek. Mountainsides featured giant claw marks, jumbled paths of unimaginable chaos.

Wood met with Jack Saunders, the county's civil defense coordinator, and set up a makeshift headquarters on U.S. 29. The open-air "control center" soon included a school bus, Chevrolet van and state police car. A tarpaulin offered shade. A portable generator provided electricity. Card tables and the trunk of vehicles served as desktops.

Officials improvised an aircraft landing strip, "Lovingston Airport." A level section along U.S. 29 served as a runway for small planes and helicopters.

Volunteers were chosen to head vital tasks: search and rescue (there'd be over 300 helicopter missions), distributing food, clothing and shelter, dispatching medical assistance, locating and identifying the dead.

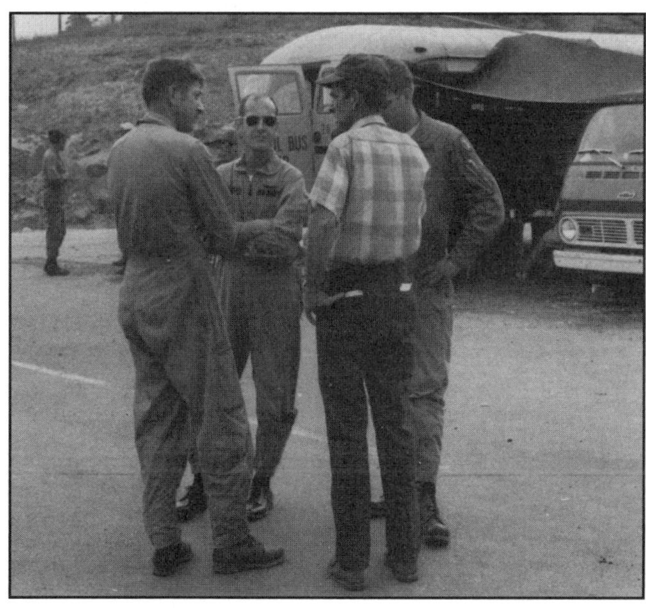

Cliff Wood confers at the emergency command center in Lovingston, Va.

The state police barricaded roads into the county and were stingy with admission. Wood instituted a rigorous pass system. "We didn't want everybody coming in to look at the disaster," he said. "It's demoralizing to have strangers come by and stare at you in your distress. And a large number of visitors would have hindered operations."

The sale of alcoholic beverages was suspended for the duration.

On Thursday evening, August 21, the men leading the emergency operation gathered at the courthouse to assess the situation and discuss plans for the coming day. Daily assessments and discussions became a ritual for weeks.

Overnight lodging was hastily procured. Wood and Tribble borrowed mattresses from the county jail. The men attempted to nap on the floor of the sheriff's office. They settled for a sleepless respite.

So much had happened. So much needed doing. The scope of the disaster continued to unfold.

Top priorities included saving lives and tending to the injured. Rumors of many deaths proved fact. Nearly all rescues occurred during or shortly after Camille's rampage.

Portable radios and emergency telephones arrived on Friday, August 22. Ham radio operators also set up a station.

Gov. Mills Godwin flew in for the first of several visits. He was shaken by what he saw. "It is impossible to describe in words," Godwin said after touring Massies Mill. "It can only be realized by one who goes there and walks down the street and sees that every house and building save two have been destroyed or damaged."

He worked closely with Nelson County.

"At first, we had no idea where we'd find the resources to do what we needed to do," Wood said. "There was no FEMA (Federal Emergency Management Agency) in those days. The governor said, 'We'll do what we have to do and worry about paying for it later.' That's a great philosophy!"

***

Whitehead started an organization in Roseland, which evolved as a satellite of the central command in Lovingston, located less than 10 impassable miles away. His area included some of the hardest-hit communities: Tyro, Massies Mill, Roseland and Piney River. From *Torn Land*:

"The people in my home district there were all just pouring to me, 'Can I do this?' 'Should I do that?' 'What should I do?' 'What about food?' 'What about water?' 'What about this?' Every problem that came up they brought to me—which is a natural thing, and to which I had no objection. I wanted to try to help them. But I still had my hands full. I just had more than I could do, so I began to set up some semblance of an organization, very similar to what they had in Lovingston, based on the practice mission that had been staged for us by personnel from the University of Virginia earlier, in which I had been an active participant, of course."

Whitehead and county supervisor Walter Hoffman handled aid requests from Massies Mill. Hoffman lived two miles west of the village. He woke during the night of Camille and immediately sensed something was wrong. Water seemed to be rushing outside his house although there was no creek or river nearby.

"I couldn't figure out what it was until I went outside," Hoffman said. "I walked out the back door and stepped into water. The house wasn't in a ravine or low spot, just on the gentle slope of a mountain. Still, the water accumulated there."

His house was unharmed. At dawn, he drove a tractor to a rise overlooking Massies Mill.

"It looked like a big lake," said Hoffman. "The whole place was inundated from hill to hill."

American Red Cross

Lovingston, Va. "... Lovingston doesn't have a stream, hardly. It has a stream that in wet weather will run and in dry weather doesn't." — Cliff Wood
A Southern Railroad tender was carried about two miles by floodwaters.

That day, he and others rescued neighbors stranded in trees and debris. They witnessed ruin throughout the Tye River valley, but that's not what caused the greatest sorrow.

"You have friends you've lost and you're more devastated by that than anything," he said. "That's worse than the physical devastation."

***

Whitehead flew to Lovingston and met with Wood on Thursday, August 21. The encounter didn't go well. The sheriff came with a long list of needs and found Wood under siege. Every time they'd confer, somebody would interrupt. An exasperated Whitehead got up and left. He returned to Roseland empty-handed.

The men met again the following Monday. They labored on too little sleep and had seen too much pain, too much death. Each believed the other uncooperative, if not hostile.

"Apparently, what he thought I was doing to him, I thought he was doing to me," Whitehead said in *Torn Land*. "So we both blew our stacks. And immediately after this we shook hands and both of us admitted that we had been wrong and had made mistakes in prejudging each other—that we had a job to do yet, and that the thing to do was to forget about petty things of that nature and to buckle down and go ahead and try to get the job done."

***

During the waning days of August there were the striking incongruities seen after every flood. Away from the grasp of waterways, beyond the carnage, life went on as usual. Kids playing ball, lawns being mowed, fields harvested—typical sounds and scenes of late summer.

But on Virginia's highways, convoys converged on flood-ravaged districts. Tractor-trailers loaded with food, clothing and other necessities raced down reopened roads, mingling with busloads of volunteers. The Red Cross, church and fraternal groups and other organizations offered assistance. Officials in Lovingston faced the task of storing and disbursing supplies, and coordinating an army of those eager to assist.

"It was remarkable," Wood said. "The desire to help others says a lot about this country."

Recovery began in earnest.

Wood served as a military policeman during the Korean War. Those dispossessed in Nelson County reminded him of the forlorn refugees he'd seen in Seoul and other war-torn places. This time they were friends and neighbors. He felt responsible for their welfare.

"We stayed busy," Wood said. "Each week there was something else. A road got opened. A house got built or (temporary) housing was set up. A streambed was dug out and the land reshaped, the rocks reburied. That sort of thing.

"People would see things happening like a big Caterpillar at work. You knew we were progressing. A helicopter flying overhead. You knew what it was doing. You saw tremendous resources doing things, building things and fixing things. It gave us hope."

The search for the dead continued into September. It was grueling and difficult work, locating bodies and bringing them to a makeshift morgue for identification.

Volunteers immersed themselves in a sweltering world of muck, stench and debris. Local teenagers proved effective, doggedly returning day after day.

Early on, Phillip Payne went to his father Dan, the director of search operations, offering his assistance and that of other teenagers. The elder Payne reluctantly agreed. Helicopters took the boys to rugged, remote locations. They'd spend countless hours working their way along stream banks, returning mud-splattered and bone-tired after locating numerous bodies.

John Gordon, pastor of Calvary Baptist Church in Lovingston, made victim retrieval his mission. As stated in *Torn Land*:

"County youngsters recovered bodies; rescue squadsmen recovered bodies and Mennonite teams recovered bodies. But when the body was particularly decayed and difficult to extract, when the stench was overpowering, when recovery seemed an impossible task, John Gordon was the man who went out to get it. Gordon personally recovered 17 bodies. Dan Payne, who coordinated recovery missions, said of him, 'He was the best there was. There was nothing he couldn't, or wouldn't, do.' "

Several residents threatened Wood and his staff because they felt officials weren't doing enough to locate missing kin, or for other reasons. He bears no grudges.

"We would take the fuss and wouldn't fight back," Wood said. "We could understand their frustration. These people came back later and apologized for being so mean. I told them they needn't apologize. We understood."

There came a time to stop searching for the dead, to return to a semblance of normalcy. The command center shut down on September 10. Relief operations transferred to county offices.

The community held a memorial service weeks after Camille. Gov. Godwin addressed the gathering.

"The governor said kind things," Wood recalled. "He had lost a daughter who had been struck by lightning. We knew that he was sincere. His speaking was important to us."

***

Challenges continued. Flood victims spent several months and more in trailers serving as 'temporary' shelter. Many homes were never rebuilt. American Cyanimid and Georgia Marble, leading employers, soon left. The area wrestled with Camille's aftermath for years.

Today, various memorials honor the dead. Nelson County will never forget Camille, but it has moved on.

The landscape still bears scars. There are other scars, too, unseen.

Whitehead lost his bid for re-election, a defeat that stung.

"I felt like this: I had done the best I had known how for the citizens of Nelson County," he said. "I certainly did a fairly good job at it. But doing a good job didn't get me re-elected. It got me defeated. I felt bad about losing the election."

In early 1972, Whitehead found a job with the state Office of Civil Defense. He soon became acting director for the region encompassing northern Virginia. That June another devastating flood struck the Old Dominion—Hurricane Agnes. Whitehead's adept handling of that crisis led to a promotion. He went on to assist jurisdictions in emergency planning and requirements. Today, every county in Virginia has a natural disaster response plan.

Wood never sought public office again, had no interest in it. He now sells real estate. His Lovingston office is within sight of the Camille command post. Memories linger.

"I had this awful feeling the first few days that we weren't getting anything done," Wood said. "The sheriff and I have talked about that. The frustration. Feeling so helpless. And all the death that occurred before we could even respond. I had that hanging over my head, which I couldn't do anything about.

"As I've gotten older I've begun to live with the idea that we did our best at the time. I remember that on the second or third day an older gentleman that I knew well and had a lot of respect for came to see me at the control center. He asked me to take a walk with him. He said, 'I want to tell you something. Years from now people will ask why you did this or why you did that. All you can say is that you did what you thought was right.'

"I can still say that. I did what I thought was right."

Cliff Wood today.

STATE TROOPER RECORDED A PORTRAIT OF DISASTER

Ed Tinsley

On August 16, 2004, Virginia state trooper Ed Tinsley sewed on a departmental record ninth service stripe, the start of his 46th year in uniform. Days later, another anniversary was on his mind. It had been 35 years since Hurricane Camille.

The night of the flood he visited his parents in Bedford County, about 40 miles from Massies Mill. The storm dropped "maybe an inch" of rain, according to Tinsley. He thought nothing of it until the telephone rang the next morning. Although it was his day off, "The secretary at the area office called and told me, 'The sergeant says come back to (Amherst) county, get in uniform, get in your car, get on the road and give him a call.' I asked, 'What's going on?' She replied, 'When you get there, you'll find out.' "

Tinsley's assignment: determine the extent of flooding, report on what roads and bridges remained open and assess what assistance might be needed. There followed an unforgettable day of blockages—roads washed out, bridges or their approaches gone, mudflows.

The trooper drove northeast, seeking passage across the James River. The closest bridge still open was at Bremo's Bluff, about 30 miles downstream from Nelson County. He crossed and turned west, skirting the county's northern boundary. At one point, Tinsley followed a tractor as a farmer led him through fields and woods, a not-on-any-map bypass of a swamped highway. He headed south, planning to drive through the Tye River Valley. He halted in the mountain hamlet of Montebello. Beyond, there was no hint of a road.

That night, Wednesday, August 20, 1969, Tinsley knew a calamity had occurred. For the next month he kept an oral diary, nightly tape recordings of impressions and reflections. The following are excerpts from his *Portrait of a Disaster*:

THURSDAY, AUG. 21

I proceeded into areas of Nelson County that I had thought about the night before, which had not been checked. After finding several routes into this area washed out, I reached (the vicinity of) Massies Mill, coming in over secondary roads. I was getting some idea of what massive damage we'd had. Every low spot in the mountains had washed out—from the very top of the mountain down—which would indicate a terrific amount of rain, of water, involved.

I continued into Massies Mill. The water was just beginning to recede. There had not yet been any count or location of the bodies and missing. This was a community of approximately 40 houses and buildings. There were only two that were undamaged enough so they could be lived in.

While at this location, I informed the sergeant of my desire to check a section of Amherst County. He agreed. We lined up a rescue squad to go in.

Coming back from Massies Mill into Piney River I picked up two boys: one, 14, and one, 16. This is all that remained of a family of seven that was living in the immediate area of Massies Mill.

The 14-year-old said that they had gone to bed and his father had awaken them when he realized that water was getting up around the house. They had gotten into their car, the whole family, and started away, when the car flooded out. They all got out and tried to get to (safety). The water was rising so fast that they were all swept away. The two boys that survived hung on to trees until helicopters and rescue teams rescued them early the next morning.

In all of this tragedy, it gave me a real good feeling to realize that in the midst of this (the boys) did not want to leave the scene. They were concerned about staying and making funeral arrangements for their mother and father and the other three brothers and sisters. It was quite heartening to realize that somebody as young as this would be concerned about such things.[4]

At this time we have 56 people missing and 26 known dead.

FRIDAY, AUG. 22

I proceeded to the Lovingston area where we had a (command center) set up which was eventually called "Control." From here I was dispatched with a helicopter into the area I had covered the day before. We picked up approximately 12 people.

During trips that I made in the helicopter, it was brought very vividly to my imagination and vision how much damage had occurred. This area of the Blue Ridge apparently had immense rain dropped on top of it. And every gully, every little valley, every low spot in the mountains has been washed out as if some giant claw had grabbed hold of it and pulled everything out. They've been washed all the way down to solid rock. Everything gone! As this built-up going down the mountains to the streams and rivers and on into the larger rivers, it carried everything with it. Highways, roads, people, houses, cars, trucks.

In one area alone, we lost two tractor-trailers completely which, up to this time, have been unaccounted for. There have been others that have been recovered, but we have two that have completely disappeared from the face of the earth.

At the end of this day we had 96 missing and 36 known dead.

SATURDAY, AUG. 23

In the past couple of days I have had the opportunity to drive north on (U.S.) 29 to the Woods Mill area, which is completely washed out for a distance of a half-mile. Every field coming down out of the mountains was completely filled—some to a depth of 30, 40, 50 feet—with mud.

At one particular location there was a row of houses (along U.S. 29). As the water, mud, debris and trees came down, it picked up three and buried them. I understand that there are nine persons missing there. These people will never be located because they're buried in too much debris. It would appear, looking at this damage, that some mighty hand had reached and picked things up, tossing them around, then washed them down with a fire hose.

I had an occasion to take a helicopter ride with some dignitaries. They were very impressed and visibly touched by what they'd seen. The day before, the governor had been up. He was visibly touched by what he'd seen to the point of very visible tears in his eyes. That is the general feeling of everybody involved.

---

[4] The 14-year-old, Warren Raines, and his brother, Carl, related a harrowing tale.

With the Tye River rising and surrounding the house, the family decided to evacuate. Four children of a neighboring family arrived, and 11 people crowded into the Raines' station wagon. The vehicle stalled on Route 56. Everyone waded through the increasingly turbulent, rising water. Most were swept away. The boys found refuge in trees. They watched telephone poles, trees, cars and houses go by, illuminated by lightning. A collision would likely have meant a quick death.

Ironically, the Raines' house survived. The upstairs remained untouched. Upon their return, Bo, the family's black lab, greeted the boys. All else was silent.

The word was passed this morning that somebody (told the media) that there was nothing but mass confusion in the whole county, which I would certainly have to disagree with. The organization here is working fine.

I don't know what we'd do without the local people. A lot of them have family that are missing and are working hand-in-hand 16 to 18 hours each day to help the search teams locate where houses were and possibly determine how many people are missing.

We have one man I've worked with who has a brother and sister-in-law missing. He's been out on missions where we've picked up bodies. I feel sure he is hesitant to go out on these but doesn't show it.

We have young people that are coming in and doing tremendous work on search teams. It's good to see people with such organization, even with such tragedy around them. There's certainly no confusion.

At the end of this day, we had 47 known identified dead, 4 unidentified dead, and 91 missing. We had the missing rate rise, and the death rate rise, too.

SUNDAY, AUG. 24

(Tinsley was reassigned to handle radio traffic at the Control Center. He remained there until Sept. 2.)

It is very obvious that the past four 18 to 20-hour workdays are beginning to show on quite a few people. Tempers are cut pretty thin. People are saying a lot of things that they will probably regret later, but it hasn't gone too badly.

At the end of this day we have 50 identified dead, 5 unknown dead, and 101 missing.

MONDAY, AUG. 25

This is my sixth day now in excess of 16 hours. I'm operating the radio again. Our crew has been cut down to two, myself and an investigator.

Again, it's just hard to believe that the damage I'm looking at, the damage I've seen, the damage I've flown over and walked through, could be so great and extensive.

There could never be an accurate description or record in the history books as to what (went on) here. Pictures will show part of it. Words will tell part of it. But it will never be accurately described or made a part of history except by the people that looked at it. If I record this now and tell it later, it will never be as great as what it's been by looking at it.

The death count is 62 dead, 88 missing. The number of missing has dropped a bit, more than the death count has climbed, which is a good sign because some of the missing are turning up. One turned up today. He had been working on a search crew for five days. So these kinds of mistakes, errors, overlooks, are happy overlooks.

However, some bodies being brought in now may never be identified due to the time that's passed since they've been dead. Of course, a lot will never be found. They're buried in the mud, under trees, and some may have washed to the ocean. But back when all this began people were talking, "If I could find this member of my family and bury them so that I know they're buried, I could put up a monument or marker where they are."

In looking at the mountains, I can't think of a more fitting or more permanent monument. In looking at the sides and faces, where the great slides have come down exposing the solid rock for distances of 200 to 300-feet wide all the way to the top—this will outlast any monument that anyone on earth could put up. So my feeling is that if part of my family was buried under this mass of trees and dirt, I'd feel like they were buried good, and a monument erected that would be much better than anything I could ever do.

TUESDAY, AUG 26

It's evening. It's been exactly seven days since the rain started that brought the earth down, the trees down, and caused the disaster we're speaking of. Seven days!

Two or three days after this happened people were talking about leaving. The people are now talking about getting the crops in—what they have left—saving what they can and where they're going to rebuild.

This is good. It bears out the truth that the people here are not cowards or such as that. They are not going to leave. You can't run them out. In fact, we've met one woman who's been living at her location for 74 years who wouldn't even come out to take her shots.

WEDNESDAY, AUG. 27

Nothing new today. Very quiet at my post. Very quiet throughout our whole operation. No bodies were recovered today. At this time we have 63 dead, 84 missing. Several missing have been dropped off (the tally) because they've been located alive.

THURSDAY, AUG. 28

Back on the radio again. Haven't had a lot of traffic through my location today. We found one more body last night, about midnight, a young child completely deteriorated, and a 14 to 15-year-old girl this afternoon. The big problem now seems to be controlling the traffic, the (outsiders) coming in, as the people try to recover.

SUNDAY, AUG. 31

It's been 12 days now since the flood. We got quite a lot of extra searchers over the Labor Day weekend. Yesterday, we recovered six bodies and today we recovered eight. Identification is being held up by the conditions of the bodies.[5]

Everybody involved where I'm located at, "Control," has just about reached the point of being what you would consider 'slap happy.' Everybody's getting so tired you either have to laugh or cry or crack-up, I guess. But things are going on and we think that in the next couple of days we can take down our operation. That will leave us with 30 to 40 bodies missing, which will probably never be found.

I talked to a preacher today who last Sunday, I found out, went to church in his work clothes and boots. I know him from seeing him go out on so many of the missions when they are picking up bodies. He had about 25 people in church and told them that there wouldn't be any sermon. They had work to do. (He told them to) get their work clothes and meet him outside, he'd put them to work. Which is what they did. This is the kind of spirit the whole community is operating on right now.

TUESDAY, SEPT. 2

This is the first day that we have not had search teams out in large numbers. We did not recover any bodies today. However, during the weekend we recovered 20. We feel at the command post that this is possibly the most that we will find. Maybe others will come to light as the construction crews clean out the debris and all from bridges. So this afternoon we moved our armored car, which we have been using as our command post, back to Appomattox. And my job from now on will be working with Investigator (R.D.) Jones in helping to identify what we have. Unless something new comes to light this will be all I'll have to put down in this, my portrait of a disaster.

[5] Eight flood victims remain unidentified as of 2006.

***

Tinsley objected when first posted to the Lovingston command center: "I wanted to be in the field going into the hollows and helping the search teams."

The trooper plans to retire in 2007. He now believes that he was the right man at the right place. As Tinsley puts it: "The Camille assignment was the highlight of my career."

American Red Cross

Massies Mill, Va. A family once lived here.

American Red Cross

Massies Mill.

American Red Cross

Mudslide.

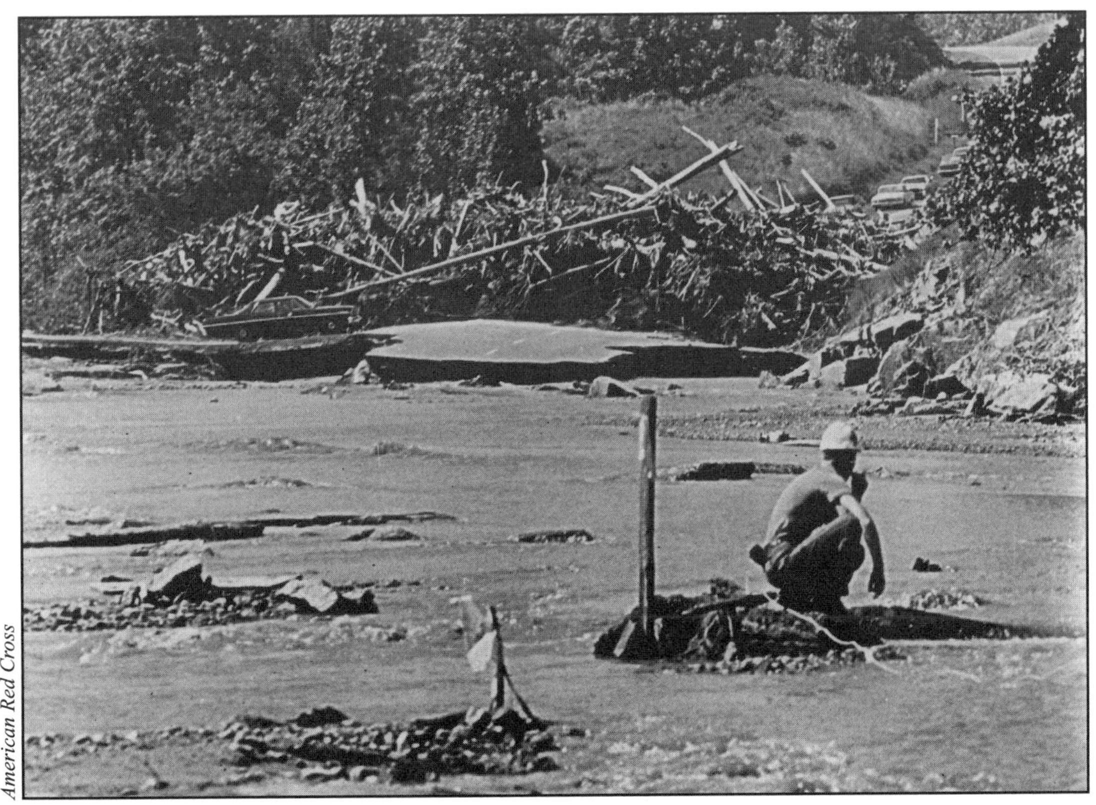

American Red Cross

At Woods Mill, Va., U.S. 29 was torn up and strewn with debris.

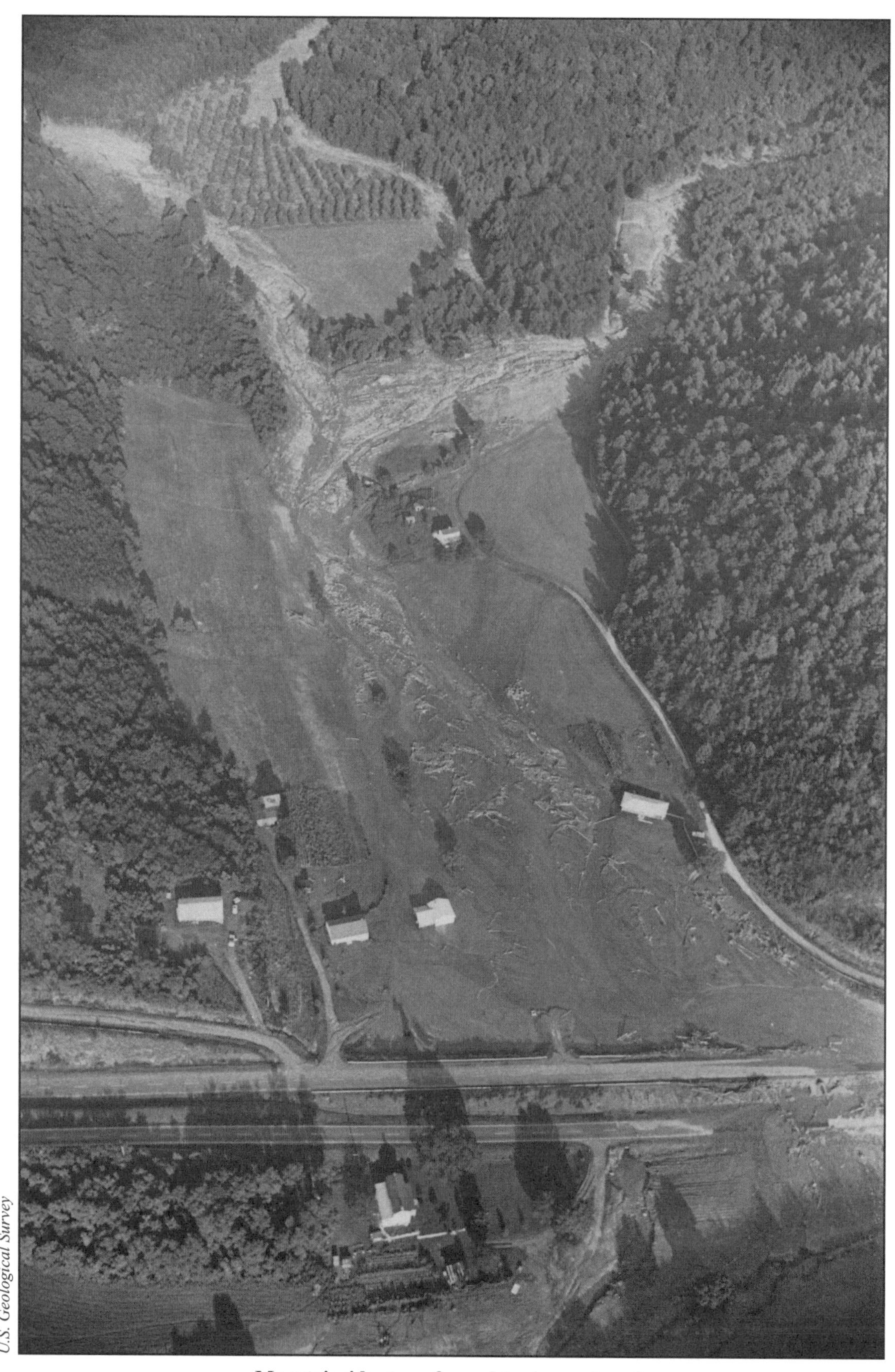

U.S. Geological Survey

Mountainsides transformed to rivers of mud.

1971

August

DORIA

Déjà vu. Doria was back, or at least an incarnation bearing that name. Once again, the storm took aim on eastern sections of the Mid-Atlantic, particularly New Jersey.

Winds gusted to 70 mph when Doria made landfall in eastern North Carolina on August 27. Gales lashed coastal Virginia, the Delmarva Peninsula and New Jersey as the storm sloshed through.

Norfolk International Airport caught a sustained wind of 52 mph. A tornado slammed Chesapeake and Portsmouth, Va., making splinters of more than 100 trees.

Doria wasn't as strong as its earlier namesake, remaining a tropical storm. But prolific rainfall and an inland route made it far more destructive. Remnants combined with a slow-moving cold front to dump 6-12 inches of rain from the Chesapeake Bay to southeastern Pennsylvania, and on much of New Jersey.

At least one weather station in 15 of the Garden State's 21 counties measured more than 8 inches of rain. New 24-hour rainfall standards were set at Trenton, 7.55 inches, and Newark, 7.84 inches.

Rivers spread disaster through central and northern New Jersey. Record or near-record crests were reported on the lower Passaic and middle Raritan rivers. The Saddle and Millstone rivers and Rancocas Creek also rose to unprecedented heights. States of emergency were declared in Elizabeth, West Orange, Saddle Brook and Union Township.

Southern New Jersey had little flooding but reported the state's only tornado. During the early hours of Friday, August 27, a twister roared ashore from the lower Delaware Bay and struck Cape May. It maintained a narrow, intermittent path for 25 miles to Woodbine, leaving downed trees and more than 20 damaged homes.

Tropical Storm Doria rainfall (August 27-28): **Delaware**—Middleton 6.92", Newark 6.85", Dover 5.32". **Maryland**—La Plata 10.10", Millington 8.82" Annapolis 8.76", Cambridge 7.40". **New Jersey**—Princeton 10.15", Bound Brook 9.39", New Brunswick 8.59", Rahway 8.77", Cranford 8.52", Trenton 8.04". **Pennsylvania**—Neshaminy Falls 11.42", West Chester 7.76", Philadelphia 5.68".

October

GINGER

Hurricanes are often unpredictable but few top Ginger. The indomitable Ginger lasted 28 days—20 as a hurricane. It tied the San Ciriaco Hurricane of 1899 as the longest-lived Atlantic tropical cyclone.

The storm developed east of the Bahamas on September 6 and churned out to sea during following days. By September 14, it was located about 1,500 miles east of Cape Hatteras, seemingly on its way to Europe. Then, reversing course, the hurricane followed a slow, erratic route to North Carolina.

It made landfall on September 30. Winds gusted to 92 mph at Atlantic Beach. Rainfall totaled up to 10 inches in northeastern North Carolina. Southeastern Virginia collected several inches. Damage was generally minor.

The jaunt over land finished Ginger. It tracked off the Delmarva Peninsula on October 3. The Weather Service issued a final advisory on October 4.

1972

June

AGNES

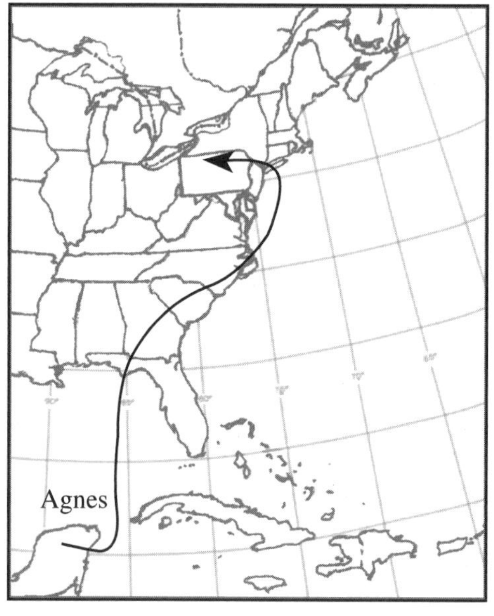

"When will it stop raining?"

That's what residents of the Middle Atlantic states wondered during June 1972, as Hurricane Agnes loitered in the region. The local creek, normally a trickle, became a river, the river became a flowing lake, the lake broke through dikes and dams and anything else in its way. "When will it stop raining?"

Hurricane Agnes. Sights that linger. An event that changed lives and communities.

"There was flooding like they've never seen here," said Frank Mazurkiewicz of Reading, Pa. "It's probably the worst I'll ever see. And the (Schuylkill) river took a long time to recede. That was an incredible experience. All these years and I can still smell the mud."

Paul Mansour of Woodbridge, Va., spent June 21 visiting friends, ignoring the downpours. There was no way to avoid Agnes when he left for home that night.

"It was unreal, the rain coming down in sheets. An incredibly hard rain and awfully dark. I said to my friend, 'This is like nothing I've ever been through.' With a bad thunderstorm, you get solid rain for a few minutes and then it lets up. This didn't let up."

Agnes affected nearly the entire East Coast. It killed 117 people and became the costliest hurricane to 1972, causing $3.1 billion in losses. Rarely in U.S. history has there been such a widespread failure of levees, dams and other flood protection measures. Rarely have so many people required emergency evacuation.

The storm offered profound lessons. A minimal hurricane doesn't necessarily mean minimal trouble. Landfall doesn't always diminish the threat from tropical cyclones—the worst may lie inland. And, most important: Don't assume that the highest known crest on a stream or river can't be topped.

Agnes struck west of Apalachicola, Fla., on June 19 with winds of minimal hurricane force. It soon weakened to a depression. However, the remnants strengthened to a tropical storm on June 21 as they reached North Carolina's Outer Banks. Once offshore, the Atlantic provided abundant energy and moisture.

The tropical cyclone made landfall again near New York City, veering west before merging with a stationary front over northern Pennsylvania. And the rain seemed like it would never end.

A state-by-state summary:

MARYLAND

"I have never seen such total destruction as has taken place in a number of areas in the state," said Gov. Marvin Mandel, after touring central Maryland.

Property losses totaled about $110 million and 19 people perished. Rainfall amounted to more than 10 inches in Montgomery, Frederick, Howard, Carroll, Baltimore, Harford and Kent counties.

The night of June 21-22 brought a fright to anyone living in a stream or river valley. Water rose unbelievably fast, incredibly high. As the flood progressed, officials in several jurisdictions worried about possible dam failures.

Lake Needwood, located in the northern suburbs of Washington, D.C., topped 50 feet, exceeding a normal depth of less than 20 feet. Water crept within inches of a natural spillway, ready to outflank an earthen dam. Officials feared the dam itself might fail.

James Gleason, the Montgomery County chief executive, declared a state of emergency at 3:30 a.m. on the 22nd. Residents living near Rock Creek, from Rockville to Chevy Chase, a distance of about 15 miles, were urged to leave. The evacuation order affected about 5,000 people. Gleason canceled the proclamation later that morning.

The Patuxent River crested as high as 51 feet, more than 30 feet above normal. Brighton Dam at the Triadelphia Reservoir, in the northeastern suburbs of Washington, and nearby Rocky Gorge Dam strained to hold the onslaught. Agnes dumped more than 10 inches of rain on the Brighton Dam, filling it beyond capacity. Water cascaded over the top although all floodgates were opened. A ruptured dam would have meant a catastrophe for the city of Laurel (pop. 35,000). The threat gradually subsided.

The Susquehanna River caused massive flooding below the huge Conowingo Dam in northeastern Maryland. Port Deposit and Havre de Grace were evacuated as excess poured in. The lake behind the Conowingo Dam rose to a depth of 111.5 ft on Friday, June 23. Superintendent Paul English warned, "the stability of the dam cannot be controlled once the water reached 111 feet."

All 53 floodgates were opened for the first time in the barrier's 40-year history. Water rushed through at 9 million gallons per second versus a normal pass-through of 400,000 gallons. The dam held.

Residents of Jones Falls Valley in Baltimore were told to evacuate when the Lake Roland dam seemed in jeopardy. It survived. Nevertheless, flooding in the metropolitan area left 14 people dead.

The Patapsco River flooded historic Ellicott City. Water rose to the second floor of many buildings in the lower section of town. Flooding damaged or destroyed 50 businesses and numerous houses. A tractor-trailer truck carried by the Patapsco demolished the front half of the Jonathan Ellicott house, a landmark dating to the early 19th century.

Agnes provided the closing chapter to Daniels, a textile mill company town nestled in the Patapsco River gorge near Baltimore. Founded in the early 1800s, Daniels had several different owners and underwent a few name changes (Elysville, Alberton). The textile mill village boasted more than 200 residents during the period the C.R. Daniels Company owned the settlement, starting in 1940. Daniels included a general store, post office, bowling alley, pool hall and three churches.

During the middle 1960s the company phased out employee housing. Once bustling Daniels was nearly deserted by 1972. Most remaining buildings washed away.

While many rivers obliterated landmarks, the Patapsco unearthed one. A section of the first 13 miles of U.S. railroad tracks, built in 1830, was discovered after the flood. It had been the site of a famous race between one of the earliest railroad locomotives, the *Tom Thumb*, and a horse. (The horse won!)

The Chesapeake and Ohio Canal National Historical Park, located along the Potomac River, suffered one of its most devastating floods. Dedicated by President John Quincy Adams on July 4, 1828, aiming to carry commerce to Pittsburgh and the Ohio River, it never got beyond Cumberland, Md. The Baltimore and Ohio Railroad, which was also dedicated in 1828, made the canal obsolete. Nevertheless, the canal survived until 1924, a quaint transportation route used by mule-hauled barges.

Bethesda, Md.

Special Collections, University of Maryland Libraries

Ellicott City, Md.

By 1972, the National Park Service owned the 184-mile preserve, a recreational oasis. Agnes obliterated large sections. Restoration took years.

Frederick dealt with twin floods. A flash flood on June 22, the result of more than 6 inches of rain, inundated areas along Carroll Creek. The central Maryland city experienced a second crisis the next day when the Monocacy River surged over its banks. The Monocacy crested at 33 ft. (flood stage 15 ft.). Water submerged several blocks along its meandering route, invading water treatment and sewage facilities.

Farmers throughout central and eastern Maryland had significant losses. Rain and gusts of 40-60 mph flattened or drowned crops.

John Swaine Jr., a weather observer and farmer from Royal Oak on the Eastern Shore, wrote: "The corn crop was blown down very badly. The corn height was 6 in. to 3 ft. Barley that was not harvested appears to have had the heads broken off and lost. The wheat crop was blown down where wheat was heavy. Most fields were flooded from the rain."

The Chesapeake Bay was whipped into high surf, the result of strong, persistent, easterly gales. Agnes claimed boats, docks and seawalls. Property owners along the bay received an ugly surprise as rivers like the Susquehanna disgorged sordid contents.

Walter Harris remembers a stupendous quantity of trash. His farm is located near Still Pond in Kent County, along the bay's eastern shore. "I found a mass of debris along the shoreline that extended about a thousand feet into the Chesapeake Bay," Harris said. "There was every odd and end that you can imagine."

PENNSYLVANIA

Agnes impacted Pennsylvania with a terrible intimacy.

President Richard Nixon declared the Keystone State a disaster area. Floodwaters killed 48 Pennsylvanians, left 220,000 homeless and caused property losses totaling $2.1 billion.

The storm pounded the sprawling Susquehanna River basin, one of the most flood-prone watersheds in the nation. According to the National Weather Service, "The Agnes flood remains the greatest flooding event known in the Susquehanna River basin in regards to both the area affected and the magnitude of the flow. Only the extreme upper headwaters escaped disastrous flooding."

Civil defense officials along the Susquehanna and its tributaries faced a nightmarish task. They worked with a dearth of information on upstream rainfall and watched the seemingly boundless flow of waterways shatter previous benchmarks. Flooding invaded neighborhoods thought immune, necessitating thousands of evacuations by boat or helicopter.

The Susquehanna River exceeded the great flood of March 1936, a modern standard. After 1936, a levee system was built along sections of the heavily populated Wyoming Valley in northeastern Pennsylvania. In 1936, the Susquehanna reached 33 ft. in Wilkes-Barre. Agnes sent the river to 40.7 feet, surpassing a flood stage of 22.0 ft.

The Wyoming Valley had received heavy, albeit unspectacular, rainfall. Wilkes-Barre reported 5.17 inches from June 20-24. Hardly the stuff of catastrophic flooding.

But Agnes was a cruel storm. While most tropical systems quickly exit the Mid-Atlantic, it reached the ocean and then returned, skirting the Pennsylvania-New York border. More than 15 inches of rain fell in the upper Susquehanna basin. This deluge rushed toward the Wyoming Valley, a fearful volume of water.

On June 22-23, thousands of volunteers attempted to raise the area's levees. They piled sandbags, putting their hearts and hopes into the effort. Sirens wailed on the morning of Friday, June 23, signaling that the river had won. Anguished workers retreated to higher ground. Neighborhoods soon merged with the Susquehanna.

The river topped its old mark early on June 23 and remained above that level until the night of the 25th.

Wilkes-Barre, Kingston and other low-lying sections of the Wyoming Valley suffered incredible devastation. Agnes damaged or destroyed about 24,000 homes, 3,000 small businesses and 150 factories. About 100,000 people were displaced.

A city of the dead washed away in the nearly century-old Forty Fort Cemetery. The Susquehanna entered hallowed ground. Caskets were unearthed and disintegrated. Bodies tumbled out and carried downstream. "Some looked like they were standing or walking on water," said the caretaker.

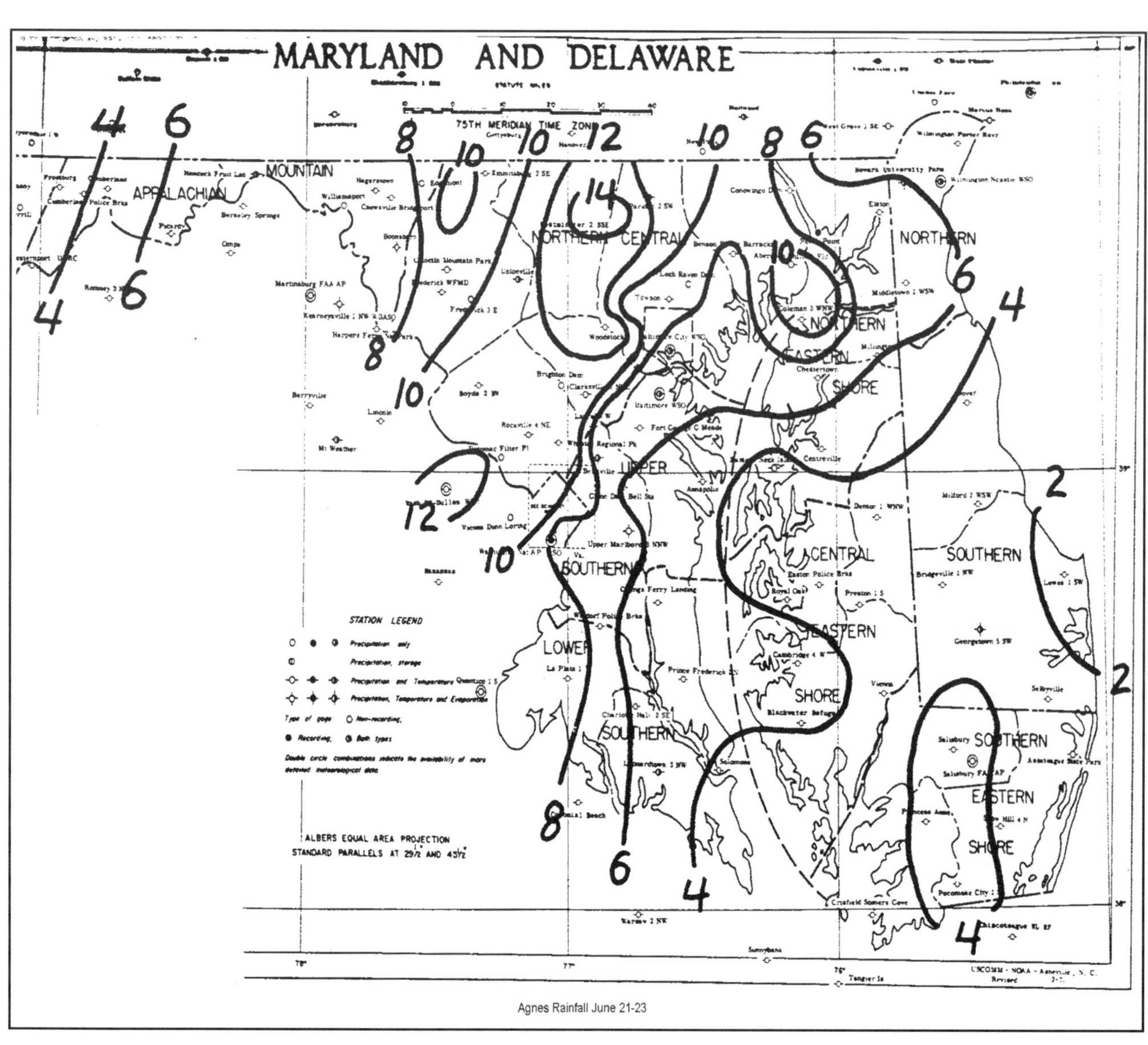

Agnes Rainfall June 21-23

Floodwaters scattered the remains of 2,000 graves, depositing them on streets, lawns and porches. National Guardsmen and volunteers handled the grisly

IN MEMORY OF
THOSE AT REST ON THIS HILLSIDE
WHOSE NAMES ARE UNKNOWN AND
WHOSE GRAVESITES IN THE
FORTY FORT CEMETERY WERE
DESTROYED BY FLOOD WATERS
OF THE SUSQUEHANNA RIVER
JUNE 23, 1972

retrieval. Only 25 bodies were subsequently identified. The anonymous dead reside today in a mass grave at the Memorial Shrine Cemetery in nearby Carverton, on a hillside, safe from the Susquehanna.

Sunbury (pop. 15,000) avoided Wilkes-Barre's fate. The Susquehanna lapped at the top of the town's protective dike, but was contained. For years, some residents complained of the floodwall being an obstruction, an eyesore, but Agnes silenced critics. After the threat subsided, a sign appeared that expressed the sentiments of many: "Wall, I love you!"

On Thursday, June 22, 7.16 inches of rain fell on the state capital, Harrisburg, for a two-day total of 12.55 inches. The swollen Susquehanna followed flash flooding.

Agnes was an equal-opportunity destroyer. The Governor's Residence in Harrisburg, completed three years earlier at a cost of over $2 million, merged with the river. Located on a bluff, it seemed out of harm's way. Yet, nearly five feet of muddy water covered the first floor when the Susquehanna River crested.

Communities near Harrisburg wrestled with water. Lemoyne, Wormleysburg, New Cumberland and Steelton were just a few walloped by the Susquehanna. Tens of thousands of workers became at least temporarily unemployed, including 5,000 employees of Bethlehem Steel in Steelton.

All waterways in eastern Pennsylvania overwhelmed their banks. One of the most destructive, the Schuylkill River, swamped many towns, including Reading, where it rose to a record 31.5 ft. The rise came after 15 inches of rain fell on the Schuylkill basin. At Pottstown, the Schuylkill crested at 29.97 ft., almost 9 feet above the previous record.

Paul Anselm, the fire marshal and civil defense coordinator for White Marsh Township, remembers June 1972.

"The flood became a lesson for us," Anselm said. "We dealt with situations that weren't in any operations manual."

For example: "There were large quantities of flammable, hazardous, and toxic material that had floated away from factories along the river," said Anselm. "We had to quickly find out what was inside the barrels and other containers going downstream, how the material would react, and track where it was heading."

York, in southeastern Pennsylvania, had a flood that rivaled the storied rise of August 1933, as Cordorus Creek plowed through the municipality. More than 15 inches of rain fell in the Cordorus watershed.

The city tallied severe losses. About 1,500 people were forced from their homes. Ironically, York applied for coverage under the National Flood Insurance Act five weeks before Agnes. A letter of approval arrived in the midst of the crisis (too late for anyone to purchase protection).

Agnes also afflicted western Pennsylvania. At Pittsburgh, the Ohio River rose to its highest level since 1942, 11 feet above flood stage.

Gov. Shapp summed up the calamity when he renamed Hurricane Agnes, "Hurricane Agony."

***

Looting plagued some of Pennsylvania's flooded towns. But for every theft there were a hundred acts of kindness.

The Lutheran Church of the West Berks District, Pa., pledged a thousand sandwiches each week

From the collections of the Luzerne County Historical Society

Volunteers at the Market Street Bridge in Wilkes-Barre, Pa., attempt to raise the Susquehanna River levee. The river was unstoppable.

American Red Cross

A fire burned in a Wilkes-Barre neighborhood even as streets flooded.

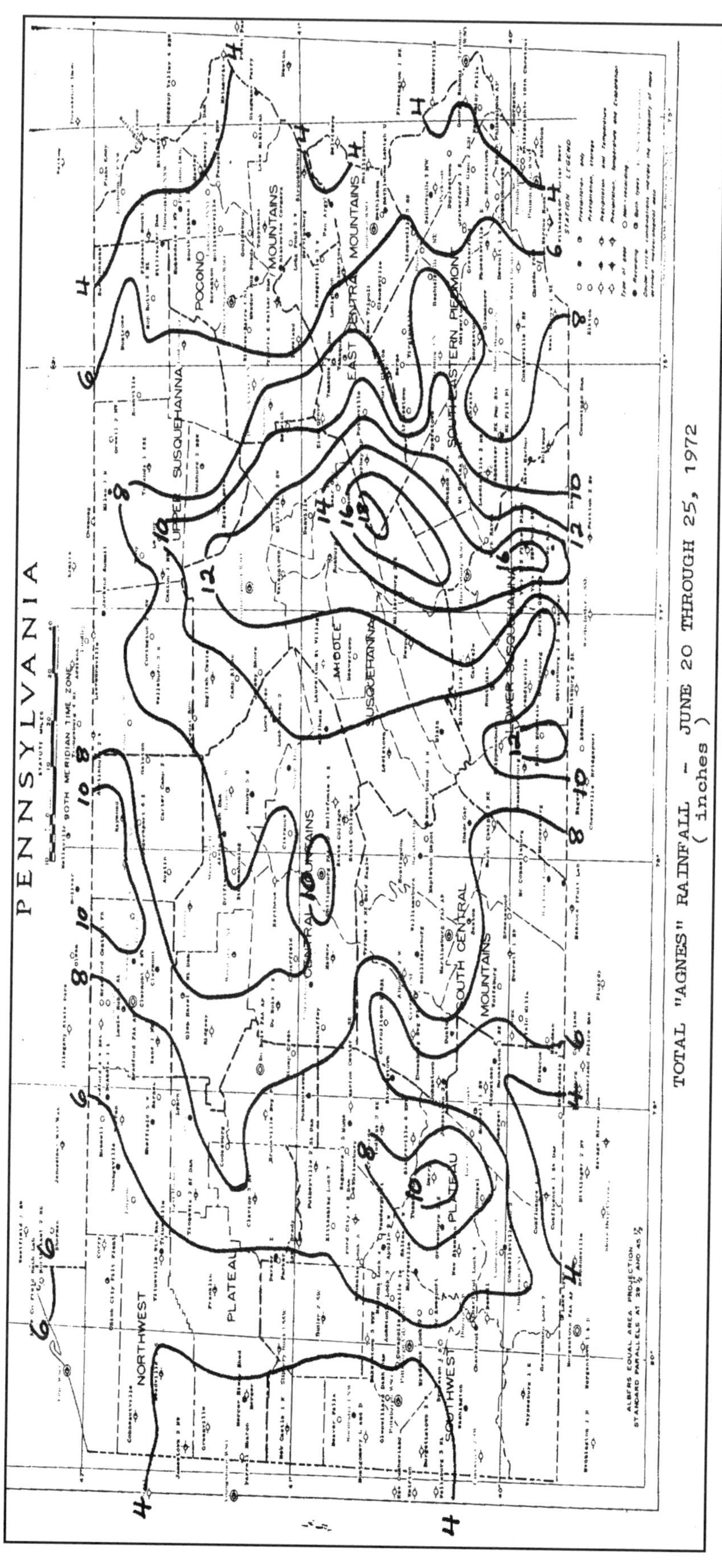
PENNSYLVANIA
90TH MERIDIAN TIME ZONE
NORTHWEST
PLATEAU
SOUTHWEST
CENTRAL MOUNTAINS
SOUTH CENTRAL MOUNTAINS
MIDDLE SUSQUEHANNA
UPPER SUSQUEHANNA
LOWER SUSQUEHANNA
POCONO MOUNTAINS
EAST CENTRAL MOUNTAINS
SOUTHEASTERN PIEDMONT
STATION LEGEND
ALBERS EQUAL AREA PROJECTION
TOTAL "AGNES" RAINFALL - JUNE 20 THROUGH 25, 1972
(inches)

for seven weeks to Wilkes-Barre flood victims. They dubbed the effort, "Operation Sandwich."

The folks of Petersburg, Michigan (pop. 800), collected bedding, clothing, kitchen utensils—anything they thought helpful—and sent a loaded trailer to Scranton.

Teenagers from St. Luke Lutheran Church in Silver Spring, Md., spent July in Harrisburg. They did grueling work, maintaining shelters, clearing mud and cleaning the homes of the elderly.

Many others assisted. Public employees toiled endless hours. Communities throughout the United States and abroad contributed volunteers and material goods. The influx of aid was a high point during an otherwise dreary time.

VIRGINIA

Agnes created record or near-record flows on most rivers in the state. Flooding drowned 13 people and left $126 million in property losses.

Much of Virginia received 5-10 inches of rain. Chantilly, in the western suburbs of Washington, D.C., collected nearly 16 inches. (Only the southeastern and southwestern corners of the Old Dominion were spared heavy rain.)

From the Weather Service: "This extreme rainfall coming after a few days with showers and thundershowers and falling over the entire watersheds of the major rivers caused near record to record floods. The Potomac, the Rappahannock, the James, the Roanoke, the Appomattox, and the New rivers all reached flood stage, along with the smaller rivers and streams. Cities and towns heavily affected included Manassas, Occoquan, Fredericksburg, Richmond, Scottsville, Glasgow, Covington, Buchanan, Farmville, Roanoke and Salem."

Faltering dams threatened sections of northern Virginia. The Lake Barcroft and Occoquan dams, near Washington, D.C., threw a terrific scare into those living downstream.

The Barcroft dam in Fairfax County, less than 10 miles from downtown Washington, held 135-acre Lake Barcroft. Water breached the side of the structure. Officials warned that complete failure would unleash a "20-foot wall of water" along Holmes Run, which coursed through the city of Alexandria. The lake gradually drained until all that remained was a massive mud puddle.

Occoquan has a long history of flooding, but Agnes remains a singular event. The town was evacuated on the night of June 21 as a dam threatened to free a large reservoir. Although the structure held, a substantial release of water inundated many homes.

(The event marked a turning point. The village claimed roots dating back to the middle 1700s. A thriving port during the Revolutionary War and into the 1800s, it declined during the 20th century. After being nearly washed off the map by Agnes, Occoquan made a comeback by reinventing itself as a folk art center.)

Flooding at Occoquan meant a water-supply crisis for Fairfax County and vicinity, one of the state's most populous sections. Damage to a water intake and treatment plant at the reservoir and flooded pumping facilities left a half-million people without drinkable water. Dry taps, followed by days of a boil-water advisory, seemed more than a bit ironic in the aftermath of the region's worst flood.

The Richmond metropolitan area also lost tap water. The James River compromised the main processing facility. Gerald Gordon worked as an operator at the Richmond Metropolitan Water Treatment Plant. Employees and National Guardsmen sandbagged the facility but the rising James River proved too much.

"The river just washed over the top," Gordon said. "I saw a thin curtain of water come over the top and it quickly became a torrent. It filled the settling and treatment basins and poured into the building."

The plant remained closed for more than a week. Potable water was gradually restored. "Initially, use was restricted to laundry, then people could use it for bathing, and finally it became safe for drinking," Gordon said.

The James River crested at 36.51 ft. in Richmond (flood stage 9 ft.), eclipsing the previous record of 30 ft. set in 1771. Downtown Richmond remained closed for days. The river left one-sixth of the city under water.

Fredericksburg faced a difficult recovery after a 39.1 ft. crest on the Rappahannock River, only exceeded by the 42.6 ft. rise of October 1942.

Heavy flooding targeted the Roanoke Valley of southwestern Virginia. In Roanoke, 380 homes sustained major damage.

WASHINGTON, D.C.

Flooding killed 16 people in the metropolitan area and routed about 12,000 residents. But Washington, D.C., had few evacuations. Swamped basements and roads were the most common maladies.

The 7.19 inches of rain measured during a 24-hour period on June 21-22 ranked slightly below the hurricane-related totals of August 1928 and August 1933. The Potomac River crested at 15.5 ft. (flood stage 7 ft.). Winds at National Airport gusted to 49 mph.

EAST COAST

Although Agnes caused catastrophic flooding along much of the East Coast, tornadoes were the main story in Florida. It spawned the largest tornado outbreak in state history (to 1972), producing 28 twisters, including a pair of F3 intensity. The tornadoes killed seven people and injured more than 140.

Heavy rain marked the storm's passage through Georgia, South Carolina and North Carolina. Agnes dumped 5-10 inches of rain on the western half of North Carolina. Notable flooding occurred on the Dan and Yadkin rivers. The Catawba, Saluda, Rock, Congaree, Lumber and Broad rivers also flooded.

Delaware suffered modest crop damage and it recorded the highest gust north of Georgia—67 mph at Dover Air Force Base. Gusts of 50-60 mph lashed much of the state.

Although Agnes churned near the New Jersey coast, rainfall in the Garden State totaled less than 5 inches. Tides rose 2-4 feet above normal but caused little damage. Much of the $15 million in property losses was a result of ruined crops.

The National Weather Service described Agnes as "the greatest flood disaster in the history of New York state." It killed 24 people in New York and caused $700 million damage. More than 100,000 people were displaced. President Nixon declared 14 counties disaster areas.[1]

Downpours pelted New York's southern tier from Cattaraugus to Chemung counties, dropping more than a foot of rain on some localities. Higher totals included: Wellsville 13.0", Alfred 12.9" and Hornell 11.1".

The Chemung River swamped the cities of Elmira and Corning, N.Y. In Elmira (pop. 40,000), nearly 20,000 residents fled as levees protecting the city were breached. A total of 18 people drowned in the greater Corning area and 6,000 people left their homes. Corning Glass Company, the city's main employer, shut down for months.

A weakened dam near Auburn, N.Y., forced the evacuation of 15,000 inhabitants. Among other towns suffering severe losses: Salamanca, Olean and Hornell.

West Virginia caught the fringe of Agnes. Destructive flooding occurred along the Ohio River, between Chester and New Martinsville.

Gales generated 15-foot waves on Lake Erie. Surf battered the south shore. The Ohio River, swollen by rain in Pennsylvania, caused significant damage between East Liverpool and Hannibal, Ohio.

***

Robert White, director of NOAA, put Agnes in perspective: "We believe that the flooding from the Gulf Coast to New York is the most extensive in the nation's history."

Hurricane Agnes rainfall totals (June 21-23): **Maryland**—Woodstock 13.85", Wheaton 12.35", Westminster 11.73", Aberdeen 11.28", Rockville 10.62", Potomac 10.19", Frederick 7.85", Chestertown 7.44", College Park 6.64", Baltimore (BWI Airport) 6.62", Baltimore (Customs House) 6.39", Salisbury 4.16". **New Jersey**—High Point 3.49", Princeton 3.04", New Brunswick 2.59". **Pennsylvania**—York 15.67", Harrisburg (Airport) 15.11", Sunbury 13.33", Williamsport 12.81", Carlisle 11.40", Gettysburg 9.91", Reading 8.53", Wilkes-Barre 4.93", Philadelphia 3.46", Pittsburgh 2.14". **Virginia** (June 20-22)—Dulles Airport 12.18", Vienna 10.30", Alexandria 8.66", Lynchburg 7.27", Martinsville 6.88", Fredericksburg 6.70", Glasgow 6.24", Ashland 5.49", Roanoke 4.75", Richmond 2.97",. **Washington, D.C.**—National Arboretum 9.19", National Airport 7.91".

[1] Although the center of Agnes passed over western Long Island and near New York City, southeastern New York received the least rainfall in the state. Storm totals were generally less than 3 inches. New York City had just 1.86 inches from June 21-23. The disaster would have been much worse had the heaviest rain targeted the New York metropolitan area.

REMEMBERING AGNES

"I told a fellow in Philadelphia—he said, 'Were you in the flood?' Yeah. 'Did you have any water?' I had a little in my basement, I replied. 'Oh,' he said. 'That's not too bad.' Yeah, I told him, but it came through the chimney."

— Sterling Lamoreux on Hurricane Agnes

That was a slight exaggeration. Water didn't come through the chimney. But it filled Lamoreux's basement and rose to within inches of the first floor ceiling of his Kingston, Pa., home.

June 1972 brought heartrending days to northeastern Pennsylvania. A time when the surreal *was* real.

On the afternoon of Friday, June 23, before his home flooded, Lamoreux watched the rising Susquehanna inundate century-old Forty Fort Cemetery, upstream from Kingston. Swirling water unearthed graves, with a vengeance.

"Caskets were coming out of the ground and floating," Lamoreux said. "The metal ones and concrete vaults would float through the cemetery and knock headstones over. There was a mausoleum there and I could see it leaning, leaning, leaning. It finally tipped over because the ground beneath it was so soft.

"The old wooden coffins would virtually disintegrate. They popped to the surface and fell apart. I saw skeletons later, up in trees, wherever they lodged."

Earlier that day, Lamoreux and thousands of others attempted to bolster Susquehanna levees. Failure wasn't an option. Their homes were at stake.

Just after 11 a.m., civil defense sirens sounded. Water tore through a levee north of Kingston. Sandbagging ended. Officials ordered everyone out.

"It was unbelievable," Lamoreux said. "Your hope is that you're going to win and we were winning where I was. A lot of people didn't want to quit. They couldn't understand it when authorities started chasing them away."

The magnitude of the flood—inconceivable. The Susquehanna River had never topped 37 feet, the height of a levee shielding Kingston. Agnes sent the water to nearly 41 feet. Only 30 homes out of 6,600 remained untouched in the town of 20,000. The water rose to 11 feet at Lamoreux's home.

He left Forty Fort and returned to a deserted neighborhood. His house was located about 10 blocks from the Susquehanna River. The area was still dry. Earlier, Lamoreux sent his wife and children to a relative. Now, he and a cousin sat on the front porch waiting, waiting…

5 p.m. The flood didn't arrive as a trickle or surge. Instead, it crept underground. Lamoreux heard a loud "whoosh," as a manhole cover levitated on a five-foot column of water, then slid off and rolled "like a coin on a table until it settles down."

Time to leave. A motorcycle served as his getaway vehicle. Lamoreux plucked the Honda from the initial stream of water and carried it up his front steps and into his carpeted living room, leaving a muddy trail. "My wife is going to give me hell for this," he thought.

Lamoreux sped through his backyard. He followed a pre-planned escape route, reaching a railroad embankment at the edge of Kingston. The rise contained the water, a relief to those living beyond the barrier but a catastrophe to those caught in what became a lake.

"It was like we were caught between two dikes (the railroad embankment and levee)," Lamoreux explained. "There was only one spot in Kingston that wasn't flooded. That included 30 to 50 homes on Church Street. There was enough rise in elevation so the water didn't cover the ground. They got seepage in their basements but didn't get muddy water."

The Susquehanna peaked on Saturday evening, June 24, and slowly receded. Water still claimed Kingston when Lamoreux attempted to return home to retrieve a wedding album and photographs of his kids. He climbed the railroad rise that separated the fortunate from the flood-ravaged. A policeman confronted him.

"I told him that I was going to the house," Lamoreux said. "He said, 'No, you can't go in there. I'd have to shoot you!' I said, 'Jonesy, you know me. I promised my wife that I'd go back for the baby books. If you shoot me it wouldn't hurt any more than it already hurts.' He said, 'It's going to blow up, there's going to be gas…' I started to walk into the water and he's yelling at me. I said, 'Go ahead and shoot!' I never even looked back.

"I swam to my house—had to kick in the door. God, what a sickening feeling that was! My kitchen, which had been all white, was virtually all brown."

Everything on the lower floor was coated in mud. The carpet, furniture, appliances—ruined. A flood's notorious companion, mold, appeared.

Lamoreux's despair was shared by thousands of families. To make matters worse, they faced uncertainty about the stability of the ground beneath their homes. Coal mining, once a mainstay of the local economy, had ended by 1972. However, a century of digging left a honeycombed network of mine shafts and caverns. Would they collapse once water drained off?

"There was concern that maybe the whole valley would sink," said Lamoreux. "No one could attest to what would happen. There were all kinds of rumors flying. There were people who did nothing for a while until they got assurance it wouldn't happen."

The ground remained stable. Cleanup and recovery began. Neighborhoods bustled with activity. Housing and Urban Development trailers and campers, lent to victims, were commonplace in the Wyoming Valley during the year following Agnes.

Summer heat turned Kingston into a festering world of mud, and later, dust and mold. Residents returned to homes coated in slime. Interiors were a malodorous mess. Little could be salvaged.

"All the curb lines, from the sidewalk to the street, were piled about eight-feet high with refrigerators, couches, beds, dressers and pianos," Lamoreux said. "Everything in the house. They came with huge front-end loaders and picked it up. By the time they cleaned the street, people brought more things out and they had to do it again.

"We use to have a lot of strip mines in the area, very deep," he continued. "You'd think they'd never be filled. They all got filled with the debris. There's millions of dollars, maybe a billion dollars, in metal dumped into those strip mines."

Even while repairing his home, Lamoreux assisted a neighbor, an elderly widow.

"If I didn't help, I think (the aftermath of the flood) would have killed her," he said. "I got my brother-in-laws to come down and they helped clean out her house. I got her electricity going. I had (my brother-in-laws) tear out the paneling and re-panel the house. They got rid of the mud. She was probably the first one on the street back together. People who are that old—it's a hell of a blow to suffer."

Lamoreux moved back into his residence days before Christmas 1973. Not everyone returned.

"My friend had a home he was going to move into on Friday night, the evening of the flood," Lamoreux said. "It was new. It happened to be on the Wilkes-Barre side of the river. He worked for the power company and didn't get (to his new home) for about two weeks. He finally got there. It had floated about two blocks from where it originally stood. Never lived in it. It was lodged between a house and a telephone pole.

"He got $5,000 forgiveness, $15,000 for relocation and a 1 percent loan. He rebuilt on a hill. My friend never wanted to experience that again. He built in Plains, which is away from the river. If the water reached him now, we'd all need an ark."

In 1975, the remnants of Hurricane Eloise again brought flood fears to the Wyoming Valley. Levees held. Lamoreux says that had the Susquehanna invaded his home again, he wouldn't have rebuilt.

"You just cannot imagine until you've lived through one what damage a flood does."

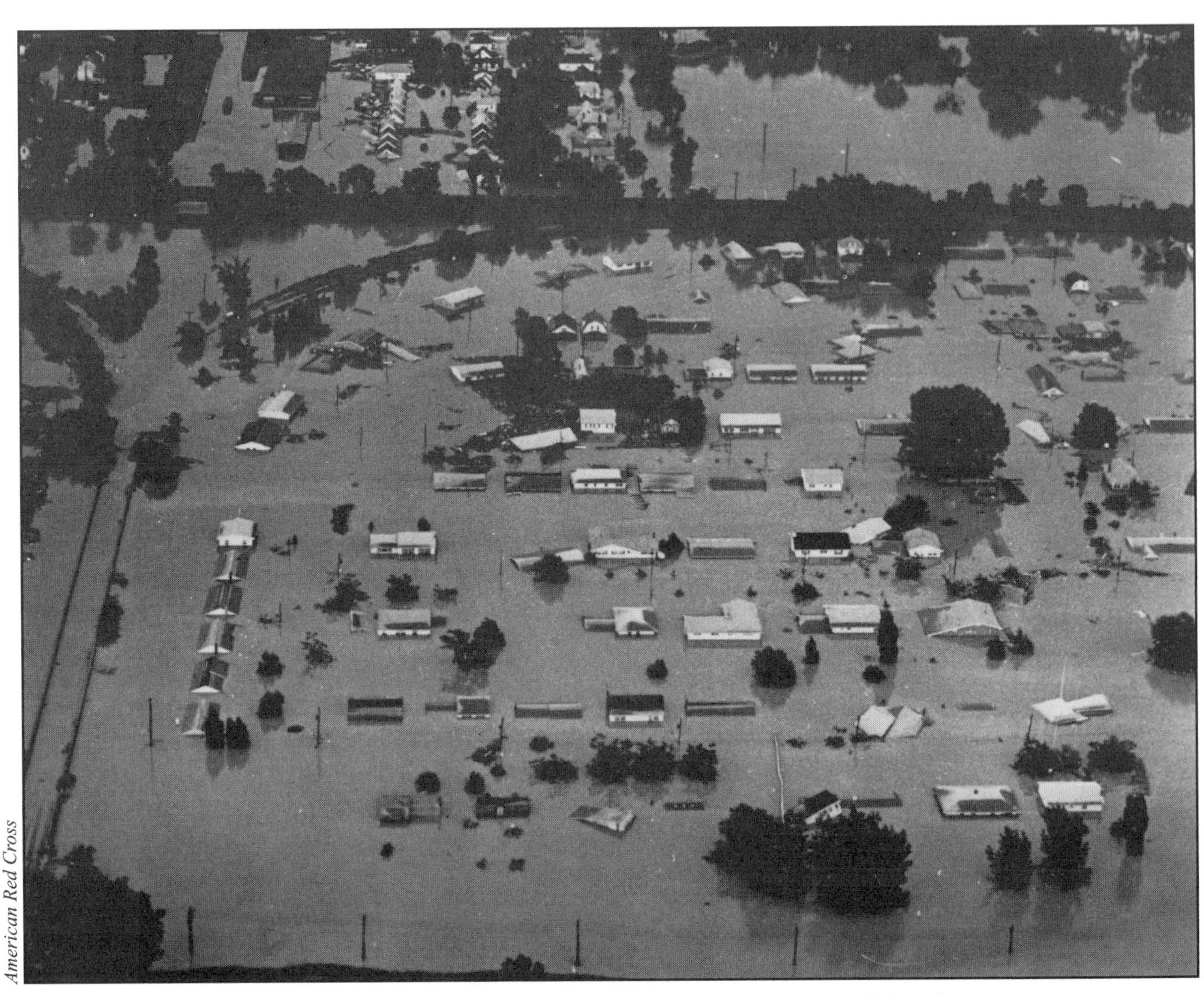
American Red Cross

Failure of the Wyoming Valley levee system meant inundated neighborhoods.

COPING WITH AGNES...

In the aftermath of the disaster, newspapers such as the Harrisburg *Patriot-News* printed editorials exhorting readers to unite and rebuild their respective communities.

The *Patriot-News* was no mere spectator. It became part of the story. For the first time in the newspaper's 120-year-history, it missed publication. The *Patriot-News* headquarters on South Market Street had been built during the 1950s. The building's lowest openings were a foot higher than the record flood of March 1936. Agnes exceeded that by nearly four feet, submerging the pressroom.

Publication resumed on June 28 with a special Flood Edition. The following editorial served as inspiration:

IT'S UP TO US

THE WORST is over—but the hardest has just begun.

Future generations will talk of the Great Flood of '72 much as our generation spoke of the Flood of '36. The rivers and streams, which normally provide us with vital water, with recreation and with an esthetic setting, have struck the Harrisburg area a cruel blow.

But it is far from a fatal blow and it need not even be a permanently crippling blow. We can clean up and bounce back—if we have the will.

Plutarch wrote: '...the truly noble and resolved spirit raises itself and becomes more conspicuous in times of disaster and ill fortune.'

In our time of disaster, there have been evidence of mean and low spirits in those who seized upon tragedy as an occasion to try to loot and, to a much lesser degree, in those whose curiosity drew them unnecessarily to flooded areas, glutting roads and hampering rescue operations.

But the overwhelming memory of the Great Flood of '72 will be the evidence of 'the truly noble and resolved spirit' raising itself in our midst. Those whose duty it is to serve in times of distress, both civilian and military, served beyond the call of duty. The volunteers were magnificent. The organizations and individuals who rallied by sharing their skills and space and goods were superb. At a time when our newspaper could not fulfill its function, radio and TV outdid themselves to keep lines of communication open with a concerned public.

NOW, as we assess the damage, pick up the threads of our personal and business lives, and face the future, we need that sense of oneness, that sense of sharing and communal effort, even more.

The Patriot-News shared in this community disaster to a far greater degree than its traditional role of journalistic observer and recorder. Our "home," too, was inundated and we suffered grievous losses. And we share now in the community's efforts to shake off the effects of the flood and to rebuild for the future.

It won't be an easy job. To succeed, we must muster not only our personal spirit but also our sense of communal spirit. We succeeded during the peak of the flood itself and we will succeed in its aftermath.

HURRICANE AGNES STILL HAUNTS THE CHESAPEAKE BAY

THE WATERWAY HAS NEVER RECOVERED

Weather maps indicated a tropical storm as Agnes romped through the Mid-Atlantic region. But make no mistake, it was a Category 5 hurricane to aquatic life of the Chesapeake Bay.

The bay is North America's largest estuary, with a watershed covering parts of six states and Washington, D.C. It offers rich diversity—about 3,600 types of plant and animal life, including 350 species of fish.

Few effects from Agnes have been as long lasting as its assault on the ecosystem. No event during the past 400 years has combined timing and an influx of freshwater and contaminants in such a lethal way. The bay's watershed collected an average of 5-10 inches of rain. Subsequent flooding carried the sum of our ills—sewage, as well as industrial, agricultural and residential waste—into a fragile world.

Agnes turned the bay into a garbage dump. Trash, especially plastics, may take more than 100 years to break down. Oils and chemicals lingered, killing birds, plants and fish. Untreated sewage contaminated shellfish beds.

The storm greatly increased turbidity (silt, pollution, debris), and added an abundance of nutrients conducive to the growth of excessive algae. The flow of freshwater significantly altered salinity. The influx killed plants, fish and other organisms.

In the aftermath of Agnes, Maryland state climatologist Joe Moyer wrote, "Among the areas and activities adversely affected by Agnes, special attention should be given the Chesapeake Bay. Here flooding streams and rivers dumped unprecedented amounts of trash, oil, silt and other pollutants and greatly reduced its salinity. The shellfish and oyster industry has sustained a tremendous loss through the destruction of vast numbers of shellfish and oysters by the bay's lowered salinity."

This after years of taking the estuary for granted. Since the 19th century runoff had carried staggering quantities of industrial, residential and agricultural wastes. Tributaries contributed raw sewage. Watermen harvested Chesapeake's waters with deadly efficiency.

Hurricanes, the great rain producers like Agnes, exploit environmental vulnerabilities and accelerate undesirable processes. The result: near-extinction of oyster beds, greatly diminished populations of clams, crabs, and various other species; and the loss of critically important submerged aquatic vegetation.

"Chesapeake" is derived from a native American word meaning "great shell fish bay." That's a sad irony. Agnes and subsequent storms, as well as continued contamination, harvesting and diseases, have left the oyster population a shadow of its former abundance. During 2003, oystermen gathered 19,000 bushels, the lowest catch to that time.

Oysters once served as an important contributor to the bay's filtration system. A century ago, they filtered the waterway's volume in three days; now, with fewer oysters, it takes an estimated 700 days.

Submerged aquatic vegetation, also known as "SAV" or bay grasses, offers shallow-water habitat for many species, providing food, shelter, and healthy levels of oxygen. It filters pollutants and helps stabilize sediments.

The influx of sediment during June 1972 smothered most vegetation. Timing couldn't have been worse; Agnes arrived during the peak of the bay grass growing season.

"Agnes almost wiped out underwater grasses," explained Bruce Michael, the director of Tidewater Ecosystem Assessment for the Maryland Department of Natural Resources. "We have aerial photography from the 1930s through 1950s of what the bay grass acreage used to be in Maryland and Virginia. We're not even halfway to where we want to be."

Excessive nutrients flowing into the bay resulted in a proliferation of algae. A limited population of algae is a natural and critical part of the Chesapeake ecosystem. The vegetation captures solar energy and supports the food web. However, a proliferation blocks sunlight and decreases dissolved oxygen. (When the blooms die, decomposition removes dissolved oxygen from the water, creating conditions that stress or kill fish and other species.) The problem continues.

"The Chesapeake Bay is like a soup," says the Maryland Department of Natural Resources. "Both are composed of many ingredients. But just as too much of any ingredient can spoil the flavor of the soup, too much of a particular substance can harm the bay. The current problem with the bay is too many nutrients. Nutrients are substances that help (algae) grow. The most important nutrients are nitrogen and phosphorus. Plant and animal matter (including human waste), fertilizer, and even deposition from car exhaust and power plants all contain nutrients. If not treated, these nutrients will find their way into creeks, rivers and eventually the bay."

The ideal weather is plenty of sunshine and little rain.

"The best situation is a drought," Michael said. "They certainly have some negative impacts for the bay, but overall a drought is the best thing because most of our nutrients are now a result of runoff from agricultural and urban areas. With dry weather, there is much less runoff. This reduces algae and allows grasses to flourish."

Public awareness of the bay's plight has resulted in the implementation of state and local nutrient reduction and water improvement programs. There is also increased monitoring of changing conditions.

Ongoing and expanded efforts are crucial. The bay is resilient. Given the chance it will attempt to restore a healthy balance—a struggle since Agnes.

American Red Cross

Salem, Va. Vast flooding in the Chesapeake Bay watershed caused ecological calamity.

IMAGES OF AGNES

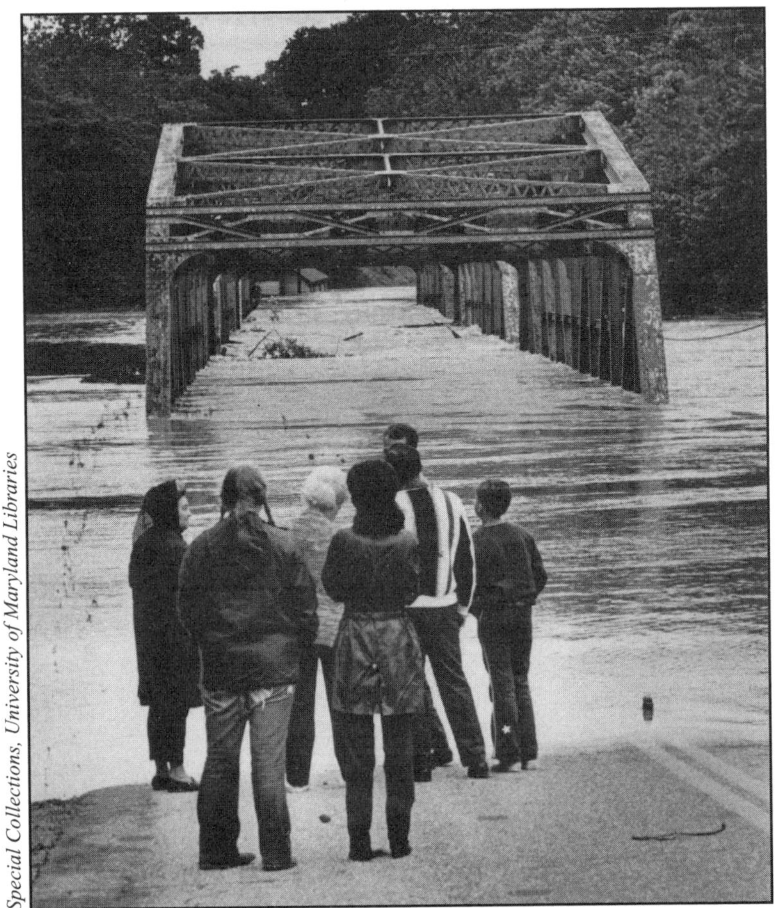

Special Collections, University of Maryland Libraries

The Monocacy River rages through central Maryland.

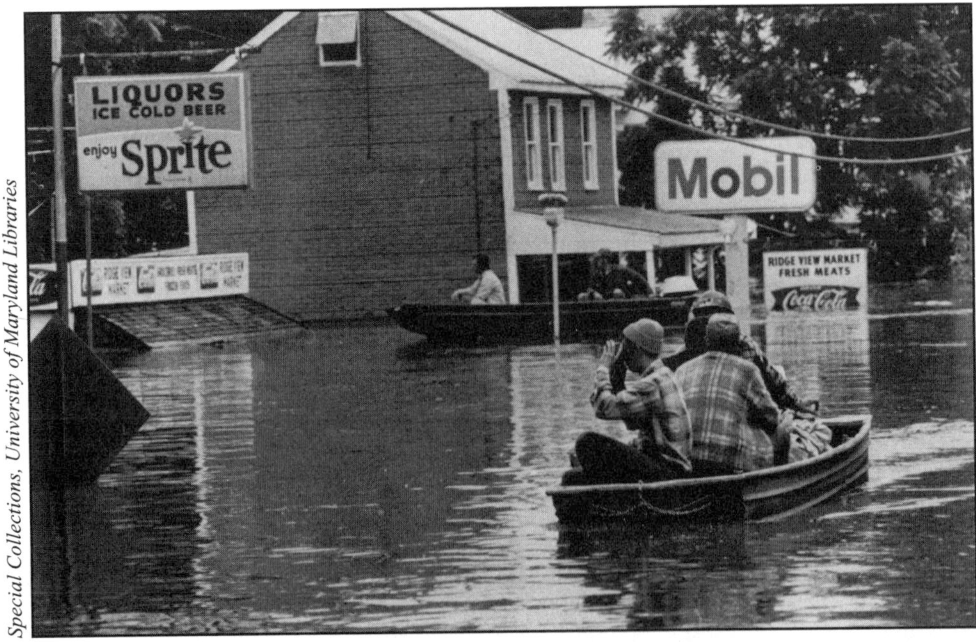

Special Collections, University of Maryland Libraries

Point of Rocks, Md., along the Potomac River.

The Historical Society of Dauphin County

Pennsylvania Governor Milton Shapp and his wife evacuate the executive mansion.

The Historical Society of Dauphin County

Harrisburg, Pa.

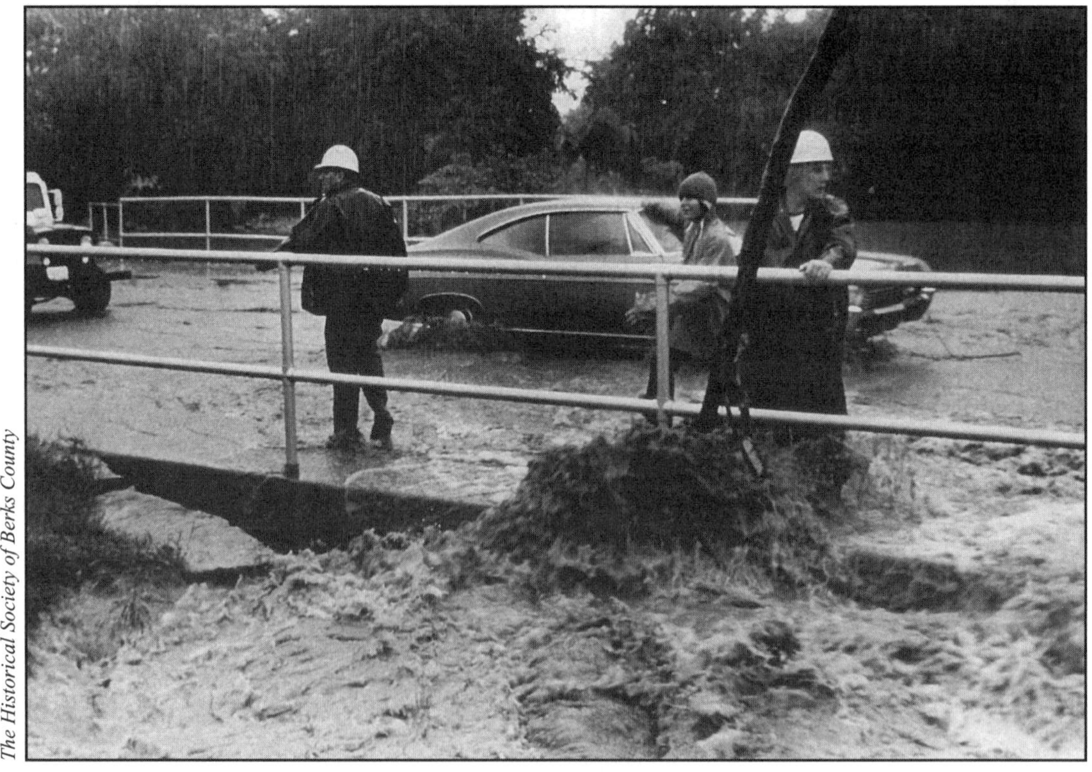
The Historical Society of Berks County

Reading, Pa.

1975

September

ELOISE

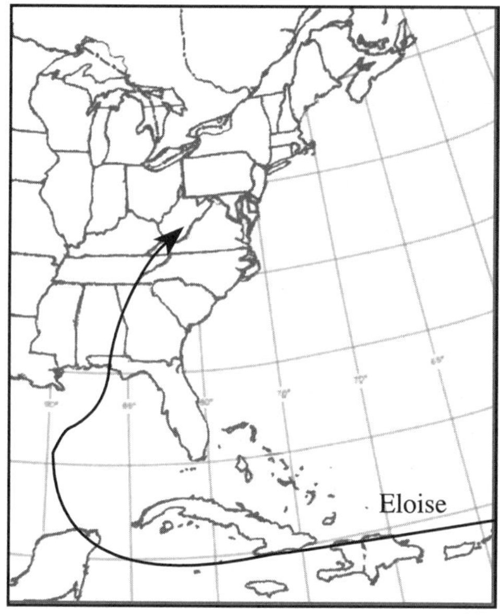

The Atlantic basin had a quieter hurricane cycle from the early 1960s until the middle 1990s. But less active is not inactive. There were regional exceptions. The Mid-Atlantic, for example, saw repeatedly hurricane-related floods from 1969 until 1979. In 1975, Eloise provided a water-logged disaster.

Eloise made landfall on September 23 near Fort Walton Beach, Fla.—only 10 miles from where Hurricane Agnes came ashore. The Category 3 hurricane pursued a track west of Agnes, through the Appalachian Mountains.

The storm soon lost bluster but not moisture. The National Hurricane Center summarized the synoptics:

"A low pressure center identifiable as the remnant of Eloise was no longer discernible by late on the 24th. However, the moisture brought northward by the hurricane combined with an old frontal system over the northeastern United States to produce heavy rainfall and serious flooding until skies cleared on the 27th."

Rainfall from September 23-26 totaled 7-14 inches from northern Virginia through eastern Pennsylvania and southeastern New York. Severe flooding occurred along the Chemung, Potomac, Shenandoah and Susquehanna rivers.

Pennsylvania again faced a watery ordeal. The National Weather Service:

"Record September rainfall over the Susquehanna Basin produced the greatest September flows of record. Flows were running somewhat higher than normal through the 23rd when significant rainfall from the remnants of Eloise began to affect the area. Almost continuous rain from the 22nd through the 26th produced totals of 5-7 inches over most of the basin and 10-15 inches over the lower and middle Susquehanna Valley. Amounts of similar magnitude were observed only during Agnes in June 1972."

Infrastructure took a beating. At least 13 water plants and 16 sewage treatment plants were knocked out of service. Even the state capital, Harrisburg, came under a boil-water advisory after 7.22 inches of rain on September 25-26 produced flooding that contaminated supply.

Eloise displaced more than 20,000 Pennsylvanians. Emergency workers plucked the marooned off roofs, trees and vehicles. Boats plied routes made familiar by Agnes three years earlier.

"It's worse than Agnes," declared James Fox, the Adams County civil defense director. The comparison was apt for scattered localities in south-central Pennsylvania and sections of central Maryland.

Gov. Marvin Mandel proclaimed a state of emergency in 10 of Maryland's 23 counties.

The Monocacy rose 14 feet above flood stage in Frederick, invading downtown. It compromised a sewage treatment plant and a pumping station that supplied the municipality's drinking water.

About 100 people spent the night stranded on a rain-swept hillside in Detour when Double Pipe Creek didn't. Westminster (about 15 miles east) reported about 14 inches of rain from September 23-26.

Rainfall in a swath between Baltimore and Washington, D.C., totaled 7-13 inches from September 23-26. A final deluge of more than 4 inches during the night of September 25-26 caused widespread flash flooding in central Maryland.

Ellicott City, Elkridge and Laurel, pounded by Agnes in 1972, again suffered a natural disaster. The

Patapsco and Patuxent rivers burst forth in frenzied fury. Homes were flooded, cars were lost and businesses, many uninsured, were wrecked. In Laurel, more than 500 residents fled when the floodgates at Rocky Gorge Dam were opened. Even so, water cascaded like a Niagara. Some refugees returned to plundered apartments. Looters used boats to gain access.

Serious flooding occurred in Washington's southern suburbs.

Hundreds of families in Alexandria and Arlington abandoned their homes. Four Mile Run, Holmes Run, and Cameron Run tumbled through residential neighborhoods.

Urbanization and inadequate drainage exacerbated flooding. Houses, apartment buildings and shopping centers had replaced field and forest during the decades before Eloise. Four Mile Run, which devastated the heavily populated border between Alexandria and Arlington, wrought major property losses.

Blinding rain created myriad difficulties in Washington, D.C. Drivers negotiated detours around impassable streets. Thousands of basements flooded.

***

Eloise found its way into a White House press conference. Ron Nessen, President Gerald Ford's spokesman, injected humor into an otherwise gloomy situation.

"President Ford has signed an emergency order directing the Pentagon to begin immediate construction of an ark 350 cubits long."

Nessen stated that the National Zoo would begin assembling two of every living species, one male and one female.

Suddenly, the sun came out.

"The ark project," Nessen commented, "will be deferred."

Hurricane Eloise rainfall totals (Sept. 23-26): **Delaware**—Dover 4.39", Milford 4.04". **Maryland**—Westminster 13.48", College Park 10.01", Rockville 9.00", Aberdeen 7.13", Baltimore 6.48". **Pennsylvania**—Gettysburg 7.75", Reading 6.13", Philadelphia 6.34", West Chester 4.79", Allentown 4.51". **Virginia**—Alexandria 7.68", Fredericksburg 7.32", Charlottesville 6.94", Richmond 4.01". **Washington, D.C.** 8.57".

Washington Post: D.C. Public Library

Four Mile Run burst its banks along the Alexandria-Arlington, Va., boundary.

1976

August

BELLE

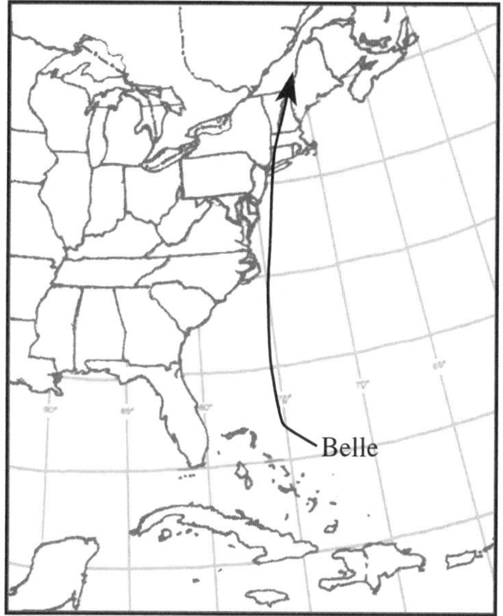

Hurricane Belle is among the rare hurricanes whose eyewalls have passed over New York City. It raced ashore near Jones Beach, Long Island, close to midnight on August 9. It packed sustained winds of 75 mph and a central pressure of 28.94 inches. New York City, on Belle's weaker western side, had peak gusts of 60-70 mph.

The hurricane brought New Jersey gales and several inches of rain. High winds uprooted trees and caused scattered power outages.

Belle dazzled sections of northeastern New Jersey with a colorful lightning display. Flickering yellow, orange, green and red flashes illuminated the night. Such hues are a result of varying particulates.

"The color of lightning is due to the air between the flash and your location," says meteorologist Ron Holle, a lightning expert. "All flashes start out white because they're so intense. However, rain, hail, drizzle, dust, sea salt, pollution, and other material in the atmosphere can cause the flash to take on colors."

Damage in the Mid-Atlantic and New England proved less than expected. Belle possessed Category 2 strength, winds of 100 mph, while off the North Carolina Outer Banks earlier on the 9th. Cooler water south of Long Island sapped the hurricane's strength, providing plenty of "What-ifs?" in its wake.

1979

September

DAVID

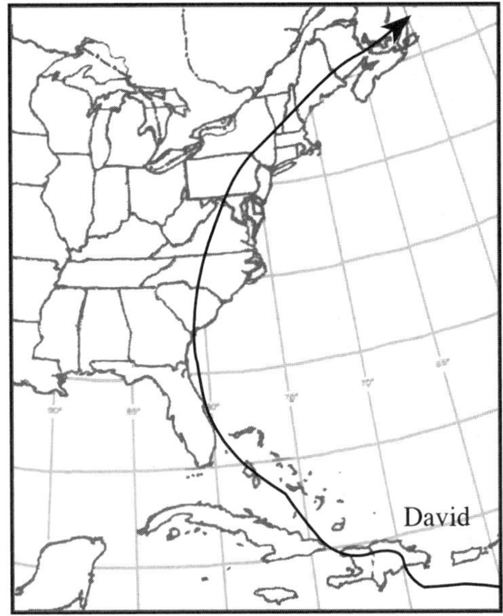

Forecasters didn't mention anything about a tornado outbreak.

Employees at Gloucester Point Marina on the lower Chesapeake Bay couldn't believe what they were seeing. A skiff took flight moments after a tornado swooped down. Other craft flew in all directions. The wind departed as suddenly as it arrived. Spectators marveled, "Did you see that?"

From the Carolinas to New Jersey, others asked a similar question on September 5. Told to expect a hurricane, they got tornadoes. Hurricane David spawned 34 twisters on the East Coast and an unprecedented outbreak in the Middle Atlantic states. Warning often came too late. Forecasters focused on the potential for gales and flooding, not tornadoes.

Days earlier, David sliced through the eastern Caribbean as one of the region's most powerful hurricanes—a borderline Category 5 with sustained winds of 150 mph. It devastated Puerto Rico and the Dominican Republic, killing at least 1,000 people.

David plunged inland near Savannah, Ga., on September 4. The following day tornadoes whipped through the Middle Atlantic states.

Several prowled southeastern Virginia, descending on Newport News and Hampton. More than 100 homes were damaged or destroyed. The outbreak moved north.

During the evening of September 5, a tornado touched down near Mount Vernon, just south of Alexandria, Va. It skipped northwest across Fairfax County. Winds reached F3 intensity, 150 mph. The twister damaged dozens of homes. One man died when a tree crashed through his Great Falls, Va., dwelling. Woodson High School near Fairfax City sustained modest losses from its second run-in with a tornado since 1973![1]

The tornado lifted briefly before mauling the Fairfax School Employees Federal Credit Union in Fairfax City and continuing a path through several neighborhoods.

A tornado ripped through Oley Township, Pa., near midnight on September 5, destroying several buildings. One occupant died and four people were injured when a tornado tracked through a trailer park in New Garden Township, near Avondale, Pa. A twister in Pedricktown, N.J., struck several homes and overturned two tractor-trailers at a truck stop. An F2 tornado left dozens of people homeless in Claymont, Del.

Gales and heavy rain advanced up the Eastern Seaboard. Gusts near David's track ranged from 40-60 mph. Rainfall averaged 3-6 inches. The combination ensured thousands of downed trees and significant power outages.

Central Virginia, the northern Shenandoah Valley and north-central Maryland had extensive flash flooding.

David produced epic flooding in Baltimore, Md. Water surged through industrial parks, businesses and homes in the Jones Falls Valley. Residents and business owners in the Mount Washington neighborhood thought David more destructive than hurricanes Agnes or Eloise. Clipper Mill and Parkdale were also

[1] A tornado visited the area on April 2, 1973. Woodson High lost part of its roof and sustained significant structural damage forcing students to attend another school for the remainder of the term.

devastated. The city logged 1,500 calls for swamped basements. Power outages were rampant. Property damage in the Baltimore area topped $30 million.

In Woodbridge, N.J., two children and the policeman who tried to save them drowned after being swept into a storm sewer. Trenton clocked a gust of 54 mph, typical of winds in the Garden State.

Gusts of 50-65 mph lashed New York City. Power outages affected more than two million people in the metropolis.

***

David Hoadley has traveled more than 700,000 miles since 1956 in a quest to observe and photograph tornadoes. He has witnessed more than 160. Fellow enthusiasts consider him "the godfather of storm chasing."

Hoadley missed the tornadoes spawned by Hurricane David, including a storm that tracked within a few miles of his Falls Church, Va., home. Curious about the one that got away, he conducted a study of the tornado's characteristics. Amid the buzz of chain saws, he toured hard-hit localities and interviewed residents.

"The Fairfax tornado of 5 September was a small storm, doing F1 to F3 damage of a very localized nature," Hoadley wrote. "Damage patterns suggested a rotating mesocyclone (supercell) with two or more satellite tornadoes moving about the overall circulation core and briefly intensifying along the northeast quadrant."

Winds wielded a potent punch in two distinct geographic areas: along the path of the tornado and in sections near the tornado, where straight-line winds (streaks) broadsided houses and trees.

Among Hoadley's observations:

- Damaging straight-line winds occurred at some sites immediately prior to the tornado, but they were separate from the tornado itself. One man witnessed "a gray wall-like fast-moving fog" sweep east to west across a soccer field as treetops began to bend. Seconds later, a tree toppled in his yard.

- The mesocyclone (parent supercell) was not sufficiently well organized to produce the persistent, highly visible condensation column or funnel of classic Midwestern tornadoes.

- There were few reports of thunder and lightning and none of hail—frequent precursors of tornadoes. Most respondents reported moderate to heavy rain just prior to the twister's passage and lighter rain afterward.

- Sounds varied. Many residents said the twister arrived quietly, without warning. But other people in or near the path of the tornado reported a noise like a jet engine. In one neighborhood, it sounded like "a buzzing saw or a million bees."

  Hoadley speculated, "These widely varying experiences may be due to critical wind speeds for a tornadic 'roar' not having been attained prior to reaching the ground, and audible sound developing only after the tornado had time to interact with surface features."

- Some observers noticed an oddly colored sky before or after the tornado. They described tones of silver-gray, a purplish haze and a golden glow. Weather radar indicated that cloud density in the tornadic cell varied. Late-day sunlight may have filtered through, creating striking hues.

- Suction vortices likely produced devastation in a few locations. One of the vortices—a miniature tornado within the larger tornado—destroyed a house even as the surrounding area remained almost unscathed. Intense wind spirals or vortices, generating incredible power, are responsible for seemingly random acts of destruction within a twister's path. "These things are so capricious," Hoadley said, "that they can't be predicted and there's no warning or way to guard against them."[2]

---

[2] The late Theodore Fujita, a designer of the Fujita tornado intensity scale, described suction vortices as having a rotation up to 100 mph faster than the overall vortex or tornado, although a fraction of the size. He cited Hoadley's report as the first documentation of this phenomenon in a hurricane-related tornado.

Hurricane David rainfall totals (Sept. 5-6): **Maryland**—Catoctin Mountain Park 9.40", Westminster 6.75", Rockville 6.66", College Park 6.33", Baltimore 4.70". **New Jersey** (Sept. 6)—Ringwood 5.77", Plainfield 4.10", New Brunswick 3.17". **Pennsylvania**—Philadelphia 2.14". **Virginia**—Big Meadows—Shenandoah National Park 8.93", Langley AFB 7.66", Newport News 5.65", Vienna 4.66", Charlottesville 4.03".

Hurricane David spawned tornadoes in the following counties/cities: **Delaware**—New Castle. **Maryland**—Anne Arundel, Baltimore, Calvert, Carroll, Charles, St. Mary's, Washington. **New Jersey**—Cape May, Gloucester, Salem. **Pennsylvania**—Berks, Chester. **Virginia**—Fairfax, Gloucester, King George, Loudoun, Stafford, Northumberland, Hampton (city), Newport News (city).

A tornado tore through Fairfax, Va.

A tornado struck Oley Township in southeastern Pennsylvania.

Oley Township.

Rough-going in College Park, Md.

Baltimore, Md. A flash flood swallowed Lombard and Market streets.

1985

September

GLORIA

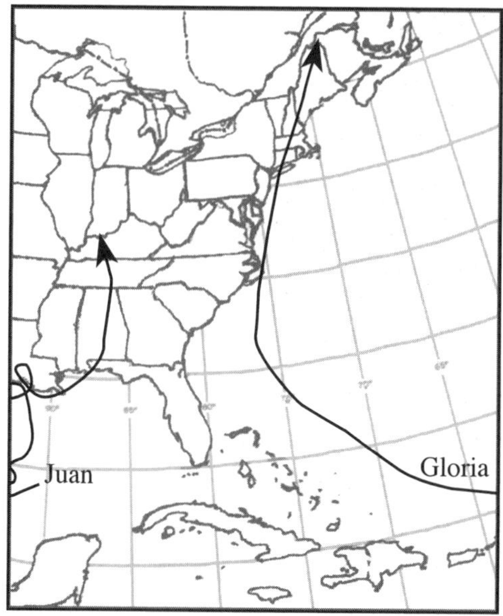

As Hurricane Gloria approached the East Coast during late September 1985, emergency management officials pondered the always vexing question: "Who should evacuate?" The Category 4 storm, with sustained winds of 150 mph, seemed on a rendezvous with disaster.

"Killer Storm of the Century," was one of the imposing monikers attached to the massive, whirling menace. On September 25, Gloria took aim on North Carolina and the Mid-Atlantic.

Highways leading from beaches clogged with bumper-to-bumper traffic. Schools and businesses closed. Resorts transformed into ghost towns. Even Atlantic City's casinos went dark. Longtime shore dwellers, some who had weathered a half-century or more of nature's worst, left.

"EVERYONE TO EVACUATE THE ISLAND," commanded a marquee in Ocean City, Md. Most folks complied.

Gloria passed over Cape Hatteras on September 27, with a barometric pressure of 27.98 inches. Winds of nearly 100 mph dropped to 6 mph as the eye tracked over the station. (When the eye's southern edge arrived, winds returned to hurricane force within three minutes.)

Gloria steadily weakened after brushing Hatteras. Coastal areas from Virginia Beach to the Jersey shore had minimal hurricane-force winds and modest flooding. The "Killer Storm of the Century" struck central Long Island as a modest Category 2.

Rain drenched eastern sections of the Mid-Atlantic. Totals greater than 4 inches were commonplace throughout the Delmarva Peninsula and Chesapeake Bay region. Annapolis, Md., had 7.18" and Cambridge, Md., received 7.00".

Gloria also soaked eastern Pennsylvania. Allentown/Bethlehem, (7.85") and Wilkes-Barre/Scranton (6.52") established new 24-hour rainfall records.

Downpours were usually benign after a dry summer. Take, for instance, metropolitan Washington, D.C., which tallied 3-5 inches.

"The Washington area received far more benefits than damage," wrote Thomas Blackburn, editor of the *Metropolitan Washington Climate Review*. "Children (and their teachers) relished a day off from school in most jurisdictions. There was some minor flooding. Although several people reported wind gusts over 30 mph, damage was mostly minor."

Final estimates put Gloria's cost at nearly a billion dollars, a figure which reflected a building boom to water's edge, soaring real estate values and the ease that even a modest hurricane has in racking up huge losses. But considering the hype, well, weather Armageddon it wasn't.

The 'storm of the century' was now "an over-Glorified storm." Critics asked, "Has the Weather Service cried 'wolf' too often?"

Blackburn took issue with second-guessers.

"Gloria was—and deserved to be—a media sensation. Just the slightest turn to the left from the track it actually took could have devastated parts of the East Coast."

Tom Hand, a life-long resident of Cape May, N.J., agrees. He has lived through more than a half-century of hurricanes. His home received wind and rain damage from Gloria.

"It could have been much worse," says Hand. "The eye of Gloria was headed straight for us and came within 30 miles before veering sharply to the northeast."

Evacuation decisions are bound to be controversial. Basing decisions on a snapshot of a hurricane at least 30 to 36 hours away—the minimum time recommended for implementation of an evacuation plan—and a necessity to err on the side of caution will, no doubt, ensure future Glorias.

PREPARING FOR HURRICANE GLORIA

Rehoboth Beach, Del. The mail must go through...

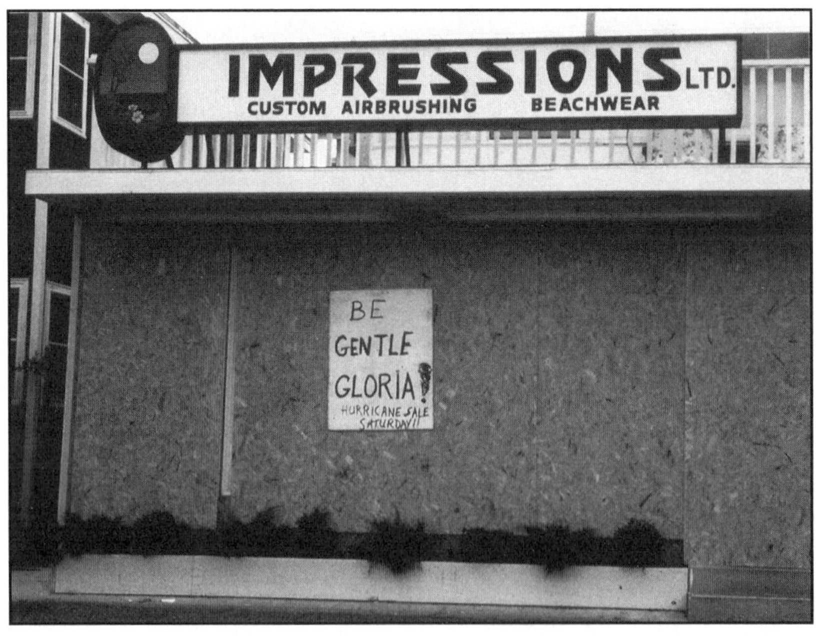

A Rehoboth Beach merchant hopes for the best.

EVACUATION REMAINS A CHALLENGE IN HURRICANE PLANNING

Emergency managers along the Mid-Atlantic coast agree that it's not a question of if a major hurricane will strike, but when.

Gloria and other hurricanes have triggered massive evacuations during recent decades. None fulfilled its billing. Rest assured, that won't last.

All coastal jurisdictions in the Middle Atlantic region have hurricane response strategies. Among the unknowns: When it comes time to leave, how many people will cooperate? How smoothly will the exodus proceed?

Determining the scope and timing of an evacuation is a sensitive issue. If too few people leave and the storm is worse than expected, officials take the heat. Ditto, when many people leave and the storm fizzles. But what if the effort begins too late?

"My greatest nightmare scenario," says Max Mayfield, former director of the National Hurricane Center, "is to have people stuck in their cars in a gridlock as the core of a major hurricane makes landfall."

Emergency managers dread a "short-fuse" evacuation, one initiated too late. Possible causes: a wavering forecast, an explosive storm-deepening prior to landfall, or an unanticipated speedup or change in direction. Officials want to get everyone into a shelter before the onset of hazardous conditions. Depending on the scope and time of year of an evacuation, they estimate at least 32 to 48 hours is needed.

"You don't want to create a panic-type environment," said Gary Schuchardt, the coordinator of regional emergency management services for Hampton Roads, Va. "Not everyone needs to evacuate. We must get the appropriate people to leave. Others can stay put with at-home emergency planning and adequate supplies."

A consideration for anyone remaining on the upper floors of a high-rise building: Wind increases about 10 mph per 100 vertical feet, potentially shattering windows and ripping off roofs. "Once the envelope is broken, you're in for the ride of your life," Schuchardt warns.

The sequence of hurricane evacuation events followed by many localities:

- **Awareness:** Notify people of the impending storm.
- **Standby:** Prepare emergency services.
- **Decision:** Decide on the scope and timing of evacuation. (This is a dynamic process that can change with the threat.)
- **Preparation:** Mobilize and place all resources in position.
- **Evacuation:** Open designated shelters, change routing on major highways if necessary (reverse inbound lanes, for example) and ensure that residents affected by a mandatory evacuation are so informed.
- **Storm Event:** Have everyone sheltered before the onset of high winds. Sheltering choices include taking refuge with friends or relatives who reside inland, booking commercial lodging or staying at a public facility.

Studies indicate that 60 percent of those who evacuate shelter with friends or relatives. Another 20 percent seek out motels/hotels. About 10-15 percent take refuge in workplaces or second homes. Shelters serve 5-10 percent.

The elderly seem most resistant to leave, says Schuchardt. Many don't want to impose on relatives, or may not have that option, and are reluctant to go to a public shelter. They may have lived through many hurricanes that left their property intact, making them skeptical of dire warnings. Yet, they're among those at greatest risk.

Schuchardt concedes that repeated false alarms might create widespread complacency. Nevertheless, he argues, evacuation of vulnerable neighborhoods remains the safest option if there's the possibility of a dangerous hurricane. The emergency manager questions anyone who would ignore an evacuation order.

"What if you decide or need to leave while the storm is in progress?" Schuchardt asks. "How are you going to get around if roads are impassable? What if you need medical or other emergency assistance? What kind of lifestyle will you have after the storm? What if you don't have enough water or food on hand? What if it takes a week to get the utilities back on?"

His advice: "If you are within an area at risk for hurricanes, take heed and get information ahead of time. Make a family emergency kit and plan for what you may have to do. Make a partnership with your local emergency management office and follow their directions. If you do your job, we can do ours much better."

WHEN THE TIME COMES TO EVACUATE OCEAN CITY...

Officials in Ocean City, Md., face many tasks as a hurricane approaches, including the timely evacuation of residents and vacationers. The resort has a population of 5,000, which swells to six figures on summer weekends. Two bridges link Ocean City to the mainland, and a coastal highway leads to the Delaware seashore. The municipality's evacuation plan includes the following stages:

PHASE 1: Anyone wanting to travel to Ocean City is asked to delay a visit until the situation improves. Mobile home residents and those living in known flood-prone areas should secure their homes and prepare for possible evacuation. Boat owners should secure or move all watercraft.

PHASE 2: Non-residents and vacationers are asked to evacuate. All mobile home and low-lying area residents are asked to evacuate. The mayor closes the beach. Municipal bus service begins to be used as transportation to temporary shelters. The drawbridge on U.S. Route 50 is closed to boat traffic.

PHASE 3: The mayor declares a state of emergency. The sale of alcohol is banned and businesses are asked to close immediately. Everyone other than emergency personnel is asked to evacuate. Incoming traffic to Ocean City will be limited to emergency personnel. All Ocean City shelters are relocated to the mainland, with municipal buses used as transportation to shelters.

PHASE 4: The mayor requests a complete evacuation as quickly as possible. No incoming traffic is allowed into Ocean City. Public transportation is shut down. Remaining city personnel are ordered to seek shelter.

November

JUAN
THE ELECTION DAY FLOOD

For all the build-up surrounding Gloria, a minimal hurricane, Juan, proved the most destructive tropical cyclone of the season. Juan caused 50 deaths and left property losses totaling $1.5 billion in the United States.

During late October the tropical storm lingered over the central Gulf Coast, dropping copious precipitation. It gradually moved north, carrying moist and unstable air east to the Atlantic. This high-octane atmospheric fuel whipped up related storms.

An offshoot tracked east to west across North Carolina on November 2 bringing moderate rain north to Pennsylvania. Then, a more vigorous low pressure system traveled from Florida to western Maryland from November 3-5. Days of sporadic showers saturated the ground, followed by a deluge. Tropical and Atlantic moisture lifted over higher elevations and drenched sections of the Blue Ridge. Montebello, in Nelson County, Va., reported the most rainfall, 19.77 inches from November 2-7.

Rainfall of six inches or more doused much of northwestern Virginia and northern West Virginia from October 31 to November 5, with most falling on November 4-5. The resulting flood took its place among the area's storied natural disasters.

The James and Roanoke rivers went on sprees in Virginia.

At Lynchburg, the James River climbed to 35 ft., shattering the 28ft. crest wrought by Hurricane Camille (flood stage 18 ft.). The city declared a state of emergency and National Guardsmen patrolled affected neighborhoods.

Virginia State police officers periodically blocked traffic over the busy U.S. 29 viaduct in Lynchburg as houses and other large objects approached, threatening the bridge. The thoroughfare survived, its concrete arches demolishing or deflecting the onslaught.

State trooper Ed Tinsley was on duty during the disaster, assisting at the Lynchburg viaduct. He had also assisted after hurricanes Camille and Agnes and knows all too well the sense of helplessness that accompanies a flood.

"You can't stop it," said Tinsley. "You can't divert it when it's that massive. All you can do is get people out of the way."

He cited another frustration. Whether out of stubbornness, financial necessity or as an accommodation with nature, property owners continue to occupy sites ravaged by floods. Known floodplains. They risk their lives and the lives of those who have to rescue them.

"It's persistence," Tinsley said, shaking his head.

Scottsville, on the middle James River, ranks the flood of 1985 among its worst. A marker in town lists the following historic levels: "Great Freshet of 1771: 40-45 ft., Agnes 1972: 34.0 ft., Juan 1985: 31.8 ft."

The James River crested in Richmond at 30.8 ft. (flood stage 9 ft.), exceeding Hurricane Camille (28.6 ft.), but short of the flood from Hurricane Agnes (36.5 ft.).

The Roanoke River at Roanoke crested at 23.4 ft., eclipsing the previous standard of 19.6 ft. set by Agnes. About 3,000 homes and 100 businesses sustained damage in the metropolitan area and property losses amounted to $520 million. The city collected 10.63 inches of rain from October 31 to November 4, including 6.61 inches on the 4th.

In Buena Vista, along the Maury River, damage amounted to $50 million, about 10 times the city's annual budget.

Incessant rain caused extensive flooding in the Shenandoah Valley. In Rockingham County alone, angry waters affected 4,000 homes, 350 farms and 95 percent of the primary and secondary roads. Four people perished.

When the downpours ended, 40 counties in Virginia were declared federal disaster areas.

West Virginia experienced its worst hurricane-related catastrophe. At least 40 people died. The National Weather Service reported:

"Along many rivers and streams, flooding of 100 to 500-year flood level frequencies occurred. Records were established in the headwaters of the Monongahela and Potomac basins, as well as along the Greenbrier and Little Kanawha Rivers. Records were also set on the Tygart, West Fork, and Cheat Rivers. The most heavily damaged towns were Parsons, Rowlesburg, Albright, Petersburg, Franklin and Moorefield. A total of 29 counties were included in a disaster declaration. Floodwaters washed away entire towns, roads and bridges. Of the nearly 9,000 homes damaged, 4,000 were completely destroyed. Total damage estimates were in excess of $577 million."

The Potomac River crested at 54 ft. in Paw Paw, W.Va. (flood stage 25 ft.), 33 ft. at Shepherdstown, W.Va. (flood stage 15 ft.), and 34 ft. at Harpers Ferry W.Va. (flood stage 18 ft.).

The Cheat, Tygart, West Fork and Buckhannon rivers, flowing north out of West Virginia into Pennsylvania, spread abundant ruin. Flooding devastated the Pennsylvania counties of Somerset, Allegheny, Westmoreland, Washington, Fayette and Green.

Moderate to severe flooding afflicted western Maryland. The Chesapeake Bay region also saw significant losses. Strong easterly winds, hours of gusts that exceeded 50 mph on November 4-5, caused a destructive rise along the western shore of the bay and on the lower Potomac River. Joseph Moyer, Maryland's state climatologist, wrote:

"Along the western shore of the Chesapeake Bay and its tributaries in southern Maryland, strong easterly winds combined with storm tides reaching 4 to 6 feet above normal, accompanied by waves of 6 to 8 feet, resulted in extensive damage to piers and sea walls as well as to buildings and roads. Considerable beach and soil erosion was reported. Water levels were reported as the highest since the Hurricane of August 1933."

According to the National Weather Service:

"The most severe damage occurred along the Potomac and Rappahannock rivers, with 75 percent of all piers having been severely damaged or destroyed. Westmoreland County (Va.) on the Potomac received over $5 million of damage, with $1 million in damage to the town of Colonial Beach. Over 150 houses along with waterfront businesses were damaged by the floodwaters. Major damage occurred to seawalls, bulkheads, and waterfront highways."

"Juan Big Storm," Patrick Michaels, Virginia's state climatologist, called it. Few would disagree.[1]

Hurricane Juan rainfall totals (Nov. 4-5): **Maryland**—Frostburg 5.57", Oakland 4.18", Cumberland 2.73", Frederick 1.47". **Pennsylvania**—Erie 4.22", Meadville 3.66", Washington 3.47", Harrisburg .85". **Virginia**—Montebello 12.20", Big Meadows 11.30", Glasgow 8.47", Covington 8.20", Amelia 7.85", Staunton 5.59", Charlottesville 4.71", Richmond 1.72", Norfolk 1.09". **West Virginia**—Canaan Valley 8.10", Petersburg 7.40", Pickens 7.16", Clarksburg 6.71", Snowshoe 6.50", Rowlesburg 5.78".

[1] And it was one big hurricane season for the Middle Atlantic states, an exception to a generally quiet decade. Hurricanes Bob (July 25), Danny (August 18) and Kate (November 22), as well as Tropical Storm Henri (September 23-24), affected the region but caused considerably less harm than Gloria or Juan. Danny was the most significant, bringing flash flooding to central Virginia and southern Maryland.

1989

September

HUGO

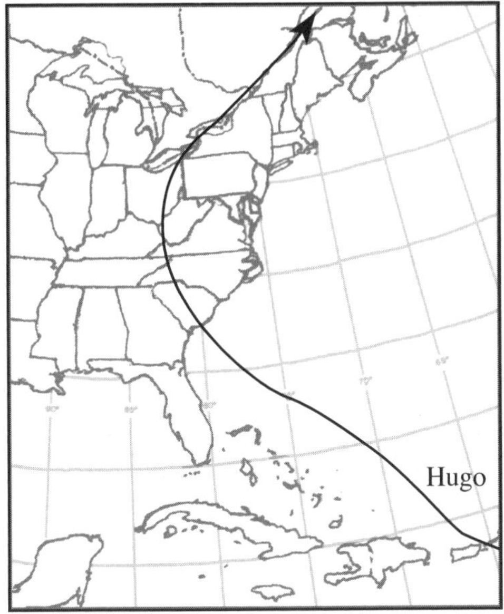

September 1989. Meteorologist Barbara Watson was where she wanted to be and thrilled to be there. Just a few years out of Penn State University, Watson had joined a select group of forecasters at the National Meteorological Center near Washington, D.C. Now, a Category 4 hurricane with the unlikely name "Hugo" churned westward, ever closer to the East Coast. She found herself in the not-so-calm eye of a media storm.

"I arrived on one of the days (of Hugo's approach) just as *Good Morning America* was packing up its cameras," Watson said. "I remember having a reporter and photographer from *The Washington Times* following me around and interviewing me as I was working. We were getting many media calls and also calls from federal agencies, including NASA and the Navy, asking questions to help them make decisions. The National Hurricane Center was overwhelmed with calls. Those who could not reach them were turning to us. At one point, there was talk of a police escort taking the meteorologist-in-charge, Jim Belville, to Annapolis to personally brief the governor on the threat.

"I was asked to plot a large North Atlantic tracking chart with Hugo's past positions on it and the forecast through 72 hours. This was then couriered to the president.

"Someone told me they were watching *Prime Time Live* that night. *Prime Time* was interviewing the president at the White House. As they were walking through a room, they saw my map posted in the background."

Watson's interest in weather took root as a child. Her father, Harry McNaught, illustrated a book on weather and she grew up "fascinated by thunderstorms." Hurricane Agnes left a singular impression when it swamped her Pennsylvania town. After stints with the National Weather Service in Fairbanks, Alaska, and Albuquerque, N.M., the meteorologist arrived in Washington a step ahead of Hugo.

Forecasters anticipated that the worst would brush Charleston, S.C., before veering sharply to the north-northeast. They expected a path through central or eastern North Carolina, Virginia, Maryland and Pennsylvania. Watches and warnings were posted accordingly.

"Hugo was forecasted to take a track very similar to the track Hazel took in October 1954, and so we were thinking it could be a similar event," Watson explained. "Hazel produced wind gusts of 90 to 100 mph. With Hugo, we were thinking of wind gusts of 70 to 90 mph."

The hurricane crashed ashore near Charleston about midnight on September 21-22. Sustained winds of 120 mph screamed through the city. A 20-foot storm surge assaulted the coastline. Hugo ranks among South Carolina's most destructive hurricanes.

The menace seemed in no hurry to turn. It roamed further west than predicted battering Charlotte, N.C., 200 miles inland, with hurricane-strength winds and widespread damage.

The storm finally curved, plowing through the highlands of southwestern Virginia, West Virginia and western Pennsylvania. Hot Springs, in Bath County, Va., had a gust of 81 mph. Jimmy Stewart Airport, Indiana County, Pa., clocked 73 mph. Hugo's rapid movement suppressed rainfall.

Eastern sections of the Mid-Atlantic, bracing for

the worst, saw little. Washington, D.C., had a peak gust of 37 mph and occasional showers. Watson relaxed.

"I was (at work) 14 hours straight before Hugo made landfall," she said. "When I got home, I had to be back at the office in about six hours. Yet, I was glued to the television watching coverage as Hugo neared and made landfall. Not that I wanted anything to happen to Washington, but the next day after the storm missed us and all of the adrenaline that kept me going on little sleep disappeared, I suddenly felt emotionally and physically wiped out. I went home and crashed."

(Watson stayed with the weather service's Baltimore-Washington field office for 15 years. She is currently meteorologist in charge at the field office in Binghamton, N.Y.)

NOAA

Enhanced infrared imagery of Hugo morning of September 22, 1989. The eye is over the coast near Charleston, S.C.

1992

August

ANDREW

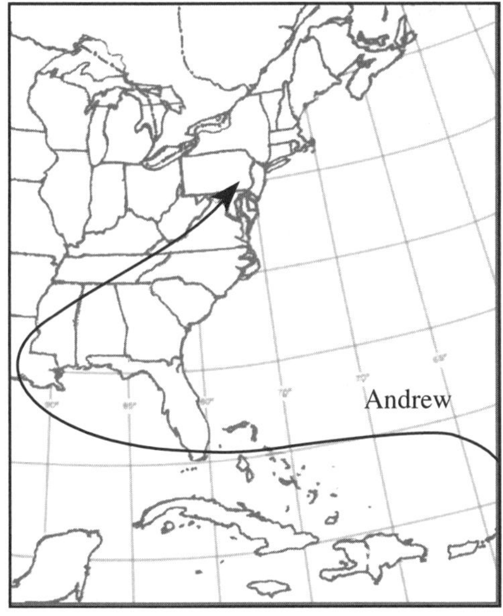

Andrew became the third tropical cyclone of the 20th century to reach the United States as a Category 5. As with the others—the Labor Day Hurricane of 1935 and Hurricane Camille in 1969—its remnants tracked through the Middle Atlantic states.

The remains moved through central Maryland and southeastern Pennsylvania during the late afternoon of August 28. They collided with a cold front moving south from the Great Lakes. The clash set off several short-lived tornadoes, including a destructive whirlwind in Howard County, Md., near Baltimore.

Several houses, power lines and cars were seriously damaged. Downed trees marked the twister's narrow three-mile path. This final gasp added a million dollars to Andrew's $27 billion tally—the costliest hurricane in U.S. history until Hurricane Katrina in 2005.

Earlier, on August 24, Andrew made landfall in Florida, strewing wreckage along a densely populated 40-mile strand south of Miami. Estimated sustained winds up to 165 mph and gusts of 195 mph battered the area. The blow rendered anemometers useless. According to the National Weather Service:

"When Hurricane Andrew hit southeast Miami-Dade County, Fla., August 24, 1992, flying debris in the storm's winds knocked out most ground-based wind measuring instruments, and widespread power outages caused electric-based measuring equipment to fail. The winds were so strong that many wind-measuring tools were incapable of registering the maximum winds. Surviving wind observations and measurements from aircraft reconnaissance, surface pressure, satellite analysis, radar, and distribution of debris and structural failures were used to estimate the surface winds."

The National Hurricane Center sustained assorted damage. Some computers overheated because the backup air conditioning system failed. Satellite dishes in back of the building and other communications equipment, as well as the instrument tower on the roof of the facility, were mangled.

Andrew by the numbers in Florida: 43 dead, more than $25 billion damage, 175,000 people homeless, 25,000 houses destroyed and more than 100,000 damaged. Anyone's guess: the number of terrified people huddled in their houses during the worst, moving from one shattered room to the next, shielded by mattresses or anything else they thought might protect them, praying for the nightmare to end.

Neighborhoods from Florida City to the southern suburbs of Miami resembled a war zone, block after block of rubble. Homestead, directly in Andrew's path, had 1,176 mobile homes before the hurricane. Only nine survived.

After crossing the Everglades, a diminished but still respectable storm churned across the northern Gulf of Mexico. It came ashore as a Category 3 in central Louisiana on August 26. Losses totaled $1.5 billion in the Pelican State.

Days after the hurricane, many South Floridians remained traumatized. Family members and friends who last met before the calamity would meet, embrace and cry. Words unspoken. Storm survivors.

***

At the National Hurricane Conference in 1995, with Andrew fresh in participants' minds, Robert Sheets, the former director of the National Hurricane

Center, didn't mince words when comparing hurricane risks with earthquake threats:

"The potential for loss of life and property seems greater for hurricanes than for earthquakes. Nevertheless, U.S. public education, research, operational warning and mitigation of potential hurricane impacts lag behind similar activities for earthquakes.

"Indeed, if we are to mitigate future hurricane-related losses, we need to emulate the earthquake programs. Earthquake program expenditures for research, education and operations exceed expenditures for hurricane preparedness programs by a factor of three or more."

Sheets predicted a grim future of $100 billion mega-disasters.

"Although the financial losses caused by Hurricane Andrew were staggering, we were fortunate they were not worse. If Hurricane Andrew had tracked only 20 miles further north in Florida, two different studies show losses would have topped $75 billion in Florida alone. A continuation of that same track across Florida would have resulted in major losses in the Fort Myers area and as far west as New Orleans. Total property damage likely would have exceeded $100 billion. We may assume the nation's insurance industry would have been in shambles and losses from rising waters in Miami Beach and New Orleans would have exhausted the reserves of the National Flood Insurance Program.

"Of even greater concern is the likelihood casualties in southeastern Florida would have been tremendous because more than 30 percent of the region's residents did not evacuate the condominium complexes in Miami Beach, Hallandale and Hollywood.

"Additionally, Andrew's inland impact could have been much more severe. It is possible to imagine a slower-moving and wetter tropical system tracking up the Appalachian Mountains and resulting in widespread devastation due to inland flooding and mudslides similar to those accompanying hurricanes Agnes in 1972 and Camille in 1969. Such flooding could add dozens of fatalities and billions of dollars in damages to losses and jeopardize already tenuous emergency response and recovery efforts at all levels."

($100 billion storms are here! The losses from Hurricane Katrina exceeded that amount.)

1995

September

ISMAEL

Hurricanes originating in the eastern Pacific Ocean occasionally impact the Middle Atlantic region. They merge with continental weather systems while crossing the United States, adding moisture and energy. Or they traverse Central America, entering the Caribbean Sea or Gulf of Mexico before heading north.

Hurricane Ismael struck the Baja Peninsula of Mexico on the night of September 14-15, 1995. Remnants drifted through western Texas late on the 15th. A weak low pressure trough picked up the remnants and pulled the moisture northward, strengthening the system. Rain reached the East Coast on September 16-17. It provided drought relief, drenching northern Virginia, central Maryland and vicinity with 1-2 inches of rain. (A year later, on September 16-17, 1996, another hurricane born in the Pacific, Fausto, brought the Mid-Atlantic a dousing of similar magnitude.)

October

OPAL

Few Atlantic hurricane seasons have been as active as 1995. It produced 19 tropical cyclones. Opal was the most significant in the Mid-Atlantic region. The hurricane's remnants spawned a tornado outbreak.

Opal approached Pensacola, Fla., on October 4, strengthening from a Category 2 to a Category 4 within hours. Caught off guard by the sudden growth spurt, officials feared the worst—a nightmarish evacuation in full swing as the monster reached the coast. But the storm weakened before landfall. It came ashore as a marginal Category 3.

Opal gradually dissipated while tracking through the western Appalachians. Its dying spasms touched off tornadoes.

On October 5, one slammed West Point, in southeastern Virginia. It overturned several small planes at an airfield before spinning a three-mile path through fields and woodland.

Many hurricane-spawned tornadoes occur after dark, seemingly less dependent on daytime heating than twisters generated by other weather systems.

That night, several struck Maryland. The strongest romped through the eastern suburbs of Washington, D.C., destroying 15 homes and damaging more than 100 others in Camp Springs and Temple Hills. Weaker tornadoes touched down in St. Mary's, Charles and Anne Arundel counties. The latter traveled for six miles, from Odenton to Glen Burnie, damaging about 20 homes.

1996

July

BERTHA

July 4, 1996. While the nation watched fireworks, the National Hurricane Center observed the earliest formation of a tropical cyclone in the eastern Atlantic. Hurricane Bertha developed in the shadow of Africa, near the Cape Verde Islands.

It made landfall in North Carolina on July 12. Camp Lejeune reported a gust of 108 mph and an eight-foot storm surge. The hurricane caused $270 million in damage during its romp through the Northeast.

Bertha reached Virginia as a tropical storm, bringing gusts of 50-60 mph to the eastern half of the state. It dumped 3-6 inches of rain from the Delmarva Peninsula to the Richmond and Washington, D.C., metropolitan areas. Short-lived tornadoes touched down in Smithfield, Gloucester, Hampton and Northumberland counties in Virginia, injuring nine people.

The remnants of Bertha, accompanied by heavy rain and gales, tracked across the Delmarva Peninsula, southeastern New Jersey and New England.

September

FRAN

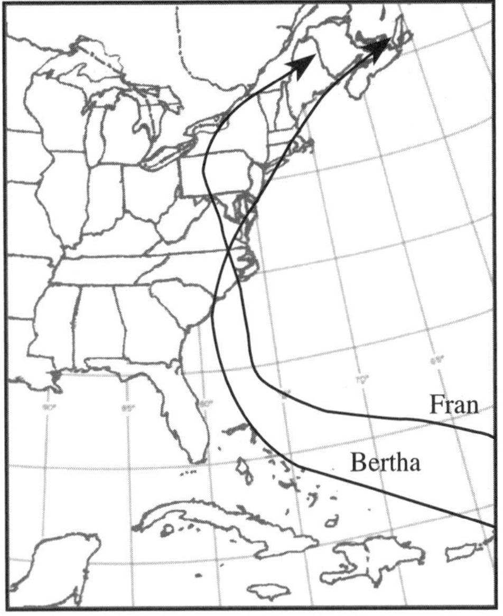

Photograph courtesy of NOAA, Department of Commerce

Hurricane Fran

Hurricane Fran came ashore in North Carolina on September 5, churning through the eastern section of the state and Virginia, Maryland and Pennsylvania. It killed 34 people. Damage totaled $3.2 billion making the storm the third costliest U.S. hurricane as of 1996.

Sustained winds of 115 mph and gusts to 140 mph at landfall diminished to half that as Fran crossed into Virginia. Strong gales lashed the eastern half of the state. Big Meadows in Shenandoah National Park reported the Old Dominion's top gust, 79 mph. Hampton clocked 71 mph, among the highest gusts in southeastern Virginia.

Fran downed thousands of trees and numerous power lines. More than 550,000 customers lost electricity in Virginia—one of the state's worst outages to that time. Homes went dark from the Blue Ridge to the Atlantic.

The hurricane caused one of Virginia's notable floods of the 20th century. Inland tidal and non-tidal waterways were affected.

Most rivers flooded in Southside Virginia. The Dan River at South Boston crested at 33.2 ft., above a 25-ft. flood stage, nearly the equal of the 33.4 ft. record rise caused by Hurricane Agnes in 1972.

Fran brought the third flood disaster within 15 months to northwestern Virginia. "We've had enough '100-year storms' during the past year," one resident lamented.

At Strasburg, the North Fork of the Shenandoah rose to a record 32.3 ft. (flood stage 17 ft.), besting the 31.2 ft. benchmark of October 1942. The South Fork of the Shenandoah River crested at 32.6 feet in Front Royal, eclipsing a 12-ft. flood stage.

The Maury River inundated Buena Vista, but the devastation caused by hurricanes Camille in 1969 and Juan in 1985 was averted, in part, by a partially completed flood control project.

The Potomac River crested at 13.8 ft. in Washington, (flood stage 7 ft.). The Rappahannock River reached 26.9 ft. in Fredericksburg (flood stage 18 ft.). The James River peaked at 23.8 ft. in Richmond (flood stage 9 ft.).

The northern Shenandoah Valley received 10-15 inches of rain. Thousands of homes were damaged. Drowned basements were legion.

Flooding closed more than 650 roads in the Old Dominion. Raging waterways also blocked hundreds in West Virginia, particularly in Hardy County where 90 percent of the thoroughfares became impassable.

Flash flooding plagued western Maryland and a three-county area west of Harrisburg, Pa. The hardest-hit sections were Frederick, Washington and Allegany counties, Md.

Lengthy gales piled up water in the Chesapeake region. The Chesapeake Bay surged 4-6 feet above normal. Battering surf destroyed seawalls, docks and piers. Many shoreline homes flooded.

Atmospheric instability in the wake of Fran triggered severe local storms in eastern sections of the Mid-Atlantic, including a cloudburst in suburban Philadelphia. On September 8, up to 10 inches of rain fell in Abington Township during a three-hour period, resulting in several deaths and millions of dollars in property damage.

Hurricane Fran rainfall totals (Sept. 4-7): **Maryland**—Frostburg 6.72", Cumberland 5.53", Rockville 4.60", Frederick 4.31". **Pennsylvania**— Newville 9.80", Biglersville 5.30", Gettysburg 4.38", Altoona 4.11". **Virginia**—Big Meadows 16.77", Luray 14.33", Staunton 8.88", Charlottesville 8.20", Front Royal 7.74", Lynchburg 7.04", Vienna 6.58", Warrenton 5.78", Richmond 2.01". **Washington, D.C.** 3.38".

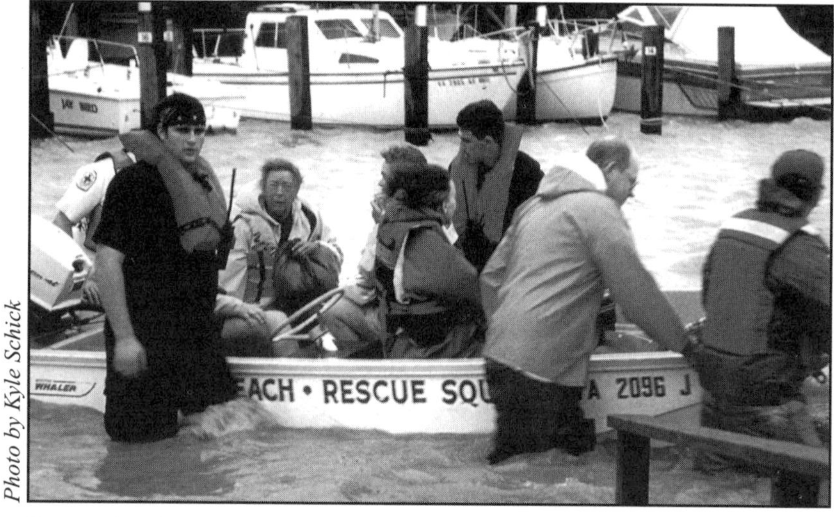

Photo by Kyle Schick

Evacuation in Colonial Beach, Va., ahead of Fran's high tides. The tidal Potomac River had moderate to severe flooding.

Piney Point Lighthouse Museum and Park

Flooding on the lower Potomac River inundated Piney Point, Md.

1998

August

BONNIE

Despite progress in the detection, tracking and forecasting of hurricanes, accurate predictions can prove elusive. Hurricane Bonnie vexed forecasters during August 1998.

The storm seemed of little concern to Virginia after a jaunt through eastern North Carolina and return to sea. However, the Gulf Stream invigorated the system. By the afternoon of August 27, a resurgent Bonnie blasted coastal sections of the Old Dominion with hours of gusts greater than 50 mph.

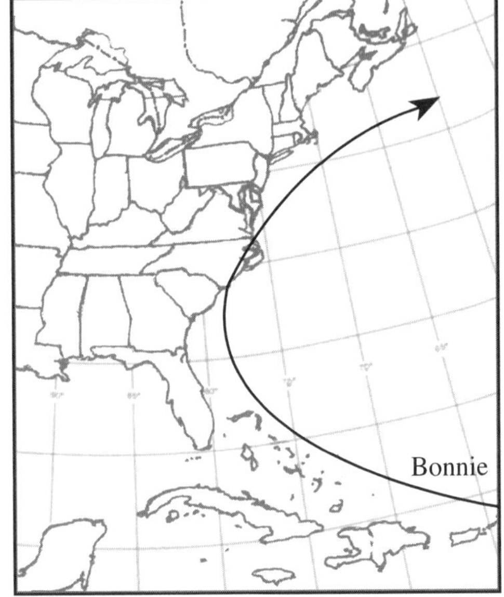

Norfolk International Airport recorded a peak gust of 64 mph and Langley Air Force Base in Hampton clocked 67 mph. Cape Henry caught a sustained wind of 81 mph and a gust of 104 mph. Vicious broadsides at nearby Virginia Beach left property losses totaling $13 million.

Winds damaged hundreds of homes and uprooted thousands of trees throughout southeastern sections of the state. Power outages affected 320,000 customers of Virginia Power, the region's largest utility. Many residents remained in the dark for days.

***

Hurricanes periodically slap coastal Virginia after an overland journey. Like Bonnie, Danny (1997) and Charley (1986) delivered parting blows.

Danny caused several tornadoes. The twisters struck Chesapeake, Norfolk and Knotts Island.

Charley gusted to 63 mph at Norfolk International Airport. South Island, about 10 miles away (along the Chesapeake Bay Bridge-Tunnel), clocked a gust of 104 mph on top a lofty tower.

1999

August/September

DENNIS AND FLOYD

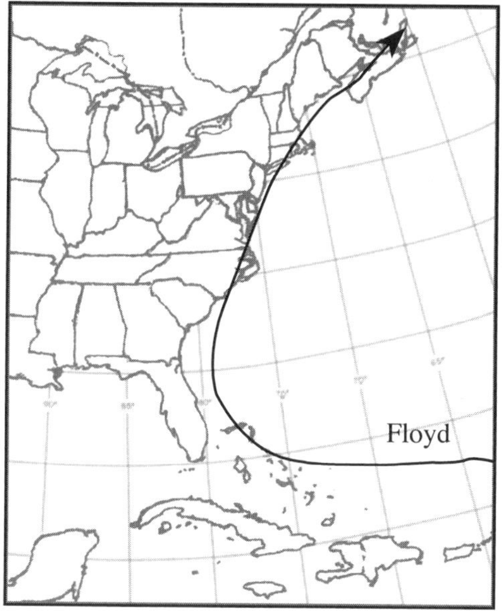

Hurricanes Dennis and Floyd. Rain and more rain.

Dennis lingered near North Carolina and Virginia from August 30 to September 6. It dumped more than 10 inches of rain near the coast and inland.

Floyd arrived on September 16, a born rainmaker. While off the coast of South America, its sprawling feeder bands tapped Amazon rain forests. A week's passage over the Atlantic Ocean added additional moisture.

Floyd steadily intensified, becoming a strong Category 4 hurricane while approaching the southeastern United States. Warning flags flew from Florida to Massachusetts.

An estimated two million people in the southeastern United States evacuated inland—the largest peacetime exodus in U.S. history. Resulting traffic jams left motorists fuming. Highways resembled parking lots. Then, Floyd weakened and missed most of the evacuees' homes, targeting an area further north.

It came ashore near Cape Fear, N.C., as a Category 2 hurricane. Tides were unspectacular, but rainfall was phenomenal. A stalled frontal boundary to the west provided the locus for steady torrents. Totals of 10-20 inches fell from eastern North Carolina to eastern New England.

At least 60 deaths were attributed to Floyd. It left a tab of $4.5 billion.

Eastern North Carolina is hurricane country. Storms occasionally drop prodigious rainfall. Floyd was no fluke. Man-made vulnerabilities greatly added to losses.

North Carolina experienced its most devastating flood. Floyd killed 51 people, destroyed 7,000 homes and damaged 56,000 dwellings. High water closed most highways in eastern sections of the state and created numerous maladies. Contamination from sewage and assorted wastes produced an environmental nightmare.

Rainfall in southeastern Virginia ranged from 12 inches to more than 20.

Nearly two feet of rain fell on sections of the Blackwater River basin, immersing Franklin (pop. 9,000). Most residents and business owners needed flood insurance and an ark (the former being about as rare as the latter). Flooding destroyed or seriously damaged 150 homes and over 180 businesses. Commercial establishments were mostly mom and pop operations, the backbone of the local economy.

"Every business downtown is, from a business standpoint, destroyed," said Franklin's mayor, Jim Councill. "We will rebuild. We will have a revitalized downtown. We will come back, but it's going to take a long time."

Gales launched 30 ships of the James River reserve (ghost) fleet. They sustained no damage but provided a considerable environmental scare. The wayward vessels, loaded with contaminants, were among 70 aging military craft awaiting disposal.

Highest winds occurred at varying distances from the center of circulation. The James River Bridge at Hampton Roads, in the hurricane's path, clocked a gust of 100 mph. The Chesapeake Bay region had peak gusts of 50-70 mph, with the Chesapeake Bay Bridge near Annapolis, Md., reporting a top gust of 76 mph (although Floyd's eye was more than 100 miles away at the time!) Other gusts included 71 mph at Tall

Timbers, Md., (along the lower Potomac River); 65 mph at the Patuxent River Naval Air Station and 54 mph at Andrews Air Force Base.

Rain overwhelmed many gauges. Chestertown, Md., received 14 inches from September 15-17, with most falling on the 16th. Totals greater than 10 inches fell throughout the central and northern Delmarva Peninsula.

A new calendar day rainfall record was established for Delaware on September 16 when 10.58 inches fell in Greenwood.

Excess water ponded everywhere. Elevated road embankments and narrow culverts created blockages on flat farmland, turning fields into lakes.

Philadelphia had its wettest day of the 20th century on September 16, 6.98 inches. More than 10 inches fell in Delaware County, Pa. Much of southeastern Pennsylvania averaged 5-10 inches.

Wissahickon, Perkiomen and Neshaminy rivers and Ridley Creek crested at unprecedented heights.

Floyd's eye remained intact as it embraced the Atlantic Ocean at the Maryland-Delaware border. Spectators got a rare glimpse of a hurricane's unique feature, a floating canyon of airy quietude. As a bonus, tides remained tame; destructive wind and rain stayed inland.

Passage of the eye brought a fleeting interlude to Ocean City, Md., and Fenwick Island, Del. The sun peeked out behind a thin veil of clouds. Winds became gentle, fitful. Rain ceased.

After about twenty minutes a dark wedge approached from the southwest. Floyd's eyewall returned with light rain but powerful gusts. Breeze became gale within minutes. Observers at the Coast Guard station in Ocean City, which recorded a barometric pressure of 28.88 inches as the eye passed, watched the instrument spike upward.

The Isle of Wight Bay reversed course, propelled by a shift in wind direction. Water, which surged north shortly before, pressed south to the Ocean City Inlet. There it wrestled with the oncoming sea, a maelstrom of clashing waves and warring currents.

Billowing gray and white clouds raced through a tropical blue sky, complemented by a brilliant rainbow. West winds restrained long lines of ragged, whitecapped breakers. So went Floyd...

***

When September 16 began, most areas in New Jersey struggled with a drought emergency. By evening, the state faced a flood catastrophe.

Floyd damaged or destroyed more than 76,000 homes and 4,000 businesses in the nine counties that were declared disaster areas, according to the

The eye of Hurricane Floyd visited Ocean City, Md., and Fenwick Island, Del.

Federal Emergency Management Agency. Property losses totaled more than $1 billion.

The hurricane was downgraded to a tropical storm while off Cape May. Wind gusts in New Jersey rarely exceeded 50 mph, but downpours sent most streams and rivers on a rampage.

The heaviest rainfall in the state, more than 10 inches, fell on central and northeastern sections. At least one weather station in 12 of New Jersey's 21 counties collected over 8 inches of rain.

The Raritan River basin lay squarely under the deluge. The river attained record crests at Manville and Bound Brook, submerging the densely populated Raritan Valley. At Manville, the Raritan peaked at 27.5 ft. (flood stage 14 ft.), and at Bound Brook it crested at 42.13 ft., (flood stage 28 ft.) About 2,000 people left Bound Brook—many by boat. In neighboring Manville, more than 1,000 residents escaped the rising water. (Emergency shelters in the region remained open for months.)

Adding to danger: Thousands of barrels of chemicals, some toxic, floated into Raritan Bay and washed up on local beaches.

A water plant serving 500,000 people in the Raritan Valley closed for a week. More than a million people in northern New Jersey were advised to boil tap water (if they could get any!).

Among other Garden State waterways that crested at record levels: Saddle River at Lodi, 13.94 ft. (flood stage 5 ft.), Millstone River at Blackwells Mills, 20.97 ft. (flood stage 9 ft.), Rahway River at Springfield, 10.67 ft. (flood stage 5.5 ft.).

***

David Robinson, the New Jersey state climatologist, attended a drought crisis meeting on the day Floyd arrived. Afterward, he shifted gears and analyzed the disaster in the Passaic and Raritan river basins. Among his observations:

- Higher river levels prior to Floyd would have exacerbated flooding somewhat. It is certain that flooding would have been worse in the Passaic River basin in northern New Jersey had a series of reservoirs not retained a considerable amount of the runoff from upstream portions of the basin. (Even so, the Passaic River and its tributaries inundated many communities.)

- A land use assessment is needed within the Raritan watershed to determine the impact development has had on the delivery of precipitation to the streams and rivers of the basin over the past 30 years. It is possible that the higher flood levels associated with Floyd, compared to Doria in 1971, were, in part, the result of the increased conversion of farmland to residential and commercial developments, creating greater runoff.

- Flooding associated with Hurricane Floyd will go down as one of the worst natural events of the 20th century in central and northeastern New Jersey. Six deaths, numerous dangerous rescues, approximately 25,000 evacuees, and damage close to $1 billion resulted from Floyd. The situation would likely have been worse, particularly in the Passaic basin, had an extended period of drought not preceded the event.

Hurricane Floyd rainfall totals (Sept. 16-17): **Delaware**—Vernon 12.36", Greenwood 10.58", Newark 9.70", Wilmington Airport 8.29", Georgetown 6.11". **Maryland**—Chestertown 14.00", Millington 11.77", Annapolis 11.60", Federalsburg 11.20", Bel Air 8.64", La Plata 8.27". **New Jersey**— Pompton Lakes 14.45", Somerville 12.64", North Plainfield 12.24", Pequannock 10.67", Princeton 10.44", Trenton 10.10", Morristown 9.40". **Pennsylvania**—Doylestown 10.07", Valley Forge 10.04", Exton 8.82", West Chester 8.26", Chadds Ford 8.25". **Virginia**—(Sept. 14-16)- Newport News 16.57", James City County 14.30", Williamsburg 14.28", Smithfield 12.50", Gloucester 11.25", West Point 10.75", Portsmouth 10.10", Richmond 6.54".

FRANKLIN, VIRGINIA

Photograph courtesy of FEMA

Photograph courtesy of FEMA

FEDERALSBURG, MARYLAND

Photograph by Charles K. Planner

The town bridge is swamped by Marshyhope Creek.

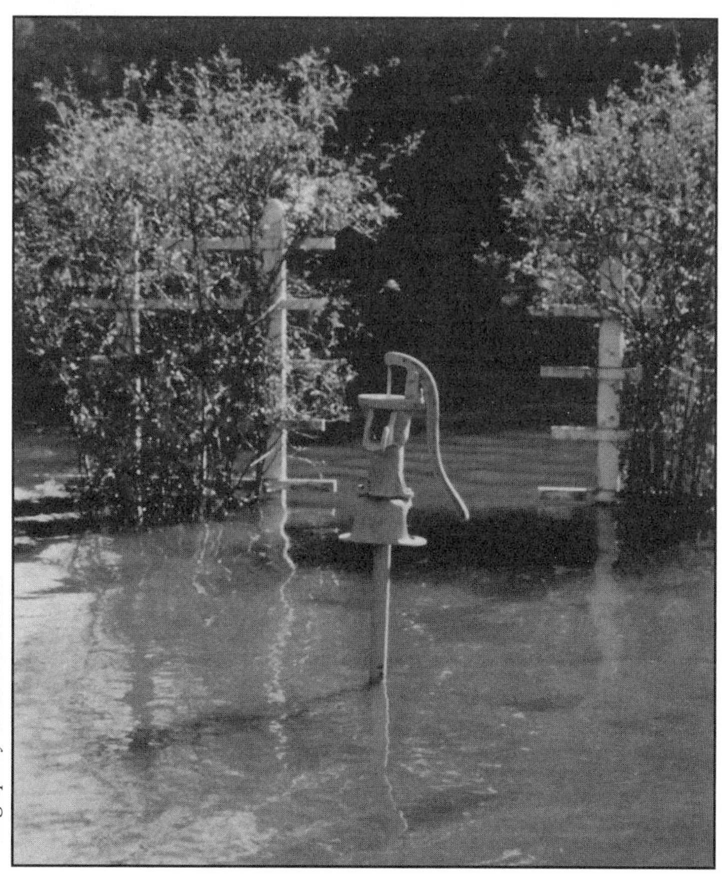

Photograph by Charles K. Planner

TRIAL BY WATER AND FIRE. BOUND BROOK, NEW JERSEY

Photographs courtesy of the Bound Brook Office of Emergency Management and New Jersey Department of Environmental Protection

Fire destroyed part of downtown.

HURRICANES
2000s

2001

June

ALLISON

Homeowners of the Huntingdon Valley Club Condominiums in suburban Philadelphia, Pa., were fed up. The remnants of Tropical Storm Allison dumped nearly 10 inches of rain, enough to chase them from their dwellings. Supposedly living in a government-designated "100-year floodplain," they discovered to their dismay that Allison was the *sixth* such disaster within a century.

The deluge wasn't expected but little about Allison was, from landfall in Texas on June 5 until its brush with eastern Pennsylvania on June 17. Allison spent five days crawling through eastern Texas. It dumped up to 37 inches of rain in the Houston metropolitan area, killing 40 people and causing nearly $5 billion in damage. Never before had a mere tropical storm caused such losses.

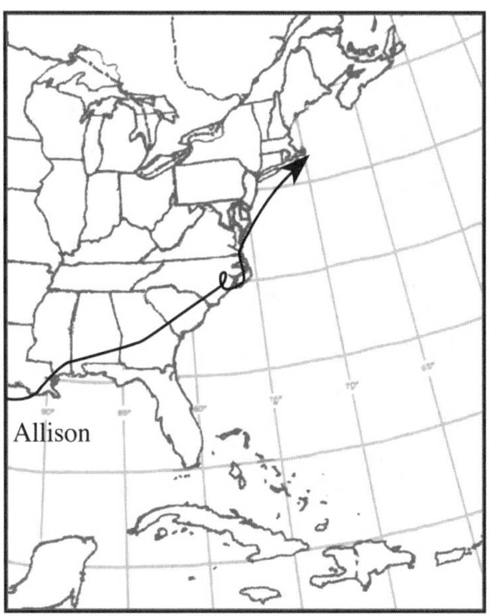

Downgraded to a tropical depression, Allison intensified over southern Louisiana and regained tropical storm strength. It tracked along the Gulf Coast and up the Eastern Seaboard. The storm unleashed 23 tornadoes from Louisiana to Virginia.

Several inches of rain fell on northeastern North Carolina. Downpours diminished as Allison traversed Virginia and Maryland.

Individual storm cells from a tropical remnant system sometimes turn severe. A cloudburst developed over Montgomery and Bucks counties in southeastern Pennsylvania. Among the heaviest rainfall totals: Chalfont 10.17", Willow Grove 10.16", Doylestown 9.35".

Flash flooding wrecked property and mired traffic throughout the area. A natural gas explosion killed six people at the flooded Village Green Apartments in Upper Moreland Township. Allison claimed another victim when a motorist plunged into turbulent Wissahickon Creek.

***

Once in a hundred years flood. Hurricanes have a way of confounding expected frequencies. Just ask residents of the Huntingdon Valley Club Condominiums.

2003

September

ISABEL

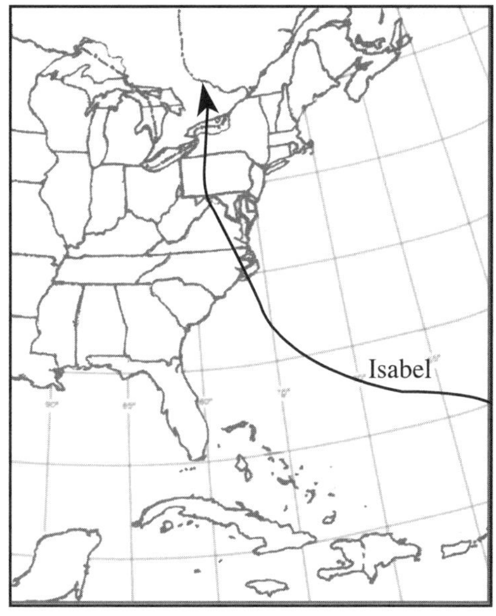

Blake Harper lived in the Caribbean region for years, experiencing several hurricanes. Now, as Hurricane Isabel approached, he was in North Beach, Md., (which he thought safe from such storms), on the roof of his house watching waves from the Chesapeake Bay roll by his front door.

"The waves were at least six feet high!" Harper exclaimed. "It looked like the surf at Cape Hatteras."

Isabel stirred the bay like no hurricane since Hazel in 1954. Water broke through the floor of Harper's cottage. Objects large and small took aim. A car floated to within a few feet, blocked by a tree.

"I was worried that the debris would come through the house," Harper said. "Slam. Slam. Slam. All night long."

His home survived but many didn't. The town lost its popular boardwalk, several shops and a grocery store. On the first anniversary of the storm, a banner along the main street advertised, "Supermarket Operator Wanted."

***

Isabel appeared formidable several days before landfall. It reached rare Category 5 strength and maintained that ferocity for nearly 48 hours.

Computer forecasting models suggested that Isabel would strike somewhere between North Carolina's Outer Banks and the Delaware Bay. The National Hurricane Center feared the hurricane might make landfall as a Category 3. However, offshore waters were cooler than normal. During the afternoon of September 18, Isabel plowed into eastern North Carolina. It struck Ocracoke as a Category 2.

The hurricane killed 40 people and caused $5 billion in property damage. Isabel packed a potent punch long after landfall. It caused most destruction after being downgraded to a tropical storm.

(The Saffir-Simpson hurricane scale understated the effects of high winds on interior sections of the Mid-Atlantic. Isabel didn't even rate a minimal Category 1 as it crossed Virginia, Maryland and Pennsylvania. Yet, wind-related damage in these areas amounted to more than $3 billion.)

Storm surge caused considerable losses along the North Carolina Outer Banks. Tidal estuaries of the Mid-Atlantic also endured Isabel's wrath.

Gusts greater than 50 mph swept areas east of the Blue Ridge, delivered by hours of periodic squalls. High winds and spongy soil resulted in the loss of innumerable trees and unprecedented power outages. The number of customers without electricity included: Virginia 1.6 million, Maryland 1.25 million, North Carolina 525,000 and Washington, D.C., 78,000.

Power remained off for weeks in some neighborhoods. Utility companies bore the brunt of public ire, vowing to improve next time.

Potomac Electric Power Company (Pepco) estimated that more than 75 percent of its customers lost power. A subsidiary, Conectiv, reported 40 percent of its subscribers similarly inconvenienced. Afterward, Pepco hired James Lee Witt Associates to investigate what went right, what went wrong, and how the company could improve responsiveness.

"Disasters are defining moments for utilities," according to the assessment. "We strongly believe there needs to be a new way of looking at utility performance in preparation for and during a disaster. If Pepco and Conectiv focus their organizations on what customers expect both day-to-day and in extreme environments, collaboratively engage those who share the responsibility for restoration of the basic functions of the community, and take advantage of organizational lessons others have learned about preparing for and recovering from disasters, they can then become leaders within the field of utility emergency preparedness and response. At least equally important, the region as a whole will be better able to withstand and recover from disasters."

A state-by-state summary:

VIRGINIA

Gov. Mark Warner described Isabel as "probably the worst storm in a generation." It affected nearly the entire state. Tidal sections dealt with destructive surf and high winds. Gales uprooted trees and wrecked power lines across much of Virginia.

Isabel by the numbers:

- Fatalities: 36
- Total damage (not including ongoing economic losses): $1.9 billion.
- Homes destroyed: 1,124
- Homes damaged: 9,027
- Businesses destroyed or seriously damaged: 1,477
- Peak gusts (mph): Chesapeake Bay Bridge-Tunnel 87, Norfolk Naval Station 83, Quantico 78, Langley AFB 76, Norfolk (International Airport) 74, Richmond (International Airport) 73, Newport News 65, Wallops Island 62.
- Rainfall totals: Big Meadows (Shenandoah National Park) 11.10", Devils Knob (Nelson County) 10.70", Urbanna 7.00", Emporia 6.41", Waynesboro 6.11", Staunton 5.80", Williamsburg 4.50", Richmond 4.32", Newport News 3.70", Fredericksburg 2.79".

Around Virginia:

The night of September 18-19, 2003, will long be remembered throughout the Chesapeake Bay region. Shorefront communities gazed upon waterways that they hardly recognized. Tides, predicted to rise 3-4 feet above normal, rose 5-8 feet. They peaked at record or near-record levels, topped by ocean-like surf, invading areas thought safe. Homes, docks and boats littered beaches.

Carnage along the Potomac River at Colonial Beach rivaled that caused by Hurricane Hazel. Waves attacked the town, destroying boats, docks and piers. The surf invaded waterfront homes and businesses, eroded shoreline.

Popular establishments like The Riverboat, Wilkerson's Seafood and the Colonial Beach Yacht Center sustained tremendous damage.

Much of the tidal Chesapeake region shared Colonial Beach's plight.

In downtown Alexandria, the Potomac River topped the mark set by the legendary hurricane of August 1933. Recent development along the waterfront funneled the Potomac up the main thoroughfare, King Street, swamping the historic Torpedo Factory and many commercial establishments.

The Potomac surged into the New Alexandria and Belle View neighborhoods. Hundreds of homes were flooded and nearly 200 cars lost. The area had no recent history of flooding, and residents received little or no warning. In the aftermath, they raced to salvage possessions.

The winds several hundred feet aloft were generally of hurricane force. However, they reached the ground unevenly. For instance, Quantico, Va., reported a peak gust of 78 mph but Fort Belvoir, only 15 miles away, had 49 mph.

Power outages plagued the eastern two-thirds of Virginia. Many residents spent a miserable night in darkened homes, some without telephone service. In Fairfax County and vicinity, 1.2 million people lacked safe drinking water.

The Fairfax County Water Authority, Virginia's largest water utility, lost power at its four processing plants. Dry taps followed. Dana Kauffman, a member of the county board of supervisors, told constituents:

"Water, in Fairfax County, is suppose to flow freely from the faucet, unimpeded by such minor inconveniences as hurricanes. At least that's what we thought up until Hurricane Isabel came calling. For several hours for some, longer for others, there was no water, then a trickle of water, then a boil water advisory that lasted for several days."

The following appeared in a Fairfax County office building:

EMERGENCY NOTICE

Due to the Fairfax County water problems, the following is effective immediately:

- Do not drink the water from any fixture (sink, fountain, etc.)
- Do not use the coffee maker
- Do not use the ice machines
- Do not brush your teeth

Potable water is available at the main entrance and ground floor. You can use water to take showers, wash your hands, and use the bathrooms. The cafeteria has taken the necessary precautions and will be open for business as normal. Some services may not be available.

A facility notice will be issued immediately when conditions return to normal.

Uprooted trees were everywhere. Consider the effect on park property in Fairfax County, a fraction of the area affected. A newsletter by the Fairfax County Park Authority included the following assessment:

"All park sites and personnel focused on response to Hurricane Isabel. It is estimated that the fiscal impact of the storm, inclusive of tree and structure damage, lost revenue and staff time, reached $1 million. More than 1,000 trees were felled by the storm."

Fortunately, Isabel did not produce the region-wide deluge forecasters feared. Most creeks and rivers remained within their banks. The storm arrived during a wet year so predicted rainfall of 5-10 inches would have caused serious problems. Some places gathered over 5 inches, but most sections east of the Blue Ridge Mountains had 1-3 inches.

Torrential rainfall pelted sections of the Blue Ridge. Remote gauges, installed since Hurricane Camille, registered more than 12 inches at scattered remote locations, particularly in the mountains surrounding the lower Shenandoah Valley.

MARYLAND

Winds in the eastern two-thirds of the state downed trees and caused record power outages. Peak gusts (mph) included: Patuxent Naval Air Station 69, Andrews Air Force Base 69, Catonsville 69, Cambridge 57, Baltimore 55, Ocean City 53, Hagerstown 52, Salisbury 51, Frederick 50.

Tides surged 5-8 feet above normal along the Chesapeake Bay. Water rushed through neighborhoods, damaging and wrecking houses, shops and restaurants. Adding to angst: Many federal flood insurance policyholders later voiced complaints about receiving inadequate settlements.

Dorchester County was severely impacted. The Chesapeake Bay encroached upon islands and marshes, driving hundreds of families from their homes. Six months later displaced residents still occupied trailers provided by the Federal Emergency Management Agency.

Record tides swamped Baltimore and Annapolis. Baltimore's Inner Harbor was awash, Even greater flooding occurred at historic Fells Point. Shops and upscale condominiums became islands in a vast lake.

The tide at Annapolis peaked 7.58 ft. above normal, besting its previous standard (August 1933) by more than a foot. Rowboats and canoes replaced cars in lower sections of the city. Flooding engulfed nearly half the classrooms at the Naval Academy. Losses totaled in the millions of dollars. "The level of flood damage is unprecedented," said an Academy spokesman.

***

The storm marooned many. John Zyla, a resident of Ridge, in Southern Maryland, recalled how Isabel brought out the best in his neighbors:

"We had a lot of tree damage around the house and were without electricity for six long days! The morning after Isabel, I got dressed, took a bottle bath with cold water and headed out to work. As I turned the corner, a huge loblolly pine tree blocked the only road out. I got my chain saw and the whole neighborhood turned out to clear away branches as I sawed. It

Old Town, Alexandria, Va.

Alexandria, Va. Hurricane Isabel caused a great loss of trees throughout eastern sections of the Mid-Atlantic.

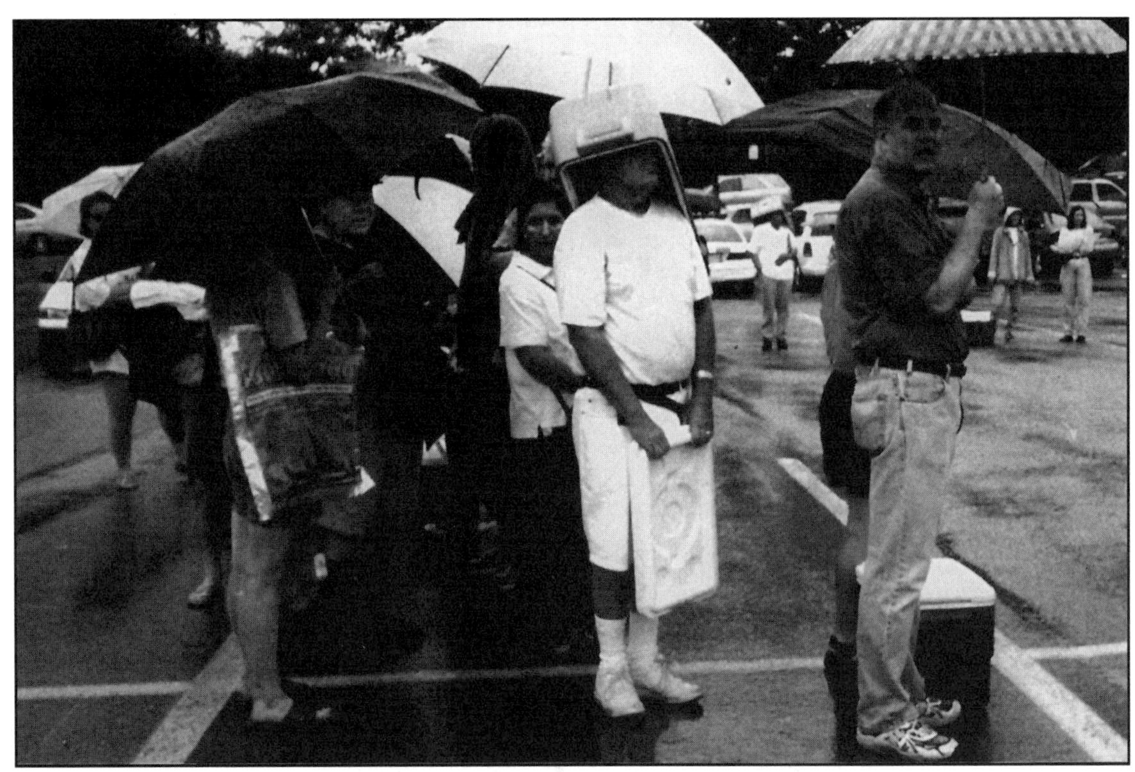

Wheaton, Md. Residents lined up at a dry ice distribution center.

was a nice neighborhood get-together. Even after all that work, we only cut a tunnel through this massive tree. A state highway crew removed the rest of the tree a week later. Other than that, we lost nine trees due to the constant wind."

In the aftermath of Isabel, thousands of people stood in marathon lines waiting for dry ice. Or they crawled through traffic hindered by blocked roads and the loss of signal lights.

"We survived Isabel," a radio broadcaster said. "Now let's survive each other."

Sheldon Kusselman, a resident of Silver Spring, recalled the sometimes maddening quirks of power restoration. "I lost power 11:20 a.m. on the 19th until (4:30 p.m.)" said Kusselman. "My next door neighbor did not get power back until the early hours of September 26—amazing and lucky (for me)."

Regina Blasic of Potomac lost electricity. She tried to save the food in her refrigerator. Efforts were futile.

"Four days without power and then intermittent power for another day," Blasic said. "I lost almost all food in (the refrigerator and freezer)."

Brian Smith of Oxon Hill brushed with near calamity when he attempted to illuminate the dark in an old-fashioned way: "I got lucky around 2 a.m. on the 19th after my smoke detector started chirping and woke me up. Wax had caught fire from a candle that I didn't put out, and it burned down! There was no damage because the candle was on the sink. I put the flames out, but the wax took an hour to cool down enough to handle it! Thank you, Lord."

Isabel offered a dazzling lightning display for some. Smith, editor of the *Washington-Baltimore Climate Review*, wrote:

"Worthy of mention was the peculiar lightning that is typical of tropical systems. There were many reports of green lightning in cloud—and when it was low in the sky, it was hard to tell whether one was seeing lightning or sparks from electrical transformers. Orange, blue, and red lightning was noted, but the vast majority of lightning observed was green. Probably many of us got a heads-up from (WJLA-TV) Channel 7's Doug Hill, who said we should be on the lookout for it. Thunder was usually not heard, however, possibly due to the general noise level of the wind and rain."

***

State officials asked the Army Corps of Engineers to help restore shoreline lost to Isabel. Erosion, the bane of the Chesapeake region, claimed substantial chunks of land.

Greater losses lie ahead. According to the University of Maryland Center for Environmental Science, "Hurricane Isabel caused more flooding and damage than would normally be expected of a Category 2 hurricane and this may be partly attributable to local sea level rise. Chesapeake Bay sea level is continuing to rise at nearly double the global average which suggests that the effects of tropical storms and hurricanes like Isabel may increase in severity in the future."

WASHINGTON, D.C.

Periodic squalls lashed the city for nine hours on September 18-19. Winds howled and whistled, accompanied by sudden, booming gusts. Reagan National Airport had a top sustained wind of 45 mph and a peak gust of 58 mph.

Clark Baker described conditions in his northwest neighborhood:

"Strong, powerful, gusty southeast winds continued during the early a.m. (19th) with moderate to heavy rain. The strongest wind gusts occurred between (midnight and 1 a.m.), accompanied by the sound of crashing tree limbs nearby. Power went off about (10:45 p.m.) on the 18th—back on (7:25 a.m.) on the 19th.

"The storm left the streets in our neighborhood paved with leaves and small tree limbs. Many larger tree limbs and entire trees had come down here and there, with mostly minor damage to cars and houses. But a few cars had been crushed, and several houses severely damaged, by large, uprooted trees—primarily curbside trees whose poorly developed root systems, restricted by the surrounding pavement, were unable to support them in the strong winds. Falling trees and limbs also brought down many telephone and power lines. There wasn't much evidence of flooding in our area."

Bob Ryan, the chief meteorologist at NBC affiliate WRC-TV (Channel 4), explained why so many trees were lost:

"After the drought of 2002, a persistent wet pattern in the East through early September had given us one of the wettest years ever. The ground was saturated; trees could not soak up all the moisture even though Washington had seldom been greener as vegetation recovered from the drought. Trees hundreds of years old had seldom been so full of leaves, nor had root systems ever been as fragile in the soft, wet soil. It was a combination for disaster especially for great urban trees that live in thin patches of soil between street and sidewalk."

ELSEWHERE

Isabel dealt a glancing blow to Delaware and New Jersey. Gusts reached 40-60 mph. Rainfall totals were generally less than 3 inches. High winds and uprooted trees caused property damage and power outages. Electric utilities in Delaware and New Jersey reported that 50,000 and 160,000 customers, respectively, lost power. Despite concern until landfall, Isabel produced few storm surge problems along the Jersey shore.

Peak gusts (mph) included: Delaware—Lewes 62, Dover 61, Georgetown 60. New Jersey—Cape May City 63, Strathmere 62, Millville 55, Keansburg 52.

The storm surge in Delaware Bay measured 3-4 feet at its juncture with the Atlantic Ocean and 5-6 feet at the head of the bay, causing modest flooding.

Isabel tracked through Pennsylvania. Central and eastern sections were whipped by long-lasting gales.

James Weber, a cooperative weather observer in Lancaster County, southeastern Pennsylvania, recorded a peak gust of 63 mph.

"Despite its far western track through Pennsylvania," Weber said, "Lancaster County sustained the greatest (wind) damage from a hurricane since Hazel in 1954—mainly from downed trees falling on power lines. I was without electricity for three days, as were thousands more throughout the area. What will be remembered about Isabel is its large wind field extending far from its center, and for the long duration of gale force winds—nine hours at this location."

***

As Isabel's first anniversary approached, Glenn Richards added finishing touches to a house along the Chesapeake Bay in North Beach, Md.

Richards and his work crew spent the year undoing Isabel's ravages. The hurricane destroyed the front and sacked the interior. Renovation didn't begin until six weeks after the storm. By then, carpeting and furnishings were junk. The washing machine seemed like an aquarium. "There were *creatures* living in it," said Richards.

Cleanup was a nightmare, particularly with ever-present mold and mildew.

"It was terrible," Richards said. "Mold goes everywhere and is almost impossible to completely eliminate."

Work gradually got done. There were inspections, permits to obtain and a pile of paperwork. Contractors were elusive. Few homes close to the bay escaped Isabel's fury. The wait for service seemed interminable.

"You see all the new houses?" Richards asked as he pointed to several homes. "That's new, that one's condemned and will need to be replaced, that's new. My wife counted 19 houses destroyed here."

Renovation is geared toward the next Isabel. Tile replaced carpeting. The hot water heater and washer/dryer are elevated. Heavy furniture is now consigned to upper floors. Items at ground level are lightweight and easily movable.

A floodwall disguised as a flower box serves to deflect the force of waves. Panels on the lower front of the house can be unscrewed to allow the bay access. Such flow-through curtails battering surf and anchors the building.

"We have no intention of fighting Mother Nature," Richards said. "We're trying to work with nature, not against it."

Glenn Richards builds for the next Isabel.

THE YORK RIVER. YORKTOWN, VIRGINIA

Photograph by Chris Stallings

Photograph by Chris Stallings

Photograph by Chris Stallings

Photograph by Chris Stallings

Photograph by Chris Stallings

Along the York River.

HURRICANES, ATLANTIC CITY AND ISABEL

Robert Levy

This is how Robert Levy, the emergency manager for Atlantic City, N.J., remembers the look of the sea as Hurricane Isabel approached:

"At first the ocean was beautiful. You got 14 to 18 seconds between each groundswell. They were nice and huge and you had these big long lines coming in. Right away I knew that they were from a tropical system. No other weather system sends impulses like that. Long fetch groundswell. As the week progressed they kept getting larger and then out of control. Whitewater as far as you could see. You'd look out and all you saw was a tremendous sea. Large waves crashing, rolling towards us—the coastline."

Levy became a lifeguard in 1960. He now directs the beach patrol in addition to heading emergency management. Weather monitoring equipment is part of the décor in his oceanfront office.

"I've always been a weather fanatic," Levy said. "I've always been interested in storms."

For a time, Isabel threatened to play spoiler to the Miss America pageant. That didn't make his job any easier. The organizers discussed contingencies and faced a potentially difficult situation.

"I went to every one of their planning meetings," said Levy. "We were trying desperately not to disrupt the Miss America pageant."

But, just in case...

"There were approximately 14 vans on standby waiting to take the various state representatives inland," Levy stated. "We looked at sending them to Cherry Hill or Vineland to wait out the storm."

Officials sought his recommendation on whether to change the location, delay the competition or cancel some preliminary events.

"No, I wasn't going to (cancel). The computer models began coming together indicating that the storm had its eye on North Carolina."

Still, for a day or two, the emergency manager sweated it out.

"This was an ongoing sweat," he explained. "I was watching the updates every cycle. When it was over, all the wind went out of me. I was worn out. You get all hyped up checking this and checking that. Fortunately, none of the worst happened. Isabel cooperated. She lost strength and went elsewhere."

Earlier in the week at least one forecast model predicted a Category 3 landfall near the Delaware Bay. What if the worst happened? What if Isabel arrived as a major hurricane?

"There would have been unbelievable damage around here," said Levy. "The Boardwalk would have littered the streets of Atlantic City.

"Isabel was a (minimal) hurricane and look what that did. Thousands of people on the mainland lost power for days. Yet, on the beach, we only had a peak gust of 58 mph. And nobody else around here had a gust that high."

Higher than normal tides caused only slight damage to the Boardwalk.

Although Isabel wasn't the Big One, it was big enough. It chased swimmers from the water and kept lifeguards on alert. Rip currents from a large hurricane may affect Atlantic City even when it's nearly 1,000 miles away. When a sprawling storm like Isabel gets within 500 miles, the sea is churning. The beach patrol makes 500-700 rescues in a normal year. If the tropics are active and the East Coast becomes "Hurricane Alley," the number can soar to 3,000.

Levy knows the danger faced by swimmers.

"When a hurricane gets close and the ocean is angry, the riptides are unbelievable," Levy said. "They not only look big, they have a totally different feel than normal waves. They have greater strength, thickness. Just talk to some of the lifeguards.

"King Neptune can humble anyone. You have to have a lot of respect and a little fear. It's good to have a little fear and know that there are powers greater than you. As good as you think you can swim, as powerful a swimmer as you may be, a hurricane sea makes everything different. You don't get the chance to swim. It's like a washing machine. It's just bubbles and foam. You can't even get your head above the foam that's blowing around."

Levy's lived through many coastal hurricanes and nor'easters. He acknowledges the risk of owning a home so near the sea.

"It's buyer beware. That's the price you pay for living at the shore. Personally, I'll take the risk. I love living here. I'd rather have this risk than, say, live in California and worry about forest fires and earthquakes."

2004

Florida hadn't seen four hurricanes in a year since 1851, but in 2004 they kept coming—Tropical Storm Bonnie and hurricanes Charley, Frances, Ivan and Jeanne. They killed dozens of people and left property damage collectively topping $40 billion. Then the storms swept north.

September

FRANCES

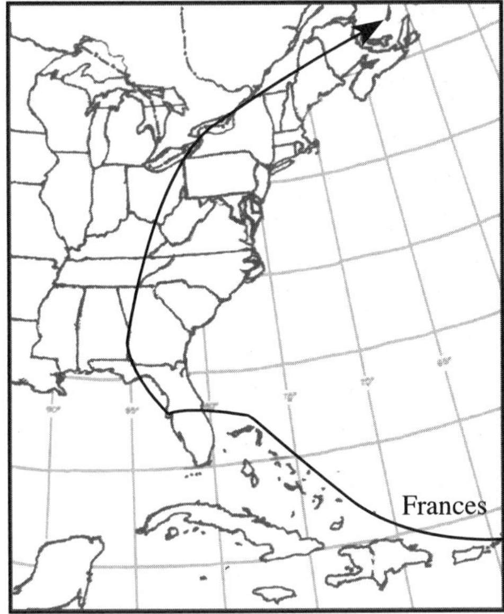

Weather patterns along the East Coast varied little during August and September. A warm ocean provided ready fuel to nourish one storm after another. Hurricanes struck Florida and tracked toward the Mid-Atlantic. The tropical systems clashed with weather fronts to the west. Atmospheric turmoil produced tornadoes and flooding.

Frances barreled into the east coast of Florida on September 5. The Category 3 hurricane's winds battered much of the northern two-thirds of the state.

The hurricane's remnants arrived in Virginia on September 8. That afternoon, 500 students at Bowling Green Elementary School in Caroline County, central Virginia, sheltered in the hallways as the sky darkened and a tornado approached. Although it missed the building, winds destroyed 200 trees in the vicinity, moved several cars and deposited the roof of a maintenance shop about a half-mile away. The tornado skipped a path through Caroline and Stafford counties, destroying nine homes and damaging more than 50 others.

A second funnel tore through Fauquier County in Northern Virginia. Bill Miller of Piedmont Growers in Bealeton heard a roaring noise and seconds later he watched a tornado wreck his greenhouse, vehicles and outbuildings. The business suffered $200,000 damage.

Twisters also affected the following counties: Amelia, Culpepper, Fluvanna, Henrico, King George and King William. A short-lived tornado west of La Plata, Md., uprooted trees along a 500-yard path.

Earlier, Frances brought calamitous flooding to western North Carolina. Nearly 17 inches of rain fell near Asheville.

Frances also produced flooding in Pennsylvania, with the worst in western and south central sections. The following counties reported significant damage: Beaver, Bedford, Blair, Butler, Crawford, Erie, Huntingdon, Lawrence, Warren and Washington.

***

The hurricane season of 2004 frustrated forecasters. Remnant systems repeatedly confounded predictions by producing tornado outbreaks and delivering tremendous rainfall. Patrick Michaels, the Virginia state climatologist, put it this way: "We are still unable to forecast death and destruction out of an overland, decaying hurricane."

September

GASTON

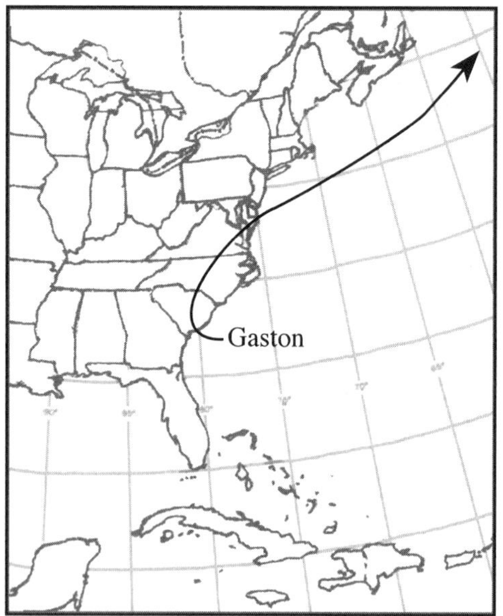

Hurricane Gaston underscored the unpredictability of tropical weather systems when they reach the Mid-Atlantic. After striking the Carolinas as a minimal Category 1 on August 30, the storm tracked into southern Virginia. Expected to churn through the state as uneventful, it stalled for hours over metropolitan Richmond. Up to 14 inches of rain cascaded down, drowning a forecasted 2-4 inches.

Downpours lasted about five hours. Rainfall rates in some neighborhoods exceeded 4 inches per hour. Richmond International Airport, about eight miles from downtown, had 6.68 inches. Ashland, about 20 miles away, recorded 10.61 inches, including 4.33 inches in one hour. Other totals included: Richmond (West End) 12.60", Mechanicsville 10.70", Sandston 8.10".

Gushing runoff targeted the historic Shockoe Bottom neighborhood, along the James River. Streets on adjacent hillsides became waterslides, simultaneously discharging their contents. The 25-square-block district, home to an age-old farmers market and upscale shops, condominiums and office buildings, became engulfed in a river. Dozens of cars floated through the streets, some with occupants pleading for rescue. Merchants, residents and tourists scrambled to safety.

Nature seemed to mock the efforts of man. Richmond's James River flood wall, completed in 1994 at a cost of $135 million, proved useless. Gaston ambushed the city by creating its own James, a watercourse that flowed behind the 'protective' barrier. (A bitter irony: Confident that the wall would protect them, many businesses and residents had no flood insurance.)

Gaston struck during rush hour, causing massive traffic jams. Floodwaters carried away vehicles, overwhelming roadways within minutes. There were scores of narrow escapes. At least eight people died.

Water reached a critical height at Falling Creek Dam in Chesterfield County, forcing the hasty evacuation of hundreds of families. The structure survived.

Gaston produced several tornadoes in southeastern Virginia. They were weak, short-lived F-0's, inflicting only minor damage.

The storm moved east by early evening. Rain ceased in Richmond.

Hurricanes don't necessarily conform to textbook descriptions about how they should behave. For example, Gaston regained tropical storm strength while its center was over land, near Yorktown, Va. It made a blustery exit from the Old Dominion.

Gusts of 50-60 mph lashed sections of the lower Delmarva Peninsula and offshore waters as the storm sped to sea. Damage was minimal. Gaston accelerated to the northeast, passing Cape Cod on August 31.

IVAN

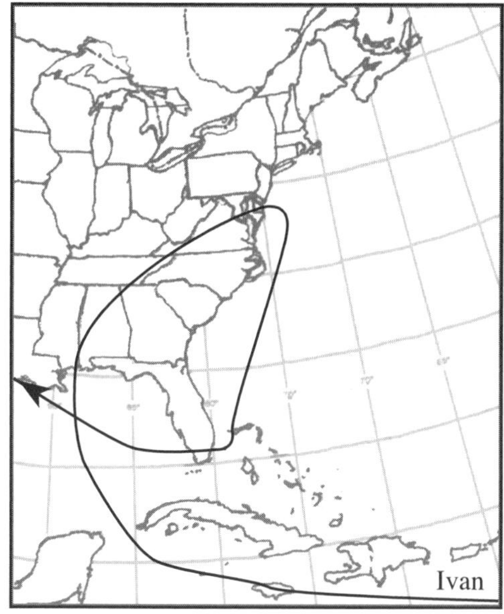

Topper Shutt, the chief meteorologist at CBS affiliate WUSA-TV (Channel 9), in Washington, D.C., seemed incredulous. Tornadoes began touching down west of the city during the late afternoon of September 17. There were so many twisters on radar that keeping track of each nearly became overwhelming.

"It's amazing how much we've seen," Shutt told viewers. "I've never seen anything like this!"

Bob Ryan, veteran meteorologist at NBC affiliate WRC-TV (Channel 4) in Washington, shared his surprise. Ryan wrote:

"Tornado Alley is the area from Texas to the Great Plains and the Ohio Valley where folks live regularly with tornado watches and warnings. But even in Tornado Alley, a day like September 17, 2004, would have been an exceptionally scary day. For us meteorologists, and anyone else who witnessed this historic tornado outbreak, it is a day we will always remember, and hope never happens again."

***

Hurricane Ivan, scourge of the Caribbean and Gulf Coast, produced a single-hurricane record 123 tornadoes along the East Coast. The numerous twisters sent thousands of people scurrying for cover and caused extensive property damage. In addition, extensive flooding plagued sections of Virginia, Maryland, Pennsylvania and New Jersey.

Ivan struck Pensacola, Fla., on September 16. Winds topped 130 mph. The storm hastened toward the Mid-Atlantic.

"I hate to think about what's going to happen inland," warned Max Mayfield, director of the National Hurricane Center.

By the afternoon of September 17, tornadoes invaded central and northern Virginia.

Dan St. Peter knew his neighborhood in Remington, Va., about 40 miles southwest of Washington, D.C., was under a tornado warning. He got his camera—just in case. Now, as if on cue, a dark sinister cloud approached.

Suddenly, the would-be tornado chaser became the chased. A furious whirlwind targeted his house. St. Peter dashed inside and went upstairs to warn his wife. They took refuge in a bathroom. The building began to shake, then—

"The roof was off in a second," said St. Peter. "The whole piece went at one time. Wham! It's gone! Just like that. It was like ripping a page from a notebook."

The bathroom walls survived amid a blizzard of insulation and little else. The couple was unharmed. A neighbor and her children in an adjacent house found safety in the basement as the tornado nearly demolished the dwelling.

WJHG-TV, Jason Kelley

An indication of things to come. One of Hurricane Ivan's earliest tornadoes touched down in Panama City Beach, Fla.

The Remington tornado was among 40 that descended on Virginia, surpassing the state's annual average of 15-20.

Several tornadic cells tracked between the Blue Ridge Mountains and Washington. They followed parallel paths, moving rapidly to the north-northeast. Funnels periodically embraced the ground, marking their presence with mutilated trees and disfigured homes.

A twister struck Centreville and Chantilly, damaging 70 buildings. Astounded motorists stuck in rush-hour traffic on U.S. 66 watched the tornado cross their path. At nearby Dulles Airport, passengers and staff scrambled for cover inside the main terminal. Meteorologists at the Baltimore-Washington field office, north of the airport, hastily took refuge in an interior room.

One tornado crossed the Potomac River near Brunswick, Md.

"It was raining a little," said Debbie Burtt. "I thought that it would be nothing more than a bad thunderstorm."

Then she saw the twister coming toward her home. There arose a tremendous noise. "The sound seemed to be all around us, inside the house," Burtt said.

Part of the roof became airborne, trees twisted and splintered, a barn turned to kindling.

"These things aren't supposed to happen here!" Burtt declared while surveying the damage. "They happen elsewhere."

"First Isabel, now Ivan!" a neighbor remarked. (Burtt lost a portion of her roof to Hurricane Isabel the year before.)

A tornado struck Remington, Va. It carried this truck 200 feet.

Another neighbor, John Wilson, watched the tornado cross his cornfield, moving east.

"I knew it was coming," he said. "I could see the atmosphere boiling. Trees (about 500 yards away) started twisting and coming out of the ground. The tornado bounced and zigzagged across the field, a weird-looking thing. There wasn't much noise until it hit."

Actually, two struck. A second twister touched down south of Wilson's house, writhing north along his driveway, leaving a trail of mangled trees. It converged with the other tornado as it reached his residence. Windows were blown out and a section of his roof was lost, but the home remained intact. A barn fell victim to the whirlwind, a pile of rubble.

Wilson has farmed his land for decades. On the day following the tornado, congregants from his church and neighbors tried to put right what nature had torn asunder. He hadn't telephoned anyone about what had happened. But they knew. Folks arrived by the carload and began cleaning up.

The farmer's thoughts turned to his closest companion, his dog, who was nearly killed. "The tornado sucked my dog out of the garage," he said, while surveying the damage. Wilson's 75-pound pet was yanked through an opening created when the door bowed out from its frame. The canine landed several yards away, terrified but unharmed.

Wilson wandered through his disheveled backyard—a bit dazed by the destruction, a bit overwhelmed by the response.

Casualties in the Mid-Atlantic were few despite the many tornadoes. An elderly woman and her daughter died in Cecil County, Md., when a tree fell on their house.

Maryland's western counties had considerable flooding. Rural Allegany County was hit hard, with over 160 homes affected, many in Mt. Savage.

Ivan produced nine short-lived tornadoes across south central Pennsylvania. Flooding, however, is the storm's legacy in the Keystone State. Moderate to major rises occurred on most rivers throughout the state. Homeowners in 60 of Pennsylvania's 67 counties filed flood insurance claims.

Much of Pennsylvania received 4-8 inches of rain, with unofficial reports as high as 13 inches. Rainfall included: Her-

The St. Peters' home in Remington.

A playset at a neighboring residence sustained superficial damage even as the adjacent house was nearly destroyed.

shey 7.90", Wilkes-Barre 7.86", Elimsport 7.50", Williamsport 6.73", York 6.02", Altoona 6.01", Pittsburgh 5.95", Harrisburg 5.52", State College 5.17".

Susquehanna River crests included: Bloomsburg 27.0 ft. (flood stage 19 ft.), Sunbury 30.4 ft. (flood stage 24 ft.) and Harrisburg 24.4 ft. (flood stage 17 ft.). The Susquehanna crested at 34.9 ft. in Wilkes-Barre, short of the 40.7 ft. rise during Hurricane Agnes in 1972, but far above a 22 ft. flood stage

The Delaware River crested at 33.45 ft. (flood stage 22 ft.) at Easton, Pa., and 30.78 ft. (flood stage 22 ft.) at Riegelsville, N.J. The river reached its highest level since August 1955.

Hunterdon, Mercer, Sussex and Warren counties in New Jersey qualified for federal disaster assistance. So did several counties in southeastern New York.

Ivan caused two episodes of flooding in the mid-Ohio River Valley. Up to 10 inches of rain on September 17 generated widespread flash flooding in West Virginia's northern panhandle and in eastern Ohio. Scores of businesses and homes were destroyed. Then, on September 18-19, the mighty Ohio River took its turn. The Ohio crested at slightly more than 45 feet in Wheeling, W. Va., highest since January 1996. The river rose to its greatest level in 40 years at Marietta, Ohio.

Hurricane Ivan spawned tornadoes in the following counties: **Maryland**—Cecil, Frederick, Harford, Montgomery, Washington. **Pennsylvania**—Bedford, Cumberland, Franklin, Juniata. **Virginia**—Amelia, Bedford, Campbell, Caroline, Chesterfield, Culpepper, Fairfax, Fauquier, Franklin, Frederick, Goochland, Greene, Greensville, Hanover, Henrico, Henry, King George, Louisa, Loudoun, Madison, Orange, Pittsylvania, Prince William, Rockingham, Stafford. **West Virginia**—Berkeley, Jefferson, Morgan.

Brunswick, Md.

Brunswick.

Ivan's twisters ravaged farms near Brunswick.

September

JEANNE

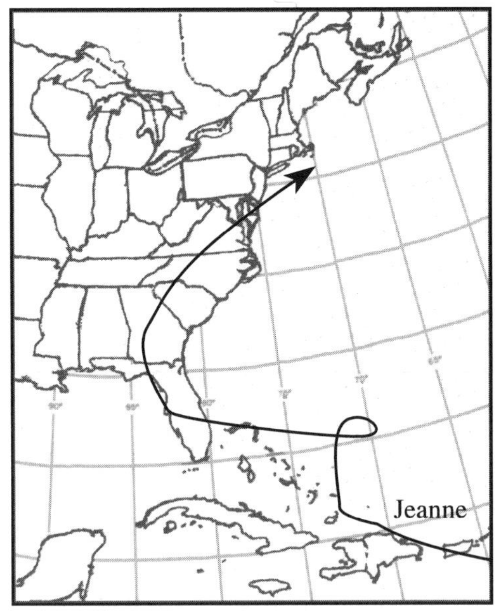

The hurricane season became a nightmare for Floridians and others. On September 25, Jeanne struck the same section of the state as Frances, pounding 200-miles of coastline from Daytona Beach to Palm Beach. Earlier, Jeanne bucketed northern Haiti with monsoonal rains of 10-15 inches, leaving 3,000 people dead and 200,000 people homeless.

Forecasters warned residents of the Mid-Atlantic to expect flooding and tornadoes as the hurricane tracked up the East Coast.

Frances, Ivan, now Jeanne. The ground, no longer able to absorb rainfall, let it flow into creeks and rivers. The Roanoke River crested at 17.9 ft. (flood stage 10 ft.) in Roanoke, Va. A moderate rise occurred along the upper James River. Flash flooding west of Washington, D.C., in Fauquier and Loudoun counties, closed many roads.

President George Bush declared that a major disaster existed in Virginia, authorizing assistance for the cities of Roanoke and Salem, and for the counties of Alleghany, Craig, Floyd, Giles, Montgomery, Patrick and Roanoke.

***

On the afternoon of September 28, Bedford Glascock heard a "freight-train" roar coming from the roof of his Solomons, Md., home. The house shook and a nearby barn collapsed as a waterspout off the Patuxent River found land.

"It was a tremendous wind," Glascock said. "I remember Hurricane Hazel, which had 100 mph winds, and this wind was higher. If it had lasted five minutes, nothing would be left standing."

His grandson, Cook, in a house less than 100 yards from the barn, didn't hear the tornado. He said that it struck without warning—no thunder or lightning, no heavy rain or howling wind.

"I got up, looked out a window and noticed the barn had collapsed," Cook said.

The twister lifted slightly as it passed over a field. It dropped on the Solomons Visitor Center, ripping off part of the roof and sending employees diving for cover. (Ironically, a display case in front of the building featured information on hurricane and tornado safety.)

Jeanne stirred up tornadoes in Cherry Hill, N.J., and near Wilmington, Del. The latter tracked from the New Castle County Airport to Willow Run along an eight-mile path. The twister damaged five C-130 cargo planes and destroyed another, scattering them around the runway. It then struck several buildings at an industrial park. About 100 employees of United Electric Supply took cover as winds tore down a wall and stripped the roof. Nobody was seriously injured.

Remnants interacted with a stalled cold front. Rainfall averaging 3-6 inches fell in central and western Maryland, eastern Pennsylvania and western New Jersey.

***

A report by Pennsylvania's climatologist summarized a difficult period:

"September 2004 will long be remembered as 'Hurricane Month' across Pennsylvania as the remnants of three potent hurricanes affected much of the Commonwealth. The substantial rainfalls within a three-week period associated with tropical cyclones Frances (Sept. 8-10), Ivan (Sept. 17-19) and Jeanne (Sept. 27-28) contributed to statewide flooding and one of the wettest months on record. Throughout the state, 7-10 inches of rain fell during these events, with numerous reports exceeding 10 inches of precipitation."

NOR'EASTERS

Hurricanes have the more fearsome reputation, but nor'easters bring a brand of misery that can match any hurricane. The strongest nor'easters produce hurricane-force winds, destructive surf and abundant precipitation. They also have a tendency to linger for a day or more.

Nor'easters may form any month but are most prevalent from October to April. Many originate along the Eastern Seaboard; some develop in the Gulf of Mexico.

Winds blow in a counterclockwise direction producing a steady northeasterly flow, hence the term "nor'easter." A few encompass more than a thousand miles, leviathans that assert power over a vast domain. Largely fueled by temperature and pressure contrasts, a trek over land doesn't tend to weaken nor'easters as it does hurricanes.

A nor'easter may develop into a hybrid—a swirling mixture of tropical and non-tropical characteristics. The hybrid usually begins as a non-tropical system and develops tropical features while traveling over warm water.

In essence, a hybrid has the guise of a nor'easter and the genes of a hurricane. Some develop tropical and non-tropical characteristics from inception such as "The Storm of the Century" in March 1993. A rare few, including the Halloween Storm of 1991 ("The Perfect Storm"), begin as nor'easters but transition to full-blown hurricanes.

This section examines some of the most severe nor'easters to visit the Mid-Atlantic region since 1950.

1950

November

reat Thanksgiving Storm. Great Appalachian Wind Storm. Storm of the Century. The blow of November 24-26, 1950, earned all those monikers. Part blizzard, part hurricane, it left 300 people dead and turned the holiday weekend into a nightmare for millions.

An explosion of the elements kicked off on Friday, November 24. A large high pressure system became entrenched over eastern Canada. It blocked a strong cold front approaching the western Appalachians. Moist tropical air streamed along the East Coast. A storm developed in North Carolina, then rapidly intensified over Virginia before meandering through western Pennsylvania and Ohio. It deepened to 28.90 inches.

A steep pressure gradient and frigid polar air clashing with tropical air ignited a disaster. Weather historian David Ludlum wrote, "The result was the greatest wind force ever known over the region, the deepest snow ever experienced, the severest cold for the season, and mighty rainfalls that raised devastating floods."

A state-by-state summary:

NEW JERSEY

Nature's fury killed 32 people. No part of the state escaped hurricane-force gusts. About 400,000 homes lost electricity. About 75,000 telephones were knocked out of service. A.E. White, New Jersey section chief for the Weather Bureau wrote:

"The great storm of November 25, 1950, will be long remembered by the people of New Jersey and adjacent areas. While the winds of this storm did not reach hurricane force of 75 miles per hour except in gusts, it is believed to have equaled the 1944 hurricane in the amount of property damage done and far exceeded the damage from the 1938 hurricane in this state. The loss of life in this storm was much greater than in either of those hurricanes."

"... By 6 a.m. on the 25th, gale winds had developed over much of New Jersey and kept gradually increasing until afternoon. (Peak gusts included): Lakehurst Naval Air Station 85 mph; Fort Dix 84 mph; Long Branch 80 mph; Teterboro Airport 75 mph; and Newark Airport 108 mph. By 3 p.m. winds had decreased decidedly in the south and central parts of the state, but strong gales continued until about 5 p.m. in the northeastern metropolitan area.

"Rainfall continued from early morning until late afternoon or evening, heavy much of the time. Amounts for the day of 3.00 inches or more were the rule, though they were somewhat less near the coast. A dozen stations recorded over 4.00 inches from the storm, while Burlington reported 6.01, Bridgeton 5.76, and Seabrook Farms 6.57 inches. The saturated soil helped loosen the root systems of trees furthering their destruction by the wind. Also, much of the damage in the Delaware Bay and lower Delaware River areas was due to the flooding of homes caused by heavy rains and wind-driven tides."

The Raritan Bay in northern New Jersey had one of the highest tides of the 20th Century. Devastation rivaled the Great Atlantic Hurricane of 1944.

The Maurice River in southern New Jersey rampaged, wrecking the villages of South Port Norris, Bivalve and Mauricetown. More than a dozen duck hunters marooned in marshes died from drowning or exposure.

Fishing villages along the Delaware Bay hadn't seen such devastation since the hurricane of October 1878. The sea, propelled by steady winds of 60-70 mph, scoured the shoreline. Few homes remained on their foundations. Every available craft in the area assisted in the removal of about 3,000 residents, the largest evacuation in the history of the Delaware Bay region.

PENNSYLVANIA

L.F. Conover, Pennsylvania section chief for the Weather Bureau, wrote:

"The 'elements' on November 24 and 25, 1950, affected more people in more diverse and violent ways than at any previous time in Pennsylvania history. Blood-chilling cold, traffic-crippling snow, violent hurricane-force winds, tree-stripping ice, flood-producing rains and abnormally high tides all combined in less than 48 hours to destroy uncounted millions of dollars in property, causing the loss of many more millions in business and the tragic deaths of at least forty persons.

"On the morning of the 24th, a large Arctic air mass began spreading eastward into extreme western Pennsylvania. This Arctic air plunged the mercury from the forties to well below 20 degrees by early afternoon east to the Allegheny Ridge. It also started the greatest snowstorm of record over the western counties. During the next 18 hours, this cold front moved only about 150 miles eastward, so that the western counties remained in the snow area of this storm. There was a temperature difference of 40 degrees or more in as many miles.

"Early on the 25th a coastal disturbance, which had formed rapidly off the Carolinas during the late hours of the 24th, was centered over eastern Maryland. It had become a very active system with strong gale force southeast and east winds, bringing a continuous flow of warm, moist air into Pennsylvania. During this memorable 25th day of November, winds rose to hurricane force over many eastern counties, and heavy to excessive rains sent streams to above flood state in southeastern counties. Extremely low barometric pressure, combined with high onshore winds, produced record high tides, which inundated tidal areas. The gales caused damage as far inland as Clinton, Centre, Huntingdon and Franklin counties."

The report continued, "The glaze storm was exceptionally severe from Fulton to Clearfield Counties with tremendous damage to forested mountainsides, power and telephone lines. Altoona lost all power as a result of breakage of ice-coated power lines and fallen ice-coated tree limbs. In some areas, the countryside was laid bare of trees."

Western Pennsylvania was buried under 15-30 inches of snow, a blanket contorted into massive drifts. Wind chill temperatures plunged below zero. More than a million people shivered in darkened homes.

Eastern Pennsylvania grappled with rain and wind. Hurricane-strength winds howled for hours. Peak gusts included: Allentown 88 mph, Reading 85 mph, Stroudsburg 76 mph, Philadelphia International Airport 74 mph.

Conover concluded: "The loss of electric power and communications due to the flooding of plants or destruction of utility cables was accentuated by the ensuing cold and wind that enveloped all of the state by dark of the 25th. The storm's cold breath did not leave Pennsylvania until the 30th. Its effects and aftermath will not leave the memory of those who experienced 'The Storm' of November 1950."

EAST COAST

Destructive winds pummeled New York, Connecticut and Massachusetts. Gusts in New York City peaked at 94 mph. Hours of strong winds sent the tide to its highest level since 1821. Albany, N.Y., registered 83 mph and Hartford, Conn., reported nearly 100 mph. On November 26, Boston clocked a one-minute sustained wind of 80 mph. Concord, N.H., had a gust of 110 mph.

Delaware fared better than its northern neighbors but sustained considerable damage. Flooding closed many roads in northern sections of the state. New Castle County Airport had a gust of 70 mph, the highest in Delaware.

Several inches of rain and brisk winds pelted the eastern two-thirds of Maryland and Virginia. Western sections endured moderate to heavy snowfall.

Tides on the eastern shore of the middle and upper Chesapeake Bay rose to the highest level since the hurricane of August 1933.

Friendship Airport, near Baltimore, had a gust of 68 mph and recorded 1.64 inches of rain. Washington had 52 mph, with 1.78 inches of rain. The temperature, which reached 58 degrees on November 25, struggled to a high of 31 degrees on the 26th.

More than a foot of snow fell in southwestern Virginia and nearly two feet covered Garrett County, Md. Pickens, in north central West Virginia, collected 57 inches from November 24-30.

Snowfall accumulations in eastern Ohio included: Steubenville 36.3", Cleveland 20.6" and Sandusky 15.1".

The polar blast accompanying the storm brought a deep freeze south to the Gulf of Mexico, shattering many November temperature records. The mercury plummeted as low as 12 degrees in northern Florida. Miami shivered at 26 degrees. Minimum temperatures also included: **Alabama**—Birmingham 5°, Mobile 22°. **Florida**—Pensacola 22°, Jacksonville 23°. **Georgia**—Atlanta 3°, Augusta 11°, Savannah 15°. **North Carolina**—Asheville -5°, Wilmington 16°. **South Carolina**—Charleston 17°. **Tennessee**—Nashville -1°, Knoxville 5°, Memphis 9°.

***

Events like the Great Thanksgiving Storm are more than the sum of the elements. Neighbors help neighbors. Residents open their homes to the stranded. Temporary loss of comfort and convenience brings renewed appreciation. Weather disrupted the lives of many on Thanksgiving weekend 1950. Yet, it gave special meaning to the holiday.

Rainfall (or equivalent) totals (Nov. 24-25): **Delaware**—Wilmington 3.54", Dover 3.35". **Maryland**—Ocean City 2.08", Cambridge 1.70", Baltimore 1.64". **New Jersey**—Seabrook 6.57", Sussex 5.50", Belvidere 4.15", Plainfield 3.40", Newark 2.74", Princeton 2.50". **Pennsylvania**—Tamaqua 6.46", McConnellsburg 4.72", Pottstown 4.69", Carlisle 3.52", Philadelphia 3.46", Lancaster 2.83". **Virginia**—Big Meadows 4.17", Front Royal 2.50", Falls Church 1.36", Norfolk .63", Richmond .31".

Snowfall accumulations (Nov. 24-26): **Maryland**—Oakland 22.0", Frostburg 9.0", Cumberland 9.0", Hancock 4.5". **Pennsylvania**—New Castle 32.0", Erie 28.3", Butler 28.0", Pittsburgh 25.4", Franklin 21.5", Uniontown 20.5", Somerset 14.6", Harrisburg 4.3", York (Trace). **Virginia**—Hot Springs 14.0", Wytheville 14.0", Roanoke 8.2", Big Meadows 4.0", Richmond .2". **West Virginia**—Morgantown 30.7", Elkins 28.2", Wheeling 26.4", Martinsburg 1.3".

Berks County Historical Society

Hurricane-force gusts toppled this giant in Berks County, southeastern Pennsylvania.

Delaware Public Archives, Dover, Del.

Flooding in Wilmington, Del.

1962

March

ASH WEDNESDAY STORM/GREAT ATLANTIC STORM

Paul Anselm, president of the Ocean City, N.J., Historical Society, opened a meeting commemorating the 40th anniversary of what many in the audience considered the storm of the century.

"By a show of hands, whose homes were in the same place Thursday that they were on Monday?" Anselm asked the audience. There was laughter, 40 years safely in the future.

Variously known as the Ash Wednesday Storm or Great Atlantic Storm, the nor'easter of March 5-7, 1962, remains singular to those along the Mid-Atlantic coast who endured its five destructive high tides.

At least 40 people died and more than 1,200 were injured. Losses totaled more than $200 million. The ocean wrecked thousands of homes, punishing the shoreline from Cape Hatteras to Long Island. Entire towns, including Ocean City, submerged. Sand dunes disappeared. Scores of temporary inlets sliced barrier islands. Nature's icy breath was felt west to the Appalachians and south to Georgia as temperatures plunged below freezing and snow piled into drifts.

The weather drama had two acts. The first, primarily on March 5-6, brought the heaviest snowfall of the winter to the Piedmont. It also buried the central Appalachian Mountains and blanketed some places in Virginia's Shenandoah Valley with the greatest snowfall on record. The second, on March 6-7, featured the Mid-Atlantic's most destructive coastal storm of the 20th century.

Meteorologists correctly anticipated a snow event on March 5-6. But coastal predictions were wrong, to put it mildly. The Weather Bureau's forecast for Delaware is typical of predictions issued to shore areas on Monday morning, March 5, on the eve of disaster:

"Snow beginning this afternoon, continuing tonight and accumulating 2-4 inches or more…On Tuesday, cloudy early in the morning but partial clearing during the day with high temperatures 32-38. Outlook for Wednesday, fair and cold."

Nothing about high winds or destructive tides.

Rain, occasionally mixed with snow, arrived early on Tuesday and continued on Wednesday. The wind reached gale, then storm force.

"The tide couldn't seem to get back out to sea," said one Ocean City resident. "Finally, water just washed over everything."

Two weather systems came together to fuel a superstorm. Massive high pressure over eastern Canada, with a barometric pressure to 31.31 inches on March 4, blocked low pressure that tracked across the Ohio Valley and Mid-Atlantic. The latter energized a coastal storm, which exploded off the Delmarva Peninsula on March 6-7. The barometer tumbled below 28.90 inches. Winds over the ocean howled to near-hurricane force and kept blowing during a period with the highest annual astronomical tides.

An Army Corps of Engineers assessment noted, "Since there was no time to recoup between high tides, each succeeding tide had less beach, dune, or bulkhead to dissipate its force and could reach further inland."

The report continued, "High waves and breakers superimposed on the high tides caused great destruction. The huge waves and breakers eroded the beaches, dunes and roads; damaged boardwalks, sea walls, bulkheads, groins and jetties; undermined and collapsed buildings; flooded streets and highways, contaminated food and water supplies; interrupted communications and power supply, and disrupted normal activities for weeks in the damaged coastal areas."

A few miles inland the weather seemed typical for an early March nor'easter—brisk winds and periodic rain or snow. At the shore, however, the ocean piled upon the shore, tossed by a bone-chilling gale. Traveling to a barrier island was like entering another world—a panorama of wild, white-streaked water.

Because of the initially benign weather forecast, evacuation operations peaked during the height of the nor'easter. By then, shore residents fled by the tens of thousands. Some traveled on their own, but many required assistance. They boarded helicopters, amphibious vehicles and fire engines—anything to get out of the ocean's way.

Bewildered folks gathered around transistor radios trying to figure out what was going on and how long it would last. The weatherman seemed to have no idea.

"After the first high tide we were told the worst was over," one woman said. "After the second high tide we were told the worst was over, and so forth. Instead, the tide kept increasing."

Ocean City, N.J., lived up to its name. Contributions came from both ocean and bay. Storm drains became ineffective, clogged by the persistent sea. Residents recalled:

"I watched a boat floating down the street followed by a car followed by another boat."

"When the storm ended, we found a boat and dock in our front yard. Somebody came for the boat. Nobody ever claimed the dock."

"There were an amazing number of fires."

(Saltwater ignited electrical systems. And some blazes were the acts of desperate property owners who had fire, but no flood, insurance.)

"There was water everywhere. Huge embers were flying over the gas plant. We were afraid that the plant would ignite and take the town with it. My mother thought the world was coming to an end."

A fiery pile of debris at an automotive service station terrified onlookers. The town's natural gas plant and an electrical sub-station lay downwind. Finally, a National Guardsman bulldozed the flaming heap away from fuel pumps.

Nothing could save about 100 houses in Ocean City, most located on the south end. Indeed, by Thursday, March 8, few buildings in the south end remained in their original location, or at least in their original condition. Most houses and shops in town sustained water damage. Miraculously, nobody died.

Photograph courtesy of the New Jersey State Police Museum

The Navy destroyer Monssen beached at Holgate, N.J.

Elsewhere along the Jersey shore:

Northern Sections: From Seaside Park to Raritan Bay, a distance of 40 miles, many motels and hundreds of homes were destroyed. Those living inland, beyond the reach of tidal waters, were amazed by the scenes of destruction on the front page of newspapers or on television. Such devastation didn't seem possible. But in places like Asbury Park, Belmar and Point Pleasant, it was all too real.

Long Beach Island: More than 600 homes were destroyed along the 18-mile strand. The ocean cut three inlets. At Harvey Cedars, more than half the houses washed away.

An unmanned Navy destroyer being towed to Philadelphia, the USS *Monssen*, was swept ashore at Holgate.

Hundreds of families fled Long Beach Island, many by helicopter. Pilots J.B. Simon and Thomas Smith counted 250 people, three dogs and three cats among those ferried in their Navy chopper.

Tragedies marred the evacuation.

The police chief of Long Beach Township, Angelo Leonetti; Beach Haven rescue squadsman Robert Osborn; and roads commissioner Kenneth Chipman died after the ocean engulfed their truck. They were attempting to evacuate residents of Holgate.

Near Holgate, a Coast Guard amphibious vehicle capsized in the surf. The nine occupants attempted to escape, but the sea snatched two couples. Their bodies were found days later, still wrapped in life jackets.

Atlantic City: A runaway barge claimed a large chunk of the famed Steel Pier. Damage rivaled the Great Atlantic Hurricane of 1944. The sea invaded lobbies of Boardwalk hotels, sending guests and staff scurrying to upper floors.

Ventnor City: Firemen responded to 50 calls on March 7, mostly for blazes ignited by salt water coming in contact with electrical circuits and fallen wires. Surf shredded the boardwalk.

Margate City: The town flooded during the five high tides. Allan "Boo" Pergament remembers trying days. He lived several blocks from the ocean. Water surrounded his house. It crept into his garage but spared living areas.

"The consecutive high tides came so fast that the water didn't have a chance to subside," Pergament explained. "It had nowhere to go. The bay and ocean kept the water from draining. Water came out of sewers, out of manholes—it came from everywhere.

"What the storm did that was most devastating to thousands of people," Pergament said, "was send water into basements where the heaters, water heaters, washers and dryers were located and flood them out. (Afterward) you heard motors everywhere you'd go, different types of pumps, sump pumps, whatever, pumping water out of basements."

Sea Isle City: Every building received damage. More than 1,000 residents were evacuated. As in many shore areas, Sea Isle City lost electricity, drinking water, sewage treatment and telephone service. Surging tides claimed nearly all vehicles.

Seven Mile Island: The strand became a chaotic scene of flooded buildings and drifting boats. Some craft caught fire, an unforgettable spectacle as they illuminated the night.

Wildwood: Fires kept crews busy. A large blaze claimed Nesbitt's Furniture Store and several adjacent offices. Embers ignited two houses a block away. The Colonial House Restaurant burned down. A bed-ridden man who refused to evacuate shot himself when the ocean entered his residence.

Cape May County: The Cape May boardwalk and Convention Hall were pounded into kindling. The sea poured into villages along the Delaware Bay. Floodwaters inundated 14 of 16 municipalities. When the ocean subsided, authorities counted 624 homes destroyed and 3,756 damaged.

For a time, 45 blazes burned simultaneously along the 30-mile coastal strip between Cape May and Ocean City. Firemen struggled to contain them. In Cape May, for example, they waded through waist-deep water to battle flames at Lund's Fisheries. The firemen could only use buckets. Flooding precluded trucks, hydrants and hoses.

DELAWARE

"This is the worst catastrophe Delaware has suffered," declared Gov. Albert Carvel.

Rehoboth Beach: The boardwalk, concessions and beachfront hotels were demolished. Homes that withstood a half-century or more of Atlantic storms succumbed to the sea. Waves of 20-30 feet lumbered ashore leaving the resort a disaster area.

Bethany Beach: Popular landmarks were lost, including a bowling alley, the Seaside Inn and the boardwalk. More than 100 homes were heavily damaged or destroyed. "You could count on your fingers the homes still standing," said one observer. Sustained winds reached 72 mph, the highest recorded on land in the Mid-Atlantic.

Delaware Seashore: Five inlets appeared between Dewey Beach and the Indian River Inlet. The bay and ocean converged at Dewey Beach. National Guardsmen patrolled beach towns in the aftermath of the disaster.

Delaware Bay/Interior: Fishing villages along the Delaware Bay suffered devastation rivaling the Great Thanksgiving Storm of 1950. Homes floated into marshes. At Bowers Beach, six children drowned as a family tried to flee in their car.

MARYLAND

Ocean City: The Ash Wednesday Storm was more severe than the storied hurricane of August 1933. The ocean rose 9.4 ft. above mean low tide, eclipsing the 7.1 ft. mark of 1933. Winds gusted to 85 mph and breakers topped 30 feet. Most of the resort's 1,200 residents left while the nor'easter raged.

Sheets, towels and blankets were hung from cottage windows to alert rescue personnel that those inside were ready to evacuate. Evacuees crowded into every sort of conveyance—fire engines, amphibious vehicles and even a dump truck. Movement took place during low tides (if they could be called that!).

Even where homes weren't threatened, occupants joined the exodus. With power out and wind chill temperatures below 32 degrees, what sense did it make to remain in a dark, unheated house?

Fires roared out of control beyond 71st Street. Their eerie glow could be seen throughout Ocean City. Engine companies could not reach them because a storm-cut inlet blocked their way. The flames destroyed several buildings, including a two-story apartment complex.

The resort's 2 ½-mile long boardwalk was torn to pieces. Flailing sections battered shorefront buildings. After the storm, an aerial survey indicated 82 bare concrete slabs—home foundations—along the five-mile stretch from Ocean City Inlet to the Delaware state line.

Crisfield: High water surged throughout the Chesapeake Bay. At Crisfield and elsewhere, boats navigated streets.

Central and Western Sections: A mantle of snow blanketed areas west of the Chesapeake Bay. The rain-snow boundary snaked through the Baltimore and Washington metropolitan areas, causing tremendous variation over short distances. Downtown Washington, for instance, measured 4 inches, while Rockville, Md., about 20 miles northwest, collected up to 19 inches.

VIRGINIA

Virginia Beach: The Weather Bureau didn't mince words about the disaster:

"The intense coastal storm brought as severe damage to the Atlantic coastline of Virginia as any extratropical storm in modern times. The resort areas near Virginia Beach in particular had heavy property losses. Many hundreds of homes on the beaches were totally destroyed and more than a thousand damaged. The long fishing pier at Virginia Beach was destroyed. The largest pile driver in the world, a $1.5 million machine, was turned on its side in deep water."

Mayor Frank Dusch declared a state of emergency, calling in National Guard troops to discourage looting. When the surf subsided, most of the sand on the beach had disappeared. There was no longer a boardwalk, and only fragments of the ocean fishing pier remained. Concessions, shops and motels along the boardwalk were left in shambles. Sand and wreckage carpeted streets.

A 50-foot wave smashed into the Chesapeake Lightship (17 miles east of Virginia Beach) on March 7, forcing the vessel to port.

Hampton Roads: Ocean View, Willoughby Spit and other places in the Hampton Roads area were inundated. The tide at Norfolk rose to 8.9 ft. above mean low water (5.6 ft. above normal), the highest generated by a storm other than a hurricane.

Chincoteague Island: Few places sustained more devastation than this town of 2,500. Winds gusted to 75 mph. Two men drowned and another died of a heart attack. Wreckage littered everywhere. The fishing fleet rested in streets and yards.

Backed-up sewers, leaking septic tanks and dead animals created a health hazard. Most inhabitants went to the mainland during or soon after the storm.

Poultry businesses were decimated. Likewise, the oyster industry. Most shucking houses were damaged or destroyed. Oyster harvest was prohibited for weeks afterward because authorities feared that raw sewage contaminated oyster beds.

The National Aeronautics and Space Administration abandoned its rocket base at nearby Wallops Island. The facility served as launch site for experimental spacecraft and housed a satellite tracking station.

About 150 wild ponies on neighboring Assateague Island drowned, nearly half the herd. However, one lucky filly and her two offspring found refuge in an unconventional shelter. "Misty," made famous by Marguerite Henry's book, *Misty of Chincoteague*, and a popular movie, took refuge in her owner's kitchen. Three days later she gave birth to a colt, which was named "Stormy."

Central and Western Sections: Record March snowfall and widespread power outages were the story here. Big Meadows (elevation 3,500 ft.) in Shenandoah National Park collected 42 inches of snow. Elevation made little difference as more than two feet blanketed the Shenandoah Valley. Winchester's 30-inch snowfall set a single storm and monthly record.

EAST COAST

The U.S. Monthly Weather Review compared the nor'easter's devastation in New York with notable hurricanes:

"In New York State, from the New York City area eastward along the south shore of Long Island to Montauk Point, tidal and wave action was most disastrous and exceeded damage caused by such great hurricanes as Donna in 1960 and the Great New England hurricane of 1938."

High winds and heavy snow in Pennsylvania and West Virginia caused widespread power outages and downed thousands of trees. Accumulations of 12-22 inches fell from York, Pa., across the southern tier of the state to Ohio. A foot or more of snow covered most of West Virginia.

Few nor'easters have caused eastern North Carolina more trouble. Dare, Currituck and Hyde counties were declared federal disaster areas. Winds gusted to hurricane force as unrelenting surf clawed at the Outer Banks. Most homes were damaged or destroyed at Kitty Hawk, Kill Devil Hills and Nags Head. The sea carved an inlet north of Buxton.

Meanwhile, snow fell throughout North Carolina's northern tier, from a few inches near the Outer Banks to about two feet in the Great Smoky Mountains.

The western Atlantic turned into a vast cauldron of frothy whitecaps. Destructive swells reached as far south as Florida. From Fort Pierce to Key Biscayne, a distance of 130 miles, combers as high as 25 feet ravaged the coastline. The surf surged through sections of Collins Avenue, the main thoroughfare in Miami Beach, halting traffic and invading shops. Officials at Deerfield Beach thought the nor'easter more devastating than Hurricane Donna (although Donna passed within 100 miles of Deerfield Beach but the Ash Wednesday Storm anchored about 700 miles away!)

***

Mayor Hugh Cropper predicted that Ocean City, Md., would be open for business as usual by Memorial Day. The public expected nothing less. In fact, summer reservations were phoned in during the storm.

Ocean City opened on time, albeit with a few shuttered motels and roped-off sections of boardwalk. The number of visitors declined that summer, but by the late 1960s vacationers flocked to the resort as never before.

***

By the early 1960s, resorts along the Jersey shore were threatened by growing blight and changing public tastes. An improving highway system, greater ease of travel and a desire to explore new places led an increasing number of vacationers to trade the beach for elsewhere.

Property owners had endured repeated hurricanes. And March 1962 brought the century's worst nor'easter.

"You could have bought the town for a song after the Ash Wednesday Storm," says Jim Campbell, historian for the Greater Cape May Historical Society.

You could have bought real estate for a song any place along the Mid-Atlantic coast. Most victims were uninsured and faced costly repairs or worse. The Ash Wednesday Storm washed away everything except their mortgages. Disheartened residents sold out at flood-sale prices. Savvy investors stepped in.

Bob Fite of Cape May remembers that during 1962 the Colonial Hotel was appraised for $150,000. "My family owned it for nearly 60 years, through good times and bad," he said. "The beachfront property sold for $5 million in 1987. It's probably worth twice that now."

A decades-long lull in destructive storms, federal flood insurance and beach replenishment projects created buyer confidence. Resorts such as Atlantic City, which obtained legalized gambling, and Cape May, which promoted itself as a Victorian-era architectural time capsule, found ways to revive interest. Growing popularity for oceanfront property fueled a run-up in prices. Values continue to soar.

Ash Wednesday Storm snowfall accumulations (March 5-7): **Delaware**—Bridgeville 2.0", Dover (Trace). **Maryland**—Oakland 30.0", Frostburg 26.0", Rockville 19.0", Baltimore (Airport) 13.0", Westminster 12.0", Hagerstown 11.0", Frederick 8.5", Leonardtown 8.0". **New Jersey**—Flemington 8.5", New Brunswick 4.0", Atlantic City 3.6". **Pennsylvania**—Hanover 20.0", Everett 18.0", Pittsburgh 15.7", Gettysburg 12.0", Harrisburg 11.8", Philadelphia 6.8". **Virginia**—Big Meadows 42.0", Front Royal 35.0", Winchester 30.0", Charlottesville 26.0", Staunton 26.0", Blackstone 23.5", Lexington 20.0", Leesburg 20.0", Lynchburg 17.9", Richmond 15.2", Danville 11.0", Falls Church 11.0". **West Virginia**— Moorefield 35.0", Martinsburg 18.0".

MEMORIES OF THE ASH WEDNESDAY STORM AT CHINCOTEAGUE

T. Stewart Baker, hurricane program manager for the Virginia Department of Emergency Management, is no stranger to hurricanes or nor'easters. He grew up on Chincoteague Island. The Ash Wednesday Storm remains a vivid memory. The following is his account of the event:

The night before the storm/flood (Tuesday, March 6) my mother was very adamant that I finish my homework in preparation for school the following day. At the same time the local doctor, a close family friend, stopped to visit my parents and indicated that the tide was swiftly rising in the downtown area of Chincoteague and that it was at the foot of Munford Street at approximately 9 p.m. Our home was on Munford Street, which was only a half block from Main Street, already under water. There was much discussion about the weather conditions and tide, as my father had a seafood business, which was located on Chincoteague Channel at Lewis Creek between the high school and downtown area.

When I awoke the next morning the house was cold as there was no electricity. My father had gone to check on his business. My mother, brother and I began raising furniture and other valuables and keepsakes as we could see that the tide was still rising, although it hadn't yet entered our home. I remember looking out my second-floor bedroom window only to see the side of a small building floating through our side yard. We began to gather some clothes and pack quickly as we knew we were going to have to go somewhere where there was heat, and was dry, as the water kept coming closer.

After a while, my father returned with the news that there had been significant damage to his business. He arrived in a work scow and instructed us to get in, that we were going to the Channel Bass Hotel. At that time my great aunt owned the hotel. Our family and neighbors converged there, as it was a safe refuge above the floodwaters and had heat and food.

The tide rose to the top of the parking meters in downtown. Navy helicopters were rescuing folks from their homes and any other dry spots where they may have gathered. There wasn't many dry spots on the island.

We stayed for two or three days, until the tide subsided so that we could evacuate to the mainland. We saw the debris from buildings, boats, docks, etc. lying in the streets and on nearby property. The townspeople that were able to make paths through the debris did so in order to assist others who were trapped in their homes. Many made their way to a local church where they waited for helicopters to pick them up and take them to the shelter at the NASA Main Base on the mainland, just inland of Chincoteague.

The building at my father's business, A&B Seafood, had been totally destroyed. He did a search and rescue operation to locate his workboats and clam floats, which had broken loose during the storm. I remember extremely large areas of debris and large fishing boats wedged between homes along Main Street. Many stores in the downtown area were destroyed beyond repair, and several homes along Chincoteague Channel and Chincoteague Bay had been battered apart by the waves.

We finally evacuated the island in the back of my father's six-wheel work truck and ended up staying with friends in Selbyville, Del., for several weeks. My father returned to Chincoteague to salvage what he could from the business and to assist others in need. My brother and I entered school while we were there. I received several protective medical injections right along with the Delaware students (due to contamination at nearby shore areas). When we finally returned home we found that our home had been flooded with approximately 16 inches of saltwater and that my grandmother's home had been flooded with approximately 36 inches. We made the necessary repairs and still reside on the island.

ASH WEDNESDAY, 1962

SEA ISLE CITY, NEW JERSEY

New Jersey State Archives, Dept. of State

New Jersey State Archives, Dept. of State

SEA ISLE CITY, NEW JERSEY

New Jersey State Archives, Dept. of State

New Jersey State Archives, Dept. of State

REHOBOTH BEACH, DELAWARE

Photograph courtesy of the Delaware Public Archives, Dover, Del.

Photograph courtesy of the Delaware Public Archives, Dover, Del.

Photograph courtesy of the Delaware Public Archives, Dover, Del.

Bethany Beach, Del.

Photograph courtesy of the Delaware Public Archives, Dover, Delaware

Dewey Beach, Del.

Photograph by Robert Conklin

Chincoteague, Va.

Photograph by Robert Conklin

Caskets floated into fields at Chincoteague.

THE NOR'EASTERS OF 1991-1993

Great nor'easters struck the Mid-Atlantic region between October 1991 and March 1993. The Halloween or "Perfect Storm" battered shore areas from the Mid-Atlantic to New England in 1991. Beaches, made vulnerable, became prey for nor'easters in January and December 1992. Just when it seemed the worst was over, a superstorm paralyzed the Northeast during March 1993.

The following is a summary of each event:

1991

October

THE PERFECT STORM/HALLOWEEN STORM

The Perfect Storm?

The weather system that developed off southeastern Canada in late October 1991 was anything but perfect. It proved frustratingly erratic, couldn't decide whether it wanted to be a hurricane or nor'easter, and refused to leave. It wasn't the strongest storm to affect the United States, but days of rough seas wrecked waterfronts in New England and impacted coastal sections of the Mid-Atlantic.

The nor'easter arrived about two months after Bob, a Category 2 hurricane that slammed New England but barely caused a ripple in the Mid-Atlantic. A 'perfect' confluence of weather features conducive to the explosive development of a storm converged northeast of New England.

A disturbance developed off the coast of Nova Scotia on October 30, drifted south and steadily strengthened. The low-pressure system received transfusions of energy from the remnants of Hurricane Grace and the jet stream, transforming a weak nor'easter into a monster.

Barometric pressure dipped to 28.70 inches and gusts reached 80-100 mph on October 29-30. A buoy off Sable Island reported a wave height of 101 feet.

Most casualties occurred at sea. The *Andrea Gail*, a fishing boat out of Gloucester, Mass., sank near Sable Island on October 29. Its six-member crew vanished. An Air National Guard rescue helicopter out of Long Island ditched off the New Jersey coast after running out of fuel. Four crewmen were rescued but another man perished.

By November 1, the storm drifted south and began tapping the Gulf Stream. The nor'easter transitioned to a tropical cyclone, becoming a hurricane off the Outer Banks of North Carolina. A routine Hurricane Hunter training flight turned anything but that day. The National Hurricane Center directed it to the low-pressure system, the supposed nor'easter, southeast of Long Island. To the surprise of meteorologists, the storm contained an embedded eye. It also had sustained winds of 80 mph and gusts of 100 mph.

The hurricane stayed well out to sea, but persistent easterly winds generated erosive surf from North Carolina to Maine. Passage over cooler water led to gradual weakening. It tracked near Cape Cod as a minimal tropical storm and made landfall in Nova Scotia on November 3.

Beaches were savaged from New Jersey to Maine, with the hardest hit in eastern New England. Even President George Bush's home in Kennebunk Port, Maine, suffered significant losses. The storm caused $1 billion in damage, including $70 million along the Jersey shore.

Sand dunes and beach replenishment projects implemented since 1962 kept flooding from being worse, especially in New Jersey. But now, as winter neared, significant stretches of shoreline were at the ocean's mercy.

1992

January

Meteorologists dread them. Low pressure systems that deepen tremendously, within hours. "Explosive cyclogenesis," as the process is known. Clark Kent turned Superman.

The sequence: Air pressure falls rapidly. Winds begin to howl and peak at gale force or greater. The ocean churns furiously.

A meager disturbance tracked across the Delmarva Peninsula during the night of January 3, 1992. Without warning, the low pressure turned destructive.

On the morning of the 4th, storm-whipped surf clawed at the Delmarva coast. Dunes were breached or washed away. The ocean provided a rude wake-up call, entering homes, shops and streets. Ocean City, Md., Rehoboth Beach, Del., and other places along the Delmarva shore suffered the worst nor'easter since March 1962. Large-scale development since then ensured considerable property losses.

A protective barrier built in the mid-1980s shielded Ocean City's boardwalk. But cottages and condominiums took a pounding in unprotected neighborhoods to the north. The wind gusted to 70 mph at Ocean City and 80 mph along the Delaware coast.

The northern third of Rehoboth Beach's boardwalk buckled or washed away. Bethany Beach lost nearly half its promenade. Several homes were washed into the ocean at South Bethany.

Gusts of 50-60 mph swept the Jersey shore. Gov. James Florio declared a "limited state of emergency" in Cape May, Atlantic, Ocean and Monmouth counties. Damage in the Garden State was less than during the Perfect Storm.

1992

December

Hurricanes avoided the Northeast coast during the summer of 1992. The lull was deceptive. On Friday, December 11, a nor'easter churned up flooding that rivaled the infamous Ash Wednesday Storm of 1962.

Events began innocuously.

A surface low pressure system developed over Georgia on Thursday, December 10, rapidly intensifying upon reaching the Chesapeake Bay on the 11th. The nor'easter continued to strengthen throughout the day as high pressure north of Maine blocked its movement. These opposites generated ever-increasing onshore winds from Virginia to New England. Gusts peaked at near hurricane force on December 11-12, and gales persisted until the 14th. Tides were already higher than normal because of a full moon.

The sea damaged or wrecked thousands of homes and businesses from Maryland to New Jersey. The Garden State tallied losses of $500 million.

"People who have lived through this storm will have lived through probably the highest tides in this century on the southern New Jersey coastline," said Wayne Albright, of the National Weather Service.

Seas of 12-18 feet attacked the shoreline. Nearly every boardwalk along the Jersey shore was wrecked or heavily damaged. Any structure within reach of the waves sustained losses. The Red Cross estimated that 3,200 homes were seriously damaged or destroyed.

The nor'easter pummeled the Delmarva Peninsula. Severe erosion again took a toll. Dewey Beach, Del., lost most of its beach.

The storm spread varying misery throughout the Northeast. Areas east of the Blue Ridge dealt with heavy rain or an icy mixture. Gales uprooted trees and caused power outages.

Tides rose 3-5 feet above normal in the New York City metropolitan area, flooding low-lying neighborhoods. Winds gusted to hurricane force.

Electrical problems shut down the New York subway for five hours during the afternoon of December 11—a nightmare for passengers on a system that averages a million riders each weekday. All commuter trains from New Jersey to Manhattan suspended service. Passengers at area airports were stranded by canceled or delayed flights.

A rain-snow mixture in Washington, D.C., turned the morning rush hour into chaos. Icy roads led to hundreds of accidents. Emergency workers in the western suburbs rescued motorists trapped by flooding as heavy snow gave way to heavy rain.

The storm dumped prodigious snowfall throughout higher elevations of the Middle Atlantic states and New England. A foot or more of snow covered the Shenandoah Valley and Blue Ridge Mountains. About two feet fell in the vicinity of Winchester, Va., and sections of western Maryland saw almost three feet. Piney Dam in mountainous Garrett County, Md., had 42 inches.

Heavy snow blanketed most of Pennsylvania. The village of Ogletown in the Laurel Highlands, southwest Pennsylvania, reported 36 inches of snow. State College (18.1 inches) had a December record snowfall. Up to two feet of snow pelted the Pocono Mountains of northeastern Pennsylvania.

***

Weather observers described conditions in their respective localities:

Mike Cerio, King of Prussia (Montgomery County), Pa.: "Intense coastal storm centered over the Delmarva Peninsula produced snow, rain—heavy at times—and hurricane-force winds. 80 mph gusts were reported by the National Weather Service in King of Prussia at 7:25 a.m. on the 11th. Hundreds of trees and tree branches felled, including several in the vicinity of this station."

Mark Dill, Westmont (Camden County), N.J.: "One of the strongest nor'easters in decades affected a large portion of the East Coast on December 10-12. Weather conditions deteriorated throughout the afternoon and evening hours of the 10th, as increasing rain and wind swept in from the southeast. By the early morning hours of the 11th, the storm's full fury arrived. Wind-whipped sheets of heavy rain accompanied by near hurricane-force gusts of 60-70 mph lashed the area for several hours. Wind damage and flooding were widespread over a large area, and some locations went without electricity for several days. Total rainfall recorded at this station was 5.17 inches."

John Drohan, White Plains (Westchester County), N.Y.: "The storm of Dec. 11-12, was called the 'Storm of the Century' for this area by the National Weather Service, causing over $700 million in damage to New York's southeast coast, Long Island and New Jersey. In our area, a TV crew videotaped a man being swept away after getting out of his car. A (teenager) tried in vain to save him. His body was found two days later in a stream on a golf course, in Mamaroneck, 10 miles from White Plains."

Gary Gallaher, Bear (New Castle County), Del.: "The storm of December 10-12 was the worst since the great coastal storm of March 1962. Steady rain driven by winds up to 51 mph pounded my station. The storm set December station rainfall records as follows: Maximum calendar day rain of 2.67 inches. Maximum 24-hour rain of 3.25 inches and storm total of 3.84 inches. …"

Ron Lehrer, Leonia (Bergen County), N.J.: "The worst coastal storm to hit New Jersey since 1950. The storm hit the area on December 11-12. Many trees were uprooted and roads flooded out. Entire neighborhoods went under water. Roofs were torn off houses and trees came crashing down on cars. Unprecedented amounts of snow in northwestern New Jersey. The New Jersey shore points were declared a federal disaster area."

Joseph Lozada, Jersey City (Hudson County), N.J.: "The metropolitan area was battered from December 10 through the 13th by one of the worst storms of this century. This classic northeaster dumped heavy rain and snow in our area while intensifying in the Eastern Carolinas and remained along the Mid-Atlantic coast for several days. Hurricane-force winds, wind-swept rain, record rainfall, heavy snow, record gusty winds, and near-record ocean tides occurred. At this site: 3.69 inches (water equivalent), 2.2 inches of snow, peak gust of 59 mph. LaGuardia Airport (in New York City) clocked 77 mph."

James Weber, Denver (Lancaster County), Pa.: "Dec. 10-11. What was described by some as a 'Century Storm', one of such magnitude that it only occurs once every 100 years, struck the Mid-Atlantic region with its full fury. At this station it certainly was the worst (wind event) since Hurricane Hazel in October 1954. Being a slow-moving storm, it pounded this station with gale force winds, and a few hurricane-force gusts, for nearly 24 hours."

Craig Ziemer, New Holland (Lancaster County), Pa.: "December 11, 1992—a powerful nor'easter brought sustained winds over 60 mph and gusts of 82 mph—highest ever recorded here. Roofs damaged, trees and road signs flattened. The local power company reported 160,000 customers without power. The worst since Hurricane Agnes in 1972."

***

Wallace Hardware in Ocean City, N.J., is several blocks from the beach. A mark on a wall inside the store denotes the high-water mark from the Ash Wednesday Storm of 1962. Another slash, a bit lower, indicates the December 1992 water level. Various beach and property protection measures were implemented after 1962. Yet, the sea came calling.

1993

March

THE STORM OF THE CENTURY/BLIZZARD OF '93/SUPERSTORM OF '93

"This could be the worst storm of the century."

— National Weather Service bulletin
Friday, March 12, 1993

Just months after the nor'easter of December, the Middle Atlantic states faced another superstorm.

Forecasters knew deteriorating weather in the Gulf of Mexico meant trouble as clusters of thunderstorms moved off the Texas coast on March 11 and were drawn into an area of lowering pressure. The arctic embraced the subtropics that day, a volatile combination. Polar, Pacific maritime and sub-tropical air coalesced to create a monster.

The National Weather Service issued the following bulletin early on the 12th:

"A dangerous and damaging major late season winter storm is forecast to develop in the northeastern Gulf of Mexico by Friday night and charge northeastward along the Atlantic Coast and into New England during the weekend. There are many indications that this storm may be unusually severe and perhaps record-breaking in many respects. All interests along the East Coast should follow the progress of this storm through local National Weather Service watch, warning, and special weather statements and be prepared for necessary action to protect life and property."

The storm blasted a path from Cuba to eastern Canada. It brought hurricane-force winds, a devastating surge and tornadoes to Florida. Blizzard conditions impacted much of the eastern third of the United States, from the southern Appalachians to New England. The storm killed 270 people and left more than $1.5 billion in property losses. It was, as the *New York Times* put it, "a monster with the heart of a blizzard and the soul of a hurricane."

Hurricane-force winds, fierce rainstorms and huge waves attacked the central and western provinces of Cuba, ruining economically vital sugar, tobacco and banana crops. It damaged hotels, factories and port facilities before tracking to Florida.

The night of March 12-13 will be long remembered along Florida's Gulf Coast. A storm surge shattered hundreds of homes, bringing surprise and terror. The surge reached 9-12 feet along the northern coast near Apalachicola. Winds in surrounding Franklin County gusted to 110 mph.

More than 20 twisters touched down, most in central Florida.

Gov. Lawton Chiles declared a state of emergency in 17 of Florida's 67 counties.

Temperature differences fuel a nor'easter and they don't come much greater than those associated with the 1993 storm. Temperatures in Florida topped 80 degrees on the 12th but gave way to bitter cold on the 13-14th. The mercury dipped to 31 degrees at Daytona Beach and 33 degrees in Orlando. Freezing temperatures covered central and northern Florida.

Much of the South shivered in a swirl of snow. Birmingham, Ala., measured more than a foot even as the temperature plunged to 2 degrees. The southern Appalachians were blanketed with snow as rarely before. Mount LeConte, Tenn., received 56 inches and Mount Mitchell, N.C., had 50 inches and 14-foot drifts.

The Mid-Atlantic region experienced a variety of wintry weather on March 13-14. A mixture of rain, freezing rain, sleet and snow pelted areas east of the mountains. Snowfall varied significantly, sometimes over short distances. National Airport at Washington, D.C., for example, reported 6.6 inches of snow while Dulles Airport, about 20 miles to the west, had 14.1 inches.

Snowfall in the Washington, Baltimore, Philadelphia and New York metropolitan areas ranged from 6-16 inches. Pittsburgh had 24.6 inches and Wilkes-Barre/Scranton, 20.6 inches. Roanoke, Va., was blanketed by 16 inches. Much of the state west of Richmond saw more than a foot.

Snowfall at higher elevations in the Appalachians generally exceeded two feet. Accumulations included: Snowshoe, W.Va., 44 inches, Seven Springs (in southwestern Pennsylvania) 47 inches, Gouldsboro (in northeastern Pennsylvania) 42 inches. Seven Springs set a state 24-hour snowfall record, 40 inches, on March 13-14.

Grantsville, Md., also set a state snowfall record when, by March 14, 48 inches fell in less than 24 hours. Ironically, that beat the previous state mark of 44 inches set in the December 1992 blizzard.

The "Storm of the Century" struck on the anniversary of the legendary blizzard of 1888 and like its predecessor paralyzed transportation. Thousands of motorists were stranded, some requiring rescue in whiteout conditions. The storm closed every major airport on the East Coast. Rail traffic was sporadic, at best.

"The volume of water that fell as snow may be unprecedented," said Frank Richards, chief of the Weather Service's special studies branch.

Peak gusts of 45-60 mph buffeted much of the Mid-Atlantic. Philadelphia reported 75 mph. LaGuardia Airport in New York had a gust of 71 mph and nearby Fire Island had 89 mph. The Jersey shore topped out at 50-60 mph.

Southeastern Virginia remained in the storm's warm sector, only cooling after the center's passage. Temperatures on March 13 soared into the 60s in the Hampton Roads area even as Richmond, less than 100 miles away, remained in the 30s. Norfolk saw heavy rain and high winds, with a peak gust of 66 mph. At nearby Hampton, gusts reached 70 mph.

Barometric pressure along the Eastern Seaboard matched readings normally associated with a major hurricane. A sampling: White Plains, N.Y., 28.38", Philadelphia, Pa., 28.43", New York City, 28.43", Washington, D.C., 28.54", Norfolk, Va., 28.54".

Coastal flooding was less than expected. There were evacuations, and the ocean invaded some sections between Virginia Beach and New York City. But an early wind shift to the west and rapid movement of the nor'easter prevented a repeat of the devastation that occurred during December.

***

So did the event qualify as the *Storm of the Century*?

Snowfall accumulations over most of the Mid-Atlantic region remained below single-storm records. Tides were only slightly above normal. Winds along coastal sections and neighboring areas didn't even match those of the December 1992 nor'easter. And while every Eastern state proclaimed a storm emergency, only Florida was declared a federal disaster area.

Still, the storm's immense coverage makes it a contender. At least then director of the National Weather Service Elbert "Joe" Friday thought so. He said, "When you take a look at the expansion of this storm all the way from the Gulf, up through the whole eastern coast of the United States, and with the devastation that this thing has wrought, I really think it is the storm of the century."

It affected more than half the population of the United States. Put another way: No winter storm, so intense, touched so many Americans.

EPILOGUE

We are in an active hurricane cycle. The Middle Atlantic states will again turn Hurricane Alley. The "Year of the Hurricane" lies ahead.

Hazel in 1954 was the last tropical cyclone to spread hurricane-force winds over a large area. The region's last devastating coastal hurricane occurred in 1944. Tropical cyclones have brought highly destructive flooding in recent decades. Expect similar events.

During 2005, Hurricane Katrina overwhelmed state and federal officials when it struck the Gulf Coast. The Middle Atlantic states will someday experience a similar test of preparedness.

Coastal areas face a great risk. Emergency managers are aware of the potential for a horrific storm along the Mid-Atlantic shore. Strategies have been formulated to deal with such an occurrence. Yet, plans were also in place in Louisiana and Mississippi as Hurricane Katrina made landfall. Still, there was chaos. Questions raised during that disaster are relevant to the Middle Atlantic region.

Coastal sections have undergone vast development. Many places have implemented beach replenishment and shore protection programs. A growing population makes such efforts critical. But the question remains: Will a hurricane negate decades of work and cause devastation in its wake?

There are other hurricane-related issues to consider. Events in recent decades suggest that flood frequency estimates understate the potential for flooding even as financial costs have risen exponentially. Flood control is sporadic. Indeed, some projects may simply provide a false sense of security. In many places, 'protection' consists of little more than hoping the Big One never comes. Should development be permitted on land meant for water? Where development exists, what are the best methods of protection? Can land use decisions afford to ignore climatological history?

We need a greater understanding of Mid-Atlantic hurricanes. Regional variations seem an afterthought in hurricane research, if they are considered at all. Tropical cyclones change as they track through middle latitudes, as they interact with surrounding weather systems and varying landscapes. Too little is known of the transitional effects. Florida weather is not Mid-Atlantic weather. A Florida hurricane is not a Mid-Atlantic hurricane.

The Saffir-Simpson Scale does not adequately gauge hurricane dangers in the Mid-Atlantic. It understates the potential damage from high winds. The region is more susceptible to wind damage than in traditional hurricane-prone places like Florida. A Category 2 hurricane here can do the work of a Category 3 further south. And the measure doesn't consider rainfall-related flooding, a paramount threat in the Middle Atlantic states. Also, Saffir-Simpson storm surge predictions, applicable to coastal sections, have less validity along the Mid-Atlantic's extensive inland waterways—as evidenced during Hurricane Isabel.

Planning and preparation requires continuous effort, community commitment and a willingness to carry out tough decisions. In the aftermath of a hurricane calamity, it's easier to blame public officials or climate change than to accept historical norms and the shortcomings of past decisions and practices.

Natural disasters bring challenges and hardships. Recovery is a wide-ranging and complicated process. But needs are predictable.

Incorporating lessons from the past is essential. The Mid-Atlantic has paid dearly for instruction. Must it contribute an ever-increasing tuition?

Everyone shares the responsibility for disaster readiness. To refrain the words of an emergency manager, "If you do your job, we can do ours much better."

Hurricane history suggests inevitable clashes with nature. The record also indicates a public resiliency. There's usually energy, a resolve, to cleanup and rebuild after a disaster. Americans, by nature, tend to be optimistic, to stand up under trying circumstances. That bent must be channeled into ongoing efforts to mitigate damage and improve our response to future events.

Recent hurricanes have left many folks wondering what coming years will bring. The only certainty is this: Storms such as Floyd, Isabel and their kind may go by a different name tomorrow, but there will be a tomorrow.

HURRICANE PREPAREDNESS AND SAFETY

Hurricane preparation must be customized for each individual. It is based on the anticipated threats—high winds, flooding rain, storm surge, tornadoes. It is based on where one intends to shelter, what property must be protected and on special considerations such as health or mobility problems. The following are suggestions, tips and guidelines:

PREPARATION BEFORE THE STORM

Learn about hurricane and flood history. Determine the risks based on past events. Local emergency management offices may have information. Many National Weather Service regional forecast offices also have material. (For the addresses, phone numbers and Web sites of Mid-Atlantic forecast offices, see the directory in Appendix C.)

Hurricane-force winds can occur far inland. If high winds are forecast, consider the danger from falling trees, power lines or other large objects. Even gale-force gusts can topple trees, especially in spongy ground. Stronger winds can take shear off roofs, blow down chimneys and shatter windows.

Residents of high-rise buildings should plan for possible window failure. Winds rise with height.

Assess insurance policies for adequate coverage of home, vehicle and other property. Which are applicable to storm-related damage? What additional coverage may be needed?

Consider purchasing federal flood insurance if in a vulnerable area. Insurance agents have information on this option. Flood coverage is usually not part of a standard home or business policy.

Determine safe evacuation routes. Learn the location of local storm shelters by contacting your emergency management office.

Plan for the needs of pets. Most public shelters do not allow animals.
(This rule may change in some places. During Hurricane Katrina in 2005, many people opted to remain with their pets. Some who refused to leave died in the storm.)

Have an out-of-state friend or relative as a family contact. Provide all family members a single point of contact in case of separation.

Make a videotaped record of your property. Store documentation in a safe, accessible place. Such information may facilitate insurance claims.

Have a plan to move valuables, keepsakes and other property out of harm's way. (Collectibles and other items may not be replaceable and can present insurance reimbursement issues.)

Assess 'what-ifs' in case of an extended loss of power, safe drinking water, telephone/cell phone service or other utilities.

If on prescription medication, have a plan for maintaining the quality and quantity required. Medications that need to be refrigerated may be at risk during a power outage.

Some smoke alarms may be dependent on electricity and could become inoperative during a power outage. If your smoke alarm uses a battery, test it before the hurricane.

Fuel your vehicle. Widespread power outages may close service stations.

Park your vehicle in a place protected from flooding and in a location safe from falling or blowing objects.

Keep a supply of cash. Power outages may put automatic teller machines out of operation.

Fill your freezer with containers of water. These help keep the freezer cold a little longer in a power outage and provide a source of fresh water if the public supply becomes unavailable.

Have a tarpaulin or other covering available as a temporary patch in case of structural damage such as the loss of roofing.

Create a checklist for last-minute preparations. Some tasks might include: unplugging all electrical appliances, turning off electricity at all breakers plus the main switch, turning off gas, removing toxic material from locations vulnerable to water, securing all outdoor objects that could blow away, closing curtains, blinds and shades to lessen the impact of flying glass, etc.

Create a disaster supplies kit. It should include:

- Battery operated radio
- NOAA weather radio
- Flashlight
- Extra batteries
- Water (three-day supply)
- Food/utensils (three-day supply of non-perishables)
- First-aid kit
- Prescription and non-prescription medicine
- Tools and supplies (paper cups, utility knife, hammer, matches, etc.)
- Supplies to maintain sanitation (toilet paper, paper towels)
- Clothing and bedding
- Necessities for children
- Necessities for pets
- Important family documents/Photocopies of identification and credit cards
- Entertainment (games and books)
- Cash and coins

SAFETY DURING THE STORM

Monitor weather and emergency broadcasts on radio or television. Anticipate a power outage. Have a battery-operated source for receiving information.

Unplug computers. A sudden power loss or surge may occur during the storm causing harm to appliances such as computers.

Do not use a corded telephone if there is lightning in the area.

Be careful if using candles, the cause of many storm-related tragedies. Keep the flame away from combustible objects and out of the reach of children.

If winds enter your home, take shelter in an interior location. Bathrooms are usually a safe choice.

The passage of the center of the storm may bring a temporary lull in wind and rain. However, severe weather often returns within a half hour.

Be alert for downed or loosened electrical wires. Assume all downed or submerged wires are live.

Smell and listen for leaking gas. If you believe there is a gas leak, immediately leave the house and keep the door(s) open. When safely out of the area, report the leak to the fire department and gas company. Never strike a match. Any size flame can spark an explosion.

It only takes two feet of water to float most cars. One foot of swiftly moving water can lift some vehicles. Nearly half of all flash flood fatalities are vehicle-related. Respect the awesome power of moving water.

Stay clear of low-lying roads and bridges. These can be washed away within minutes by a rush of water carrying mud, debris, boulders and uprooted trees. A car and its passengers can easily be carried off in such a torrent. If you encounter water flowing across a road, turn around and find a safer route.

Flash flood deaths often occur at night.

Don't count on flooded roadways being blocked by authorities. Events may occur too quickly.

Low-lying neighborhoods in urban areas may be prone to flash flooding. During a torrential downpour, roads and other impervious surfaces may act as conduits, channeling vast amounts of water downhill.

People often ignore flash flood warnings because they cannot see the floodwaters or believe their location safe. They look outside, see no immediate danger, and do not feel threatened. However, danger may be developing upstream, out of sight. For example, debris may lodge against a culvert or elsewhere and create a dam. If the jam breaks, water rushes into supposedly safe areas.

Never assume that a stream or river can't exceed the highest level in the memory of the oldest inhabitant.

Prolonged heavy rain may cause landslides/mudflows in mountainous terrain.

POST-STORM SAFETY

Notify the power company if there is an outage.

Assume all wires on the ground are electrically charged. This includes cable television feeds.

Never enter flooded areas or touch electrical equipment if the ground is wet unless you are certain that the power is off. NEVER handle a downed power line.

If your house was flooded, have a licensed electrician check for damage.

Danger doesn't end with the hurricane. Many injuries occur during cleanup.

Operate all gasoline-powered devices such as pumps, generators and pressure washers outdoors. NEVER bring them indoors. Improper use of portable generators can be deadly due to carbon monoxide from generator exhaust. Many people have died during or after a storm from noxious fumes such as carbon monoxide.

Perishable foods that haven't been refrigerated for more than two hours should be discarded.

Foods that have been contaminated by floodwater should also be discarded.

Discard all household items that have been soaked in floodwater and cannot be adequately cleaned, such as soft furniture, mattresses, stuffed toys and carpeting.

Water may percolate between walls, creating an environment favorable for mold. Spores can cause respiratory problems or allergic reactions.

Remove mold and mildew from walls, floors and other surfaces with a detergent solution, household bleach or commercial surface cleaner.

Make sure work areas have adequate ventilation. Use a respirator or mask with a rating of at least "N95," which means the pore size is small enough to block mold spores.

Be careful when driving through storm-ravaged areas. Darkened signal lights and hordes of sightseers may contribute to traffic jams. Debris may increase the risk for flat tires and other vehicular damage or personal injury.

Property crimes often increase after a hurricane disaster. Offenses run the gamut from looting to bogus contractors to the selling of flood-damaged items such as vehicles.

Price gouging may also occur. Individuals, neighborhood associations and local governments should anticipate the downside of human nature and plan accordingly.

ALL HAZARDS NOAA RADIO

All hazards NOAA radio, "the voice of the National Weather Service," broadcasts continuous local forecasts, watches and warnings. It also relays information during various non-weather emergencies.

Taped messages are repeated every four to six minutes. Stations transmit on one of several high-band FM frequencies, ranging from 162.40 to 162.55 megahertz. These frequencies are not receivable by standard AM/FM radios. They require a weather band capability. Radios dedicated to those frequencies are available at many electronic stores.

Weather band radios come in many sizes, with a variety of options. Some models offer an alarm that sounds when watches or warnings are issued. They generally cost less than $50. Information on NOAA Weather Radio is available from local National Weather Service field offices and on the Internet at http://www.nws.noaa.gov/nwr.

THE NATIONAL FLOOD INSURANCE PROGRAM

In 1968 Congress created the National Flood Insurance Program, the primary insurer of flood losses in the United States. Nearly 20,000 communities across the nation and its territories participate in the government-subsidized program, managed by the Federal Emergency Management Agency (FEMA).

Flooding ranks as the most common natural disaster in the United States. And flood losses are not usually covered by a standard homeowner's insurance policy.

Federal policies are available to any property owner or renter located in a community participating in the National Flood Insurance Program. Coverage is limited to $250,000 for the structure and $100,000 for the home's contents. Renters are eligible for up to $100,000 coverage on their possessions.

Many people forego flood insurance. Only about 40 percent of eligible property owners in high-risk areas purchase a policy, according to FEMA. The percentage is much lower elsewhere. However, neighborhoods not considered high-risk generate 25-percent of all claims.

A standard policy covers the following:

- structural damage
- basement water damage
- loss of appliances like a furnace, water heater or air conditioner
- debris cleanup
- replacement of floor surfaces such as carpeting and tile

(There are limitations on reimbursable losses. For example, while flood insurance covers the structural elements of a basement, it does not cover "basement improvements" such as finished walls, floors or ceilings, or personal belongings kept in the area. Flood insurance does not cover living expenses if displaced, or the loss of land or business. Also, the coverage pays a depreciated value for damaged belongings rather than replacement cost.)

A 30-day waiting period is required for a policy to go into effect. Contact an insurance agent or visit the FEMA Web sites www.fema.gov or www.floodsmart.gov for more information.

WEATHER WATCHES AND WARNINGS
(NATIONAL WEATHER SERVICE)

Coastal Flood Watch: Significant wind-generated flooding is possible in the watch area.

Coastal Flood Warning: Significant wind-generated flooding is imminent or occurring in the warning area.

Flash Flood Watch: Flash flooding is possible in or close to the watch area. Flash flood watches are issued for flooding that is expected within six hours after heavy rain has ended.

Flash Flood Warning: Flash flooding is occurring or is imminent in the warning area.

Flood Watch: High flow or overflow of water along a river is possible during the given time period in the warning area.

Flood Warning: Flooding is occurring or is imminent on a river in the warning area.

Gale Warning: Sustained wind speeds of 39 to 54 mph are expected within 24 hours.

Hurricane Watch: Hurricane conditions (sustained winds greater than 73 mph) are possible in the watch area within 36 hours.

Hurricane Warning: Hurricane conditions (sustained winds greater than 73 mph) are expected in the warning area within 24 hours.

Severe Thunderstorm Watch: Conditions are favorable for the development of severe thunderstorms in and close to the watch area.

Severe Thunderstorm Warning: A severe thunderstorm has been observed by spotters or is indicated on radar in the warning area.

Small Craft Advisory: A notice issued by the National Weather Service advising boaters to stay in port.

Tornado Watch: Atmospheric conditions are conducive to the development of tornadoes in and close to the watch area.

Tornado Warning: Spotters have sighted a tornado in the warning area. A tornado warning is also issued when rotation is indicated on radar (although a twister may not have touched down).

Tropical Storm Watch: Sustained winds from 39 to 73 mph, associated with a tropical cyclone, are possible in the watch area within the next 36 hours.

Tropical Storm Warning: Sustained winds from 39 to 73 mph, associated with a tropical cyclone, are expected in a specified area within 24 hours or less.

APPENDICES

APPENDIX A
BEAUFORT WIND FORCE SCALE

British Admiral Sir Francis Beaufort (1774-1857) designed a nautical wind scale in 1805. He refined the measure during following decades,. The scale is based on the wind's effect on sea and sail. In 1838, the Royal Navy adopted it as an official standard. As a visual measure, its use required no special equipment. The Beaufort Scale became popular with mariners throughout the world. Gradations ranged from Force 0 to Force 12, a wind "which no canvas could withstand."

Beaufort's creation has been adapted to land use, as follows:

FORCE	WIND (mph)	WMO CLASSIFICATION [1]	WIND EFFECTS ON LAND
0	0	Calm	Smoke rises vertically
1	1-3	Light Air	Smoke drift indicates wind direction
2	4-7	Light Breeze	Wind felt on face, leaves rustle
3	8-12	Gentle Breeze	Leaves and small twigs constantly moving
4	13-18	Moderate Breeze	Leaves and loose paper lifted, small tree branches move
5	19-24	Fresh Breeze	Small trees in leaf begin to sway
6	25-31	Strong Breeze	Larger tree branches moving, whistling in wires
7	32-38	Near Gale	Whole trees moving, resistance felt walking against the wind
8	39-46	Gale	Whole trees in motion, greater resistance felt walking against the wind
9	47-54	Strong Gale	Slight structural damage occurs, slate blows off roofs
10	55-63	Storm	Seldom experienced on land, trees uprooted, considerable structural damage
11	64-73	Violent Storm	Widespread damage
12	74 and higher	Hurricane	Widespread damage

[1] World Meteorological Organization

APPENDIX B

RETIRED NAMES OF DESTRUCTIVE HURRICANES

The names of devastating tropical cyclones are "retired" by an international committee of the World Meteorological Organization of the United Nations. The monikers are withdrawn for sensitivity reasons. Since tropical cyclones were first named in 1953, 67 of the Atlantic basin names have been retired. They include the following:

1954: Carol, Hazel
1955: Connie, Diane, Ione, Janet
1957: Audrey
1960: Donna
1961: Carla, Hattie
1963: Flora
1964: Cleo, Dora, Hilda
1965: Betsy
1966: Inez
1967: Beulah
1968: Edna
1969: Camille
1970: Celia
1972: Agnes
1974: Carmen, Fifi
1975: Eloise
1977: Anita
1979: David, Frederic
1980: Allen
1983: Alicia
1985: Elena, Gloria
1988: Gilbert, Joan
1989: Hugo
1990: Diana, Klaus
1991: Bob
1992: Andrew
1995: Luis, Marilyn, Opal, Roxanne
1996: Cesar, Fran, Hortense
1998: Georges, Mitch
1999: Floyd, Lenny
2000: Keith
2001: Allison, Iris, Michelle
2002: Isidore, Lili
2003: Fabian, Isabel, Juan
2004: Charley, Frances, Ivan, Jeanne
2005: Dennis, Katrina, Rita, Stan, Wilma

APPENDIX C

NATIONAL WEATHER SERVICE FORECAST OFFICES IN THE MIDDLE ATLANTIC STATES

BALTIMORE/WASHINGTON WEATHER FORECAST OFFICE

(northern Virginia, Washington D.C., south, central and western Maryland., northeast West Virginia)
44087 Weather Service Rd.
Sterling, VA 20166
703-260-0107
http://www.erh.noaa.gov/er/lwx/

BINGHAMTON WEATHER FORECAST OFFICE

(central New York, northeast Pennsylvania)
32 Dawes Drive
Johnson City, NY 13790
607-729-1597
http://www.erh.noaa.gov/er/bgm/

BLACKSBURG WEATHER FORECAST OFFICE

(southwest Virginia, southeast West Virginia, northwest North Carolina)
1750 Forecast Drive
Blacksburg, VA 24060
540-552-0084
http://www.erh.noaa.gov/er/rnk/

CENTRAL PENNSYLVANIA WEATHER FORECAST OFFICE

(central Pennsylvania)
227 W. Beaver Ave. Suite #402
State College, PA 16801
814-234-9412
http://www.erh.noaa.gov/er/ctp/

PHILADELPHIA/MOUNT HOLLY WEATHER FORECAST OFFICE

(southern, central New Jersey, southeast Pennsylvania, Delaware, northeast Maryland)
732 Woodlane Rd.
Mount Holly, NJ 08060
609-261-6600
http://www.erh.noaa.gov/phi/

PITTSBURGH WEATHER FORECAST OFFICE

(western Pennsylvania, northeast Ohio, northwest West Virginia)
192 Shafer Road
Moon Township, PA 15108
Main Office: 412-262-1591
Weather Forecast Recording: 412-262-2170
http://www.erh.noaa.gov/er/pbz/

UPTON WEATHER FORECAST OFFICE

(northern New Jersey, southeast New York, southwest Connecticut)
175 Brookhaven Ave. Bldg. NWS-1
Upton, NY 11973
631-924-0593
http://www.erh.noaa.gov/er/okx/

WAKEFIELD WEATHER FORECAST OFFICE

(southeast, central Virginia, northeast North Carolina)
10009 General Mahone Hwy.
Wakefield, VA 23888
757-899-4200
http://www.erh.noaa.gov/er/akq/

(TROPICAL PREDICTION CENTER/NATIONAL HURRICANE CENTER)

11691 SW 17th St.
Miami, FL 33165
http://www.nhc.noaa.gov/

APPENDIX D

DIRECTORY OF CLIMATOLOGIST OFFICES IN THE MIDDLE ATLANTIC STATES

DELAWARE STATE CLIMATOLOGIST

Center for Climatic Research
210 Newark Hall
Department of Geography
University of Delaware
Newark, DE 19716
www.udel.edu/leathers/stclim.html

MARYLAND STATE CLIMATOLOGIST

Department of Meteorology
University of Maryland
College Park, MD 20742
www.atmos.umd.edu/weather.html

NEW JERSEY STATE CLIMATOLOGIST

Department of Geography
Rutgers University
54 Joyce Kilmer Ave.
Piscataway, NJ 08854
http://climate.rutgers.edu/stateclim/

PENNSYLVANIA STATE CLIMATOLOGIST

Department of Meteorology
503 Walker Building
University Park, PA 16802
http://pasc.met.psu.edy/PA_Climatologist/index.php

VIRGINIA STATE CLIMATOLOGIST

Clark Hall
University of Virginia
Charlottesville, VA 22903
http://climate.virginia.edu/

GLOSSARY

Anemometer: An instrument that measures the speed or force of the wind. Although invented in the 1600s, reliable anemometers weren't available until the late 1800s.

Barometer: An instrument for determining atmospheric air pressure. The normal air pressure at sea level is 29.92 inches. Hurricanes generally have pressure less than 29.00 inches. The strongest tropical cyclone on record, Typhoon Tip (1979), had a minimum central pressure of 25.69 inches.

Barrier Islands: Narrow islands running parallel to the Mid-Atlantic mainland. They shield the mainland from the open sea. They help absorb an invasive ocean.

Beaufort Scale: An incremental measure used to estimate wind speed by visual observation—no equipment required. Developed in the early 19th century by British rear admiral Sir Francis Beaufort. The scale includes 13 degrees of wind strength. It ranges from "0" (calm) to "12" (hurricane). Initially a maritime aid, it was later adapted for land use.

Bermuda High: A semi-permanent, subtropical weather feature usually located near Bermuda. Its size, strength and position influence the track of many western Atlantic hurricanes.

Bucket Survey: An alternative to a standard rain gauge. During a bucket survey, meteorologists measure the rainfall found in containers known to be empty prior to the storm. Bucket surveys are typically used to measure intense rainfall in rural areas.

Calendar: Great Britain adopted the Gregorian calendar on September 14, 1752. At that time, an additional number of days were added to the historical record based on a particular century. From 1400 to February 29, 1500, nine days were appended. From March 1, 1500 to February 18, 1700, ten days were added. The eleven-day addition applied from February 19, 1700, to September 3, 1752. (In this text all dates prior to September 3, 1752, are given in double form—the first, old style, or Julian, and the second, new style, or Gregorian.)

Cape Verde Islands: Islands in the eastern Atlantic Ocean, off the coast of western Africa. Some of the most intense Atlantic hurricanes originate in this region. Many track toward the Caribbean or United States. They generally develop in August or September and take 7-10 days to cross the ocean.

Cloudburst: The National Weather Service defines a "cloudburst" as rainfall of 4 inches or more within an hour.

Computer Modeling (Numerical Forecasting): Computer forecasting models offer guidance on atmospheric patterns based on established formulas/equations and observational data taken from automated stations, trained weather observers, ships, weather balloons and other sources. Models act as guides to forecasters, who combine computer output with experience to issue a prediction. They consider several models when making hurricane track and intensity predictions.

Coriolis Effect: A deflective effect on all free-moving objects (including hurricanes) as a result of the earth's rotation. Deflection is to the right in the Northern Hemisphere and to the left in the Southern Hemisphere. The Coriolis effect is most pronounced at the poles and is non-existent at the equator.

Cyclone: Any counterclockwise rotating weather system in the Northern Hemisphere or clockwise rotating weather system in the Southern Hemisphere. These include low pressure systems, nor'easters, hurricanes and tornadoes.

Easterly Wave: Starting in June these low pressure troughs move off the African coast about every three to five days. They travel west toward the Caribbean region. Easterly waves occasionally give birth to tropical cyclones, particularly during late summer.

El Niño: A warming of the Pacific Ocean currents along the coasts of Peru and Ecuador that is associated with changes in weather patterns, including those affecting Atlantic hurricanes. El Niño seems to inhibit the frequency and development of strong storms in the North Atlantic basin. However, intense hurricanes still may occur. For example, Category 5 Hurricane Andrew formed during the El Niño year of 1992.

Equinoctial Storm (or Gale): A term used interchangeably with "hurricane" during the 18th, 19th and early 20th centuries. Equinoctial storms were expected near the autumnal equinox (late September) when, it was believed, changing seasons would bring one or more severe storms.

Extratropical: A term used to indicate that a cyclone has lost most, if not all, tropical characteristics. Extratropical storms that track through the Mid-Atlantic region, remnants of a hurricane, usually have a mixture of tropical and non-tropical features. For example, the storm may retain feeder bands although the eye is no longer discernible. An extratropical cyclone develops as a result of temperature differences between two or more air masses and such differences help fuel the storm.

Eye: A circular area of light winds or calm at the center of a hurricane. The eye is surrounded by a band of intense storm activity, the eyewall. The calm center is a distinctive characteristic of a hurricane.

Eyewall: Cumulonimbus clouds surrounding the eye, or center, of a tropical cyclone. This region usually contains a hurricane's highest winds, heaviest rain and steepest drop in air pressure.

Feeder (or Spiral) Bands: Thunderstorms that spiral into and around the center of a tropical system. Feeder bands carry heat and moisture, energy for a hurricane.

Fetch: The distance over water in which an unimpeded and steady wind generates waves. The height and energy of waves is dependent upon the wind speed, the fetch length and the amount of time wind blows over the water.

Forward Speed: The rate of movement of a hurricane in miles per hour (mph) or knots. Average speed is about 15 mph, although movement may range from a stall to 70 mph.

Front: A boundary or transition zone between two air masses of different density and temperature. A moving front is named according to the advancing air mass—a cold front if colder air is advancing and a warm front if warmer air is advancing.

Fujita Tornado Intensity Scale: Introduced by the late Theodore Fujita. The Fujita Scale rates the intensity of a tornado on the basis of winds and structural damage.

Gale: The Beaufort Scale defines "near gale" as 32-38 mph, "gale" as 39-46 mph, and "strong gale" as 47-54 mph.

Geography: The following geographic areas are referenced in this book:

Allegheny Mountains—a section of the Appalachian Mountains. The Alleghenies extend from southwestern Virginia to northern Pennsylvania. Some peaks top 4,500 feet.

Appalachian Mountains—the main mountain range in the eastern United States. The Appalachians extend from Alabama and Georgia to Maine.

Blue Ridge Mountains—the eastern range of the Appalachian Mountains, extending from northern Georgia to southern Pennsylvania. The peaks are generally 2,000 to 4,000 feet.

Chesapeake Bay region—includes the Chesapeake Bay and its tidal tributaries.

Delaware Breakwater is the name for anchorage areas behind the outer and inner breakwaters north and west of Cape Henlopen, Del. "Harbor of Refuge" is the outer and deeper of the two; "Breakwater Harbor" is the inner area. The Harbor of Refuge generally offers boats protection during hurricanes.

Delmarva Peninsula—includes the sections of Maryland and Virginia east of the Chesapeake Bay, and also includes Delaware.

Eastern Shore—includes the sections of Maryland and Virginia east of the Chesapeake Bay.

Hampton Roads—The name for the southeastern region of Virginia, located along and near the lower Chesapeake Bay. Norfolk, Portsmouth, Hampton and Newport News are located here. Hampton Roads is home to 1.6 million people.

Mid-Atlantic/Middle Atlantic/Middle Atlantic states—The region encompasses Delaware, Maryland, New Jersey, Pennsylvania, Virginia and Washington, D.C. (New York, North Carolina and West Virginia are sometimes included in this region.)

Piedmont—the geographic section between the Eastern coastal plain and the Appalachian Mountains.

Pocono Mountains—located in northeastern Pennsylvania. Peaks generally range between 2,000 and 3,000 feet.

Shenandoah Valley—a valley in northern Virginia, between the Allegheny Mountains and the Blue Ridge Mountains, about 150 miles long. The valley's continuation in Maryland is known as "The Great Valley," and in Pennsylvania it is known as the "Cumberland Valley."

Southern Maryland—a section of Maryland south of Washington-Annapolis and west of the Chesapeake Bay. (It does not include areas east of the bay.)

Southside Virginia—includes the southern tier of Virginia between Hampton Roads on the east and the Blue Ridge Mountains on the west.

Gulf Stream: A current of warm water transporting heat from the tropics to the North Atlantic Ocean. The conveyor belt travels east of Florida and north until it reaches North Carolina's Outer Banks. It then turns to the east-northeast and flows toward Europe. Hurricanes often feed off the warm Gulf Stream.

Hurricane: A tropical cyclone in which the maximum sustained surface wind is 74 mph or greater. "Hurricane" is the term for tropical cyclones of the Northern Hemisphere east of the International Dateline (Pacific Ocean) to the Greenwich Meridian (Atlantic Ocean). Hurricane is also the term for Indian Ocean tropical cyclones with winds of 74 mph or higher.

Hurricane Hunters: The nickname for the 53rd Weather Reconnaissance Squadron of the U.S. Air Force Reserve, based out of Keesler Air Force Base in Biloxi, Miss. Hurricane Hunter flights record the position of a tropical cyclone and its intensity by flying into the eye or circulation center.

Hurricane Season: The time of year having a relatively high incidence of hurricanes. The hurricane season in the Atlantic, Caribbean and Gulf of Mexico is June 1 to November 30.

Jet Stream: Rivers of fast-moving, undulating air currents up to 300 miles wide and 35,000-50,000 feet above the earth. The jet stream is surrounded by slower-moving air. A northern polar jet and southern subtropical jet may affect weather patterns over the United States, including the track of hurricanes.

La Niña: Periodic cooling of the central and eastern Pacific Ocean. Cooler water in the Pacific seems to favor the development of tropical cyclones in the North Atlantic.

Landfall: The intersection of a tropical cyclone's surface center (the area of lowest barometric pressure) and the coastline. Because the strongest winds in a hurricane are not located precisely at the center, it is possible for peak winds to occur on shore even if landfall does not occur. Conversely, a storm may make landfall and have its highest winds remain over water.

Major Hurricane: A hurricane with a wind speed of at least 111 mph. Category 3 or higher on the Saffir-Simpson Scale.

National Hurricane Center (NHC): A branch of the Tropical Prediction Center under the National Weather Service, it is responsible for tracking and forecasting tropical cyclones over the North Atlantic, Caribbean, Gulf of Mexico, and the Eastern Pacific. The NHC is located in Miami, Fla., at Florida International University.

National Oceanic and Atmospheric Administration (NOAA): NOAA operates the National Weather Service. It is headquartered in Silver Spring, Md., and is an agency of the Department of Commerce.

NEXRAD (Next Generation Weather Radar): A network of advanced Doppler radar implemented in the United States between 1992 and 1996. Doppler radar detects the location and intensity of precipitation. The radar pinpoints the location and strength of storm cells and the motion of air inside a cell. It also indicates precipitation intensity; hail size, and any rotation—potentially a precursor to a tornado.

North Atlantic: The Atlantic Ocean north of the equator, including the Caribbean Sea and Gulf of Mexico.

Nor'easter (also northeaster, northeast storm): A low pressure system that tracks along or near the Atlantic coast. A nor'easter generates strong northeasterly winds. October to April is the peak of nor'easter season, but they can develop during any month. The strongest storms generate hurricane-force winds.

Orographic Lifting: Mountains cause surface air currents to rise. Warm air rises and moderates as it reaches cooler levels of the atmosphere. Cooler air cannot hold as much moisture and rain may develop or increase. The combination of tropical moisture, orographic lifting and weather fronts have caused many destructive floods in the Middle Atlantic states.

Perigean Spring Tide: When the moon is new or full, the sun, earth and moon align so that the gravitational pull of the sun is added to the lunar effect. Twice each month, this creates higher-than-normal spring tides. ('Spring' refers to the elevated tidal level, which seems to spring forth, and not the season.) If during a spring tide the moon is at perigee, its closest approach to earth, a perigean spring tide results. These highest of astronomical tides occur twice each year—within days or weeks of the spring and autumnal equinoxes. A perigean spring tide is particularly dangerous in conjunction with a coastal storm.

Rip Current: A narrow, fast moving, channel of water. Rip currents can occur hundreds of miles from a hurricane. The powerful current can carry even the strongest swimmer away from shore. Swimming parallel to the beach rather than directly toward it may break the sea's grip, particularly in a milder rip current. Rip currents account for over 80 percent of the rescues performed by lifeguards at ocean resorts. (Also known as a riptide or undertow.)

Saffir-Simpson Hurricane Intensity Scale: A measurement that categorizes a hurricane's potential for generating destructive tides and wind-related (but not rainfall-related) damage. It is divided into five levels, or categories, based on the destructive potential of a hurricane. Each level includes an expected range for barometric pressure, wind speed and storm surge. The National Weather Service has used the Saffir-Simpson hurricane scale since the early 1970s.

Stationary Front: A stalled or very slowly moving boundary between two air masses, neither of which is capable of pushing the other away. When a tropical cyclone interacts with a stationary front, the slow movement of rain bands near the front may result in flash flooding.

Storm-Force Winds: The Beaufort Scale defines "storm force" as winds of 55-73 mph.

Storm Surge: An abnormal rise in sea level accompanying a hurricane or nor'easter. Surge height is the difference between the observed level of the sea surface and the level that would have occurred in the storm's absence.

Storm Track: The path of lowest barometric pressure associated with a tropical or non-tropical weather system.

Supercell: A long-lasting thunderstorm that produces strong winds and heavy rain. It may also generate hail and tornadoes.

Sustained Wind: The National Hurricane Center defines "sustained wind" as "a one-minute average measured at a 33 ft. above the surface in an unobstructed exposure." (Gusts are measured as a 3-5 second wind peaks.)

Syzygy: The sun, moon and earth form a straight, or nearly straight, line twice each month (at the new and full moon). The scientific term for this alignment is syzygy. Syzygy creates higher than normal tides.

Tropical Cyclone: A warm core non-frontal storm originating over tropical or subtropical waters. It contains organized deep convection, thunderstorms, and a closed surface wind circulation wrapped around a well-defined center.

Tropical Depression: A tropical cyclone in which the maximum sustained surface wind speed (using the U.S. one-minute average) is 38 mph or less.

Tropical Disturbance: A tropical weather system of organized/organizing convection—generally 100 to 300 nautical miles in diameter. It originates in the tropics or subtropics, is not attached to a weather front, and maintains its identity for 24 hours or more. From such seedlings, hurricanes grow.

Tropical Prediction Center: The National Weather Service office that includes the National Hurricane Center. It is located in Miami, Fla., at Florida International University.

Tropical Storm: A tropical cyclone in which the maximum sustained surface wind speed (using the U.S. one-minute average) ranges from 39 mph to 73 mph.

Tropical Wave: A weather feature that is generally an elongated south-north region of low barometric pressure that migrates westward across the Atlantic Ocean. Tropical waves create atmospheric instability and sometimes generate tropical cyclones. They are also known as easterly waves.

Tsunami: A seismic sea wave—not associated with hurricanes. A tsunami is triggered by an underwater earthquake, landslide or volcanic eruption. (Intense hurricanes may produce a destructive wave or series of waves that resemble a tsunami. The hurricane-induced onrush is sometimes described as a "tidal wave" but has nothing to do with tides.)

Typhoon: A tropical cyclone with a wind speed of 74 mph or higher that occurs in the western Pacific Ocean, specifically west of the international date line—180th meridian—and north of the equator. Typhoons are more numerous than their Atlantic hurricane counterparts. June to December is typhoon season.

Watershed (basin): The geographic region supplying water to a stream, river, lake, bay or ocean.

BIBLIOGRAPHY

The author consulted numerous sources when writing this book—too many to list here. Various publications have been cited throughout. Others include:

GENERAL

Ambrose, Kevin, and Henry, Dan, and Weiss, Andy. *Washington Weather*. Historical Enterprises, Merrifield, Va., 2002.

Barnes, Jay. *Florida's Hurricane History*. The University of North Carolina Press, Chapel Hill, N.C., 1998.

Barnes, Jay. *North Carolina's Hurricane History*. The University of North Carolina Press, Chapel Hill, N.C., 2001.

Brickner, Roger. *New York City Weather*. The Museum of American Weather, Haverhill, N.H., 2006.

Chaston, Paul. *Hurricanes!* Chaston Scientific, Inc., Kearney, Mo., 1996.

Dunn, Gordon and Miller, Banner. *Atlantic Hurricanes*. Louisiana State University Press, Baton Rouge, La., 1960.

Gelber, Ben. *The Pennsylvania Weather Book*. Rutgers University Press, New Brunswick, N.J., 2002.

Ludlum, David. *Early American Hurricanes, 1492-1870*. American Meteorology Society, Boston, Mass., 1963.

Ludlum, David. *The New Jersey Weather Book*. Rutgers University Press, New Brunswick, N.J., 1983.

Nese, Jon and Schwartz, Glenn. *The Philadelphia Area Weather Book*. Temple University Press, Philadelphia, Pa., 2002.

Neumann, Charles, Jarvinen, Brian. McAdie, Colin and Elms, Joe. *Tropical Cyclones of the North Atlantic Ocean, 1871-1992*. U.S. Department of Commerce/NOAA, Silver Spring, Md., 1993.

Pouliot, Richard and Pouliot, Julie. *Shipwrecks on the Virginia Coast and the Men of the Life-Saving Service*. Tidewater Publishers, Centreville, Md., 1986.

Savadove, Larry and Bucholz, Margaret. *Great Storms of the Jersey Shore*. Down The Shore Publishing and The SandPaper, Inc., Harvey Cedars, N.J., 1993.

Sheets, Dr. Bob and Williams, Jack. *Hurricane Watch*. Vintage Books, New York, N.Y., 2001.

Simpson, Robert. *Hurricane! Coping with Disaster, Progress and Challenges since Galveston, 1900*. American Geophysical Union, Washington, D.C. 2003.

Tannehill, Ivan. *Hurricanes: Their Nature and History*. Greenwood Press, New York, N.Y., 1969.

Truitt, Reginald. *High Winds...High Tides/A Chronicle of Maryland's Coastal Hurricanes*. Natural Resources Institute, University of Maryland, College Park, Md., 1968.

Williams, Jack. *The USA TODAY Weather Book*. Vintage Books, New York, N.Y., 1993.

The National Weather Service and its predecessors have published the *Monthly Weather Review* since the early 1870s. Monthly state summaries began in the early 1890s. These resources were used extensively, particularly when referencing climatological data and storm commentary. The following Web sites also provided historical and statistical information:

http://weather.unisys.com (Track maps of every Atlantic hurricane since 1851).
www.hurricanehunters.com/ (Web site of the Hurricane Hunters).
www.nhc.noaa.gov (National Hurricane Center).
www.hpc.ncep.noaa.gov/research/roth/vahur.htm (Virginia Hurricane History by Weather Ser-

vice meteorologists David Roth and Hugh Cobb).
www.erh.noaa.gov/er/lwx/Historic_Events/va-floods.html (National Weather Service in Sterling, Va.—compilation of historic Virginia floods by meteorologist Barbara McNaught Watson.)
www.ocmuseum.org/shipwrecks/storms.asp (Ocean City Life-Saving Museum—summaries of significant local hurricanes).

HURRICANES: AN OVERVIEW

Chaston, Paul. "Hurricane Manual." Spring 1992. Blue Hill Observatory Bulletin, East Milton, Mass.

Saffir, Herbert. "Hurricane Risks: Communicating Hurricane Damage Potential; Preventing Hurricane Damage." Delivered at 5th United Kingdom Conference on Wind Engineering, University of Nottingham, Nottingham, U.K. 2002.

Stewart, George. *Storm*. Random House, New York, N.Y., 1941.

HURRICANES: FORECASTING HISTORY

Fleming, James R. *Meteorology in America, 1800-1870*. Johns Hopkins University Press, Baltimore, Md., 1990.

Hawkins, Harry, Pardue, Leonard and Reber, Carl. "The National Hurricane Center." June 1961. Weatherwise (magazine).

Hughes, Patrick. "Hurricanes Haunt Our History." June 1987. Weatherwise.

Laskin, David. *The Stormy History of American Weather*. Anchor Book/Doubleday, New York, N.Y., 1996.

Ludlum, David. "The Espy-Redfield Dispute." December 1969. Weatherwise.

Reichelderfer, Francis. "Memorandum for the Secretary…" (Letter to the Secretary of Commerce on Reichelderfer's impressions of the first electronic computer.) 18 Feb. 1946. Library of Congress, Washington, D.C.

1609

Strachey William. "A true reportory of the wracke, and redemption, of Sir Thomas Gates, Knight; upon, and from the Islands of the Bermudas…" London, England, 1611.

1667

Andrews, Matthew. *History of Maryland: Province and State*. Doubleday, Doran & Co., 1929. Reprinted by Traditional Press, Hatboro, Pa., 1969.

Andrews, Matthew. *Tercentenary History of Maryland*. Vol. 1. S.J. Clarke Publishing Company, Baltimore, Md., 1925.

Browne, William H. (Editor), *Proceedings and Acts of the General Assembly of Maryland, April 1666-June 1676*. Maryland Historical Society, Baltimore, Md., 1884.

Brugger, Robert J. *Maryland, A Middle Temperament, 1634-1980*. Johns Hopkins Press. Maryland Historical Society, Baltimore, Md., 1988.

Scharf, J. Thomas. *History of Maryland from the Earliest Period to the Present Day*. Vol I. Tradition Press, Hatboro, Pa., 1967 (Reprint of 1879 edition).

1693

"Philosophical Transactions" (London). 19 August 1697, 659.

1769

Extracts from the Journal of Elizabeth Drinker. J.B. Lippincott Company, New York, N.Y., 1889.

Extracts from the Diary of Jacob Hiltzheimer of Philadelphia. William F. Fell & Co., Philadelphia, Pa., 1893.

"Letter from Virginia." Stratford Hall Plantation, Jessie Ball duPont Memorial Library, Westmoreland, Va., 1769.

Mason, Frances Norton. *John Norton and Sons, Merchants of London and Virginia.* The Dietz Press, Richmond, Va., 1937.

1775

Hume, Ivor Noel. *Another Part of the Field.* (P. 310-323). Alfred A. Knopf, New York, N.Y., 1966.

Shomette, Donald. *Shipwrecks On The Chesapeake, Maritime Disasters on Chesapeake Bay and Its Tributaries, 1608-1978*. Tidewater Publishers, Centreville, Md., 1982.

The Diary of Landon Carter. Jack Greene, editor. University Press of Virginia, Charlottesville, Va., 1965.

1788

The Diaries of George Washington. Jackson, D. and Twohig, D., editors. University Press of Virginia, Charlottesville, Va., 1979.

1795

The Papers of Thomas Jefferson. John Catanzariti, editor. Princeton University Press, Princeton, N.J., 2000.

1821

Mariner, Kirk. "The Great September Gust." Summer 1982. Virginia Cavalcade (magazine), Charlottesville, Va.

Pyle, Howard. "Chincoteague. The Island of Ponies." April 1877. Scribner's Monthly, New York, N.Y.

1846

Millas, Jose. *Hurricanes of the Caribbean and Adjacent Regions, 1492-1800*. Academy of the Arts and Sciences of the Americas, Miami, Fla., 1968.

Perez, Louis A. *Winds of Change, Hurricanes & the Transformation of Nineteenth-Century Cuba*. The University of North Carolina Press, Chapel Hill, N.C., 2001.

1861

The War of the Rebellion: A Compilation of the Official Records of the Union and Confederate Armies. U.S. Department of War, Washington, D.C., 1882.

Gallman, J. Matthew (general editor). *The Civil War Chronicle*. Agincourt Press, Crown Publishers, New York, N.Y., 2000.

1869

Allison, Frederick. "Letters to the Editors of the Express." 1 Oct. 1869. The Evening Express, Halifax, Nova Scotia.

Bowers, Emily. "Storm Surge." 5 Oct. 2002. The Halifax Herald Limited, Halifax, Nova Scotia.

Rao, Joe. "Is it lunacy to think that 'Saxby's Gale' could recur this October?" September/October 2002. Weatherwise.

1876

Moore, Mickey D. "Providence United Methodist Church, Swan Quarter, North Carolina, 'The Church Moved by the Hand of God'." Fall 1997. High Tides—bulletin of the Hyde County Historical and Genealogical Society, Fairfield, N.C.

The Diary of Jacob Engelbrecht. Vol. III (1858-1878). The Historical Society of Frederick County, Frederick, Md., 2001.

1877

Adams, Charles, and Seibold, David. *Great Train Wrecks of Eastern Pennsylvania*. Exeter House Books, Reading, Pa., 1992.

1878

Beitzell, Edwin. "The Wrecking of the Steamboat Express in the Hurricane of October 23, 1878," (an excerpt from "Life on the Potomac River"). October 1965. Chronicles of St. Mary's, St. Mary's County Historical Society, Leonardtown, Md.

Bryan, E.D. *Ho! For Collins' Beach!* Choice Graphics, Ipswich, Mass., 1997.

Cobb III, Hugh D. and Roth, David M. "Re-analysis of the Gale of '78—Storm 9 of the 1878 Hurricane Season." www.hpc.ncep.noaa.gov/research/galeof78.htm.

Holly, David. *Chesapeake Steamboats, Vanished Fleet*. Tidewater Publishers, Centreville, Md., 1994.

Ramsey, Kelvin and Reilly, Marijke. "The Hurricane of October 21-24, 1878." Special Publication No. 22. Delaware Geological Survey, University of Delaware, Newark, Del., 2002.

Scattergood, David. "Collins Beach," lithograph, Delaware River Illustrated: from Trenton to the Sea, 1861.

Sword, Gerald. "Who Goes There? Ghostly Manifestations at Point Lookout." July 1982. Chronicles of St. Mary's, St. Mary's County Historical Society, Leonardtown, Md.

"The October Gale of 1878." Spring 1973. South Jersey Magazine, Millville, N.J.

1882

Cass, W. Earle. "The Great Storm of Sep. 20-23." New Jersey Weather Review, Newark, N.J., 1882.

1888-89

Ambrose, Kevin. *Blizzards and Snowstorms of Washington, D.C.* Historical Enterprises, Merrifield, Va., 1993.

Kocin, Paul. "An Analysis of the 'Blizzard of '88'." November 1983. Bulletin of the American Meteorological Society, Boston, Mass.

Maner, Adrienne. "Derelict Ships." August 1992. Sea Frontiers, The International Oceanographic Foundation/Nature America, Miami Fla. (Reprinted in the Mariners Weather Log, October 1992 issue, National Weather Service, Silver Spring, Md.)

1888

Forman, Chanlee. *The Rolling Year On Maryland's Upper Eastern Shore*. Chanlee Forman, publisher, Chestertown, Md., 1985.

Usilton III, William. *History of Kent County Maryland, 1628-1980*. William Usilton III, publisher, Chestertown, Md., 1979.

1889

Covington, Priscilla. "I Remember an Ocean City Storm of 75 Years Ago." 14 June 1964. Sunday Magazine, Baltimore Sun, Baltimore, Md.

1891

Crockett, Fred E. *Special Fleet: The History of the Presidential Yachts*. Down East Books, Camden, Maine, 1985.

U.S. Coast Guard. "A History of the Life Saving Service."

1893

Bowen, Dana. *Shipwrecks of the Lakes*. Freshwater Press, Cleveland, Ohio, 1952.

Marscher, Fran and Marscher, William. *The Great Sea Island Storm of 1893*. Mercer University Press, Macon, Ga., 2004.

Rosenfeld, Jeff. "The Forgotten Hurricane." August/September 1993. Weatherwise.

1896

(More than two-dozen newspapers and the Weather Bureau's national and state summaries served as source material.)

1899

Stick, David. *Graveyard of the Atlantic*. The University of North Carolina Press, Chapel Hill, N.C., 1952.

1903

Leighton, Marshall O. *The Passaic Flood of 1903*. U.S. Geological Survey, Washington, D.C., 1903.

1915

Muller, Mary M. *A Town At Presque Isle, A Short History of Erie, Pennsylvania to 1980*. Erie County Historical Society, Erie Historical Museum and Planetarium of Gannon University, Erie, Pa., 1981.

1928

Kleinberg, Eliot. *Black Cloud: The Great Florida Hurricane of 1928*. Carroll and Graf Publishers (Avalon Publishing Group), New York, N.Y., 2003.

Will, Lawrence. *Okeechobee Hurricane, Killer Storms in the Everglades*. The Glades Historical Society, Belle Glade, Fla. Third Edition. 1990.

1933

Adams, Charles and Seibold, David. *Shipwrecks Off Ocean City* (N.J.). (P. 50-53). Exeter House Books, Reading, Pa., 1986.

"Hurricane Disasters of August and September, 1933." Official Report of the American Red Cross, Washington, D.C., 1933.

Sayre, David. *Memoirs*. "The Great Flood of 1933." St. Mary's County, Md.

Thompson, Stephen. "The Coast-Line." October 1933. Shore and Beach. Journal of the American Shore and Beach Preservation Association, New Orleans, La.

Veitch, Fletcher. "Hurricane of 1933." August 1985. Chronicles of St. Mary's. Bulletin of the St. Mary's County Historical Society, Leonardtown, Md.

1934

Burton, Hal. *Tragedy at Sea*. The Viking Press, New York, N.Y., 1973.

Thomas, Gordon and Witts, Max. *Shipwreck, The Strange Fate of the Morro Castle*. Stein and Day, New York, N.Y., 1972.

1935

Dye, Willie. *Storm of the Century, the Labor Day Hurricane of 1935*. National Geographic Society, Washington, D.C., 2002.

Goslin, William R. *History of the Federalsburg Flood*. January 1936.

Keyser, Jean W. "Flood in Federalsburg—1935." December 2003. Newsletter of the Federalsburg Historical Society, Federalsburg, Md.

Merriken, Ellenor R. *Herring Hill*. Baker Printing Company, Denton, Md., 1969.

"Marshy Hope Creek, MD." (Report from the chief of engineers, U.S. War Department), Washington, D.C., June 1938.

Potter, Sean. "September 2, 1935." September/October 2005. Weatherwise.

The Federalsburg Times (Various issues during Sept. 1935). Federalsburg, Md.

1936

Lee, Christine and Morrison, H. Robert. *America's Atlantic Isles*. National Geographic Society, Washington, D.C., 1981.

Wallace, Frederick W. *Roving Fisherman*. Canadian Fisherman, Gardenvale, Que., Canada, 1955.

1938

Allen, Everett S. *A Wind to Shake the World, The Story of the 1938 Hurricane*. Little, Brown and Company, Boston, Mass., 1976.

Brickner, Roger. *The Long Island Express, Tracking the Hurricane of 1938*. Hodgins Printing Company, Batavia, N.Y., 1988.

Freak Winds, New Hampshire 1938. Souvenir booklet. Lew A.Cummings Co, Manchester, N.H., 1938.

It Did Happen Here, An Illustrated Review of the Damage Wrought in the Western Part of the Monadnock Region by the Hurricane and Flood of 1938. Souvenir booklet. The Granite State Studio and Sentinel Printing Company, Keene, N.H., 1938.

New England Hurricane. Federal Writers' Project of the Works Progress Administration in the New England States. Hale, Cushman & Flint, Boston, Mass., 1938.

1940

Bostnick, M.L. "Report on Flood Damage Following the Rain on Night of August 31 and Morning of September 1, 1940." U.S. Engineer Office, War Department, Philadelphia, Pa., 1940.

Brooks, John. "South Jersey Flood of September 1, 1940." Engineering staff, State Water Policy Commission, Trenton, N.J., 1940.

"Flood Plain Information, Mantua Creek, Gloucester County, New Jersey, Chestnut Branch and Edwards Run." U.S. Army Corps of Engineers, Philadelphia District, Philadelphia, Pa., 1972.

"Flood Plain Information Report On Rancocas Creek, Burlington County, N.J." U.S. Army Corps of Engineers, Philadelphia District, Philadelphia, Pa., 1967.

1942

"Flood Plain Information, Rappahannock River, Fredericksburg, Spotsylvania and Stafford Counties, Virginia." U.S. Army Corps of Engineers, Norfolk District, Norfolk, Va., 1970.

"Interview with Blanche Moran." The Oral History Project. Historic Fredericksburg Foundation, Fredericksburg, Va., 1998-99.

1944

Bruder, Jessica. "Terror on the Boardwalk." (Article on a proposed homeland security museum.) Oct. 12, 2003. The New York Times, New York, N.Y.

Gannon, Peter. "Coastal Damage to New Jersey During the September Hurricane." October 1944. Shore and Beach Journal. American Shore and Beach Preservation Association, Newark, N.J.

Godfrey, Bill. "Old Cape Mayers recall the infamous Hurricane of 1944." Sept. 16, 2004. Cape May Star and Wave, Cape May, N.J.

Mooney, James. *Dictionary of American Naval Fighting Ships*. Volume VIII. Naval Historical Center, Department of the Navy, Washington, D.C., 1981.

"The North Atlantic Hurricane, September 14, 1944, Official Report of Relief Operations." The American National Red Cross, Washington, D.C., 1944.

Wexler, Harry. "Hurricane Detection by Radar." August 1948. Weatherwise.

Wexler, Harry. "The Structure of the September, 1944, Hurricane When Off Cape Henry, Virginia." May 1945. Bulletin of the American Meteorological Society, Boston, Mass.

Wood, Floyd. "A Flight into the September, 1944, Hurricane Off Cape Henry, Virginia". May 1945. Bulletin of the American Meteorological Society, Boston, Mass.

1954

Fredericksburg City Council Meeting of Oct. 15, 1954 (transcript). Fredericksburg, Va.

"Hurricane Hazel Lashes Coastal Carolinas, The Great Storm in Pictures." Souvenir booklet. Wilmington Printing Company, Wilmington, N.C., 1954.

"Hurricane Hazel, October 15, 1954." Souvenir booklet. The Bell Telephone Company of Pennsylvania, 1954.

Kennedy, Betty. *Hurricane Hazel*. Macmillan of Canada, Toronto, Ont., 1979.

Mook, Conrad. "The Distribution of Peak Wind Gusts in Hurricane Hazel 1954." August 1955. Weatherwise.

1955

Brown, Helen. *The Flood of 1955*. Videotape. Produced by East Stroudsburg University, East Stroudsburg, Pa., 1998.

Cody, Michael. "The Sinking of the Marvel". Aug. 20, 1995. The Sunday Capital, Annapolis, Md. Article appeared on the Web site: http://www.rosehavenmaryland.com/pages/marvel/marvelone.html.

Diane Drowns Delaware Valley. Souvenir Booklet. The Easton Express, Easton, Pa., 1955.

Gelber, Ben. *Pocono Weather: A History of Eastern Pennsylvania, the Poconos, and Northwestern New Jersey*. Uriel Publishing, Stroudsburg, Pa., 1998.

Gentry, Robert. "The 1955 Hurricane Season." February 1956. Weatherwise.

"In Disaster, a Friend." Brochure on Hurricane Diane. American Red Cross, 1955.

Lindsay, Drew. "Mayday! Mayday!" August 2003. Washingtonian Magazine, Washington, D.C.

O'Connell, T. and Sumner, H. "Hurricane Rains Cause Devastating Floods." October 1955. Weatherwise.

Shafer, Mary. *Devastation On the Delaware, Stories and Images of the Deadly Flood of 1955*. Word Forge Books, Ferndale, Pa., 2005.

"The Effects of a Threatening Rumor on a Disaster-Stricken Community." National Research Council report. National Academies Press, Washington, D.C., 1958. Available online at http://books.nap.edu/books/ARC000010/html/5.html.

Wyckoff, Jane. "How Worst Flood Tragedy Was Averted in Valley Camps." Sept. 2, 1955. Delaware Valley News, Frenchtown, N.J. A reprint appeared on the following Web site: http://www.hunterdon-online.com/life99/html/tragedy.shtml.

Zimmerman, Tim. "The Wreck of the Levin J. Marvel." August 2001. Chesapeake Bay Magazine, Annapolis, Md.

1957

Goodson, Susan and Ross, Nola Mae. *Hurricane Audrey*. Nola Mae Ross/Adams, Lake Charles, La., 1997.

1960

Articles on Hurricane Donna in Florida, North Carolina and the Northeast. October 1960. Weatherwise.

Moore, Paul. "The Hurricane Season of 1960." February 1961. Weatherwise.

1961

Davies, Pete. *Inside the Hurricane: Face to Face With Nature's Deadliest Storms*. Owl Books (Henry Holt and Company), New York, N.Y., 2001.

1967

Pelissier, Joseph. "The Hurricane Season of 1967." February 1968. Weatherwise.

1969

Bechtel, Stefan. *Roar of the Heavens*. Citadel Press Books (Kensington Publishing). New York, N.Y., 2006.

Buchanan, William…et.al. "The 100-Year Flood: Reactions to Hurricane Camille in Nelson, Amherst and Rockbridge Counties, Virginia." Report. School of Commerce, Economics, and Politics, Washington and Lee University, Lexingotn, Va., 1970.

"Flood Disaster Review and Analysis, Nelson County, Virginia." Report. Commonwealth of Virginia, Governor's Office, Division of State Planning and Community Affairs, Richmond, Va., 1970.

Hayden, Bruce P. *Atlas of Virginia Precipitation*. University Press of Virginia, Charlottesville, Va., 1979.

Hurricane Camille (various articles). October 1969. Weatherwise.

Kelly, Donovan. "The Virginia Flood of 1969, the effects of Hurricane Camille in the James River Basin of Virginia". Report. U.S. Geological Survey and Virginia Department of Conservation and Economic Development, Information Bulletin #505, Richmond, Va., 1971.

Michaels, Patrick. "Camille, The Twentieth Anniversary." Virginia Climate Advisory, Office of the State Climatologist, University of Virginia, Charlottesville, Va., 1969.

Simpson, Jerry H. Jr. and Simpson, Paige S. *Torn Land*. Nelson County Chamber of Commerce, Lovingston, Va., 1971.

Swift, Earl. "When the rain came." (A series of articles published in *The Virginian-Pilot* and *The Roanoke Times* from Aug. 15-22, 1999.)

Zebrowski, Ernest and Howard, Judith. *Category 5, The Story of Camille*. University of Michigan Press. Ann Arbor, Mi., 2005.

1972

Briggs, Peter. *Rampage*. David McKay & Co., New York, N.Y., 1973.

Griffith, William and Romanelli, Carl (editors and compilers). *The Wrath of Agnes*. Media Affiliates, Wilkes-Barre, Pa., 1972.

Hagemeyer, Bartlett and Spratt, Scott. "Thirty Years After Hurricane Agnes-The Forgotten Florida Tornado Disaster." (25th Conference on Hurricanes and Tropical Meteorology, American Meteorological Society.) National Weather Service Forecast Office, Melbourne, Fla., 2002.

"Hurricane Agnes: The Most Costly Storm." August 1972. Weatherwise.

"Weather Watch Reports During Agnes." June 1972. Metropolitan Climatological Summaries, National Capital Area. (Clarence Woollum, editor), National Weather Service, Silver Spring, Md.

Rygiel, John and Warnagiris, Paul. *The Great Flood of 1972*. Observer-Rygiel Publishing Co., Wyoming, Pa., 1972.

Shank, William . *Great Floods of Pennsylvania*. Buchart Horn, York, Pa., 1974.

The Flood of 1972. Souvenir booklet. The Times Newspapers and Allied Graphics, Ellicott City, Md., 1972.

"The Flood of '72 In Elmira, Chemung County." August 1972. The Chemung Historical Journal, Elmira, N.Y.

1975

Eloise Flood '75. Souvenir booklet. Huggins Printing Company, Steelton, Pa., 1975.

Hebert, Paul. "Atlantic Hurricane Season of 1975." February 1976. Weatherwise.

Schlegel, Jay. "A Comparison of Hurricane Eloise and Hurricane Agnes." April 1976. Weatherwise.

1979

Hoadley, David. "A Tropical Storm David Tornado in Fairfax County—September 1979." April 1981. Bulletin of the American Meteorological Society, Boston, Mass.

1985

Bittinger, Wayne (editor). *The Flood of November 4-5, 1985 in Tucker, Preston, Grant and Hardy Counties West Virginia*. McClain Printing Company, Parsons, W.Va.

Clary, Mike. "Hurricane Gloria—Were We Overwarned?" December 1985. Weatherwise.

Grunig, Susan. "Next! Hurricane Gloria." November 1985. The American Weather Observer, Belvidere, Ill.

Metropolitan Washington Climate Review. September and November 1985 issues. (Thomas Blackburn, editor). National Weather Service, Silver Spring, Md.

Teets, Bob and Young, Shelby (editors and compilers). *Killing Waters, The Great West Virginia Flood of 1985*. Cheat River Publishing, Terra Alta, W.Va., 1985.

1989

Hurricane Hugo, Storm of the Century. William Macchio (publisher/editor), BD Publishing, Mount Pleasant, S.C., 1989.

1992

Andrew! Savagery from the Sea. Sun-Sentinel staff, Sun-Sentinel, Fort Lauderdale, Fla., 1992.

Metropolitan Washington Climate Review. August 1992. (Tom Blackburn, editor), National Weather Service, Silver Spring, Md.

Sheets, Dr. Bob. "Stormy Weather" from "Hurricanes...Different Faces in Different Places, 17th Annual National Hurricane Conference." (Compiled by Lawrence S.Tait), Tallahasee, Fla., 1995.

1995

Metropolitan Washington Climate Review. September 1995. (Thomas Blackburn, editor), National Weather Service, Silver Spring, Md.

1999

Fisher, Gary and Tallman, Anthony. "Flooding in Delaware and the Eastern Shore of Maryland from Hurricane Floyd, September 1999." Report. (Fact Sheet FS-073-01). U.S. Geological Survey, Washington, D.C.

Robinson, David. "Hurricane Floyd Rainfall in New Jersey." Report. Office of the New Jersey State Climatologist, Rutgers University, Piscataway, N.J., 1999.

Smith, Wayne. "A Flirtation With Floyd." July 2001. Chesapeake Bay Magazine, Annapolis, Md.

2003

Gendell, Dave. "Waterworld." October 2003. SpinSheet Magazine, Annapolis, Md.

"Hurricane Isabel in Virginia, Facts and Figures: Sept. 18, 2003 to April 30, 2004." Report. Virginia Department of Emergency Management.

Kauffman, Dana. "Water in Fairfax County." November 2003 (P. 40). Beulah Corridor (newspaper), Springfield, Va.

"Pepco Holdings, Inc., Hurricane Isabel Response Assessment." Report. James Lee Witt Associates, Washington, D.C., 2004.

Washington-Baltimore Climate Review. September 2003. (Brian Smith, editor), Oxon Hill, Md.

Ryan, Bob. "A Monster Named Isabel." *Bob Ryan's 2004 Almanac and Guide for the Weatherwise,* NBC 4, Washington, D.C.

Stone, Steve. "Isabel wasn't close to being 'The Big One'." Sept. 28, 2003. The Virginian-Pilot, Norfolk, Va.

2004

Grenci, Lee. "Another Charley Horse For Weather Forecasters," and Rippey, Brad, "Weatherwatch." November/December 2004. Weatherwise.

Washington-Baltimore Climate Review. August and September issues, 2004. (Brian Smith, editor), Oxon Hill, Md.

Ryan, Bob. "Ivan's Remnants Turn DC Area into a Tornado Alley." *Bob Ryan's 2005 Almanac and Guide for the Weatherwise*. NBC 4, Washington, D.C.

NOR'EASTERS

1950

Bristor, Charles. "The Great Storm of November, 1950." February 1951. Weatherwise.

"Flood Plain Information, Tidal Lands and Maurice River, Cumberland County, New Jersey." U.S. Army Corps of Engineers, Philadelphia, Pa.

1962

Cooperman, A. and Rosendal, H. "Great Atlantic Coast Storm, 1962." May 1962. Mariners Weather Log, Weather Bureau, Washington, D.C.

Dorwort, Jeffrey. *Cape May County, New Jersey: The Making of an American Resort Community*. Rutgers University Press, New Brunswick, N.J., 1992.

Dryden, Beryl and Dryden, Bill. *The Tides of March in Ocean City, Maryland*. The Eastern Shore Times Press, Berlin, Md., 1962. (souvenir booklet)

Richardson, Ann. "Forty years ago '62 Storm devastated Ocean City, Eastern Seaboard." March 6, 2002. Ocean City Gazette, Ocean City, N.J.

"The Great Mid-Atlantic Coastal Storm, March 5-6-7, 1962." Report of the American Red Cross, Washington, D.C.

"The March Storm, New Jersey and Delaware," and "The March Storm and Ocean City, Maryland." April 1962. Shore and Beach Journal, American Shore and Beach Preservation Association, Newark, N.J.

1991

Junger, Sebastian. *The Perfect Storm.* HarperTorch (Harper Collins), New York, N.Y., 1997.

1992

Thompson, Robert. "December 1992 Northeaster." Winter/Spring 1993. Blue Hill Observatory Bulletin, Milton, Mass.

"Year in Review—1992." February 1993. The Association of American Weather Observers.

1993

Iacovelli, Debbie. "IWW Members Chronicle the Storm of the Century—March 13, 1993." March/April 1994. Weather Watcher Review, International Weather Watchers, Washington, D.C.

INDEX

INDEX

HURRICANES
and the
MIDDLE ATLANTIC STATES